THE MAKING OF A MOTION PICTURE EDITOR

THE MAKING OF A MOTION PICTURE EDITOR

Thomas A. Ohanian

Published by Tablo

Author Photograph by Lisa M. Surmeian

Book Cover Design by Alexander Vulchev

Falcon Icon via Flaticon/Freepik/Animal Kingdom

TABLE OF CONTENTS

For Lisa and Eliz

INTRODUCTION

Although I had written textbooks on Digital Nonlinear Editing and Digital Filmmaking, it's not as if I woke up one day and decided to do a book on motion picture editors. Rather, after decades of meeting some of the most accomplished editors in the world, I began thinking of all the experience, guidance, and advice that they could impart to a reader. I had, in the past, spent time preserving oral testimonies (from Armenian Genocide survivors) and historical music recordings. And the process of transferring analog audio and video tapes to digital, cleaning, normalizing, editing, and even writing liner notes, was enjoyable because the result was the preservation of historical experiences. And that was my only thought—preserving the experiences of these gifted artists.

Here were craftspeople who have edited some of the most famous, beloved films in the world. What happens when they pass away? What could they impart to aspiring editors? What had they learned—both positive and negative? And who would I interview? I had to adhere to some criteria and after some time it seemed somewhat logical to try and interview every Academy Award Best Editing recipient, either active or retired. Sure, there are BAFTA, César, Golden Bear, but that Oscar statuette—let's face it—is recognizable all over the world.

Thus began "the list". There were practical problems. How to make contact? What if enough didn't agree? And there were names that kept coming up—editors who had never received an Oscar. And those editors didn't receive just one nomination. Gerry Hambling? 6 nominations, amazing editor, never won. Richard Marks? 4 nominations, terrific editor, never won. And there were more. And it would be foolish not to include people, who, in any other year, would surely have won.

I thought that the book would go relatively quickly. Silly me. It ended up taking six years. Paris, Los Angeles, New York, Santa Fe, U.K., Italy, Australia—country after country. Interviews in person, by email, via phone, via video conferencing. Editors who were in the middle of really big films. Some were retired while others were jumping from film to film. Françoise Bonnot, Anne V. Coates, Jim Clark, Jerry Greenberg, Gerry Hambling, Tom Rolf, Thomas Stanford, Neil Travis—what a blessing that I was able to interview them before their passing. Regrets, too. I was two weeks away from interviewing Quentin Tarantino's great editor, Sally Menke, before her passing as a result of a hiking accident. The loss of all these great editors to the editing community is significant. Interviews that were started in one country and finished in another. Revisions. Establishing the right timelines of credits amidst a lot of conflicting dates and information.

Remarkably, the interviews have minimal content revisions. When changes did come, editors (because, of course, they are editors) mostly wanted to make sure that the narrative flow was clear. There was always an issue of length!

Editors who had no intention of entering the motion picture industry and then winning an Academy Award. Editors who were terribly discouraged—careers that were going nowhere. The editor who was so dispirited that he was going to leave the profession. The next call? It led to the Oscar. People who were going to be scientists, mathematicians, photographers, architects…

And as I listened to these fantastic stories, I started to compile a list of themes that kept coming up:

Perseverance: staying with it despite the difficulties that arise.

Awareness: being ready and aware to see the opportunity when it presented itself.

Forthrightness: Asking for the job when you know you can do it.

I think that the editors who agreed to be interviewed did so for two reasons. The first I think was straightforward. I had been at the forefront of digital nonlinear editing system creation and many editors knew me because of that. But I think the second, and the much more important reason, was that I knew their work—who they apprenticed under, the directors, and I knew the films quite well. And I think they knew, given those things, that they and the profession would be fairly represented. There were several editors who I did not know. A conversation would go something like this: "You don't know me, but you did this and that and you apprenticed with so and so...", and pretty much from there we were talking like colleagues.

I was amazed at how many editors had no idea how many awards, in aggregate, the films they edited had garnered. Many did not realize how much money the films had made.

What you are about to read are the recollections, learnings, and guidance from some of the world's finest motion picture editors. If you don't know their names, you'll know the films. And I hope that you will seek out those films you haven't seen now that you know what went into making them from an editor's viewpoint. Watch those films if you haven't seen them—they're well worth your time.

And in the Stranger Than Fiction section?

You don't speak a word of French and yet your very first feature is Fahrenheit 451 for François Truffaut.

You find yourself editing West Side Story for the director who edited Citizen Kane.

You edited a few feature documentaries, but your first non-documentary feature is Francis Ford Coppola's The Conversation working alongside Walter Murch.

You're editing a pivotal scene in The Silence of the Lambs and you need something—a very specific shot—to make it work. And you look and look and it's driving you nuts. And then you look up and that little piece of film you need is hanging—all by itself—from a hook in the trim bin.

Just by chance, you get a job to redo the lined script in Godfather II and then find yourself editing Apocalypse Now.

You wind up working for one of the most famous directors in motion picture history based on a five-minute conversation where he asks you, "Are you a good editor?" And, so far, you win three Academy Awards for editing.

You leave Apocalypse Now to go and edit Kramer vs. Kramer and you're nominated for both films during the same year.

You write a letter to the producer telling him that you just got married and you can't do the film. But you never send that letter. And then you win an Academy Award for Lawrence of Arabia.

The director looks at you, looks at the scene you just edited and says, "Do you have any idea what we went through there? How could you do this?' And then he leaves. So, you work all night and eventually win an Academy Award.

And the life of an editor? Most of the time it's a 6-12-month commitment on each film. Sometimes it's 6-7 days a week. It can be hectic, or it can be much more relaxed.

You don't think about a nomination and you get nominated. You know there's absolutely no chance you'll win, and you do. You thank your family. You forget to thank them. You go right back to work the next day. You wait for a year until the next job comes.

My profound thanks to the editors who agreed to be interviewed and who demonstrated great patience throughout the process. These editors gave their precious time, welcomed me into their homes, their editing rooms, interrupted family and vacation time, and made themselves available across long distances and many time zones. There are some editors who I could not interview—scheduling conflicts and, sometimes, a view that an editor felt that what they do is best left to the imagination. I had to respect those wishes. Perhaps in time…

My thanks to Steve Cohen and Michael Tronick—they were the first people I told about the book and they were terrifically enthusiastic. Alan Heim graciously believed in the project and led me to Jenni McCormick at the American Cinema Editors who was so helpful in tracking down the many needed photographs.

So, read on about these remarkable individuals and revisit their films. They have imparted valuable information about the profession, the films, and the considerations of pursuing a career in editing. An editor's responsibility is not, as many have thought, "to cut out the bad parts", but to form and shape the material according to the director's vision in support of the story. Editing is based on decisions—hundreds, thousands—and everything you see and hear has a decision behind it.

At the time of this writing, the editors who are interviewed in this book have been involved in films that have won a staggering 360 Academy Awards and received an additional 785 nominations!

Finally, imagine you have two million feet of film (or the digital equivalent!) and you must create a two-hour finished product. You're starting with over 370 hours of material. Layer in the realities of a release date that barrels down at you like a freight train coming down the track. Add in a $30 million marketing budget. And a myriad of other issues and multiple constituents whose input must be processed. Editing is a wonderful craft, and it is my hope that you will enjoy hearing about it directly from those who are masters.

Thomas A. Ohanian
July 2018

A BRIEF HISTORY OF MOTION PICTURE EDITING

Traditionally, for theatrical motion pictures, footage was captured on film. For television, footage was captured on either film or videotape. Eventually, of course, technological developments and improvements changed these workflows. Content for theatrical films can be acquired on film, videotape, or digital. Camera sensor technologies have and will continue to improve to the point that there will be no difference between film and digital acquisition. All of these changes are well documented in those countless resources. To keep this section somewhat brief, I have glossed over the specifics of the editorial process, but what is included herein is sufficient for a better understanding of the interviews.

Structurally, film "editing" was first done without actually physically cutting the film. The term, "editing in the camera" meant that in whatever order the final images were desired, they would have to be shot in exactly that order. In other words, you had to plan the shots that would be photographed in their final order. For example, actor "Ace" sees an apple, takes a bite, and his wife "Sue" reacts. First, Ace would be filmed. Then the shot of the apple. Then the shot of Ace taking the bite. Then the shot of Sue reacting. The film would then be developed (now you could see the film's negative) and then printed to a positive (read: workprint) which resulted in a viewable image. That film was projected, and you would see the shots in the same order that they were filmed: 1. Ace, 2. Apple, 3. Ace bites the apple, 4. Sue reacts.

If any of the shots were too short or too long, so be it. They were shot that way and for that length. But if the shot of Sue was what we wanted to see first, how could that be accomplished? The answer is physically cutting the film. The four individual shots would be cut out of the printed film roll. Now, we would have four strips of film, each at the exact length they were when they were shot. At that point, we could rearrange the shots in any order that we desired.

Ah, but not so fast… What order should we choose for the shots? We have four of them. Those four shots yield 24 possible permutations:

1: 1 2 3 4; 2: 1 2 4 3; 3: 1 3 2 4; 4: 1 4 2 3; 5: 1 3 4 2; 6: 1 4 3 2; 7: 2 1 3 4; 8: 2 1 4 3; 9: 3 1 2 4; 10: 4 1 2 3; 11: 3 1 4 2; 12: 4 1 3 2; 13: 2 3 1 4; 14: 2 4 1 3; 15: 3 2 1 4; 16: 4 2 1 3; 17: 3 4 1 2; 18: 4 3 1 2; 19: 2 3 4 1; 20: 2 4 3 1; 21: 3 2 4 1; 22: 4 2 3 1; 23: 3 4 2 1; 24: 4 3 2 1

And that is just four shots. What about eight shots? Now there are 40,320 possible combinations. And what happens when the director has decided to do three takes of each shot? While we still have eight shots, we now have three choices for each of those shots.

Splicing film involved joining the film strips together using a liquid referred to as film cement or film glue. A small section of emulsion of both shots to be spliced together would be slightly scraped in order to make the "cement" adhere to the film workprint. Film cement was eventually supplanted by tape splicing where adhesive tape was used to join both film ends. A film splicer—known as a guillotine splicer—was used to cut the film. A piece of film would be laid into this metal guillotine splicer and a razor blade affixed to the vertical arm would be pressed down, cutting the strand of film into two pieces. At that point, two different film strands could then be spliced together, affixed with tape.

Obviously, cutting the film then led to not only the reordering of the different film shots, but also to be able to adjust the length of the shots.

The Magnasync Moviola from the 1960's. Film viewer on the right and the two magnetic tracks (audio) on the left.

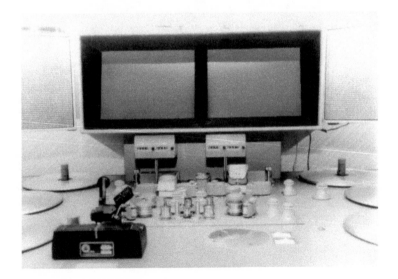

A two-picture head playback flatbed film editing system, particularly useful for A and B (two camera) scene coverage.

The film synchronizer is used to keep reels of film in synchronization with other reels. Picture and audio track(s) with common starts are thus kept in sync. Any change to the length of any track (shortening or lengthening) will result in the audio to picture synchronization being affected.

VIDEOTAPE EDITING

In 1956, Ampex, a U.S.-based company introduced a videotape recorder. Videotape editing was similar to film editing in that the videotape was actually cut. The recorded track could not be seen with the human eye. By applying a liquid to the videotape, the recorded tracks became visible. The videotape would then be cut in the same manner as film, but the joining of two pieces had to be done quite precisely. A solution was applied to the videotape, a microscope was used to see the tracks, and then they were aligned while being held in the splicing block, and then spliced together.

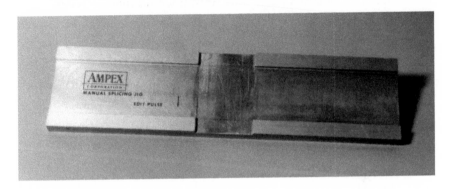

The Manual Splicing Jig from Ampex Corporation. Note the arrow indicating placement of the editing pulse.

Over time, the editing of videotape transitioned to electronically re-recording segments. Videotape was no longer cut and spliced. Instead, most often using the original source recordings, shot by shot was re-recorded onto a new videotape, creating the desired final sequence. While this became easier than physically cutting the videotape, the process was now linear—any change in the recorded sequence could not easily be undone—or reordered. Instead, the changes would have to be re-recorded due to the now linear process.

In other words, let's say that you started to put together your program in this order:

Shot A then Shot B then Shot C

And then, you wanted to switch the order to:

Shot A then Shot C then Shot B

With electronic videotape recording, recall that videotape is no longer physically cut. As a result, the master tape (which has the re-recordings of the original tape), would be wound back to the end of Shot A (since that shot is not changing its position). At that point, Shot C would be recorded at the spot where the previously recorded Shot B had been and at the point where Shot C ends, Shot B would then be recorded. It is this "recording over" process that is necessary with linear, electronic videotape editing. It's easy to see how time-consuming this can be when shots need to be re-ordered. And that brings us to some important terms that are specific to the editing of motion picture images:

Analog
Digital
Linear
Nonlinear
Random Access
Sequential Access

In the case of film, for example, we can classify the editing of film as being analog and nonlinear but not random access. Certainly, the film was not in digital form, so it's analog. Editing the film could be done in a nonlinear fashion (it could be cut and re-ordered) but it was not random access. Because you need to move either forward or back through the film roll (and could not jump from place to place within the film roll), film is sequentially accessed.

Using these terms, we can classify videotape as being either analog or digital. It is linear (isn't physically cut), and sequentially accessed (can't jump around).

ELECTRONIC NONLINEAR EDITING SYSTEMS

To provide a solution which would attempt to combine the best of film editing (nonlinear) and videotape (ability to easily erase and record over), electronic nonlinear systems appeared. These were not digital, and they typically consisted of multiple videotape machines. The videotape cassettes in each machine contained the same material. Thus, by using Machine 1 to play back Shot A and Machine 2 to play back Shot B and Machine 3 to play back Shot C, the nonlinear aspect of film was achieved. We would see Shot A, then Shot B, and finally Shot C. If we wanted to change the order to Shots A, C, and B, Machine 1 would play back Shot A and Machine 2, instead of playing back Shot B would, instead, play back Shot C, and Machine 3 would play back Shot B.

The Ediflex Nonlinear Editing System. Note the bank of multiple videotape machines which provided a limited amount of random access to content.

THE LASERDISC-BASED SYSTEMS

These systems introduced multiple laserdisc players instead of videotape players. Because the read head could jump around the analog video that was recorded onto the discs, fewer machines were necessary than the videotape-based alternative. Another significant benefit was that if an editor was creating a sequence which necessitated a greater number of cuts, there was a much better chance of the laserdisc machines being able to move quickly to the required shots. The laserdisc-based systems can be classified as electronic, analog, nonlinear and random access.

The CMX 6000 Nonlinear Editing System. Here, the bank of multiple videotape machines has been replaced with laserdisc machines which provided random access.

THE DIGITAL NONLINEAR SYSTEMS

By the late 1980's, the combination of computer technology, video compression, hard disk and optical disc storage systems led to the development of digital nonlinear editing systems. Video compression was used to reduce the size of each frame due to the fact that computer storage was quite expensive—$15 per megabyte. The images were compressed at 250:1 and the resulting resolution was quite pixelated.

The CL-550 JPEG compression chip from C-Cube Microsystems, 1990. This chip provided the hardware JPEG compression that was used by the first set of digital nonlinear editing systems.

Because they are digital, the methodology of creating a sequence out of the various shots is akin to how a word processing application functions. You can cut, copy, and paste words to modify a sentence, and a digital editing system enables shots to be easily rearranged and trimmed. These systems can be classified as electronic, digital, nonlinear and random access. Within a 7-10-year period after their introduction, these digital systems became the standard for editing motion picture content.

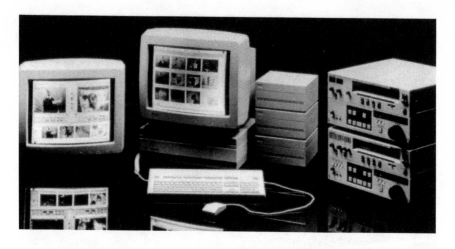

The Avid/1 Media Composer, circa 1990. The videotape machines to the right were used to play back footage which was then converted from analog to digital form and stored as digital files onto the computer hard drives to the left of the machines. The editing software ran on the Macintosh computer under the central monitor which displayed content in the form of thumbnail images.

As you read through these interviews, you will come across the various systems and different forms of workflows which these editors had to employ on their films. Knowing how manually intensive film editing is, or how time consuming it is to change your mind in editing film or videotape makes it all the clearer as to the amazing work that these editors accomplished. Imagine a couple of million feet of film, winding through it, cutting out the takes, splicing and trimming them and doing all of it manually. Two hundred, three hundred hours of film—10, 20, 50 takes of a shot—and now the unique aspect that is the craft of editing becomes clearer.

And through it all, the editor is busy cataloging and making mental or physical notes—the slight moment that an actor made an eye movement that may be of use later on or a shot that was stolen from another take to make a scene work.

There are many fine books and online resources that track the history of how motion picture images are edited. Rather than duplicate those efforts, this brief section provides the necessary background information to better understand the references over the course of the interviews.

THE EDITORS

DEDE ALLEN, ACE

Photograph courtesy of the American Cinema Editors and ACE Eddie Awards

VIA EMAIL

Partial Credits: Wonder Boys, The Breakfast Club, Reds, The Wiz, Slap Shot, The Missouri Breaks, Dog Day Afternoon, Night Moves, Serpico, Slaughterhouse-Five, Little Big Man, Alice's Restaurant, Bonnie and Clyde, America America, The Hustler.

By far, it is Dede Allen who was referenced the most by the editors in this book. Eventually, I was able to contact her, and she was kind enough to reply. She left us a short time afterwards. As you read on, you will find quite a lot about Dede through the words of editors who worked with her and who still admire her work.

✄

Dear Mr. Ohanian,

I appreciate your offer to interview me for your book, but I must decline. I'm retired now. Just about everything I would have to say is in the public record. I started in this business in 1943 at Columbia Pictures as a messenger and moved from there into sound effects editing and editorial assistant. I didn't really start editing until after I got married and moved to New York with my husband.

In my time at Columbia in Hollywood, an editor was considered a craftsman or a technician. It was a back-lot occupation. You were the tool of the studio, not the colleague of the director. That was the conventional wisdom in regard to film editors in those days. In my view, film editing is an art, and belongs in the same category as the writer, director, production designer and cinematographer.

Working in the freer environment of New York, I believe I made an important contribution to the status of the film editor, principally in being the first to get a head credit for the film editor along with the other arts on the film. I wish you success on the book. You are certainly working with some of the best film editors I know.

I hope this is of some value to you.

All the best,
Dede Allen

KIRK BAXTER, ACE

Photograph courtesy of the American Cinema Editors and ACE Eddie Awards

LOS ANGELES, CA

Partial Credits: Gone Girl, The Girl with the Dragon Tattoo, The Social Network, The Curious Case of Benjamin Button, Killing Joe, Zodiac.

Back-to-back Academy Awards, shared with Angus Wall. What I found fascinating when I spoke with Kirk is how the term "editing" takes on additional depth and meaning and where sophisticated techniques are being used to manipulate image and sound. Kirk is on the leading edge of this transformation.

✂

TO: Kirk, you are a two-time Academy Award recipient for best editing, which you shared with your co-editor, Angus Wall. How did you get started?

KB: I started in Sydney, Australia in commercial production. I was a runner for a company that had three cameramen, five directors, an editorial department, two stages, grips, gaffers—the whole nine yards. So, I spent a year assisting everyone, kind of like the dog's body. I really found that I enjoyed editing the most.

TO: That's a great start—to be exposed to every facet of the business.

KB: I was working with one of the best commercial editors there at the time, Mervyn Lloyd.

TO: Were you editing in video?

KB: No, that was still on Steenbecks. So, my first two years were assisting on film and then Avid sort of stormed the scene. I think it was a good and bad thing. When it was film, the editor was sort of clouded in mystery and no one quite knew what they were up to. You had to sit in the back seat and wait for it to be done. And it all got demystified with nonlinear. I found myself within two years working on what I think were the best commercials to offer in Australia. I decided that I was going to go to England. I got very lucky and English directors would bring me to New York and to Los Angeles when they did American campaigns.

TO: How long had you been out of Australia?

KB: I was in London for about six years working and then I hit New York and opened up my own company. So, when I did commercials in Los Angeles, I would work at Angus's company. And Angus and I would do a back and forth so that when he came to New York he'd use my company.

TO: What finally got you to move from New York?

KB: My daughter was born and that was the moment where I decided that I was going to live in one city or the other. So, I joined with Angus. And Angus knew I had always wanted to do movies and there was a moment during Zodiac where David (Fincher) wanted to reshoot a bunch of scenes. Angus had to fine cut those scenes to make sure they were done. So, Angus needed a second pair of hands. I got off a plane from Australia and Angus said, 'Great, you're doing nothing right now. Come and help me.' So I became a member of the (Editors') Union.

TO: You started working on Zodiac as an assistant editor?

KB: No, as an additional editor. I wasn't vetted by Fincher. I was vetted by Angus. So I met David on a Saturday while he was looking over my scenes. And he gave me feedback and I started executing, and it was that simple. And it was supposed to be a couple of weeks to help out and I think I was on it for three or fourth months and that was the baptism. And then David asked me to edit Benjamin Button.

TO: Did the commercial editorial background help you in features?

KB: I dunno. It's taught patience. They have great filmmakers behind them; the coverage is extensive so your film ratio is through the roof just like feature filmmaking. And it really teaches you diligence in finding the absolute best of everything.

TO: How about movies that you saw coming into Australia?

KB: Oh, yeah. I remember sitting in the theatres. The biggest one I remember knocking me out was Seven—that whole title sequence.

TO: And then you wind up working with Fincher...

KB: Right, it ends up bizarrely being Angus who cut that. And it kind of floored me. I remember being knocked out by Pulp Fiction and by (The) Usual Suspects. I started to collect laserdiscs when I was 19. And then I got to understand the experience of Scorsese and Ridley (Scott).

TO: Do you feel each film is a natural challenge?

KB: Yeah. I've gotten so lucky with Fincher. David is an expert at what he does. With David, the amount of coverage is so extensive that you can always be wherever you want to be. So, the editing takes a lot longer. And not only that, but you also start digging into the audio performance extensively and within the frame.

TO: You're taking audio from one take and putting it under another picture take and even more sophisticated things like...

KB: Splitting things up, retiming things, making sure that there is no continuity mistake. People often talk about continuity mistakes but due to the amount of takes and repetition, to get the very best of each thing, we can always correct it. It's story-led and performance-led. And then technically, you can get really accurate.

TO: Are there other editors whose work you admire?

KB: I've tracked filmmakers and their careers but never really tracked their editors. Thelma (Schoonmaker) is the exception to that. When I started to edit at an early age, there were moments in every movie that she and Scorsese did that I found myself watching over and over and over. It was the things that were incredibly dynamic with how you got seven angles into three seconds. And that, I found, just so impressive and I found it even more impressive when I got to meet Thelma. And physically she looks like my Mom! (Both Laugh) And there is this endearing thing where you want to have dinner with her but she is so cutting edge and aggressive about how she constructs these things that's just wonderful.

TO: Any particular examples?

KB: There's this scene in After Hours and I spoke to Thelma personally about this. And they dropped a set of keys out of the top story of this window in New York and someone down at the bottom went to catch it. And there are six or seven shots in this sequence and I watched it so many times. So many times because it just looked incredible. The pool breaks in the Color of Money—I just watched those over and over. All the freeze frames in Goodfellas. I watched all of them over and over again before the trunk got shut. The splashing bucket of blood in Kundun that got thrown across the sand...

TO: That high angle shot...

KB: Oh, it was awesome.

TO: You really studied these. And, really you were sort of deconstructing them...

KB: Oh, what's the name of the editor who won for The Bourne Identity?

TO: Chris Rouse.

KB: He did a movie with the same director before that.

TO: United 93.

KB: That's one of the best-edited movies I've ever seen.

TO: When you did Benjamin Button, was it difficult to work on the film regarding the performance replacements?

KB: No. Again, that was more patience. It's classic David—it just had to be done in a three-step process. We would cut the film using the actor who played the body. And I put a big, black circle around his face so that it wasn't distracting us and so you weren't judging the performance—it was just big black hole. And I would use the actor's voice, as well, for my timing. So first it got blocked out like that. And then we got Brad Pitt in and he did readings of everything. So, you're cutting it almost like radio.

TO: Right, the picture at this point isn't that important—it's the line readings.

KB: Yes, you're putting Brad's stuff into it and he'd retime it slightly. Then he'd do it on camera so now I was able to have these little side pictures in the frame of Brad's head. So, now I'm doing a sort of separate performance and an audio performance and a main picture performance. So, it's this three-tiered thing and once you've locked it off, the actual image started to get created. To me, it's classic Fincher. You're not just picking a shot—you're doing it three times.

TO: I'd like to ask you about The Social Network and The Girl with the Dragon Tattoo. You had a huge amount of footage on these films.

KB: Yeah. David tends to shoot for about nine months. And we're on from the second day of shooting. An assembly goes for nine months and tag another three weeks at the end of that for us to have our first assembly. So, almost ten months to have an assembly and then we go in and fine cut and that's going to take as long as it needs to take. Probably just under 14 months by the time we're done.

TO: That's a long time.

KB: Dragon Tattoo—the coverage on that and some of the scenes were very difficult. It was the hardest to do so far. It was exhausting. I actually don't know how that could have been done with one editor in that time frame.

TO: You and Angus didn't expect to win...

KB: With Social Network, it was so well covered and so well written. Angus and I still had to do our work, but I feel like we were given four Aces. And, Dragon Tattoo, the same thing again. But, we really worked our asses off to make that come together.

TO: I saw a video interview with you and Angus where you talk about dealing with so much footage and how hard a film it was to work on.

KB: It was much harder. I have no guilt about getting that award whatsoever! (Both Laugh) I sweated blood for that. Dragon Tattoo, based on the movie, was much more modular for us.

TO: How so?

KB: Because it took so long for these two characters to meet and intertwine. And because of the book, there were three different endings to it. You had to continue to work out how to make that work for viewers. Whereas Social Network I think we changed one line.

TO: You and Angus achieved back-to-back Academy Awards for best editing. The last time that had been done was Ralph Dawson in 1935 and 1936. And he actually won a third time in 1938.

KB: Respect to Ralph! (Both Laugh)

TO: Okay, I have some other questions that I want to ask you. They are off-the-cuff, okay?

KB: Sure.

TO: What did you think when you saw J.F.K.?

KB: Oh, my God, I forgot about J.F.K. I loved that! That was a very aggressively cut film. There was a moment when Donald Sutherland comes out…

TO: Mr. X.

KB: Yeah. And he sits in the park and he's rattling off all of the reasons why this happened with his fingers. And everything stops. And talk about a scene landing—that scene fucking lands! It lands so well. I remember seeing that in Sydney at Avalon at this tiny little beach theatre. And they even had an interval…

TO: An intermission?

KB: Yeah. And I remember walking outside, just pacing around until it got started again. Because that film is just slapping you across the face for so long and then Donald Sutherland came in and it was so powerful.

TO: There's so much information in that section. It's like a mini-movie.

KB: It just forces you to stop and pay attention because it was clarifying and clearing up and it stops you from being dizzy. God that was so well cut.

TO: Is there are particular film period you like the most?

KB: The moment that I got into loving film was during that '70s movement.

TO: I loved that period. And it wasn't just the two Godfathers. There was Dog Day Afternoon and Serpico.

KB: The French Connection. Kramer vs. Kramer.

TO: Think about the '79 Best Editing Candidates—All That Jazz, Apocalypse Now, The Black Stallion, Kramer vs. Kramer, The Rose.

KB: Fabulous.

TO: Jerry Greenberg was double nominated that year. For Apocalypse and Kramer.

KB: Wow. Kramer vs. Kramer, I think, is such a good film.

TO: I really never would have thought you'd call out Kramer. That's great. Remember, he won for French Connection.

KB: Funny—I went and rattled off two of his movies and didn't even realize it.

TO: Fincher's films seem richer to me. An example is sound—it's not an afterthought in his films. It's not tacked on.

KB: When he's covering a scene, he knows where that camera needs to be and he knows how to get deep into it. He's not going to just give you the wide and the over and the over. He's going to get right into the depth of it so that you can always construct the scene to the best of what it's supposed to be. There are a lot of takes because he's going to make sure that all the beats are landing for each angle. There's never going to be 'Oh, that's okay, we've got it in the close.'

TO: That's pretty amazing to have that.

KB: Right and we're not going to be dictated by, 'Oh, on this line we're going to have to be in the close because that's the best time they said it.' And there's so much repetition in the footage that you can still be somewhere else and take that audio performance from the close-up and put it somewhere else. And when a scene comes in, he's thought it through. You've got all the ingredients you need to cook that properly.

TO: What would you be doing if you weren't editing?

KB: I could be a lifeguard. I like surfing. I like sand between my toes. (Both Laugh)

TO: What do you like most about your craft—your profession?

KB: I like making things. I like making a difference. I like things getting better. I enjoy it a lot. A hell of a lot.

JOHN BLOOM

Photograph courtesy of the American Cinema Editors and ACE Eddie Awards

LONDON, ENGLAND

Partial Credits: Charlie Wilson's War, Closer, Wit, Notes on a Scandal, The First Wives Club, A Chorus Line, Under Fire, Gandhi, The French Lieutenant's Woman, Magic, The Lion in Winter, Funeral in Berlin, Georgy Girl.

Comedy, Drama, Suspense, Music... John moves effortlessly across genres but when he started he didn't even know what editing was! The suspenseful assassination scene in Gandhi to the great comedic timing in The First Wives Club. There is an assuredness in his work that becomes evident from the very first cut.

TO: John, you are a three-time Academy Award nominated editor and you received your Oscar for Gandhi. You are a two-time ACE Eddie recipient. It's a pleasure to speak with you.

JB: Thank you, Tom.

TO: How did you get your start in the film business?

JB: Oh, gosh. It was an incredible piece of luck. It was just before I had to do my two years Military Service in England. My mother asked my sister's (Claire Bloom) agent, Olive Harding, if she knew of a job to fill in my time before I got called up. Olive's best friend ran the Story Department at Pinewood Studios. So I went into the Story Department for a few weeks and got on well enough to be told that there would be a place for me there when I finished my two years away. My mother's request changed my life. We used to read books and scripts searching for something that might interest the resident Studio producers.

TO: That's an important job to be just thrown into like that.

JB: When I did come back there were two others in the department. One, Ted Hughes, was to become the English Poet Laureate and the other was my mentor, Lukas Heller.

TO: Lukas Heller wrote many of the Robert Aldrich movies—The Dirty Dozen, The Flight Of The Phoenix.

JB: Yes and Whatever Happened To Baby Jane. We became good friends and after being in the story department for a year and a half, he said, 'Did you ever think about going into the editing department?' And I didn't even know what editing was at that time.

TO: What a start! You edited Man In The Middle, which was directed by Guy Hamilton who went on to direct Goldfinger and other James Bond films. Music was by John Barry who scored many Bond films, and it starred Robert Mitchum.

JB: Yes, it was a biggish picture, originally called The Winston Affair.

TO: In 1965, you edited Georgy Girl, which became a big hit.

JB: I knew Otto Plaschkes, one of the producers, and I asked him if he would consider me as the editor of Georgy Girl. And that was a real watershed for me because the film was a tremendous success.

TO: And the song was a very big hit.

JB: I have a story about that. During post-production I had put a song sung by Barbra Streisand over the main credits. It was the title song from the stage musical Funny Girl.

TO: I didn't know that.

JB: And it really did work like a charm. In fact, the producers tried to obtain the rights only to find that the price would be larger than the budget for the film. (Laughs) So they were forced to drop the idea and began a search for another song. Eventually I left the film for another project and they came up with the song people know and love. But the truth is that when I first heard it I really hated it. (Laughs) Funny Girl was such a sophisticated number and "Hey There Georgy Girl" was...

TO: More Pop?

JB: Yes. (Laughs) There you go. But the song went on to probably make more than the film itself! I was delighted in the end. The film was such a success.

TO: Georgy Girl, Funeral In Berlin, The Last Safari, and The Lion In Winter. You were doing a couple of movies a year.

JB: When I look back on my career, the truth is that there's an extraordinary mix of things. Very, very good films or films in which one feels one has made tremendous input to make something that was poor into something that was presentable. I think there are films for which I was highly credited, and which were not very complicated or difficult in terms of editing.

TO: Are there films that you think should be revisited?

JB: Who'll Stop The Rain in the late 1970's for director Karel Reisz and a young Nick Nolte. He's amazingly wonderful in that film. The subject matter was how the aftermath of the Vietnam War affected peoples' judgment and it was extremely black. But it was a marvelous film. It was a remarkable and tough film, but it was lost without a trace.

TO: You worked with Richard Attenborough on three very different films—Magic, Gandhi, and A Chorus Line.

JB: With Richard, I felt such a true kindred spirit because here was a man of the theatre and an actor. And he had such a wonderful feeling for actors and performances. And I expect what I've prided myself on over the years, if I have anything to offer, is my judgment and feeling for performance. There is a consistency with Richard in that sense—of attention to everything that goes into the making of a performance. We just saw eye to eye in what we did. Chorus Line was a marvelous experience for me. I never dreamt that I would work on what would be termed a Hollywood musical.

TO: With Gandhi, did you feel the pressure of the public figure?

JB: No, I don't think one thinks of that. We just think of it as a film. The other thing about Gandhi is that I actually tried to talk my way out of doing it! (Laughs)

TO: You're kidding.

JB: No. I was already doing The French Lieutenant's Woman at the time and the two films were going to overlap and I just didn't see how it was going to be possible. At the time, Richard was having to make the film under studio-type conditions. By that I mean he was feeling he had to get a big Hollywood star to play Gandhi. I remember that when we finished Magic, Tony Hopkins was asked to play Gandhi.

TO: Was there a lot of material?

JB: Yes, there was a lot of footage, but you have to remember that we shot for almost six months. There was a lot, but it was spread out. It wasn't like getting 15,000 feet a day with ten cameras. It was much more controlled.

TO: Did you have any idea the film was going to be so well received and so well awarded?

JB: No. Absolutely not. I did think we had a very, very good film. I suppose at that time I wondered if anyone was going to be interested in it. Would the western world in the mid-80's be interested in it? I was absolutely amazed at the attention that it started to get. I think it was the first time that the studio publicity machine used words like "A World Event" and it really did get people going.

TO: Where were you when you heard you received your nomination?

JB: I was in Los Angeles working on the film Under Fire.

TO: Did you feel like you had a good chance?

JB: I did win the ACE award that year and it seemed that if you won the ACE you were the favorite. In some sense, though, you could say I had everything to lose rather than everything to gain!

TO: It's Gandhi, Das Boot, E.T., An Officer And A Gentlemen, and Tootsie. Very big films.

JB: Yes, they were, actually.

TO: And when they announced your name?

JB: (Laughs) Oh my God, I don't know! I think I was in a trance, actually! You know, I forgot to kiss my wife and I don't think I ever recovered from that! I sort of wandered onto that stage. And I'm a pretty shy person. But I memorized my speech and got through it. And then they take you into a pressroom for interviews and I was with Tom Selleck and Raquel Welch.

TO: What do you think you've learned along the way?

JB: When I started I knew absolutely nothing about editing or how films were put together and every moment was learning along the way. I think in truth, every film I do comes to me as fresh and as a surprise. I find every film just as difficult as the previous one. I don't think they've gotten easier over the years.

TO: How do you mean?

JB: I don't mean in the technical sense. I just don't feel that one gets to the stage where one knows it all.

TO: You're evolving as the films change as well?

JB: Yes. Put it this way—however many films I've done, every film is fresh because it is new and the relationships one has to make are new.

Don't forget that the biggest thing on a film is how one relates to the director. And every time you work with a new director it really is a different kettle of fish.

TO: What stands out from dailies that you've received over the years?

JB: Oh, my. Ben Kingsley. We saw the test of him playing Gandhi and I was absolutely knocked back by it. I thought, 'Wow, this could be a really interesting film!' Another example was working with Meryl Streep on The French Lieutenant's Woman who completely bowled me over.

TO: Are there films that you admire as well as other editors whose work you admire?

JB: I think anything that Dede Allen edited. I find her work breathtaking. Thelma Schoonmaker. Claire Simpson. I think they're all wonderful editors.

TO: What films are among your favorites?

JB: The films of Dede Allen, like Dog Day Afternoon. That's a perfect example of a film that I will watch at any time. The editing is superb but I watch films that I happen to love.

TO: Guy Hamilton.

JB: Solid. Professional. I enjoyed working with Guy very much. He was technically masterful.

TO: Karel Reisz.

JB: He was a most wonderful director. We had such a wonderful rapport and understanding. I loved what he did and admired him immensely.

TO: Mike Nichols.

JB: Working with Mike Nichols was a most wonderful time for me.

We seemed to have a true rapport, especially on the first three films. Wit, Angels In America, and Closer are among the most satisfying and enjoyable of my career.

TO: You also received an Eddie award for Angels In America and an Emmy for Wit.

JB: Yes, well, it's nice when they come to you, either early or late in one's career! Very nice indeed. I was very nervous when I started editing Wit. Showing your first cut of a scene is always a nerve-racking experience if you haven't worked with that director previously. Fortunately, Mike was thrilled with what I showed him and thus began a wonderful period in my professional life.

TO: Any advice to budding editors?

JB: Go to the theatre as much as possible because that is where you are going to see what performances are really about.

TO: What keeps you editing?

JB: (Laughs) I still think and hope that there will be (another) interesting subject, an interesting director, and that all the elements can come together in a good environment.

FRANÇOISE BONNOT

Photograph courtesy of the American Cinema Editors and ACE Eddie Awards

PARIS, FRANCE

Partial Credits: The Tempest, Across the Universe, Frida, Titus, Place Vendôme, Mad City, The Apartment, 1492: Conquest of Paradise, Fat Man and Little Boy, The Sicilian, Year of the Dragon, Hanna K., Missing, The Cassandra Crossing, The Tenant, Massacre in Rome, State of Siege, Four Flies on Grey Velvet, The Confession, The Army of Shadows, Z, Guns for San Sebastian, The 25th Hour, A Monkey in Winter, Two Men in Manhattan (assistant editor).

I had loved Z but after I saw Missing, I became a real fan. And there I was, on quite a cold night in Paris where Françoise was just delightful in answering my questions. Her mother was a film editor, but Françoise didn't want to follow in her footsteps—the craft was too time consuming. But she did follow and has such a remarkable career.

TO: Francoise, you are an Academy Award recipient for best film editing for the motion picture, Z. Over a period of three decades you edited eight films for the renowned film director, Costa-Gavras and it is my great pleasure to speak with you, in person, in Paris. Your mother was a very accomplished film editor.

FB: She was an editor and a widow—my father died when I was seven. And she was working, sometime late hours, sometimes during the weekend. And I used to go to the cutting room and I would play with the (film) cores and make splices. And you know at that time you had to scratch the film…

TO: You had to scratch the film so that the glue would adhere to it…

FB: Yes, and so I was going there just to play. When I was a little bit older, I would say to her, 'If I come, can I do something to help you so you wouldn't have to stay so late?' And that was the beginning of mag (magnetic) sound and syncing on mag.

TO: Right. So, you'd come in and sync dailies for her?

FB: My mother would say, 'Do you want to try cutting?' So, I learned editing as you learn how to write and read. When I was 18 years old, I said that the one thing that I did not want to do was to have my mother's job! (Both Laugh)

TO: How funny…

FB: Because I thought you can't have a private life and I still think that's true. I wanted to be an architect. In fact, I think that editing is not so far from architecture. My mother was in Italy, editing Barrage contre le Pacifique (This Angry Age) for Rene Clement. There was a person who was doing a documentary who called and I said, 'Well, maybe I can do what you want.' And that's how it started.

TO: But in a very short time, you moved on to your first full picture editing credit.

FB: Yes and I had married the director, Henry Verneuil.

TO: He was an amazing film director and won the National Cinema of France Academy Award and he won a César Award for Lifetime Achievement.

FB: Yes.

TO: I want to show you something. When I got on the plane from the States to come here, my father gave me some newspapers to read. I brought it with me so I want to show it to you. It's The Armenian Reporter and it had an article about Henry Verneuil…

FB: He was Armenian—his name was Ashot Malakian.

TO: In 1962, you were editing Any Number Can Win.

FB: Yes, in French it was Mélodie en sous-sol.

TO: And then you followed very quickly with Guns for San Sebastian and The 25th Hour. Were you intimidated at all?

FB: When I start a film, even today, I still ask myself, 'Will I be able to edit this film properly?'

TO: You still have butterflies?

FB: Yes. (Both Laugh) Each film is different and then once you start, it's easier.

TO: But we're only talking about seven years and then you start working on Z. And how did Costa-Gavras come into your life? You did eight films with him.

FB: The editor who Costa had been using was not available. And by then I had gotten separated, so I called Costa and said, 'Well, if you want me, I can edit your film!' (Both Laugh) And that's how I did Z.

TO: Amazing. And that you then went on to win an Academy Award for it. The film is as timely and relevant to what is happening in the world today.

FB: Yes.

TO: And it is timeless. Slow motion, flashbacks, flash forwards, the retelling of things from different perspectives a la Rashomon. It's a narrative feature film, which looks every bit like a documentary.

FB: For each film, I have a different style. To me, it's the material that you have that provokes or creates the style. The editor doesn't create the style. It depends on the story you are telling. If it needs to be fast, if it needs to be slower, you stay with a shot longer.

TO: The point of view shots are incredible in Z. For example, when the senator is in the back of the truck and you see his point of view of the gang coming forward. You don't see a lot of those shots these days.

It's a visceral thing where they're coming right at you.

FB: Yes, yes. I can tell you that the thing about having the slow motion, fast, not fast—I had a lot of fun, but at that time, there was no machine that could do this. So, I had to decide which frame I would have to ask the lab to print for three feet. And then I was trying to put this frame in for three frames in still and then the next one in motion for this amount of frames and so on.

TO: Sure. You were sometimes step printing but really, you're describing speed ramping up and down.

FB: Yes. So I wound up with splices on every frame. (Both Laugh) And in the screening room, it was almost impossible to see it because there were too many splices.

TO: Were you editing while he was shooting?

FB: No. He had already shot everything when I started. He had shot in Algeria and they used the lab in Algeria and brought back everything to Paris. And then I started.

TO: Were you working with him at the start or did you work alone?

FB: With his previous editor, he was used to being there and trying things with his editor. And after the first day of working like that with him, I said, 'Costa, I can't work like that. I would like to look at the dailies several times with you and you can tell me what you like and don't like for shots and actors and reactions and then go away.' But he loves being in the cutting room.

TO: Were you prepared for the reception the film would get or of your possibility of winning?

FB: I was sure I wouldn't get it.

TO: Really?

FB: I didn't even hear my name.

TO: Well, here are the films that were nominated that year for Best Editing. Hello Dolly!, Midnight Cowboy, The Secret of Santa Vittoria, They Shoot Horses, Don't They?, and of course, Z.

TO: Did you think you had a chance?

FB: No. Well, Claudia Cardinale and James Earl Jones were the presenters. And she said the names of the nominees and it was in alphabetical order by the film name. And she said, 'And for Z, Françoise Bonnot'. And then she opened the envelope and said, 'The winner is Françoise Bonnot'. But it was so close to what she had just said that I didn't hear it. (Laughs) So, I'm there and the American distributor who was next to me says, 'Françoise! You've got it! You've got it!' (Both Laugh)

TO: That's great.

FB: So, the editing was the first award for Z and I got up and I didn't even think to thank my mother who was an editor. I didn't think to thank my kids…

TO: The blur set in! (Both Laugh)

FB: Yes. I was looking for Costa and I said 'I want to thank Costa who gave me the opportunity to do that film and to have a great time doing it.' And that's it. And then after they take you for pictures. And the next thing—that's absolutely incredible—is that finally Z gets best foreign film.

TO: I want to talk about The Tenant. It has become a cult film now. It's an unusual film and of course you edited for Roman Polanski.

FB: It was difficult because I started at the same time that he started shooting. The film had to go to Cannes so it meant having it in English and also in French. So from the start, production said we had to work six days a week. Roman was working five days a week. Roman was the actor and director and every night we would go and see the dailies.

And from the four or five takes, he'd say which he preferred. So we would actually go, between his shooting, into the screening room and look at them.

TO: Between his setups?

FB: Yes. And the first assistant would arrive and tell Roman that they were ready. So, after a while, I decided that I was going to choose myself and if he wanted a different take, I would change it. I couldn't wait. The first time I showed him some cut scenes, he wasn't happy. And you know, I don't know how to do, in French we call it a 'Bout a bout' (literally translated 'end to end' or perhaps as 'head to tail').

TO: Rough cut.

FB: Yes, a rough cut.

TO: You want to edit fine…

FB: I want to edit, the first time, as close as I think it should be at the end. Because I think if you don't, how can you decide, see, and feel if it's the right rhythm? How do you know if it works or is too slow or too long? And that's what I did with Roman. And he said, 'No Françoise, I don't want you to make so many cuts. Do it with as few cuts as possible and then you can decide if you want to have a close-up.' And I really didn't know how to do that. And I thought, 'I have to be happy with what I'm doing.' So I worked all-night and then early Saturday morning my assistants and I came in. I had the whole film cut. That afternoon, around 1:30, Roman came in and we went into the screening room. I think we had about an hour and fifteen minutes total by then. And we watched everything, and he didn't say anything. And, at the end, he stood up and said, 'Françoise, even my English editor wouldn't have done that!' And then he kissed me.

TO: That's great.

FB: And from that time on, it was great. And you know, it was the same with Cimino. I didn't know him.

TO: Okay. You first worked with him on The Year of the Dragon and then The Sicilian.

FB: Yes. And I wanted to see at least one set of dailies with him.

TO: And another thing that I wanted to bring up is that these films were after Heaven's Gate and there was a lot riding on these films for him and there must have been some pressure.

FB: When I arrived in New York, he had shot Year of the Dragon in Vancouver. So there were already 70 reels of dailies.

TO: Okay, so I always try to figure a minimum of nine minutes out of a ten-minute roll. So that's at least 630 minutes.

FB: Yes, but that was just for two weeks! (Both Laugh)

TO: God bless you!

FB: Yes. (Both Laugh) So I asked Michael if we could look at one scene together. And the next day he said he didn't have any time and that I should move out to Wilmington to start working.

TO: Okay, this was Wilmington, North Carolina. He was shooting in Vancouver but they were going to use the soundstages in North Carolina.

FB: Yes. And that was the first film where I was just in the States by myself. And then I started hearing all these stories about the editors on Heaven's Gate.

TO: And you thought, 'What have I gotten into?'

FB: What have I gotten into? Yes! (Both Laugh) And then Michael says, 'You go and start editing.' So, I started and the continuity girl was fabulous. And for every shot, I would have one page and she had written, 'Michael likes the reading of that sentence, he likes that, he doesn't like that.' So I thought, 'Well, I may as well edit the way I like it, and then we'll see.' So, he arrived in Wilmington and I wanted to show him some cut scenes. And he said, 'Oh, there's no hurry.' I thought, 'He's postponing! Maybe he's going to send me back home!' (Both Laugh)

TO: He probably just wanted to postpone!

FB: Yes. And almost every night I was having dinner with Michael and I asked him when he was going to come and see. And this time I told him that he had to come. So he said, 'Fine, I'll come tonight.' He arrived with ten people around him, sits at the KEM and I showed him a ten-minute reel. He looked at it and didn't say anything. And then he went back, full speed, and looked at it again. And then he said, 'How long did it take you to cut that scene?' I said, 'This one, three or four days.' And he turned to all the other people and said, 'It's great. It's great.'

TO: What films did you work on that you thought should have done better?

FB: I mean, the one, to me, is Across the Universe. Because everyone who has seen it calls me. Because I was sure it would have been universal. The Beatles. I just don't understand why Sony just didn't do anything to market it.

TO: What have you learned during your editing career that wasn't so apparent when you started?

FB: The amount of hours. Very often, the non-recognition of what you bring to a film.

TO: Okay, Missing. Critically acclaimed when it came out. Hey, look at this: it opened tomorrow, a day after we're talking now.

FB: Missing, to me—I mean the performance of Jack Lemmon was so great...

TO: They're in the stadium, he has a pipe and his voice hitches, it breaks, it cracks. It's remarkable.

FB: He's absolutely, really, extraordinary.

TO: I learned that the film was smuggled into Chile so that people could see it. Which is amazing.

FB: It remains a remarkable film. And I think it also helped Americans because it told the story through the eyes of just an ordinary, American middle-class family. And I thought it was such an intelligent way of telling the story.

TO: And this was 16 years before the truth finally was revealed to the world about these thousands and thousands of people who had gone missing.

FB: Yes.

TO: The gunshots that you hear in the distance on Missing are almost a character in the film. They're ominous.

FB: Yes.

TO: And you don't have to hear a lot of them.

FB: No.

TO: Sometimes they sound far away. Sometimes they're a little closer. And as a viewer, you dread hearing those as do the people on the screen.

FB: The woman (Michèle Boëhm) who was doing the effects for Costa was a great sound editor. She worked on many of his films, going back to Z.

TO: We haven't talked about Frida.

FB: Yes, I loved it. When I was in Mexico with Costa for Missing, I had seen paintings from Frida Kahlo and Diego Rivera, so I knew about her. So when Julie said she was going to do the film, I was thrilled. She shot in Mexico and even in the (Frida Kahlo) museum. You know, with Julie I did two films about Shakespeare—Titus and The Tempest.

TO: You've worked with her four times.

FB: I think she's a remarkable person and she is so creative. Titus was her first film and it's just amazing the imagination she has. The visual style is amazing.

TO: Why do you keep editing?

FB: Because I still love doing it. Because I'm probably good at it—yes, I think I'm good at it! (Both Laugh) I still do it will passion. If I didn't, I would stop.

DAVID BRENNER

Photograph courtesy of David Brenner

LOS ANGELES, CALIFORNIA

Partial Credits: Justice League, Batman v Superman: Dawn of Justice, Escobar: Paradise Lost, 300: Rise of an Empire, Man of Steel, Pirates of the Caribbean: On Stranger Tides, Wall Street: Money Never Sleeps, 2012, Wanted, The Patriot, Independence Day, The Doors, Born on the Fourth of July, Talk Radio.

One of the most important things that David talks about is how persistence is key to a prosperous career in editing. It's a lesson in the lows and highs of the profession. While he thought it would be hard to talk about editing, he did a marvelous job of relating what it is like to be one of the top editors working today.

TO: David, you are an Academy Award recipient for your work on Born on the Fourth of July. How did you get your start in the film business?

DB: I got out of college and I knew that I wanted to be in film, somehow. I was at Stanford, but it didn't have a great film program at that time. So I applied to USC and UCLA but I didn't have enough of a portfolio, so I got wait listed. My sister Leslie was an assistant to Les Charles on Cheers and I finally got a job as an extra for a showrunner she knew for a couple of days. I was a PA (Production Assistant) on a non-union picture and it was a really humiliating experience. I spent the whole day standing by a generator and making sure it didn't run out of gas.

TO: Oh, gosh, what a start.

DB: Some AD called me away and, of course, it did run out of gas.

That gig didn't work out. Finally, I found a job as a post-production intern on a movie called Radioactive Dreams. I was excited about the editing room because I had some mentors who were editors. I knew Richard Chew through a friend of my father's. And I went up to the Lucas Ranch and saw him cutting Star Wars on a KEM.

TO: Talk about an introduction to the craft.

DB: He had two eight-plate KEM's in interlock and I remember him cutting the scene where Darth Vader was holding up his general by the neck. I remember talking to him about his experience editing The Conversation and One Flew Over The Cuckoo's Nest. He is just an amazing guy. They hired three interns on Radioactive Dreams. I was just reconstituting trims, but in doing that I learned that there was an ingenious system, which connected this film I was holding to the script itself. The key numbers from the negative were transcribed to a coding system (Acmade codes) that were carefully logged and could point you to a shot and take number from a scene in the script. That concept of a connection between photography and writing turned me on right away.

TO: I think it's great that something as easy to identify as that really got you going quickly.

DB: I really gave that job everything. And my boss at the time, one of the Firsts, was Joe Hutshing.

TO: You're kidding.

DB: No. After the job ended I was unemployed for like six months and it was Joe who called me about an apprentice gig. This show he was on had an immediate need and my job was to sync dailies in a lab in San Francisco, drive them up to Santa Paula, and show them to everybody. And I was crashing in the production coordinator's house in San Francisco. Those were quite tough times.

TO: Sure. It's really hard to get started sometimes and, as you said, many people just give up.

DB: I got through it, though. The movie was called The Blue Yonder and we posted at Lionsgate in Santa Monica. While we were posting the movie, I heard that they needed an assistant across the lot on this movie called Salvador by the guy who wrote Midnight Express. And the word was that people were afraid of him and people were working seven days a week, but that it was a really fun and intense project. So, I got my foot in the door to interview and that's when I met Claire Simpson.

TO: It just goes to show that with passion and perseverance you can make your way through the industry, which can be hard to get in and stay in.

DB: A lot of it is persistence. It's talent. The industry can be very discouraging. I try not to discourage people because the elements can come together. But you have to get through the hard times.

TO: You worked with Claire on Salvador and then Platoon, for which she won her Academy Award for editing. And then you became an additional editor on Wall Street. What did you learn from your time with her?

DB: Everything that's important about editing. She had learned to cut in the English documentary world and then eventually found herself in the cutting room of Dede Allen. She was Dede's First, I believe. So what Claire learned from Dede trickled down to all of us early Oliver people—me, Julie Monroe, Joe Hutshing, Pietro Scalia, others. And then the people who we all mentored, Dede's knowledge trickled down through all of them I like to think. Me, I really started to learn on Platoon. On Salvador, I was one of three assistants. It was an eye-opening experience to working with such a challenging director. I think that experience for me was about facing often grueling hours and intense personalities. It was saying to me, 'This is your little window of what the world can be like.' And it was really about 'Okay, do you really want to do this?'

TO: It's pretty amazing that you recognized the moment for what it was.

DB: And it can be difficult on relationships. Horrendously difficult. I was there sometimes seven days a week. But, then, when Claire said, 'Do you want to be my first assistant on Platoon?' I said yes. And that's when I really started to learn. And I think the answer is that I learned everything. As an editor, you realize how much of your knowledge comes from watching films. As far as the technical side, I learned everything from sitting next to Claire in the Philippines while she was cutting on a Moviola. And when editors were on the Moviola, the first assistant was really important, because the first assistant was like the source machine.

TO: Sure, and you had to be thinking one step ahead.

DB: Yes, I basically had to watch what she was doing and know, with all the material that we had, what she would want. And I had to get that material, open up the trim roll, hang it on the bin, and open up the lined script so that when she wanted an extension, you had to be able to get that quickly—using that coding system that I described. And all of it was intense in terms of being on top of your game, the state of the lined script, the state of the trims. Because you were there the whole time, you got to see every edit and how it was made. And you got to look as she looked at the script and looked at the material and to just see how she made decisions.

TO: What a great opportunity to see, first hand, how it was done!

DB: For instance, I saw that when she was cutting a scene, one of the first things she would do was to cut the dialogue. Make that work, almost like cutting a radio show in terms of the performance. And that's what I learned from her—that dialogue editing is really the driver for picture. It's something that Paul Hirsch, who I had met on The Blue Yonder, had told me. He said, 'Cut the sound and the picture will follow'. And I didn't really understand that until I was sitting with Claire and then I got it. That was the big foundation that I got from her creatively. But it wasn't just that. Once we got back to L.A. and were posting, I learned a lot about the importance of music and the importance of temp music in shaping a scene.

TO: Temp music can have a major influence early on in cutting a scene can't it?

DB: Yes, and music will totally change your feeling about a dry cut. Claire was the person who found the Samuel Barber piece (Adagio for Strings) to use on Platoon. And I just remember how that shaped and changed the mood of the scenes and how you felt about them.

TO: Right. It's a heart-tugging type of feeling when you watch the images with that music.

DB: That became really important on the first Wall Street. Claire wasn't available for the first cut because she was cutting Someone to Watch over Me for Ridley Scott. So, Oliver said, 'Brenner, do you want to be my editor until Claire comes back?'

TO: That was a terrific compliment and vote of confidence.

DB: It was the most terrifying moment in my life. Because you have to remember that I had only been a first assistant only one time in my life on Platoon and Claire won the Academy Award. But I said yes. Oliver said, "That's good, and David, don't fuck it up." I went to New York and later Claire came on and that's when she started to treat me as a second editor. I had done an entire assembly and we walked through it and, of course, she was very critical. And she taught me a lot. We really got into the music for the film and I think helped us get it down from a long two hours and forty-five minutes to the final length.

TO: I think that when sound and picture are so perfectly matched, they seem to be like a character themselves.

DB: It's really true that the tighter that picture design is to sound design and music design, the rhythm of everything becomes one. Look at the movie Wanted, the movie that I did with Timor Bekmambetov. If I could think of one movie that I've done that had the best relationship between picture and sound, it might be that movie.

TO: That's surprising. I thought you would have said Born on the Fourth of July.

DB: Born was awesome. But on Wanted, the way I built scenes from the beginning had to drive the way sound was going to work. For instance, there was a story point that when James MacAvoy's character got afraid, his heartbeat would go up to an insane rate.

TO: Right, it's off the charts.

DB: And when that would happen, the picture would change. He would start to see pulses, and as the pulses happened, the picture would slow down. Almost every shot in that movie is affected with some sort of varispeed. He would also have these experiences on the train and the "click clacking" of the train rails had to be in the same rhythm as the picture cuts, the temp music we chose, and eventually the final music. I'm very proud of that film because of the way that sound and music work on that film. Couldn't have done it without Wyle Stateman and his co-designer on that film, Harry Cohen.

TO: You don't realize all of that's going on in the film.

DB: Sure, because you're not dealing with the most complex story, and we knew that we had to make this about style. Normally, we always temp (mix) our movies, but with something like this, the temp mix is so ingrained on every shot.

TO: You made the move to electronic editing on The Doors and used the EditDroid.

DB: Joe Hutshing and I. Yes, we were looking at a lot of systems. We looked at Montage and we looked at Ediflex, which was the lined (script)-based system. There was Touchvision, which used a bank of VHS machines all running to try and chase source material. EditDroid worked the same way, but with laserdiscs. EditDroid had to cue two laserdiscs to "cut" from one machine to another. It wasn't a nonlinear system by any means. I had been cutting on a Steenbeck (Claire Simpson's flatbed of choice) and the EditDroid sort of reminded me of that. The 20 laserdisc machines made it fun to cut those concert scenes in The Doors. And I loved, for the first time, being able to preview dissolves and fades to white and things like that. We did our first cuts on the EditDroid and we would work through the cuts with Oliver. And when we got to a certain point where we were happy with the scene, we would conform the film. And it was a mess. The conforming process was a completely different program!

TO: Was Born difficult for you to do because of the emotional material?

DB: Yes, there's a scene where Tom Cruise's character shows up on the beach and it's a bright, sunny day. It's late afternoon and the sun is really low and in everyone's eyes. And it's loud and the waves are crashing and someone fires an accidental discharge and then everyone starts to fire. And they go into this village and into a hut where they had killed these women and babies. The scene was emotionally wrenching to say the least. The footage was really challenging—great, amazing, brutal footage and a lot of it. It wasn't a script-driven scene, though.

TO: There was no blueprint.

DB: I mean, the script basically said what happened but it wasn't that much of a help. Right, it was very subjective in how it might be edited shot to shot. There was a point where you had to cut out of the hut and to a Lieutenant who finds out that there's going to be an incoming airstrike so they have to get out. He comes in and tries to pull Tom Cruise's character, Ron Kovic, out of the hut. But Kovic wants to get the baby. And I remember when I first showed that scene to Oliver, I forgot to cut outside to the Lieutenant. I was so involved with Kovic was witnessing that I just had the Lieutenant enter and start pulling him out. When I finished showing that to Oliver, he hit stop on the Steenbeck. It was a Friday. He turned to me, gave me a long unfathomable look and said, 'Do you have any idea what I went through there?'

TO: Oh, my goodness…

DB: And he just stared at me and said, 'Do you have any idea what we went through there?' And he said, 'How could you do this?' And he looked at me for another long beat and then he left. Those were his notes to me on the scene.

TO: What did you do?

DB: So, with those notes, I came in on Saturday and I re-cut the scene. And he came in on Monday and he looked at it and said, 'Much better. Now let's work on it.' You know what? He was right about one thing, I did not know on more than a surface level what he went through back there, so there was something I could only discover in the scene through time, a lot of thought, and suffering. There was so much psychological pressure he had on himself to tell that story the right way.

TO: A tremendous pressure for you and Joe Hutshing on the film…

DB: And that was present constantly.

TO: Was there a breakthrough when you realized how to handle the scene?

DB: I think the main thing I realized that I was too cutty.

TO: You were cutting too much.

DB: Yes, I realized that the true moment came from Tom Cruise's single (angle) and I think I was away from him too much. I had been so blown away by the wealth of these great Steadicam shots and I think the emotion of his character didn't track. That's usually what's wrong with a cut of a scene. Oliver will say, 'I'm not getting the emotion of the character enough' and you have to figure out how to get there. Oliver Stone is a notes director. He doesn't want to be there in the editing process because he wants to have a fresh eye.

TO: March 26th, 1990. Born on the Fourth of July, Driving Miss Daisy, The Fabulous Baker Boys, Glory, and The Bear. At the ACE awards, Glory was chosen and sometimes that's an indication of what will be chosen at the Oscars. Did you think your chances were good?

DB: No, I didn't think we were going to win because I thought they were going to give it to Glory, which was an amazing film. But then we won and it was a surprise. I will say that Born on the Fourth of July really stands up.

TO: It has longevity.

DB: It really is an amazing film. Sometimes as an editor you can't go back and look at a film for a long time, because you think about the cut that you made or the disagreement that you had over a scene, or the long nights disappointing your family. It's too hard. After a while you can go back and look at the film. And you know what? They don't make films like that anymore.

TO: Have there been films that you edited that didn't do well but you think should have done better?

DB: Heaven and Earth opened so close to Schindler's List that no other dramatic film could really get attention because Schindler was such a phenomenon. I would say besides Heaven and Earth, it would be Lolita.

TO: You edited that for Adrian Lyne.

DB: Julie Monroe and me. It's one of the films that I'm most proud of as an editor.

TO: Tell me why.

DB: It's a beautiful masterpiece. Gorgeous cinematography. The attention to detail that Adrian Lyne gave. Every shot, be it a wide landscape or a close-up on one of his actors. It's a disturbing story and it's told in a way that Jeremy Irons made this character so sympathetic. And I think, in a sense, it was difficult for people, but Adrian was very faithful to Nabokov's book. It's a film that people were afraid of. On top off all this, the production company, Carolco, went under while we were editing so we had no distributor.

TO: It's unfortunate.

DB: We really had to search for a domestic distributor. It was a film based on a literary property, a period film, and a subject of a disturbing nature and financially there was a risk that the studios were probably not willing to take. Even Paramount, the studio for which Adrian had made almost a billion dollars. Finally, the Samuel Goldwyn Company bought the movie, and realized it in some theaters for a couple of weeks. Then it was released on Showtime.

TO: You used split screens very nicely in Wall Street: Money Never Sleeps.

DB: Those split screen montages are sort of old fashioned. They come from the '70's from films like Airport and The Andromeda Strain. And the first Wall Street had these split screen montages when they were making trades and Oliver loved them. Remember the Steve McQueen film…

TO: The Thomas Crown Affair?

DB: Yes, The Thomas Crown Affair. We tried to do them ala that film.

TO: I thought it was great the way you did it.

DB: And with all the people talking, it was not easy to cut. The way I approached it first, was to remember once again—make sound work first. I cut it in a certain way where the audio was very clear and then I'd look at the picture and then it became where to place the boxes and what size should they be and what draws your eye. I tried to make it so there was only one person whose mouth is moving.

TO: Really? That's interesting.

DB: Yes, it's something I found out. It's better to have everyone else listening because your eye will go to the moving lips.

TO: Starting with Salvador, you've thus far worked on nine films with Oliver Stone.

DB: As an editor, I did Wall Street with Claire Simpson, then Talk Radio, Born on the Fourth of July, and The Doors with Joe. I was on The Doors for about a year and a half.

TO: That long?

DB: Yes, and that was a thrilling experience for me. Later I did Heaven and Earth with the late and truly great Sally Menke. World Trade Center and Wall Street Money Never Sleeps with Julie. My favorite of those films as an editor was probably Doors. It was everything you can imagine. The images that Bob Richardson shot on that film are some of my favorite images that I ever got to cut. And the montages intercutting concert footage with story beats were the most exciting. There's a song, Not To Touch The Earth, that the Doors play at this huge outdoor concert where there's an enormous bonfire and Jim Morrison has these hallucinations of Indians around him.

TO: It's a very memorable moment in the film.

DB: We intercut this with him fighting with his wife. Then he burns the house down and he and his buddies get in a car and are driving around. And finally he gets married in this witch ceremony. And all of these things are intercutting and you have to come back in the song at the moment that is dynamic visually and musically… then you have to choose the right moment to cutaway once again. It was usually with the completion of camera movement or a musical statement… or it could be something more surprising and off-putting. And it all has to build. This is just the most wonderful, challenging thing for an editor. The film had so much of that. When we were on the mixing stage, I don't think I had had a week off since Talk Radio—three films, back to back. I said to Oliver, 'You know, I need a break after this.' And he said, 'You don't understand what I'm doing. The next film I'm doing is J.F.K.' And he described the film to me and it was 'Oh, my God, how can I not do this?' But I was so exhausted. I didn't think I could do it. It was just sheer exhaustion.

TO: Well, you had been going for four straight years, at the very least.

DB: I backed out of the film and it turned out to be one of his greatest, if not the greatest film that he ever made. And all the things that The Doors offered was just a tiny hint of what they did on J.F.K. and the ground broken by Joe, Pietro Scalia, and also Hank Corwin on that film.

TO: But you continued with Oliver Stone after J.F.K.

DB: And Heaven and Earth was a great experience. During our post, he went off to shoot Natural Born Killers. We had to take copies of our edits to where he was shooting in Arizona and it was very difficult to finish the film because of that. But we had a long post and Sally and I got to really explore a lot.

TO: You worked pretty much non-stop between Heaven and Earth and World Trade Center. Here are the films: The River Wild, Fear, Independence Day, Lolita, What Dreams May Come, The Patriot, Kate & Leopold, Identity, and The Day After Tomorrow. Talk about variety. There was a long gap before you worked again with Oliver Stone on World Trade Center.

DB: You know, for the next eight films or so, Oliver was always on a different schedule and we could never line up. With World Trade Center, he wanted to go back to something that was very simple.

TO: It's not easy to do a whole film with these two men trapped for the majority of the film.

DB: At first, we didn't know that he wanted that simpler approach. So, we really amped up the scenes and aggressively cut with a lot of sound design. We even had some subliminal cuts. And Oliver gave me no indication that he didn't want to do that. So, when I showed him a cut of one of the scenes, he said, 'No, no, no—I want to make this way more like a documentary. I want to make this very simple. I don't want to pump this up.' He was talking about the first act of the film, through where the buildings fall. Once they were under, the situation lent itself to more license. But even those sections aren't too stylized.

TO: You know the critics wrote something like 'Stone is restrained' but I liked the film. It was about these two men and the style supported that.

DB: And it let the actors and the story take center stage because the story was still absorbing and disturbing.

TO: Given all the experience you have, do you get asked to talk about editing a lot?

DB: You know most of us get a little tongue-tied when we talk about editing. Walter Murch is very articulate about it. He's a great theorist. For me, I just know what works for me, and, I know when it feels good. Editing is a physical thing and you're using your gut all the time. And when it's really working, you're in this zone where time flies, and you're really sailing.

CONRAD BUFF, ACE

Photograph courtesy of the American Cinema Editors and ACE Eddie Awards

LOS ANGELES, CALIFORNIA

Partial Credits: The Equalizer 2, American Assassin, The Huntsman: Winter's War, Snow White and the Huntsman, Rise of the Planet of the Apes, Training Day, Thirteen Days, Titanic, True Lies, Terminator 2: Judgment Day, The Abyss, Spaceballs, Jagged Edge.

Imagine being a visual effects editor on The Empire Strikes Back building complicated layers in an optical printer. And then the ability to shape performances of CGI characters as a cut scene evolves. That shows the breadth of experience that Conrad has. He just has this ability to get every bit of kinetic energy that the footage has and highlight it.

✂

TO: Conrad, you are an Academy Award, Eddie, and Golden Satellite Award recipient. How did you get your start in the motion picture industry?

CB: I had an early interest in film, which was born out of an interest in theater. When we were kids, we were always endeavoring to get a part in a play and to see plays. And we put on plays at the ripe old age of seven years! One day I was visiting my grandfather, who was an artist and a painter. He had cameras that he used to take reference photos for his paintings. So that really began an interest in photography. And eventually the light bulb went on in terms of the connection between theater, photography, and cinema.

TO: Were you also going to a lot of films?

CB: Yes, this all manifested itself as my mother was taking me to see films by Ray Harryhausen and the early Hammer films. And then somewhere around age eleven I did a lot of odd jobs and saved up forty bucks and bought an 8mm film camera. I wanted the single frame capability so that I could emulate the stop-frame animation of Ray Harryhausen. And eventually through my teens, I was making films with my friends and eventually graduated to 16mm. And in the '60's I was being bombarded with these great films that were coming out.

TO: Which films come to mind?

CB: Darling by John Schlesinger. Morgan! (Karel Reisz). Far from the Madding Crowd by Schlesinger. This Sporting Life by Lindsay Anderson. And all of a sudden, my tastes changed and I gave up my interest in visual effects and I was very much interested in cinematography and not in editing.

TO: When did editing come onto your radar screen?

CB: In the late '60's when I saw Bullit. Not as a career, but as an appreciation of the contribution of the editor. So I went to Pasadena City College but I got drafted and ended up in the Navy. I wound up in Washington, making films for the Office of Information. We had a small, 8-10-person group and we made documentaries.

TO: It sounds like a great training ground.

CB: I was able to experience all the technology and equipment of filmmaking. We had Steenbecks and Arriflexes and it became my film school.

TO: Before your first picture editing credit, you worked on many groundbreaking films in the area of visual effects as a visual effects editor and editorial supervisor. Films such as "Raiders of the Lost Ark", "The Empire Strikes Back", and "Ghostbusters".

CB: After the Navy, I spent five years working in high-end commercials for clients like United Airlines and Budweiser. And in those days, commercial editorial was all film. And, frequently, the commercials had a lot of complicated effects work, all of which were composited on optical printers. But, after five years, I wanted to move on.

TO: But you had all the visual effects compositing experience.

CB: Right, and one day I got a call from someone who asked me if I knew anyone who knew about optical printing and visual effects. And I said, 'Me', without knowing what it was for. I ended up working at Industrial Light and Magic when John Dykstra was running things. This was right after they had done the first Star Wars and they were doing Battlestar Gallatica for television. And that was really my transition to features. And while I was there, an old friend—Dennis Muren—who I had known since I was a teenager—was working there as was Richard Edlund. They said they were moving up north to establish ILM in the Bay Area and were going to do The Empire Strikes Back. And they asked me if I would run the editorial department.

TO: And ILM grew very rapidly.

CB: The company was very successful and then Raiders of the Lost Ark came along and I worked on that. Then Poltergeist and then E.T., and I had a minor hand in all of them. Then, when George Lucas decided to do the last of the Star Wars films, I asked if I could move into live action as an assistant and they agreed, which was wonderful. And that really was my initial break. And my desire at that time had really grown into wanting to be an editor. Marcia Lucas was editing as well, and she was quite amazing. She was very influential and helped my appreciation of what one can do with the craft. It wasn't just about assembling what you saw—it's sometimes completely reengineering a scene. That was quite enlightening and made me want to do more. I was fortunate to meet Sean Barton, who was Richard Marquand's editor, and that's how I wound up on Jagged Edge.

TO: Jagged Edge did very well at the box office. I love that John Barry score.

CB: I did too. I was Sean's assistant on Jedi and he called me. I was just finishing Ghostbusters and I was first hired as an assistant editor. But, really, I only cut a few scenes and Sean cut that movie with Richard. However, it allowed me to share a credit with a friend and it catapulted me into being able to do a film on my own. And the apprentice was Billy Goldenberg who then went on to do a lot of work with Michael Kahn. It was a great transition for me into the editing world.

TO: When I went to see Training Day, I wasn't sure what to expect. Denzel Washington is just scary.

CB: Training Day was one of my favorite experiences as an editor. Denzel was so shot out of order that it wasn't until very late in the game that I had enough material to begin to connect scenes. I liked the script, I liked Antoine Fuqua, the director very much, but I didn't know if it was gelling. When I connected the scenes, I ran out my cutting room and across the patio at Warner Bros. to my assistant's room. And I said, 'This is actually a really good movie!' And there was a real joy and excitement about that one to me.

TO: What were some of the challenges on the film?

CB: Editorially, the performances were a challenge because I had a huge amount of material. And there were so many choices to make. Denzel was experimenting wildly from take to take. There were variations physically, emotionally, and there were hours of material with these actors who spend a lot of time being towed in their car. So, you had the ebb and flow of performances and it was a real challenge. I'm quite possibly more proud of that movie than almost anything else I've worked on. I know I had a big contribution in making it work as a film.

TO: It did very well with audiences.

CB: Yes, but its success was a bit of a surprise. We tested it at screenings and it never tested all that high.

TO: Really?

CB: Yes, no matter what reengineering we attempted. And Lorenzo di Bonaventura, who was running the studio at the time said, 'You know, I like this movie. I don't care what the numbers are. Let's release it.'

TO: You made the transition from film to digital editing on The Getaway.

CB: A lot of my friends in the commercial world were using the Avid on a daily basis. I was interviewing for The Getaway and the studio had an accelerated post schedule. They suggested using Montage, with the multiple tape decks. And I said, no, either I'm going to edit this on film or I'm going to edit it digitally. So I gave Roger a demonstration and he loved the idea.

TO: And then after The Getaway you went on to True Lies.

CB: And I never went back to film. I introduced Avid to Jim Cameron on True Lies and he was dubious but then decided yes—because he's intrigued by technology—and came to appreciate what it could do for him.

TO: You've done a lot of films where there have been multiple editors. How do you approach that?

CB: Both The Abyss and Terminator 2: Judgment Day were edited on film. I still very much like T2. Jim has a wonderful ability to shoot beautiful material and write very compelling pieces that are great movies. What I most appreciate about him is that he does so much homework. He is not winging it when he's out there and hoping it's going to come together. He has researched, written, determined approaches and is also fascinated by the technology. Jim shoots a lot of material but, unlike a lot of people, he shoots a lot of really good material.

TO: And both The Abyss and Terminator 2 had tremendous visual effects. Can you recall your reactions when you first saw what was being developed?

CB: Astounding! (Both laugh) And ironically, it was my old friend Dennis Muren who was the visual effects supervisor. The water tentacle in The Abyss was mind blowing. The first time I saw the test it was—Oh My God—staggering. But this is Jim and honestly he is the guy who pushes all this—witness Avatar, Titanic, True Lies, and Terminator 2.

TO: True Lies is great because of the balance between action and humor.

CB: He's very good at the balance between story and character and incredible action sequences. His films are always events and they're always wonderfully thought out and that's what's great about working with him. One of my favorite moments in The Abyss is a scene that Joel Goodman edited. And I thought he did an absolutely brilliant job. And it is the scene between Mary Elizabeth Mastrantonio and Ed Harris where she is essentially drowning. It was so well put together and the choices were staggeringly good.

TO: It is so suspenseful and so hard to watch.

CB: It's beautifully done. In Terminator 2, I have a fondness for what we called 'The Canal Chase', when the bad terminator pursues the boy and Arnold rescues him. I cut that scene and it was all on KEMs and Moviolas and I'm quite proud of that scene.

TO: It's great.

CB: It's very satisfying. Now, on True Lies, one of the most complicated sequences I ever worked on was the Harrier sequence when Arnold is trying to rescue his daughter. And that took me weeks and weeks because of the amount of footage, the techniques that were used that Jim devised, and how to blend them seamlessly. It was very challenging so I'm proud of that one area. On Titanic, the concept was that Jim was going to edit the film himself. And he just got too busy. So, I went over to his house and he showed me some footage from his dive to the actual Titanic, which was used for all the R.O.V. exploration. And it was magnificent and stunning material and it was just jaw dropping. It was way beyond your expectation. And that doesn't happen very often.

TO: Did you realize how successful the film was going to be?

CB: I started getting dailies and immersing myself in the film, but I had no idea how impactful the film was going to be.

TO: What did you start with?

CB: The first scene I was assigned was the 'Poop Deck Sequence', which sounded rather benign when I signed up. Well, the poop deck sequence involved the final moments of Rose running to the end of the ship as it's going down. And she and Jack are clinging to life along with a handful of others as the ship is descending for its final plunge. It was technically very complicated because there were multiple techniques employed and multiple camera crews had shot material. Jim had done the principal photography and stunt work and then there were miniature units, things that had to be composited, and things you had to imagine. And the challenge was to marry all these different techniques and make it seamless.

TO: How much was length an issue in the cutting room?

CB: At one point, Jim and Richard (Harris) and I were discussing the length and I suggested the David Lean approach of putting in an intermission. But Jim felt that there was no way to break it up and he was right.

TO: If you had done that, where was it going to be?

CB: It would have been somewhere near spotting the iceberg. But it wasn't necessary. Even though it's a very long film, it's compelling enough.

TO: Let's talk about Oscar night.

CB: You don't want to think about being nominated and you try to dismiss it. And when I heard my name called at the Academy Awards, it was exhilarating. You sort of float to the stage hoping that you don't blow the acceptance speech!

TO: Are there films that you edited that, for whatever reason, didn't do as well as they should have and that you feel the reader should revisit?

CB: One of my personal favorites is Jennifer Eight and another is Seraphim Falls. And they both have flaws but the experiences were great.

TO: When you edited Rise of the Planet of the Apes, what was unique to you as a new experience?

CB: That was a new challenge for me and it keeps you going and I learned a great deal on that film. Andy Serkis flat out did a wonderful job. It was his performance that we were trying to harness. I was, initially, stymied because I wondered how in the world I was going to make editorial selections based on the performance. Here is an actor, in a gray suit, with all sorts of reference markers on him, being captured by various cameras. And he is interacting with actors.

TO: So what specifically was challenging about that?

CB: One of the difficulties is that the interaction with Andy Serkis and Freida Pinto, James Franco, and John Lithgow was that they, as actors, responded best performance wise in the shots where Andy Serkis was present. Very often we had to utilize what we call clean plates, where we would shoot the scene again without Andy Serkis in it. And the actors would try to emulate the performance and the physicality of the previous takes that Andy was in. And I found that incredibly difficult to harness his performance and integrate and structure the scenes. And remember, at this point, you're still watching a cut that has actors interacting with people in gray motion capture suits.

TO: Right, the ape characters aren't there yet.

CB: Yes, and it was hard for the studio to experience the emotionality that we had gotten used to in the cutting room. Act two was virtually without dialogue. So there were vast passages where we had motion capture actors pretending to be apes. Is the scene working? Is the second act working? It was enormously challenging and I credit the director, Rupert Wyatt, who was able to endure a year of shooting and a year of post-production and being able to overcome the challenges of limited visual information.

TO: Other than the intensive use of motion capture, was this like working on a normal feature?

CB: No, it was, for me, like working on an animated film.

TO: What do you mean?

CB: We had the ability to change not only the performance but also the physicality of how a character would get from A to B in a shot or in a scene. We could alter time and space.

TO: This is an important point you're making. Because you could also alter the performances of the apes.

CB: Yes, and that's the first time I've ever been able to do that! And it was incredibly educational and challenging. It's yet another tool in the arsenal.

TO: You're rewriting yet again.

CB: Yes, exactly. And we did a lot of rewriting.

TO: That's pretty amazing. What have you learned along the way?

CB: The thing that I didn't realize initially was what an amazing impact editorial has on a film. How you can truly have a significant impact on reactions and how people perceive the film. Just through the manipulation of imagery, sound, and music. But I think the biggest thing for me was you can significantly alter peoples' perceptions.

TO: Are there any films that come to mind where you really admire how they were put together as well as other editors whose work you admire?

CB: Films that specifically hit me were Day of the Jackal, Fred Zinnemann's film, edited by Ralph Kemplen. That film to me is a masterpiece. You know what the outcome is going to be because Charles de Gaulle did not die. And yet, the tension is unbelievably great. The rawness, the documentary quality of it all, the performances, it's a beautiful piece of work. In the Name of the Father, Gerry Hambling's editing work. Everything I ever saw Gerry Hambling do was so strong. A film that I think is absolutely wonderful and it is all about editing is Duel, edited by Frank Morriss—good God, it's beautiful. And I liked Charley Varrick. And I was also influenced by Dede Allen's work in the '60's. Jim Clark for Darling and The Killing Fields.

TO: If you weren't editing what would you be doing?

CB: Cinematography still holds that fascination. I'm not sure. Medical? Airline Pilot? (Both laugh)

RICHARD CHEW, ACE

Photograph courtesy of the American Cinema Editors and ACE Eddie Awards

LOS ANGELES, CA

Partial Credits: Music, War and Love, The Way, The Runaways, Bobby, The New World, I Am Sam, Shanghai Noon, Hope Floats, That Thing You Do!, Waiting to Exhale, Singles, Men Don't Leave, Clean and Sober, Real Genius, Risky Business, My Favorite Year, Goin' South, Star Wars: Episode IV - A New Hope, One Flew Over the Cuckoo's Nest, The Conversation, The Redwoods (Documentary Short).

Richard has had an amazing career and is still at the top of his game. The first feature? The Conversation, working alongside Walter Murch. Then Cuckoo's Nest. Then Star Wars. All back to back! Each decade has brought memorable films and timeless work from this soft-spoken and talented editor.

TO: Richard, you are an Academy Award and two-time BAFTA recipient for Best Editing. You received your Academy Award for Star Wars and your BAFTA Awards for One Flew Over the Cuckoo's Nest and The Conversation. What led you to editing?

RC: I really enjoyed shooting documentaries, interacting with those subjects and travelling and seeing places as a cameraman. I shot a documentary called The Redwoods, which won an Academy Award for Best Documentary short back in 1967.

TO: I didn't know that.

RC: When I got into the editing room with Trevor Greenwood, who was the director, he showed me what he was doing with the images. And the images took on a different meaning in editing than when I was on location shooting. You can talk about it. You can read about it.

Then when you're doing it, you become intoxicated with the power of it.

TO: You've edited many different genres. Do you have a favorite?

RC: I would probably favor comedy because you have to be so much more adept at timing. Comedy has its own subtleties and timing. My new interest is a style of narrative and I think it's nonlinear versus linear storytelling.

TO: Can you explain?

RC: Well, the moviegoer has been conditioned to see stories in a linear fashion.

TO: Beginning, middle, and end.

RC: Right. Something happens to our protagonist and there's a conflict and this is what he does in response to it. And then the villain does this, the protagonist does that, and there's a resolution and an ending. In the last 10 to 15 years, we've seen the growth of much more sophisticated storytelling. You take these events that seemingly are not associated with each other at the beginning of the film and you begin to interweave them in a way that makes sense to you at the end of the picture—like Babel.

TO: Great example. In the past, audiences could understand flashbacks and then flash- forwards, but it took some conditioning.

RC: It's much more demanding of the viewer.

TO: 1973 to 1977. The Conversation, One Flew Over the Cuckoo's Nest, and Star Wars.

RC: I was in the Bay Area when Francis Coppola, Milos Forman, and George Lucas were in the prime of their careers. What sticks in my mind is how much I learned from each of those films and those directors. I was pretty naïve about the power of editing.

TO: Can you give some examples?

RC: I had the good fortune to work with Walter Murch on The Conversation. I began to put together the first cut because e Walter was unavailable. After I put the film together in the order that it was scripted, Walter showed me, with the encouragement of Coppola, how to restructure the scenes and create scenes from fragments of other scenes. And we worked on that film for almost a year and a half.

TO: What do you think when you see the film today?

RC: What I learned when I see it now is the flexibility—the plasticity—of structure and how editing can accomplish that. On Cuckoo's Nest, Milos Forman is a director who is a really good editor. And I learned how to use reaction shots. How to use the characters that did not have dialogue and incorporate them into a scene. On the ward, most of the dialogue was from the McMurphy character—Jack Nichols on—and Nurse Ratched. Milos taught me where to put the reaction shots of the other patients —Billy Bibbit, Cheswick, Harding— these other people who then contributed to the atmosphere of Nurse Ratched's dominance of the ward.

TO: The reaction shots are so perfectly placed throughout that film.

RC: Yeah. And I thought it was wonderful—you're advancing the story and the characters by the use of these wordless moments. Milos shot all these other characters with two cameras. If the main camera was on Jack Nicholson, then a second camera would be on Brad Dourif, who played Billy Bibbit, as an example.

TO: Real Genius is like that as well—characters react without saying anything and it is very funny.

RC: Right. On Star Wars, what I learned was the power of cross-cutting. When I was putting together the first cut, especially the opening third of the movie when the Storm Troopers invade Princess Leia's spacecraft, the script had them as extended scenes. In working with my co-editor Marcia Lucas, I learned the power of cross-cutting from her. We broke up those extended scenes into sections that were ten to twelve seconds long. And then we would intercut them as parallel action. So, that was a new device for me to learn how to use. When I think back, not only did I have the chance of working with really good directors, but also with really good editors. Whether it was Walter Murch or Paul Hirsch or Marcia Lucas or Lynzee Klingman. It was a wonderful way for me to start my feature career.

TO: With Star Wars, were you surprised at winning?

RC: Yes. Some of the other nominees that year were Michael Kahn and Walter Murch. These guys are kinda superstar editors. It's really a tribute to George Lucas, his imagination, his unique vision.

TO: Bobby is a great film. It didn't get the attention it deserved.

RC: It was a remarkable experience. Another one that has endured is the sequence in Risky Business where Tom Cruise and Rebecca DeMornay make love on the train. And I think that people react to the sensuality of it. It's very mesmerizing and seductive.

TO: Are there films that you edited that people should revisit?

RC: One is Men Don't Leave. It was a really insightful take on depression and how a single mom goes about raising two boys in a strange city. Jessica Lange plays the mother seeking romance and she's not able to control how her sons are growing up outside of her home. The audiences never warmed up to it.

TO: Why do you think the audience response wasn't there for Bobby?

RC: I think, in retrospect, that maybe audiences thought it was too didactic or too overtly political. I'm not sure about this but maybe it hurt the picture that the whole closing credits dwelled on the Kennedy family. That wasn't the original impulse behind the film as written by Emilio Estevez. It was because of Harvey Weinstein's adopting the picture as one of his own. And he did exert some pressure, requiring us to cut the movie in order to include more of Bobby Kennedy. To the point where the whole closing credits are all photo stills of the Kennedy family.

TO: Right.

RC: So I don't know if that was a turn off for people who may have liked the story if it were more self-contained and not as a tribute to the Kennedy family. I don't know, but that's just a guess.

TO: Joel Cox told me that he thought it is a beautifully edited movie.

RC: Really?

TO: Yes.

RC: That's very kind of him. Joel's a terrific editor himself. I would add I Am Sa m. I think Sean Penn is so good in it. And Dakota Fanning —she was six years old when she acted in that. I think she was just astounding.

TO: How about films that you like to watch?

RC: Well, I was in law school at the time that I saw the picture that led me to want to work in film: Nothing but a Man.

TO: Okay, one second. I don't know it. Let me look it up. Okay, I see it—1964.

RC: Right. It was made by these two guys who had gone to Harvard, and starred Ivan Dixon and Abbey Lincoln. The story takes place in the South and her character's father is a pastor who opposed her seeing this blue-collar worker played by Dixon. Their courtship, the opposition by the father, the white co-workers and customers of the place where Dixon works all add up to a layered story. Before I saw this, movies were entertainment in my mind, not thought-provoking. This was the first time where I became aware of an American film that seemed relevant for the times.

TO: And had a social aspect to it...

RC: Yeah. I hadn't seen To Kill a Mockingbird yet. And the sound effects and music track added such rawness to each of the scenes. It really opened my mind to thoughts of 'Hey, this is really great. What if I could learn to do that? Can people do this for a living?'

TO: It's great that you can trace it back to a single film and an experience like that.

RC: I am forever grateful to Michael Roemer and Robert M. Young, the filmmakers. It wasn't overtly political, but by showing the hardships of two African-Americans who were just trying to pursue a normal life against certain societal odds made the film implicitly political. I like to mention that film because it led me to the career I have. Robert Young gave me a lot of guidance at the beginning.

TO: You made the transition to editing electronic nonlinear...

RC: I wasn't raised with computers but learning to work with them wasn't difficult for me. The first film I edited on computer was Waiting to Exhale. And it was a really good match because I found the digital equivalent to what I was used to doing on film.

TO: That's why when we created it we used those very similar film concepts.

RC: Well, you succeeded with me, buddy. (Both Laugh)

TO: It was all timing.

RC: Digital editing has created the misconception that it would speed things up. Whether it's Pietro Scalia, Paul Hirsch, Lynzee Klingman—it's a creative task and you don't create faster because you have a computer in front of you. That's why directors shoot so much—because they want options. All of a sudden, the editor now has

15 takes per angle — instead of three—and so our task becomes more time consuming.

TO: Are there films that stand out where you were particularly challenged?

RC: The Conversation for sure, because it was such an editorial puzzle. Credit has to be given to Walter Murch for solving that. I was just too inexperienced. But the one that I was more intimately involved with and that took much longer is Bobby. As I mentioned, after it was shot, there were issues that Emilio and I had to solve. And when Harvey Weinstein picked it up for distribution, he had some ideas, which led to reediting portions of the picture. Now, none of those ideas were bad, but they were different from what was intended in the script.

TO: So, you had to go and do things that you hadn't planned on?

RC: Yes. They were to introduce the character of Bobby Kennedy earlier. The original script didn't have Bobby enter the picture physically until the last act when he enters the hotel and Anthony Hopkins greets him. Once Harvey Weinstein got involved, he thought—probably correctly— that the name Bobby Kennedy wouldn't mean anything or have an attraction to audiences in 2006 unless we introduced him earlier and interspersed him through the picture. So, to create the prologue and to set the time frame was challenging.

TO: You were in California at the time that Kennedy was campaigning and when he was assassinated. It must have been emotional for you to see the recreation.

RC: I marched with the anti -war movement in the '60's and it meant a lot to be offered the chance to work on Bobby. It was very meaningful for me to revisit that time and it was emotional. After he is shot, the picture ends with a voice-over of the speech that he gave a day after Martin Luther King was assassinated.

TO: It's an incredible speech—it really is. I looked it up and it's the one that he gave in Cleveland. It's the "On the Mindless Menace of Violence" speech.

RC: The power of ending the film with that speech led us to change how we presented the political remarks Bobby made in Ambassador Hotel ballroom before he stepped into the kitchen where he was shot. Emilio wanted to use those remarks because it's the last documentary footage we have of him. But those remarks were overtly political, and it would have diminished the powerful speech that we use at the very end. I had to convince Emilio to use what Bobby was saying in the ballroom only as a voiceover supporting images of the Vietnam War and street protests. We didn't want to take away from the final speech. That was something we had to discover as a solution along the way.

TO: Anything else that comes to mind?

RC: On Risky Business, I used second unit footage to show a lot of trains passing each other in rapid succession. Then at the end there was a train giving off a spark that was to symbolize a sexual climax. I showed it to Paul Brickman and that inspired him to reconceive the sequence. Eventually he returned to the location in Chicago and shot a new scene to precede what I had shown him. By step printing to slow down the action and that, combined with the music that we picked, gave us the feeling we wanted. From the Tangerine Dream music and the step printing of the footage and how it fades to black, we created the whole feeling we were after.

TO: What films and editors do you admires?

RC: Apocalypse Now, The Godfather I and II, Raging Bull. In more recent times, City of God—just the use of the parallel characters and how they were introduced. I like Slumdog Millionaire, Into the Wild, Babel, and Traffic in terms of how they were put together.

TO: Because of the sequencing?

RC: Yes. They had nonlinear structures which we talked about earlier. I talked to Jay Cassidy who edited Into the Wild, and he said originally it was a linear story. It wasn't until much later in post-production that they decided to start with the end of the story. I thought about how much it sounded like what I had experienced with Walter on The Conversation and how you have to manipulate these things and see how they work.

TO: What else?

RC: Babel and Traffic were both edited by Stephen Mirrione and I admire his work. Slumdog Millionaire has a clever story structure alternating the character's past with the present time. I liked 127 Hours a lot. When you realize the confined time period and location, how can you present that story and the development of that character and still tell a story full of tension? I thought it was brilliant to be able to do that.

TO: What editors come to mind?

RC: Walter Murch has worked with Fred Zinnemann, Anthony Mingella, Francis Coppola. Walter is so special that he's able to bring his uniqueness to the works of these different directors. I think the same of Anne Coates—being able to work with everyone from David Lean to Wolfgang Petersen to Stephen Soderbergh. Alan Heim because his career goes back some 30 years, to the work he did with Bob Fosse, such as Lenny and All That Jazz… Today there's a new guy on the block whose work I like. Hank Corwin.

TO: Yeah. You know, Hank's name doesn't come up as often as it should, I think. He's really talented.

RC: Right. He isn't as well-known as some other editors, but his work is so unusual. I worked with him on The New World. His style is so unique because of how he sees things. Even though Natural Born Killers doesn't have the story impact of some of the other films we've been talking about, but the stylistic pizazz—Wow.

TO: Speaking of style, what did you think of J.F.K.?

RC: It's right up there. It's one of those experiences where you look at it as an editor and think, 'How is that even possible?' The editors that work with David Fincher...

TO: Kirk Baxter and Angus Wall.

RC: They've come on like gangbusters. The late Sally Menke and Quentin Tarantino.

TO: Waiting to Exhale did really well.

RC: Yeah, it did box office because the book was so popular. Forest had a difficult job. He had to babysit a diva —Whitney Houston—who was hard on the crew. Once she got out of the trailer she was fine with cast members. Forest's job was to balance a huge megastar with an accomplished actress —Angela Bassett—who comes with formal training from the Yale School of Drama.

TO: What have you learned along the way?

RC: Not to take anything for granted. At the beginning of my career the critical response to the movies I edited was pretty good. I made the mistake of thinking 'Oh, everything I work on is going to be great' and I was too young to appreciate how difficult it was to get to that level. There are people who work for decades in this industry and try to achieve that level of recognition and here I was, this young guy who basically was not schooled but acting on instinct.

TO: What is it about your profession that you like the most?

RC: I get to work with such creative minds and visionary spirits. I'm just amazed that I get to be in the same room and exchange ideas with smart people. Arguing with Milos Forman. Listening to Marcia Lucas or George Lucas talk about their theory of cutting.

TO: And each film is a new experience.

RC: A new experience and the goals are different for the story and the film. This is why I value having worked with so many different directors. I get so many different views on life and I love that aspect of my career. I get paid to do this, so I feel 'How much better can this be to get paid to do what I love?' And I feel very, very lucky

JIM CLARK

Winning the ACE Career Achievement Award in 1999
Photograph courtesy of the American Cinema Editors and ACE Eddie Awards

LONDON, ENGLAND

Partial Credits: Happy-Go-Lucky, Vera Drake, Kiss Kiss (Bang Bang), The World Is Not Enough, The Jackal, This Boy's Life, The Mission, The Killing Fields, Marathon Man, Charade, The Innocents.

It was difficult for Jim to speak on the phone and easier to respond via email. Relive the suspense of The Jackal, Marathon Man, the sheer delight of Charade. In Jim's words, "You have to invest a lot of your soul in the work."

✂

TO: Jim, you are an Academy Award and BAFTA recipient for Best Editing for your work on The Killing Fields. Are there films that you edited that did not get the attention they deserved?

JC: Day Of The Locust is a film that was buried due to commercial failure and has a lot of visual riches within it.

TO: You edited The World Is Not Enough. Is there a different form of pressure you feel when you are editing a film that has a significant legacy—such as the James Bond films?

JC: The James Bond films are made within the confines of an ever-developing formula born of enormous financial success. One always feels a pressure with any film but with Bond there were so many precedents to adhere to.

TO: Did you ever feel that there were scenes that you had so much difficulty with that you had to leave them until the time was right for you to work on them?

JC: I've always tried to deal with difficult scenes as they come up but sometimes one is overwhelmed and the pressure you refer to in your previous question is a constant factor in putting a finished movie together. There were several scenes in This Boy's Life where I was constantly banging on to the director that they needed attention and it was he who put off dealing with them. In some instances scenes have to be reshot which, of course, is very expensive. We had to do this on The Mission and, in my opinion, never quite succeeded.

TO: Was editing The Killing Fields emotionally difficult for you or are you able to develop a distance between the material and yourself?

JC: Editing any movie is emotionally draining. You have to invest a lot of your soul in the work. The main problem with The Killing Fields was making the storyline coherent and in the early stages of shooting, getting enough coverage for the scenes. Of course on that film I also had to overcome a prejudice the director had against me as I was cutting in London while they were shooting on the other side of the world and David Puttnam had instructed me to say what I thought of the rushes coming back. It wasn't until I went out there and met with Roland Joffe that he began seeing me as a collaborator rather than a threat.

TO: Who are some of the film editors you admire and why?

JC: Artie Schmidt, Michael Kahn, and Sam O'Steen. Each film is its own world and though I admire the work of many editors, we all have our failures and successes. We can only function if we're given good material to work with.

TO: What advice would you give someone who wanted to be an editor?

JC: Study every aspect of film making as a good editor must pull all the elements, visual and audio, into a totality, which serves the story being told.

ANNE V. COATES, A.C.E

Photograph courtesy of the American Cinema Editors and ACE Eddie Awards

LOS ANGELES, CA

Partial Credits: Fifty Shades of Grey, The Golden Compass, Unfaithful, Erin Brockovich, Out of Sight, In the Line of Fire, Chaplin, Raw Deal, Greystoke: The Legend of Tarzan, Lord of the Apes, The Elephant Man, The Eagle Has Landed, Murder on the Orient Express, Those Magnificent Men in Their Flying Machines, Becket, Lawrence of Arabia, The Pickwick Papers.

What do you say about an editor who has been working in motion pictures for over 70 years? Who, in every decade of her work, has made significant contributions to cinema? Sitting in her home for our interview, there are two awards that sit high atop a wooden shelf. The Oscar and BAFTA awards for Lawrence of Arabia. Gracious, patient, and terrifically funny.

✂

TO: Anne, you are an Academy Award Best Editing recipient for Lawrence of Arabia. You have been recognized with a BAFTA Academy Fellowship and an ACE Career Achievement Award. For your contributions to the industry, you received an honorary Oscar 53 years after winning for Lawrence of Arabia. You were awarded the Office of the British Empire (O.B.E.) and have been an inspiration to filmmakers and editors around the world.

AC: Thank You.

TO: And while so much has been written about Lawrence of Arabia—deservedly so—I think Beckett is just incredible.

AC: I think it's such a beautiful film.

TO: How did you get started on this journey?

AC: To begin with, when I was a kid, I wanted to be a horse race trainer. (Laughs) I began to go to the cinema. The school started taking us to see the classics—Jane Eyre and, particularly, Wuthering Heights which changed my whole life. Apart from falling in love with Laurence Oliver, it opened up a whole new concept to me of storytelling. I think we were reading it in school and it's quite heavy going. And to suddenly see it there in pictures alive with real people!

TO: This is the William Wyler directed film.

AC: Yes, and I knew very little about films. So I started to look into ways of getting into the film industry. Now you think it would have been easy for me because my Uncle was Lord Rank.

TO: He headed up the Rank Organization, which owned film studios and theatres.

AC: Yes. I was very fond of him but he didn't really want me going into the film industry. I had to convince him that I was not going into it for the glamour or the actors and that I really wanted to make films and tell stories. But he put me into religious films, which is why he got started in the business in the first place. He was very religious and taught Sunday School and thought film was a good way to get through to people. And he probably thought 'That'll damper her ardor!' (Both Laugh) But it didn't! And that's the first time I saw 35mm film.

TO: What did they have you do at that time?

AC: I did all sorts of jobs. I was a P.A. I made the tea and the coffee, looked after people. I became quite a good projectionist. I did sound, repairing films.

TO: That was a great way to learn all the basics.

AC: I loved it. I really did. I heard there was a job for a second assistant in the cutting rooms at Pinewood Studios. And they asked if I knew how to do opticals and I said yes and that I could splice. But most of the things they asked me about I had no idea what they were, let alone do them! (Both Laugh) But I said yes to all of them. And it's a bit of advice that I give to students always. I say, 'If you've got confidence in yourself, say yes, and then find out'. And hope for the best!

TO: Sure.

AC: I went to friends of mine who were in proper cutting rooms and spent two weeks with them, learning the routine and that sort of thing. And then I reported to work.

TO: That's great.

AC: I had gotten the job and an amazing thing happened. It was a film called The End of the River, being produced by Michael Powell and Emeric Pressburger. I was mostly splicing and hanging up trims. And apparently Michael and Emeric didn't like the job the editor was doing, so they gave the film to their top editor, who was cutting The Red Shoes—Reggie Mills. Reggie didn't want to use the first assistant. He said, 'No, send Anne up with the film'. So, there I was on my very first picture, working with one of the very best editors.

TO: That's amazing.

AC: Yes, it was amazingly interesting. I wish I were a little more experienced—I would have learned more than I did, but I learned a lot. And I also had the opportunity of helping out on The Red Shoes with some of the splicing and syncing of their dailies. And I got to spend time on the floor watching Mickey (Michael Powell) directing, which was very interesting. And I was very, very lucky because within about five years I was editing. I did a few jobs as a first assistant and then I got a break on a live action Robin Hood that Disney was making.

TO: Okay, so that was The Story of Robin Hood and His Merrie Men, directed by Ken Annakin.

AC: Yes. I was cutting the second unit because the editor couldn't keep up with two units and they liked what I did. And I did some cutting and then went back and was an assistant again.

TO: So, constantly back and forth...

AC: Yes, exactly. I always thought that it was more important to keep working. And then I was working with my friend, Clive Donner, and he was offered Pickwick Papers, but he couldn't do it. I knew the producer and said to him, 'Why don't you put me up for it?'

TO: This was going to be your first feature as a full editor...

AC: Right. So I went for an interview with Noel Langley, who was a first-time director. You know, there's a lot of luck in not only getting your first feature but also beyond and being in the right place at the right time. It usually works out. Only once in my life have I been offered two really top pictures at the same time. And I think I made the right choice.

TO: I can't wait for you to tell me.

AC: One was Lolita with Stanley Kubrick and the other was Lawrence of Arabia.

TO: I had no idea...

AC: Yeah. You know, it was funny at that time because Kubrick was a red-hot director. And I was quite tempted.

TO: How did you decide?

AC: My husband said, 'You can't even dream of not working with David Lean if he wants you!' (Laughs) And you know, a funny thing happened. And I haven't actually told this story before because it only just happened the other day. I was turning out some paperwork here, and I came across some old letters. And one started, *"Dear Mr. Spiegel, I'm afraid that I can't cut Lawrence of Arabia because you're not offering enough money."* Now it wasn't worded exactly like that, but I did explain at length that I wasn't going to work for that kind of money on a film that was going to be working day and night, etc. *"Thank you very much. Goodbye."*

TO: That's amazing.

AC: But the interesting thing is that, because I have it, I never sent it! (Both Laugh) Because if I had sent it, my life might have been totally different! (Both Laugh)

TO: Yeah.

AC: But I know why I didn't send it when I think about it. I'm sure my husband said, 'Don't you dare send that letter!' (Laughs) But, you know, I was so angry and we were negotiating and they were offering so little money. And typical me—to leap into that without stopping to think...

TO: But it was David Lean. Coming off of The Bridge on the River Kwai...

AC: Yes, but it's funny. If I had of sent it, it wouldn't have happened. So, I'm going to give it to the Academy museum.

TO: What a great story. (Both Laugh)

AC: Yeah and I just found it and remembered the story. I haven't really told it before.

TO: Thanks for telling me. So much has been written about Lawrence that can be found in many books and documentaries. And because I didn't want to ask you a question that you've probably answered hundreds of time, one of the things I've wanted to ask you is that when you look at this body of work that you have been involved with, what stands out?

AC: Well, I don't know if there are moments that stand out—it's the whole film. After David finished shooting it, we had 16 weeks before the Queen saw it. Which as you know, being an editor, 16 weeks to finish a film that's three hours and forty minutes? I had the whole picture cut except for the last battle scene, which David was still shooting. He came off the battle scene and straight into the cutting room. And we were working day and night to get the film ready. Seven days a week, 16 to 17 hours a day. And sometimes I think that if we had more time we may have done some things differently. So, we finished the film and everybody's consensus was that it was a great film, but it was too long. After we had shown it to the Queen, I went back with David and we cut out about 15 minutes from it. And I think I was even more upset than David was about that because I thought all the scenes were great and very beautiful.

TO: Was it overwhelming to get all that material?

AC: The difficulty was that I could make another film out of the outtakes! (Both Laugh) We had such beautiful stuff. The mirage work was amazing. In fact, we cut one of the mirage sequences out just before we finished it.

TO: Was that difficult?

AC: You know, David... I so admired him. He was so brave with taking stuff out. Much more than me and he taught me two or three things about editing that were invaluable. Things like holding shots and visualizing them with music and all sorts of things like that. Whereas I would have been chopping it down a bit more I think. He also taught me to have the courage of my conviction. He said, 'If you think you're right, say it! Work on it and show people what you think. And always follow your own truth and be truthful about what you do.'

TO: It's interesting that when you watch documentaries about filmmaking almost always there is the clip of the match. I watched one the other day on the magic of film editing and of course it was right there. It has taken on such an iconic status in our little world of film editing.

AC: (Laughs) I know! I don't know why. One of my children said to me the other day, 'Mum, why is that cut so famous?' (Laughs) I mean, I couldn't explain why. Some journalist from Australia rang me up at three o'clock in the morning once to ask me what I was thinking when I did it! (Both Laugh) Ten years later!

TO: That's hilarious.

AC: I can't put my finger on the magic of that, really.

TO: A captured moment in a film full of them.

AC: I'll tell you an interesting thing about it that I've thought about since that I didn't at the time. I was cutting on a 35mm Cinemascope print and because the film was butted together and just had the crayon marks on it where the dissolve was going to be. And when we took it into the theatre, we saw the cut going from the match blowing to the sunrise.

TO: It was going to be a dissolve instead of that cut…

AC: Yes, and we would never have done that had it been on digital because we'd have done the dissolve in the machine, probably, and never really looked at it. But we saw—David and I—the potential of that. Because I had gotten David into direct cutting.

TO: What do you mean?

AC: I had gotten him to go see some of the French films before we started. They were doing all of this direct cutting and David loved it when he saw it. And I think we did it as well as anybody. But again, if we had been on digital, we might not have seen it. But on film, we saw it and we thought, 'My God, it works as a cut'. And we rubbed the lines off and looked at it again. And he said to me, 'It's not quite right, Annie, take it away and take a few frames off and see if you can make it really perfect.' And I literally took two frames off, took it back, and he said, 'That's it.'

TO: That's a great story.

AC: Yeah (Laughs).

TO: Were you astonished about the awards it received and that you won an Academy Award?

AC: I was totally astonished that I won an award. I didn't even know what a nomination was! I knew so little about the Academy Awards. They flew over Peter O'Toole and Omar and people like that.

Anne's Oscar and BAFTA awards for Lawrence of Arabia
Photos by Tom Ohanian

TO: So how did you find out?

AC: David rang me in the morning and said, 'Well, you won and then I knew we were going to do fairly well.' Because he said that if editing won, that was a fairly good omen. But, no, I didn't expect to win.

TO: What films are some of your favorites?

AC: Wuthering Heights is still my very favorite film, ever. I just think it was fantastic. Have you ever seen Les Enfants du Paradis?

TO: Sure. I know it as Children of Paradise, the English name.

AC: I love that film. I definitely have that on my top ten.

TO: What highlights stand out in this amazing career of yours?

AC: You know there was always something that Carol Reed once said to me that's always been a highlight. He said, 'I've worked with many really good editors, but you're the one with the most heart.' And I think that's something that I really treasure. There have been so many ups and downs in life. You know, things I've been disappointed about. I mean I really wanted to cut A Man for all Seasons.

TO: What happened?

AC: They wanted me to do it. And they rang up who they thought was my agent. And he said, 'She's not free, she's busy.' And they hired somebody else. And by that time, I thought, 'I'm going to ring up myself and ask Bill Graf (Executive Producer) if they were thinking of me. And he said, 'Are you free? I thought you were busy! We just hired somebody yesterday. If you had rung up yesterday, it would have been yours.'

TO: Oh, no.

AC: Well, there was disappointment. There's a funny story that I actually think is rather sweet about (The) Horse's Mouth.

TO: You did that for Ronald Neame, with Alec Guinness.

AC: Yes, and that was really my step up in my career. It wasn't Lawrence, as everyone thinks, because before that I had done Horse's Mouth and Tunes of Glory, which I think was Ronnie Neame's best film, actually.

TO: That's a great film.

AC: Lovely film. Both of them. I rang up for an interview and Ronnie said, 'Well, actually, I don't like employing women.' (Laughs) And then he said, 'And I certainly wouldn't employ a married woman because they're always trying to get home to their husband and children.' But then he said, 'But I'll take a chance with you' and it was a great break and I was very excited about it—working with Ronnie Neame and Alec Guinness! Ronnie and I became the closest of friends for many years.

TO: There's a really cool Criterion DVD for the film…

AC: And just a few months before I had met my future husband. After I was on the film for a month, we wanted to get married. And I thought, 'Well, I can't tell Ronnie!' (Laughs) We were going to have a big, white wedding. And I said, 'Let's go get married secretly and we won't tell anybody.' So we did. We had a two-day honeymoon and our families came. I used to take off my wedding ring and hang it on a gold chain around my neck when I drove in to the studios.

TO: Hmm…

AC: For three months this went on. And then one day we were in the office and Ronnie was saying something and then I said, 'Well, as a matter of fact, Ronnie, I have been married for three months and have you noticed any difference in my performance?'

TO: Good for you.

AC: Yeah. And the producers were there. And they all clapped and said, 'No! Absolutely not!' And Ronnie said, 'We're very happy with you.' And then he said, 'Next thing you'll say is that you're pregnant.' And I said, 'Yes, I am!' (Both Laugh)

TO: You know, I wish that people would re-discover Beckett.

AC: Isn't that a beautiful film?

TO: It's a great film.

AC: The dialogue is unbelievable. It's one of my favorites because of the script, the dialogue, and the characters. When I first got the dailies,

I was terribly disappointed.

TO: Why?

AC: (Laughs) Because I was used to having big landscapes coming in. But then it all started coming alive and it was a beautiful film. And to cut those performances—they (Peter O'Toole and Richard Burton) were both so good. The only time I've come across that recently was when I did In The Line of Fire with Clint Eastwood and John Malkovich.

TO: Eastwood and Malkovich are great together.

AC: They're so brilliant. (Laughs) You didn't know who to be on, because you wanted to be on both of them! Particularly on the telephone conversation.

TO: You do Lawrence and then you do Beckett and yet this is the same woman who does Erin Brockovich and In The Line of Fire. She can do anything. That's how I think of you.

AC: (Laughs) And then we got an acting nomination for Diane Lane in Unfaithful. I like to think of myself as an actor's editor, actually. John Malkovich thanked me and I thanked him for the great work he did.

TO: Your work in Out of Sight is really remarkable.

AC: George Clooney and I are great friends and have been for many years. He actually leapt over the railings at the Oscars to come and give me a hug.

TO: There was a lot of controversy on how to end Unfaithful...

AC: We had three completely different endings. And we reshot the scene in the car and finally we went back to the original.

TO: How involved do you get in being consulted in situations like that?

AC: Very involved in that particular case. Adrian Lyne liked to involve you a lot. I was very involved in the ending and we previewed it this way and that way. And I always knew which ending I liked and we stuck to it. Richard Gere liked that ending to begin with but we got sidetracked with a lot of opinions, which led to the reshooting. Eventually we went back to the original ending.

TO: Where the car just sits at the intersection…

AC: Yes. Which was allowing people to make up their own minds.

TO: It's a much more interesting film that way, though…

AC: (Laughs) But, of course. That's the best ending. You know, everyone I was talking with and even my crew—they all had different ideas. Some thought he should go into the police station. Some thought he should fly off. So, everyone was divided. But if you left it like that, then people could make up their own minds.

TO: Can you recall when you first started seeing Lawrence with that majestic score?

AC: Yes, but the thing was that we were scoring the music on one stage and our music editor was laying it up in the cutting room. But, they weren't always happy with what Maurice (Jarre) was doing. So, they were redoing the music overnight and we were getting new pieces of music to lay up the next day. I remember they wanted more timpani. Sam wanted more theme because he knew he could sell it. David wanted more violins because he loved violins.

TO: Well, I suppose that would make sense. There was Bridge on the River Kwai with Colonel Bogey's theme and Bridge and Lawrence had that commercial cross over to selling music.

AC: That's right. Exactly. I'll tell you—you go all over the world and you'll hear the Lawrence of Arabia theme being played. I've been amazed. I was in India and China and there it is—always being played.

TO: Incredible. It's kind of like a triple play—Colonel Bogey's March, the theme from Lawrence, and Lara's theme from Dr. Zhivago.

AC: But, yes, it was exciting seeing the music on it. It was also exciting seeing and hearing it in stereo. I was adjusting the audio levels on the camels as they were going across the screen because we didn't have enough hands! (Laughs)

TO: During mixing? That's funny. In recent times when you see the films that are coming out, are there films that stand out for you?

AC: I thought (The) Social Network was a beautifully edited film.

TO: Why?

AC: Because I was always looking at who I wanted to look at. The emotions were right, the rhythms were right. It was cut fast but not so fast that I couldn't appreciate what people were thinking and what was happening. And I like that. I like fast cutting but I don't like fast cutting when it's just things flashing past my eyes and I have no idea what it is. That's television to me! (Laughs)

TO: I think you hit the nail on the head when you said that you were always looking at what you wanted to be looking at.

AC: Yes.

TO: Were there films that you edited that didn't do as well as you thought they should have?

AC: Yes, yes. One is I Love You to Death. Have you seen that?

TO: Yeah, yeah, that's with Kevin Kline.

AC: I think that's a brilliant film. A wonderful cast. Tracey Ullman, William Hurt, Keanu Reeves, Joan Plowright, River Phoenix. Some of it is so funny even now when I see it. And I loved working with Larry Kasdan. We had such a good time. We were so happy on it. We thought we had a really good film. And we got the most terrible ratings. They hated the film.

TO: Why?

AC: Black comedy does not go well in America. We spent three million putting another ending on it and the marks went up only something like three percent.

TO: Do you think previews are useful?

AC: I think they make the film worse. Studios will lose all enthusiasm for a film if it gets low marks. When I did Chaplin, we did the preview and got an 84. And everyone was totally flabbergasted. So they decided to do a preview out of town and they got an 82. So they were even more astounded. And that film—I don't think it made more than 30 or 40 million worldwide. I mean it absolutely didn't make any money. So, you can't tell.

TO: There was the best actor nomination…

AC: Robert was wonderful. When I showed Robert's The Little Tramp scene to Chaplin's daughter, Geraldine, who was playing her mother, she burst into tears. She said, 'He's so lifelike—just like Daddy.' It was just extraordinary—he was very good. But I think they advertised it wrong. They did a really nice poster of him as The Little Tramp but the story wasn't about that. It was about him and the women. You know, in talking about moments that really stand out, do you know how I got Lawrence?

TO: No.

AC: I cut the tests of Albert Finney. David had done a week's testing of Finney. Three days of him as 'The Arab' and a couple of days of him as 'The English'. I got a call from John Palmer, who was a Line Producer. And he said, 'Do you want to come in? So I went down and David was very austere but friendly. And he shot the first scene, which was the Arab scene. He gave me some notes on how he wanted it to go and I took it away and cut it. Then we were running dailies on the English scene. And he said, 'Have you cut that first scene yet?' And I said, 'I have. I'd like to show it to you tomorrow if you have time.' And he said, 'No, no, show it to me now.' And the whole crew was there and I said, 'David, not in front of the whole crew!' And he said, 'Go ahead and run it at once!' So I went away, terrified...

TO: I'll bet.

AC: And I came back and I had to show it to the whole crew. I was so terrified; I think I had my eyes shut. My mind was so frozen when I ran it for David. And he got up and said, 'That's the first time I've ever seen anything cut exactly as I would have done it myself.'

TO: That's fabulous.

AC: And that was a lovely moment. The tests with Albert Finney are amazing. They're in the BFI (British Film Institute) in London and you can see them.

TO: I have to do that someday.

AC: Peter made it his own and nobody can imagine anyone but Peter in that role. But, in fact, Albert Finney did a wonderful test.

TO: I wanted to go back to In The Line of Fire for a moment. It seemed an unusual choice for you at the time. What drew you to it?

AC: Well, I had a very good reputation but when I came over (from England) I couldn't do union films because I wasn't in the union. I mean, they wanted me to do Fatal Attraction and the union wouldn't let me.

TO: I didn't know that.

AC: My then agent got me an interview with Wolfgang Petersen. There were three editors they were interviewing: Me, Tom Rolf, and another who I can't remember. My agent acted very quickly and said to them, 'Anne is only going to be here for three days and maybe you could see her.' Wolfgang agreed and I went to his house and I told him how interesting the film was, particularly the telephone conversation. I said, 'They really interest me. I think they'll be so exciting to cut.' And apparently that's what he really liked. That's what attracted me—these two personalities, dancing around each other.

TO: I think that's the best part of the movie.

AC: Yes, that's what I loved. Clint and John were both equally interesting actors.

TO: Kwai came out in 1957. Had you seen it?

AC: Of course, but that was edited by Peter Taylor. And he thought he was going to do Lawrence.

TO: Okay, so you meet Lean and he had just done this huge picture. What did you think about Kwai?

AC: I thought it was a fantastic film. I knew Lawrence was going to be enormous but it really didn't scare me.

TO: No?

AC: You're confident at that age; do you know what I mean?

TO: Sure. Did you have a good working relationship with David Lean?

AC: I was initially really scared of him because he was a top editor and I was up and coming. And particularly when he was on the floor shooting, he was very severe. But he loved the work I had done on the tests and then we got on really well in the cutting room day and night. Working with David was so exciting—almost exhilarating. Sometimes we argued, but mostly we were in total step. David used to say to me, 'Now if you've got an idea, Annie, don't keep it bottled up, tell me.' And I'd do so and he'd say, 'Oh, that's the most idiotic thing I've ever heard.' But he'd do it in such a nice way. And then a few days later, he'd come 'round and say, 'You know what you came up with the other day? Well, there are bits of rubbish in it but out of it, I did start to think that if we did this, and this, and this…'

TO: Well, at least he admitted it…

AC: And I thought, 'Good…Good… One can do all these little things from behind the scenes that make a big difference.'

TO: Of course.

AC: (Both Laugh) But I could see my crew cringe when David would say, 'It's rubbish', but I would mentor them and tell them, 'Do you realize that if I hadn't said that, we wouldn't be doing this?'—meaning to better the film. And the two assistants I had went on to become really good editors.

TO: Who were they?

AC: Norman Savage. When I couldn't do Doctor Zhivago, Norman did it. David offered me Doctor Zhivago, but I couldn't do it because I was having a baby—my daughter. And Ray Lovejoy, who cut 2001 and Dr. Strangelove for Kubrick. I actually got Ray the job. They were both top editors, but they both died very young, unfortunately.

TO: It's wonderful to know that you mentored them and then they went on to edit those films.

AC: I really believe in helping young people as much as possible. You don't have to wait to be an editor. If you've got the gift for it, you should take your opportunity when it arrives.

TO: Anne, it's been an absolute pleasure speaking with you today. I want to thank you for all your time. Any parting words?

AC: I love my work. I love editing and thank you very much!

STEVEN COHEN, ACE

Photograph courtesy of the American Cinema Editors and ACE Eddie Awards

LOS ANGELES, CA

Feature Films: Reach Me, Before the Rains, Material Girls, The Prince and Me, 15 Minutes, Blood and Wine, Three Wishes, Angie, Lost in Yonkers, Rambling Rose, No Man's Land.

Television Movies: Five movies in the Jesse Stone series,Don King: Only in America, Teamster Boss: The Jackie Presser Story, Crazy in Love, L.B.J.: The Early Years.

Television Series: Bosch, Wayward Pines, The Bridge.

I met Steve during the earliest years of my work as a co-inventor of the Avid editing systems. He was instrumental in shaping the development of editorial products across several companies. A talented editor and Emmy recipient, he has been deeply involved in the rights of motion picture editors and deserves a unique place in the industry's adoption and transition to digital editing systems.

✄

TO: Steve, you won an Emmy for your work on LBJ: The Early Years, an American Cinema Editors Eddie Award for Don King: Only in America, and the ACE Robert Wise Award for "journalistic illumination of the art of editing." You were the first to use Avid Media Composer on a studio feature film, Lost in Yonkers. How did you get your start?

SC: I was lucky enough to get a scholarship to Yale, and though I'd focused on the sciences in high school, I ended up studying art and made a student film, a documentary about elementary school education. My mother's sister was a script supervisor. She had just finished Alice's Restaurant, and introduced me to a lot of people. The first call I got was from an editing company making commercials. I started there as a bicycle messenger, delivering film cans in midtown Manhattan. The understanding I had with the owner—a wonderful guy named Mort Fallick—was that if I could find time to learn, he would teach me. It didn't take long for me to start assisting. About a year later, he decided to move to California and offered to take me along.

TO: You had a really good storytelling background due to the commercials and documentaries.

SC: I always enjoyed the mechanics of film. We worked in 35 and did most of what you would do on a feature, but in much less time. I learned a lot—synching dailies, organizing the editing room, cutting negative, ordering opticals.

TO: What were you doing at Paramount?

SC: Primarily carrying film around—very monotonous. But there were a lot of films in production, and if they needed help, they'd see who they could get. So, I was always going off and working on shows.

TO: How long were you in the apprentice pool?

SC: Roughly a year. The first feature I assisted on was Foul Play in 1977, with Goldie Hawn and Chevy Chase. Pembroke Herring was the editor.

TO: What did you learn from watching those editors?

SC: I assisted Pem on two shows and then began working with Dann Cahn. Both taught me a great deal, but I really learned how to cut from Dann, because he gave me scenes to edit—sometimes quite challenging ones.

TO: You worked in television before going to features.

SC: I cut TV movies for several years, eventually winning an Emmy working with director Peter Werner on LBJ: The Early Years. I eventually had a chance to interview with Martha Coolidge for a TV movie she was doing, which was going to be cut with the Montage.

TO: This was Bare Essentials.

SC: Yes. We did that show and then went on to do Rambling Rose and many other pictures.

TO: Winning an Emmy for Best Editing must have been a great morale booster.

SC: It was very exciting.

TO: Did you expect it?

SC: No! (Laughs) I mean, we knew we had made a good show, but I didn't think I'd win an Emmy. I was surprised to get nominated and very surprised to win. The other thing that happened in those years was that I got involved helping to reform the Editors Guild.

TO: I've talked to a lot of editors who had a great amount of difficulty getting into the Guild.

SC: There was a rule that you had to assist for eight years before you could become an editor. You could get a medical degree in less time than that! A group of us came together and worked to change the rule. We put together an organizing campaign. All we were trying to do was to get it down to five years. But we did our homework and when the vote was finally taken, we won easily.

TO: If it's a director you haven't worked with before, what's that interview like?

SC: You inevitably talk about the script, because the story you're telling is the foundation of the meeting. But you might also talk about personal stuff because a director wants to know that they can get along with you for months at a time. And I have the same kinds of questions—how easy will it be for us to collaborate? Will our tastes and storytelling instincts complement each other?

TO: You were an early user of nonlinear, tape-based editing systems.

SC: I started using the Montage, and I was very eager to try it. I had written some fairly sophisticated software in the early '80s and was very excited by the personal computer revolution. And I came to believethat the potential for computers in editing was huge. I did a couple of shows on the Montage, and I found the system to be brilliant and seminal. But it was also limited and at times, maddening. I ended up writing them a 30-page letter, describing what I thought they should be doing, and I worked with them for a while, helping to build a digital prototype. As a stepping stone, they had a hybrid system, which they called the Montage IIH.

TO: Can you describe that?

SC: The Montage had 17 tape drives shuttling dailies around to preview the show without actually cutting anything. The hybrid had an 18thdrive which was a bunch of SCSI hard drives. Same editing methodology, same controls, but digital speed. In practice, you cut everything off the 18thdrive, but if you had a problem you could check your work on the tape drives, which we knew worked.

TO: You mean check for picture quality, focus, and so forth?

SC: Yes, and also to make sure the cuts were accurate. I believe there were only two users of the hybrid. I used one, and Godfather III used the other. The biggest problem was systemic: a 30-frame system cutting 24-frame material.

TO: Because of the phantom frames.

SC: Exactly. I really got to understand why, and that turned out to be pivotal later on. The picture I did with the IIH was called Crazy in Love, also directed by Martha Coolidge. We were working with exposed drives perched on shelves, no cases, tied together with SCSI ribbon cable. A big drive back then held less than a gig, cost two thousand dollars and weighed about ten pounds—so storage was limited! Then I did another show for HBO, and by that time Montage had begun working with digital optical discs in an early RAID configuration.

TO: What show was that?

SC: Teamster Boss, written by Abby Mann. We set up the IIH, now with optical drives, and went a full week with the drives not working and film coming in every day. I had met Eric Peters at NAB and saw an early Avid, and later met Bill Warner at a tradeshow in L.A. called Digital World.

TO: That would have been NAB 1989. Bill was Avid's President, of course, and Eric was the Chief Technology Officer.

SC: At NAB that year there were several early systems competing. It was very clear to me that Avid had the best. I was working on Teamster Boss, with film piling up and problems with the Montage. I had talked hypothetically to Bill and Eric about what would be needed to do a show. At the last minute, I decided to take a chance and do Teamster Boss on the Avid. One big issue was that we had to cut negative. This was HBO, and in those days, they required a conformed negative—you couldn't just deliver a tape master.

TO: Right. We had developed MediaMatch, the film matchback software, to deal with that. Just so we have everything clear for the record—this was film shot at 24 fps, transferred to video at 29.97 fps, edited at 29.97 fps on Media Composer, and then you needed a negative cut list created from the 29.97 EDL (Edit Decision List).

SC: Right. The original MediaMatch was a HyperCard stack, right?

TO: Yes.

SC: We ended up using Avid version 3. It worked very well but we definitely had some problems. At one point, one of the engineers came to L.A. and was actually tweaking the code in our cutting rooms. Larry Jordan, Mort Fallick's son, was assisting me—he's since become an accomplished editor. We got through the show, cut the negative, and I learned a tremendous amount about how hard it was going to be to do a feature with matchback. You know this, of course, but to clarify, every cut has to be conformed to the nearest frame in material running at a different frame rate. To keep picture in sync, the software can adjust cuts by a frame. This isn't a major problem in television, where you conform only once. But in features we had to be able to conform the picture over and over again for screenings[SC1]. That was the beginning of a long association between me and Avid and led to Lost in Yonkers.

TO: I remember coming out to Cincinnati to see you on location.

SC: I remember! I was eager to use an Avid for that show, and Martha Coolidge, the director, was very supportive. Her openness to the new technology, her willingness to take a risk and embrace it, was absolutely pivotal. Eric had sent me a white paper that described a hypothetical 24-frame workflow, and I understood immediately that this would solve our problem. I realized that it would let you make a perfect change list, which was essential. At the time, there was a lot of skepticism about digital editing for features, partly because of the frame-rate problem.

TO: Just for clarification, editing at 24 fps offers you a 1:1 relationship with film shot at 24 fps. Therefore, no video pulldown to deal with, no matchback to deal with, and no phantom frames. You cut on the exact frame that was shot. The change list is a way of comparing two versions of the show and allowed you to conform your workprint for multiple screenings.

SC: Correct. The video we were working with wasn't good enough for screenings, so we had to project film, and do it regularly as the editing progressed.

TO: Right.

SC: Eric knew that 24-frame editing was essential, and the underlying architecture for it was in the code, but it hadn't been implemented. That's what I helped with. Eric made a commitment to deliver the change list software by the time we would need it, when we had a first cut. So we had a window in which to make it work. It was an exciting time.

TO: You have a unique position in history in relation to this.

SC: Later, Martha and I did another show called Angie, and again I used early beta software. A lot of the features that editors now take for granted were developed during that period: JKL trimming, asymmetrical trimming, replace edit, and many other things that I advocated for and helped design. My assistants during that period were pioneers, too: Scot Scalise, Alexis Seymour, Kate McGowan and Chris Brookshire.

TO: What does it take to be an editor?

SC: It takes tremendous tenacity. That's the first thing. The I Ching says, "perseverance furthers"—stick with it, but don't expect it to happen quickly. You need to be very comfortable working alone in a room, and you need to be at least somewhat egoless. An editor has to find the right balance between their own point of view and working within someone else's point of view. You can do one or the other well but doing both is harder.

TO: Are there things that stand out from the films you've done?

SC: You inevitably love the films that came out well. But a lot of what I'm proud of is that the films meant something to people, that they represented a complete, coherent statement that had a strong emotional impact on an audience. One of the most satisfying things is to reveal and shape a character in a way that moves people.

TO: That has to be one of the most underrated qualities regarding what an editor does.

SC: People inevitably focus on what the actor did, not how you molded it. I want to be seen as an actor's best friend—someone he or she can trust to find the most honest moments and weave them together.

TO: What films have you liked over the years?

SC: I often find that I like smaller pictures, that maybe aren't as well known. And I sometimes love stuff that doesn't have a lot of cuts. The scenes in Children of Men or Gravity with those incredible long takes, for example. But my favorite movie from an editing perspective is Terrence Malick's Days of Heaven, edited by Billy Weber. It's rarely praised for its editing, though in recent years I think that's changed somewhat.

TO: Why Days of Heaven?

SC: It's a poem and a montage from the first frame to the last. I've seen the movie many, many times and it never ceases to move me. It remains a kind of wonderful mystery that always has more depth to it. It's really a tragedy that we can't see it anymore in the way it was intended. It was such an immersive experience in 70mm and six-track sound.

TO: If you weren't an editor, what would you be doing?

SC: I almost became a psychologist, and before that, I figured I'd go into the sciences. So I probably would have pursued one of those paths.

[SC1] Repeated below. Didn't seem necessary to say it twice.

SCOTT CONRAD, ACE

Photograph courtesy of the American Cinema Editors and ACE Eddie Awards

LOS ANGELES, CA

Partial Credits: Crazy on the Outside, The Virgin of Juarez, Alison's Choice, Mortal Kombat (Action sequences), Wagons East, Masquerade, The Bedroom Window, The Wraith, Cat's Eye, Heart of Steel, Cheech and Chong's Next Movie, Up in Smoke, Outlaw Blues, Rocky, A Boy and His Dog, The Making of Butch Cassidy and the Sundance Kid, The Long Goodbye (assistant film editor).

Scott started in the mailroom at Twentieth Century Fox and has worked in every major genre. And what's one of the most important things he's learned? "You have to be very honest with opinions of the script and it's the same way with the film. You have to be honest with it."

TO: Scott, you have been working in the film industry since 1964. You received an Academy Award and an Eddie for "Rocky" along with Richard Halsey. You started in the mailroom at Twentieth Century Fox in 1964 and that led to some work on a documentary of the making of Butch Cassidy and the Sundance Kid. But, your career was over almost before it began. What happened?

SC: You needed eight years of editing experience before you were allowed to cut. George Roy Hill gave his assistant, Ron Priceman a 16mm Bolex with a 12:120 Angenieux zoom lens and told him to shoot some material. I started to put something together at night after I finished my assistant job.

I would call Ronnie and say, 'Hey, why don't you do an interview with Newman and with Redford' and we would talk constantly about what he needed for the documentary. We showed how the "Oh Shit" jumping off the cliff scene was done. They shot part of it in Colorado and then when they got back to Los Angeles at the Fox Ranch, they put the two actors on a crane against a blue background and shot them jumping off into a tank. Then they married that with the footage done in Colorado. It won an Emmy. I cut this on the side and it violated the eight-year rule because I had only been in the guild for four years. I got called up before the union and they were very possibly going to kick me out. I explained that I thought it was only going to be an educational piece and I wound up talking my way out of it.

TO: What a start. You were an associate editor to Lou Lombardo who edited for Robert Altman and Sam Peckinpah on The Long Goodbye.

SC: Louie and Danny Greene, who cut M*A*S*H, were two of my very strong influences. Bob Simpson was one of the most incredible editors I ever came across.

TO: He was nominated for editing for The Grapes of Wrath.

SC: Yes. And Louie was a very strong influence because he had done some very cutting edge editing on The Wild Bunch, mixing slow motion with regular speed and I admired his style. I cut quite a few scenes on The Long Goodbye.

TO: You've edited across almost every film genre. When do you say yes as opposed to no to a project?

SC: It's the script and the personality of the director. I love being able to go across genres. I started out with comedies, with Cheech and Chong and I didn't want to get pigeonholed, so I went to T.V. to be able to do dramas.

TO: And you got the Eddie award for Heart of Steel.

SC: Yes. Then I did thrillers for a while. And after doing drama and thrillers, no one thought I could cut comedy (Laughs). Did you know that Up In Smoke was the first film of its kind to break $200 million?

TO: Really?

SC: Yeah. Wagon's East was one of the funniest scripts I ever read. John Candy, as everyone knows, died halfway through the making of the picture. His death, besides being a real tragedy, presented a lot of challenges. I found myself trying to take him out of one shot and putting him on horseback going across a river digitally and it was a very difficult experience.

TO: Tell me about The Temp.

SC: That's an example of what can happen in Hollywood. It was written as a black comedy and it was directed, shot, and cast as a black comedy. Because of an administration change at Paramount, they wanted to turn it into a straight thriller. And it just wasn't that. They brought in some top writers in Hollywood—Ron Bass and Frank Pierson to do rewrites and to reshoot about a third of the movie. And it just didn't work. It was a very painful experience, both for me and Director Tom Holland.

TO: Rocky. It was made for $1.1 million and made over $117 million during its original theatrical run. How did you get involved?

SC: I had assisted Dick Halsey on Payday and he called me because they were about two-thirds of the way through shooting in Philadelphia. Dick had been on location and had just returned to L.A. He said there was a lot to cut. I started pretty much at the fight and worked my way backwards to the middle of the movie. The fight was, at that time, a lot of footage—it was 84,000 feet and six cameras.

TO: About 15 and-a-half hours of film for the fight.

SC: Yeah and on film you loaded each 1,000-foot roll up on the KEM and pulled your pieces. Our styles were very similar, and it was very homogenous. You can't tell who cut what scene.

TO: Sound effects and music are important elements to Rocky.

SC: We were very lucky on that with Rocky because Bill Conti was brought in early and one of the best situations is where you are able to tailor the music to the film at an early stage.

TO: So, scenes like the training montage were tailored to the music and vice versa while you were editing.

SC: Yes, he was doing piano tracks that we would use to cut to or adjust the picture to and that's why everything was in rhythm, both the training montage and the fight. When I did my first cut of the fight, I cut it to a Bad Company song.

TO: You're kidding!

SC: No, and the director had an idea of using more classical music and the producers wanted something more popular. And that's what Bill Conti achieved—a cross between the two. It has a classical lilt to it, but it has a very contemporary feel. The majority of the film was not difficult, but the fight was a big challenge. We just had so many pieces and there was so much to do because we were editing on film.

TO: Do you recall seeing the entire completed film for the first time?

SC: When we finished and locked the cut, I moved on to another film. We had done a lot of the sound effects for the fight scenes, but Richard was on the dubbing stage when it was all finished. I had only heard parts of the final score so the first time I saw the whole thing completed with the music was at the Academy screening.

TO: What was that like?

SC: It was an extremely rewarding experience because for your peers to give you a standing ovation at the end of the film was outstanding.

TO: Did you realize how big the film was going to be?

SC: I don't think anyone really knew. We knew we had something really good.

TO: March 29th, 1977. Rocky, All The President's Men, Bound for Glory, Network, and Two Minute Warning. William Holden was the presenter. Do you remember the moment?

SC: (Laughs) Richard's mom taped that and I still have the VHS tape of our segment where Bill Holden gives us the award and it's probably one of the most precious pieces of film that I have. You have no idea what's going to happen. And then they said, 'the winner is'…

TO: And you figured it wasn't going to be you and Richard.
SC: Our hopes dropped because we thought it wasn't us. And then he said, 'Uh, excuse me, the winners are…' and at that point, we knew we had it.

TO: To the very end…

SC: It's a very daunting experience being in front of that many people and how big it is around the world.

TO: You moved from film to the digital nonlinear systems pretty early on.

SC: Yes, in 1993. But at first, it was a very big transition I have to admit.

TO: How so?

SC: Because on a Moviola or a KEM, you can stop on a dime and the frame is at your fingertips and there's a different kind of timing. On an Avid, it's more like cycling through and you're working at the speed of the machine. As soon as you get used to it, it's great. I was one of four editors on Sister Act 2. And the director, Bill Duke, who's a wonderful guy, shot a lot of film—850,000 feet. Disney had a very tight release schedule and that's why we had four editors on it. And every musical sequence had 30,000-40,000 feet of film.

TO: You had something like 157 hours of material.
SC: Right and I was working with two KEMs, both with three heads on

them, and you had to load everything up and then take everything down and then load everything up...

TO: People today forget how physical film editing was...

SC: I thought that Avid was just the way to be doing this. I tried to convince them to make the jump, but it was just too late in the process. With Wagon's East, we started that on film, but then we moved to Lightworks. In all fairness to Lightworks, it was very early, and we had a lot of technical problems. On the next picture, I went back to Avid and I never looked back.

TO: What are some favorite films?

SC: Oh, my gosh, there are so many. Clear and Present Danger Clear is one of my favorite movies of all time. My wife or son will tell you I probably look at that about once a year. The editor did a great job on that film.

TO: Neil Travis.

SC: I just really have always admired his work, from Dances With Wolves and Patriot Games to Clear and Present Danger. He was just an excellent editor and I told him that. Lawrence of Arabia influenced me tremendously. The Wild Bunch influenced me in another way. When I really love a film, I go back and see what made that film tick and where. I'll look at the individual scenes and in the overall rhythm.

TO: What have you learned along the way?

SC: I've been fortunate to become close friends with many of the directors I've worked with. I think it's a collective learning experience—that you learn how to read the personalities. You learn how to accomplish what you want to accomplish while working within the framework of that director's personality. Over the years I figured out that you might as well be truthful up front because if the Director doesn't agree with your opinion, you probably won't be a great team anyway. And if he does agree with your opinion, you're off to a great start. And it's the same way with the film. A director has his or her point of view and you have to hope that the vision and the point of view is something that's going to connect with the audience. So, you have to be honest as a director and honest as an editor.

TO: Have you had a job interview go a different way than how you thought it would go?

SC: One of the funniest things that ever happened to me on an interview was with Kirk Douglas. He was going to direct a film called Posse. I had read the script and I was waiting outside. They called me in and I shook hands with Kirk and he says, 'Have you got your script with you?' And I said no and he hands me a script and says, 'Go to page 38. The part of so and so.' And he tells me to read that part and that he's going to read the other part. And I say, 'Okay...' And I do a couple of lines and you can tell he's acting with me.

TO: You must have been, like, 'what's going on?'

SC: I had some acting experience growing up, but I asked him why he wanted me to read the part. And he said, 'Well, you're here for the part, aren't you? You're an actor, right?'

And I said, 'No, I'm here for the film editor job.' And he says, 'Well, you don't look like a film editor, you look like an actor! I couldn't possibly use you as an editor.'

TO: You're kidding.

SC: And that was the end of that interview! (Both laugh) I walked out shaking my head, thinking I should have said that I was there to read for the part! Who knows, maybe I would be an actor now instead of an Editor.

JOEL COX, ACE

Photograph courtesy of the American Cinema Editors and ACE Eddie Awards

LOS ANGELES, CALIFORNIA

Partial Credits: Den of Thieves, American Sniper, Jersey Boys, Prisoners, Gran Torino, Flags of Our Fathers, Million Dollar Baby, Mystic River, The Bridges of Madison County, A Perfect World, Unforgiven.

Joel came through the Warner studio system, starting in the mail room. When he edits, he makes a cut and only watches the scene after he's done. No second guessing. He played back a scene—one that he had just cut right in front of me—it looked terrific. That's skill, experience, talent, and confidence. Four words which are apt descriptions of Joel.

TO: Joel, you received your Oscar for Unforgiven. How did you get your start?

JC: (Laughs) I actually got my start in front of the camera at six weeks old and I continued to do bit pieces like that until I was twelve!

TO: I never knew that.

JC: When I graduated from high school, I started going around the studios to get a job working in sound. And I got a job in the mailroom here at Warner Brothers.

TO: What's amazing about your career is that you have only worked here, at Warner Brothers.

JC: (Laughs) I was here for about six months, just pushing mail around, and I got an opportunity to go to the editorial department to be a film messenger for one day. Rudy Fehr was the head of the editorial department and one Friday night he called me into the office and said 'We'd like to offer you the next opening here. Are you interested?' And I said, yes, absolutely, I'll take it.

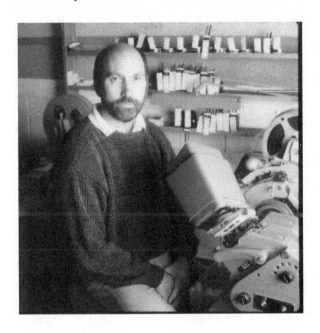

In the Cutting Room
Photograph courtesy the American Cinema Editors and ACE Eddie Awards

TO: Then what happened?

JC: (Laughs) I sat three more years in the mailroom waiting for the opening to happen!

When someone in editorial got sick or went on vacation, I got to go over there and I kept learning and learning. I eventually got in, during the summer of 1964 and learned how to put dailies together.

TO: You had a real apprenticeship program in place.

JC: Right and as an apprentice in the system, I was used by the studio in various departments - so I worked in sound effects as an assistant, music as an assistant, ADR as an assistant. The only way assistant editors moved up was when an editor left or retired or passed away.

TO: Both 1969 and 1970 were very interesting years for you. You worked as an assistant editor on Sam Peckinpah's The Wild Bunch, Francis Coppola's The Rain People, and Michael Wadleigh's Woodstock.

JC: The Rain People was actually the first one. It was a little film that Francis went out on the road and shot. Barry Malkin was the editor. They brought it back to the studios and the studio had to assign an assistant; I worked with Barry hand in hand. The studio moved you around, and that was when I met Bill Phillips and Bill Stevenson who worked in the sound department for Quinn Martin on The FBI.

TO: The television show ran for nine years.

JC: Right. When that show was over they asked me to come and work with them and so, for two seasons, I worked in television—in fact that was my only work in television.

TO: So you worked in sound?

JC: Yes, I worked as a sound effects assistant and a music assistant and Kenny Wilhoit was the music editor and I learned my music editing skills from him. Yeah, it was two years in the trenches like that, and I learned a lot! I was working in the office and there was a George C. Scott film, Petulia...

TO: That's Richard Lester who directed it—1968.

JC: And Rudy Fehr called and said, 'Listen, get this reel out of the show."

TO: Because they wanted to see something in just that part of the film.

JC: Right. Now, it was a very unfortunate time in life because Bobby Kennedy had just been assassinated. In the film, George C. Scott makes a derogatory comment about Bobby Kennedy and Jack Warner wanted that removed. The film was already done, finished, and in the exchange ready to go into the theatres. So we ran it and we marked the film, took it out of the projector, came out to one of the cutting rooms and over my shoulder, as I edit, are Jack Warner and Rudy Fehr.

TO: Talk about pressure!

JC: And, as I made the very first edit I ever made in my career, both of them werestanding over me while I made this positive print. What that means is that you have the track running 20 frames ahead. I made this cut and it worked perfectly and they loved it.

TO: You got your first full picture editor credit in 1975 for Farewell My Lovely.

JC: Right, but just before that I did Rafferty and The Gold Dust Twins and that was when I met Walter Thompson.

TO: He was nominated twice for editing This Above All and The Nun's Story.

JC: Walter and Ferris Webster were old school. They never grew up with the director in the editing room. When the director came in, they put me in front of the Moviola and I got to do all the changes.

TO: That's great.

JC: Yes, which is, again, training and learning on the job, how to work with a director. If you go right back to the very beginning when I was riding on the bike as a messenger, I got to watch Bill Ziegler...

TO: He did Rebel Without A Cause and My Fair Lady.

JC: Yeah and Folmar Blangsted...

TO: Rio Bravo, The Summer of '42.

JC: Right and you're just watching. But the one who took me under his wing, really, was Sam O'Steen.

TO: He had an amazing career—The Graduate, Chinatown, Cool Hand Luke...

JC: Sam took me to his editing room and gave me my basic skills of how to run film, mark it, and pick the pieces you want. And then you'd run it and if it was good, that was it. If the director walked in, you could show him what you'd done. Whether you were one minute in the scene or four minutes in the scene, everything up to that point in the film, was done.

TO: It wasn't just an assembly, it was already finely tuned.

JC: Right, it was done. Not a work in progress. Now that we have the Avid, I still edit the same way. I'm old school.

TO: When did you make the transition to digital editing?

JC: I think it was 1995. We did a little film here...

TO: The Stars Fell on Henrietta. That's when I met you, here on the lot.

JC: There's no doubt that because of electronic editing producers and studio heads think you can do things faster. It's still 10,800 feet of film in two hours. Clint says it's the greatest invention to filmmaking that he has ever seen in his career, because of what we can do with it that we couldn't do before. The downside he says comes when you have a director who can't make up his mind.

TO: You need real discipline to know when it's done.

JC: I remember a Director's symposium where there were different directors speaking and they asked a question about what do the directors do after they finish shooting. And Clint said, 'Well, I take about a week or so off and then I get with Joel and I make my cuts.' And one of the other directors says, 'A week?' And Clint says, 'Yeah, it takes us about a week and we're done.'

TO: You have such a long relationship with Clint Eastwood. But only three of them are westerns.

JC: I love doing westerns. But working for Clint—we've done everything. We've done music, we've done comedy, we've done adventure, we've done drama, a little sci-fi stuff. I think I'm the luckiest guy in the world at the job that I have, where I am today. I'm very fortunate and very lucky.

TO: And you've worked incredibly hard at it.

JC: Well, it's not that I didn't earn it and not that I wasn't ready for it. But once the opportunity is there, you still have to make the opportunity work. But I do want the world to know that I am very fortunate and very grateful for where I am.

TO: What do you tell people who want to get into the craft?

JC: Well, when you've got two or three people in a room pulling three different ways, you've got to know how to make everyone kind of happy and that's a personality thing and not everyone has that and fortunately I have the kind of personality that always seems to work with people.

TO: I've sat with you while you were editing. You make it look easy. But have there been times when you've had difficulty with scenes?

JC: (Laughs) Well, I wouldn't say it's difficult. I only read the script one time. Clint has a vision for a film and he brings that vision to the film but it may change. Clint lets the actors breathe, and lets the film breathe; I think the awards and accolades that he's received have proven that his style is pretty accurate on how to do it. Most actors will tell you that after they are finished, it was the greatest experience they ever had. Remember, he's an actor first. Clint did give me this piece of advice and it's really the only one. 'Do as I do as a director. First instinct and never look back.'

TO: So simple and so hard to do for most of us.

JC: Yeah. I remember Walter and Ferris would cut a scene and we'd look at it and they'd go home and the next day, they'd come in and take it apart and play with it. And Sam O'Steen told me, 'That's not what you want to do.' And Clint Eastwood told me, 'You don't want to do that.' He says, 'The minute you start second guessing yourself, you've taken yourself out of the realm of that fresh approach and there's something that might be there that you'll never get again.'

TO: When you started to get the dailies for Mystic River, did you realize you had something very special in those performances?

JC: Absolutely. From day one and the first scene I put together, I thought 'Wow, if this continues, this is going to be some film.' Now, this is a bit of an unknown thing but basically, starting that film, we started tracking music. Clint started writing music and he'd bring it to me. And he'd say, 'Try this and tell me what you think.' And he'd give me four or five pieces and I'd go through the film putting this piece here, this piece there…

TO: Million Dollar Baby came right after Mystic River. When you read the script and you put together the ending did you realize how powerful it was going to be for the audience?

JC: Well, as we went along, yes, I started to see the performances. I had met Hillary when they were working down in the gym in Los Angeles. I was on the set and she came up to me and she said 'How's it going?'

TO: Boy, if that's not a leading question to an editor…

JC: And I said, 'You'll be pleasantly surprised.' And she said, 'Really?' And I said, 'Yeah.' Well, the film went on and became what it became and it won Best Picture, Best Director, Best Actress, and Best Supporting Actor. The day after the awards, we had an interview here. And after the interview was done, Hillary comes over and looks at me and she hugs me and starts crying. And she said, 'You and I both know that I have this award because of your work.'

TO: Wonderful.

JC: And I told her that I was honored that she said that. Because they have to give me the performance. A compliment from an actress of that caliber is something.

At the ACE Awards for Unforgiven
Photograph courtesy the American Cinema Editors and ACE Eddie Awards

TO: It sure is. You received your Academy Award for Unforgiven.

JC: You know, you put a film together as an editor and you always hope that the work is good. You hope that you captured what the writer and the director envisioned for the film, and the actors... It's not an individual thing. We're all working together to make the film. It's about attaining the director's vision of the script. And there are a lot of moments in that film. There is some humorous stuff in Unforgiven.

And there's some tragedy in it, too.

TO: You draw out the suspense and the tension.

JC: Well, we did that. We were working a tempo where we were trying to get the audience to squirm in their seats. To realize and to feel that they were in this pressure cooker.

TO: Do you ever go back and look at it, considering it was a real high point of your career?

JC: Some years later when I saw the film on television one day, I watched it. And I watched it for about ten minutes because I've seen the film somewhere between 50 and 70 times. Yeah, when I'm done, I'm done. When Clint's done, he's done. But I just sat and watched it. And that film really is good.

TO: Are there examples of films that you worked on that didn't do as well as they should have? One of my personal favorites that didn't get its due recognition is A Perfect World.

JC: (Laughs) That's the one I was going to tell you!

TO: Really?

JC: Yeah. It's my belief that the film was released at the wrong time. It came out near Thanksgiving. And if there is a time of the year that a child endangerment film does not belong out it's Thanksgiving to Christmas. People don't want to see that. So, we release it in this country and we do $35 million worth of business. Then the film releases in Europe, after the first of the year, and does $100 million. I mean Kevin Costner. I think it's one of the best things he's ever done.

TO: Are there films that you admire or other editors whose work you enjoy?

JC: There are too many. It's way beyond four or five. I've been in this business all my life. Ben Hur, West Side Story—a marvelous film.

Richard Chew did Bobby and I was watching (the Robert Kennedy) assassination on television and when I saw that in the film I felt that they recreated exactly what happened that evening. Integrating the original footage with what they shot, I thought was brilliantly done. JFK is also a marvelous film. There are so many.

TO: Do you ever see your films with an audience?

JC: No. But I'll tell you why. And Clint's right on this. We're either filmmakers, or we're not. Clint says, 'We either know what we're doing, or we don't.' We either have a gut feeling or an intuition about making a film or we shouldn't be doing this. When we did Gran Torino, Clint said to me, 'There are a few people who think I shouldn't do this because people are going to think that's who I am.' But, of course, it's just a film. He saw this character in the book, he thought it would be interesting to do and he did it. And it's a huge hit film.

TO: And it's incredible because it was done very fast…

JC: And nobody—just like with Million Dollar Baby—nobody saw that ending coming and no one saw the ending in Baby. And the press kept it quiet. So it was a shocking ending. Is it hard to take? Absolutely. But real life is hard to take. In real life, things happen that we don't want to see.

TO: But that's what makes the film special. It doesn't cheat for a happy ending.

TO: What do you think is the most satisfying part of your job?

JC: Seeing the finished product, because I look back at where we were going with it, and I see how it finished. It's very gratifying when a film comes out the way you planned it.

GABRIELLA CRISTIANI

Photo courtesy of Gabriella Cristiani

LOS ANGELES, CA

Partial Credits: Teleios, Match, Kandagar, Moths, One Night with the King, Savior, The Sheltering Sky, The Last Emperor, Tu Mi Turbi, Luna, 1900 (Associate Editor), Last Tango in Paris (Associate Editor).

When you speak with Gabriella, the feeling you get is, well, the best way I can term it is: ageless. She simply has an amazingly positive outlook. And she really downplays the successes she has achieved but they are substantial. Gabriella—the first native Italian who was nominated for and won an Academy Award for Editing.

✄

TO: Gabriella, you are an Academy Award, Eddie, David, and Silver Ribbon recipient for Best Editing. It is my great pleasure to be speaking with you. How did you get started in the film industry?

GC: I was kidnapped by a brilliant, genius film editor when I was 17! (Both Laugh) And I saw what he was doing and I was totally fascinated. And so I blackmailed him that if he didn't teach me what he was doing I would leave him forever! (Both Laugh)

TO: I'm laughing so hard. I can assure you no other interview started like this!

GC: (Laughs): I was only 17 and at the beginning of life. But I was fascinated with him—Franco Arcalli.

TO: Okay. He was a co-writer of Last Tango in Paris and also one of the editors.

GC: Yes. He edited The Conformist, 1900, Once Upon a Time in

America and hundreds of movies he did in Italy. He was a brilliant mind to learn from. And it really happened by accident because I went to pick him up for lunch at his editing room. And I was watching what he was doing and it was fascinating because he was watching dailies very casually.

TO: Oh, I see, you didn't really know what film editing was about.

GC: Yes. And he was going back and forth, watching these images. And without even looking at what he was doing, he was cutting pieces of film and putting them together. And he'd run them through the Moviola and it was the most fascinating, brilliant thing that I had ever seen in my life.

TO: The magic of editing—putting one piece against another to make a meaning.

GC: Yes. And I saw him do it and I saw the screening and it was fascinating how you can create from apparently not connected images a scene. And that possibility—to make something like that was really...

TO: The creation of emotion by juxtaposing images...

GC: Exactly. It was striking to see that.

TO: Franco Arcalli really was a brilliant editor. You began your long relationship with Bernardo Bertolucci as an associate editor on The Last Tango in Paris and 1900. What was it like working on those two films and what did you learn?

GC: I was Arcalli's assistant for seven years from 1967-1974. I did a lot of movies with him and I saw his patience and his creativity. I learned a lot. He was my mentor. Kim and I were working on Last Tango but Kim got sick and was in the hospital for three weeks. The production didn't want to stop so they brought in Roberto Perpignani and I edited with Roberto for three weeks. After that, Kim came back and he and I finished Last Tango. Roberto had a different approach to editing—more intellectual and theoretical. Kim didn't talk much—he was very much discovering as he watched the images and what was there to be created.

TO: Kim was Franco's nickname, right?

GC: Yes. And then with Bernardo, I continued through Sheltering Sky.

TO: Much has been written about The Last Tango in Paris regarding the subject matter, but the story that is often not covered is what happened to the film in Italy and how it was seized and Mr. Bertolucci being imprisoned. Is that true?

GC: We were laughing because we never expected that to happen like some terrible scandal. No, Bernardo was not put in prison—the movie was.

TO: It was confiscated?

GC: (Laughs) Yes, and for 20 years they kept a copy of it in a criminal museum. Which is absolutely ridiculous and bizarre. And Bernardo did not go to prison, thank God, because that would have been horrible. Professionally, it was really fun. We were saying to ourselves, 'Who's going to watch this movie?' We were hoping because Marlon Brando was in it. But we didn't know.

TO: Sure, it's one thing to see him as the Godfather, but this film was very different.

GC: Yes, and one funny episode was one day I went back to the cutting room. I was the assistant and in charge of the film and everything. And I used to put the separate takes on a counter and one day two takes of Marlon Brando naked disappeared! (Both Laugh)

TO: Well, I guess someone really wanted that footage and knew it existed...

GC: We don't know who stole them. We don't know how they stole them. The only people who had keys to the cutting room were me and the cleaning people. But we never knew or found out!

TO: It must have been pretty interesting to see the dailies for the film, though...

GC: You must remember that in that studio in Italy they were making all kinds of amazing movies. And to us that movie was just another movie. Of course, it had Marlon Brando, but after one week of dailies, it becomes just another actor...

TO: And the work that has to be done.

GC: Yes, and of course, it was also very challenging because there was a lot of work for me to do and to be on top of. I never scratched one frame of film because I wanted to give it to the editors in immaculate condition. I was really concentrating on the technical preparation.

TO: Okay, I'd like to ask a question on 1900. The film was really controversial because of the running time of the film and then change of control over it.

GC: That was a very bad story. Kim was the editor, but you know, the movie was taken to America and the story, which we never believed, was that it was re-cut by an American editor. And it was very sad because what was done was something that Kim could have done very easily. And probably even better, having known the story so well. But the producers did all that and it was very unfair and they did something very bad, which was that they cut the negative.

TO: This was all done without Bertolucci?

GC: Yes, they did it before Bernardo could see it or approve it. And Bernardo was on trial.

TO: So at the time he was still on trial in Italy on the obscenity charge relating to Last Tango?

GC: Yes, and then he won. So, we finally got the movie back.

TO: 1900.

GC: Yes. And I had to go to Technicolor and rebuild everything, back-to-back and piece- by-piece. And, as you know we lost frames.

TO: Right, because they cut the negative and you lost frames any time they cut into that negative.

GC: Yes, and so I went back and replaced each cut so you would not see that it was missing a frame.

TO: Only three years after working on 1900, you were the editor on the first of four films you edited for Bernardo Bertolucci—La Luna. What was that like now that you were in the full editor role?

GC: Well, the reason I edited that movie was that Kim died. And Bernardo was thinking about using another editor, but he really couldn't decide on anyone else. And eventually he asked me. But I really didn't want to do it.

TO: Well, I'm sure it was probably too soon.

GC: I didn't want to take Kim's place, of course, for emotional reasons.

TO: Of course.

GC: So, Bernardo and I had a very sad conversation because we were both missing Kim enormously. And Bernardo found a solution and he said, 'Okay, let's do this. I don't want to put the weight on you so much. You and I will edit and if we need someone else to come in and supervise we will call them.' And then he said, 'But, until then, just relax. I'm very confident you can do it.' And remember, I had already edited two or three movies and he knew that I could edit.

TO: It was just following in Kim's footsteps…

GC: Kim was such an important collaborator and had an important role in Italian film history in the '70's. He worked with all the important directors and was the central point for these people. He was brilliant. And I say this not because he was my mentor and my companion but because he was a genius.

TO: He has a very impressive filmography. In addition to the films we already talked about, he edited Zabriskie Point.

GC: Yes, and we took that decision and I started editing. Of course, at the beginning, it was really emotionally hard. But then I felt fine.

TO: The Last Emperor was released in 1987 and went on to sweep the Academy Awards, winning nine, including your Academy Award for Best Editing. It was an enormous undertaking. How long did you work on the film and what were some of the major challenges you experienced?

GC: Well, that was the easiest movie I've ever done in my life. Believe it or not.

TO: Really? That's the last thing I expected to hear. I'm shocked to hear that.

GC: (Laughs) I know, it is shocking. But it is true! I'm not making this up. It was the easiest movie.

TO: You had a lot of footage…

GC: Two million feet.

TO: And you were editing on film.

GC: We had a ton of footage. But I believe that the more you have the easier it is to edit.

TO: Why?

GC: Well because whatever you take is fine and whatever you throw away is fine! (Both Laugh). No, honestly, I was really trying not to do that movie because I was terrified and horrified to find myself in that situation. And there was the different language as well. I didn't know if I could make it or if I wanted to make it.

TO: So, what happened to make you get off the fence?

GC: Finally, Bernardo said, 'Shut up, just get on and work!'

TO: That's funny.

GC: Yes. You know, this was the first movie I did with Bernardo where I didn't go on location with him because I was doing another movie.

TO: Okay, that was High Season with Jacqueline Bisset, right?

GC: Yes. And Bernardo waited for me. So, when he came back from China, I saw tons and tons of footage. Hours and hours.

TO: Okay, I calculated the amount—it's over 370 hours of footage!

GC: They locked me in a room for ten days with Bernardo to look at all the footage! (Both Laugh) And I was speechless—complete speechless from the beauty of what they shot. And Bernardo was getting worried and he asked me, 'Why don't you say anything?' And I told him that I was completely mesmerized.

TO: He must have loved that.

GC: Yes, and so my first thought was that what they shot was so beautiful. That was my concern. It was 'My God, there is so much beauty here that maybe people will be turned away.'

TO: Okay, I know what you mean. Right, there's a majesty in those widescreen vistas. Probably the same kind of thinking for Lawrence of Arabia, where you can't help but be impressed by the landscape but you still have to concentrate on the story or you'll get overwhelmed.

GC: Yes. And so I started editing and that was probably January 1987 and on August 21st—I'll never forget that date—we finished the movie.

TO: Where were you when you heard you were nominated for the Academy Award?

GC: For a week, I didn't understand that I was nominated—I thought it was for the movie and for Bernardo!

TO: Really?

GC: I didn't realize it was a personal nomination! You know, with the education I received from Kim, I never thought about being recognized with awards but only the pleasure of doing what you like to do and what you want to do. So the Oscar, to me, was something that didn't belong to me. It was not in my consciousness. It was not something that I could possibly even think about. First of all, it's not my culture. Secondly, no one Italian editor—not even Kim—was nominated.

TO: That's right. You were the first native Italian nominated for an Academy Award for Film Editing. And when they announced your name?

GC: When they announced my name, I was out in the lobby!

TO: Really?

GC: Yes! I had to run to the stage because I was outside! And I was congratulating Vittorio Storaro because he won just before me. And then they went to a break and were going to do documentaries. And so we went out to congratulate Vittorio and we were all out. But then they changed the order (of the awards). So then they said my name and one of the (film's) producers who stayed inside came out and took me in!

TO: What a story! That's amazing.

GC: I almost missed it!

TO: You made the transition from editing on film to electronic nonlinear editing on The Sheltering Sky using the CMX 6000.

GC: Yes. Bernardo was very against electronic but now he loves everything that you can do on electronic systems. But at the time he was very resistant. And also, I felt very guilty because I edited Sheltering Sky in 28 working days.

TO: That's crazy!

GC: And that was shock. Shock. But also you think, 'Wow'. And I was fast without digital because think about when I edited Last Emperor I did that in seven months including sound and everything. And that was film.

TO: Yes.

GC: So, electronic gave me even more speed, but that was a mistake.

TO: Why?

GC: In fact, a big mistake. Because Bernardo was in Cannes where he was the President of the Jury. And he came back and the movie was done and he went in shock. And he said, 'No way.' And I said, 'Yes, it's done. I don't know how I did it!' (Laughs) And the first thing he did was that he had me send back the CMX 6000 and we went back on film!

TO: What films do you like to watch? Any favorites?

GC: Oh, yes. One movie that I watch again and again and again is Shall We Dance? I think it's a masterpiece.

TO: Yeah, I love that movie. The one directed by Masayuki Suo. It's great.

GC: It is great. In every aspect. Dramaturgically, comedy, poetic, sentimental. I mean everything. That is a movie that I would tell people to watch again and again because it's full of details. It's so powerful and profound. Another one is Babette's Feast. That story tells you the story of a woman's consciousness and desire and capacity to please one's self and others. And in that movie it is very clear how women can be so much better to rule because all we like to do is to please. You know, I recently saw, In Bruges.

TO: Sure, Colin Farrell and Brendan Gleeson.

GC: I'm not very much for violent movies, but this movie... It's something else! I also just saw City Island with Andy Garcia. Oh, it's very nice, very sweet, and very well done. You can see the joy they had making the film.

TO: It's a lovely pleasure for me to spend so much time with you.

GC: You're welcome. My pleasure.

CHRIS DICKENS, ACE

Photograph courtesy of the American Cinema Editors and ACE Eddie Awards

LONDON, ENGLAND

Partial Credits: Mary Queen of Scots, Genius, Macbeth, The Double, Les Miserables, Paul, Submarine, Slumdog Millionaire, Hot Fuzz, Shaun of the Dead

What a genuinely nice man. When you talk with Chris, he will tell you that one of the most important things is to not be afraid of throwing away the work and finding a new approach. He's fearless in the cutting room when it comes to starting over. "You have to have the courage to tear things apart and start again."

TO: Chris, you are an Academy Award, ACE Eddie, and BAFTA award recipient for best editing for your wonderful work on Slumdog Millionaire. You started off with a great interest in filmmaking and painting, right?

CD: Yes, my Dad had a Super-8 camera and like a lot of people at that time, we made little movies when I was nine and ten years old. When I was 16, I went to art school and I was very interested in modern sculpture. And that gave me a lot of insight into the working process of artists. But I knew that I was not going to make a living at that! (Laughs) So I thought that going back to filmmaking made sense. And the part of filmmaking that I was always interested in was joining shots together.

TO: So, that Super-8 camera and editing your movies really showed you the power and fun of juxtaposing images and editing.

CD: Yeah, the nuts and bolts of making a film. And even my painting and sculpting was using the notion of moving images to tell a story. I chose editing and went to school for that and when I got out of school I started working.

TO: As a sound editor?

CD: Yes, I did work as a sound editor but I also did picture editing on smaller things. Originally, I thought that sound editing would be the choice for me, but as I got working in the industry, I felt that picture editing was going to give me more control over the final film and also to be able to work more closely with the director. So that was really what led me to the decision. I had worked as an assistant picture editor and what I learned the most is that you shouldn't be afraid to start over again. The art teachers always said that if you weren't happy with the work that you should have the courage to scrub out the lines and start again.

TO: Right, don't be afraid to change...

CD: Yes, and that advice stood me in really good stead as an editor because you're constantly reworking and rewriting and revisiting an ongoing process. And if I hadn't learned that it was important to go back, it would have been harder. You need to have the courage and look at it and say, 'is that right?' The thing about the film industry is that even if you think something right, you may have someone who comes along and tells you that it isn't! (Both Laugh) And you still have to change it whether you like it or not! And often you realize that the request is a different way and it may not be your way, but it's very important to remember that.

TO: You can't stubbornly be wed to an idea.

CD: Yeah, and it's hard because emotionally you're involved. But being an editor, that is absolutely essential—to be open-minded.

TO: Some editors feel that they get typecast by doing just one type of film and you, thankfully, don't have that problem.

CD: Slumdog Millionaire has lots of different things in it and many things rolled into one. It has drama—it's a thriller—it has comedy. If I hadn't of had that kind of variety previously, I don't think I would have been capable of editing it.

TO: I think a perfect run-up to that has to be your work on Shaun of the Dead. This was a really successful film with a very loyal following.

CD: I didn't realize it would have such a long life and a cult following. I mean, Slumdog Millionaire is known everywhere in the world and Shaun isn't. I knew I loved the film and the mixture of genres. It was a simple film without a big budget and in a way that comes through. I think that's why people like it—it's not pretentious in any way. I'm just pleased people enjoyed it and really that was my big break because it got noticed so much.

TO: I love the single take where Shaun—Simon Pegg—goes into the convenience store at the beginning and he's oblivious to everything around him. And then he goes in again and everything has changed.

CD: Yeah. You know, I'm in that.

TO: Really?

CD: Yeah, I'm the jogger.

TO: You pulled your Hitchcock. (Both Laugh) How did you come to edit Slumdog Millionaire?

CD: By accident.

TO: Really?

CD: As a lot of things, you're typically working on something else when a director calls you and you just might not be free. And Chris Gill, who had cut several films for Danny wasn't available. Danny quite liked Hot Fuzz because it was fast and frenetic in terms of the editing but not ridiculously so. And Danny wanted that for the film—a very kinetic kind of approach.

TO: Had you read the book?

CD: I hadn't read the book, but I loved the script. I had heard about it and I just had to do the film. And I think Danny is just a great director and he doesn't mess around—he knew that I really wanted to do it and he offered me the job. Danny has a drastic approach to editing.

TO: How so?

CD: Just trying things. And Danny did start shooting things a couple of weeks before the main shooting started. And we thought they were just camera tests.

TO: You were on location in India with him?

CD: Yes. And actually that footage was proper shooting.

TO: That was going to be the style…

CD: Yeah and he does ask for feedback and works that into his shooting. And so if we had something edited, he'd go back and shoot some extra things and some new things for scenes.

TO: Was it a hard film for you to edit?

CD: Well, all of it was challenging. It was hard for many reasons. Going to India and working with locals was difficult because I was helping the assistants and doing more than normal. But while it was challenging and hard, that's why the film works and why it's successful. I loved the material and I grew to love Mumbai and the people. And because I was there while they were filming, I understood the city and that the film was not just about the story but that it was also about how India is growing and changing. And having an understanding of those changes really helped. It more than helped. It meant that I was able to go through the process that Danny and the producers wanted me to go through.

TO: Did you have a lot of material?

CD: The first assembly was three and a half hours long. The script was really good but there were a lot of details about the game show and things were playing out in real time. And on the page, it was fine. But, when you put it together, it worked, but it didn't feel whole. It felt like parts of a whole while you were watching it. And essentially that was the challenge of the film—getting it down to length.

TO: I never got the feeling of repetition.

CD: Danny wanted to get it to 100 minutes. And it was just not possible—it was a two-hour film and possibly a little more than two hours. And we condensed it to join it so that it was one story and not four stories joined together.

TO: What was your working style with Danny Boyle?

CD: It was very inclusive. We had a lot of screenings with the writer and the producer together and a core group of people. And Danny likes to try a lot of things before deciding what works best. And that's a good challenge. We didn't spend a lot of time editing the film, but we had enough time. Danny likes to work very quickly.

TO: So, really the big challenge was to make it cohesive?

CD: Yeah, joining the four stories together and finding visual ways of joining those different timelines was really the work. And we found things that really helped.

TO: Can you give me an example?

CD: Simple devices like cutting from similar angles like cutting from the back of Jamal's head as a child to the same shot as an adult when he's on the show. Or hearing the sound of the "Who Wants to be a Millionaire?" show coming through from one scene to another. Or, the other way around, having score coming from one scene to another.

TO: These were all used as motivating a scene forward...

CD: Yeah, and it was a good way of condensing things. The script was created as a multi-layered story and you had possibilities in the editing. Often in a film you have an A-B-C order and you can't easily change that. But this one always had all those different possibilities. And as an editor it's brilliant because you could really play with that. You could work with flashbacks and really develop those. And Danny knew he needed to shoot enough material to be able to do that in an edit. He had a lot of cameras running and then he went back for scenes three or four times.

TO: Even though you had a lot of material and possible ways of structuring the film, the challenge as you describe it was a good challenge to a better end. Sometimes, you don't even have those possibilities.

CD: That's right. I've found other films harder because they're more restrictive because of what you can do creatively. And that can be really frustrating. You have to remember that Slumdog was a small film—it had a budget of 12 or 13 million dollars, if that. And it was not a well-known book. It could have gone many ways in a different director's hands. Simon (Beaufoy) is a great writer and he thought about the elements and he wrote something great. But he wrote something really ambitious—children and adults at different ages and it looks great on the page but you think, 'how are we going to do that?' And if the budget was larger, maybe we wouldn't have been able to do the things we did.

TO: The suspense that you create during the song rehearsal / blinding sequence is absolutely excruciating. I think it is marvelous work. Did it take a long time?

CD: Not that one. Weirdly, I think because of what's happening, it was always excruciating. Other things took longer. I think because what you were seeing was so extreme, I found it easier to do. The thing about Slumdog is not the scenes themselves. It's about how they work together. And that was the challenge. In other words, we could have a scene that was beautifully shot and edited well and just not work in the whole.

TO: Right.

CD: And that's why I think the film did well. And I hope that doesn't sound as if it's bragging. But I think that all the elements of the film worked together. And that's when a good film becomes a great film or a memorable film. And where that scene was in the film, and getting that right, was work.

TO: Did you have a lot more scenes with the kids?

CD: Oh, yes. We had to cut a lot of it out and in hindsight perhaps that was the right decision. Too much of the cute kids running around would have made it that much harder to have a scene like that. The blinding scene is hard and really difficult to watch. And it's a question of tone, isn't it? If you start the film off in the right way, you're going to get scenes like that and the audience will stay with it.

TO: Sure, I guess it's the type of thing where you haven't lied or misled the audience that they're going to see one type of thing and then the film delivers something else.

CD: Yes, and getting the tone right for the film was another big challenge. The script was a lot lighter than the film ended up being. The script had a lot more comedic scenes, but the film couldn't end up like that because of that one scene. The first major scene in the movie is when Jamal is hanging and is being electrocuted by the police commissioner who is trying to get the truth. And it was written in a way where it was supposed to be more comedic but it can never be funny.

TO: Sure, I'm baffled about how that could work.

CD: Especially at the start of the film because you've got no context for that. And we were very much on the edge with things that are difficult to watch, and things that are funny, and things that are beautiful.

TO: Some things that are very humane and others that are very inhumane.

CD: Yes, exactly.

TO: I want to take you back to February 22, 2009. It was a very competitive night for editing. The Curious Case of Benjamin Button, The Dark Knight, Frost / Nixon, Milk, and Slumdog Millionaire. All very different films and any one of which could have been chosen that night.

CD: Dan Hanley and Mike Hill who did Frost / Nixon leaned over and said 'It's going to be you.' I was probably more dazed than anything else! (Both Laugh) Everyone was very accomplished and anyone could have won.

TO: What are some of the things you've learned?

CD: I think there are two things. The first is to be open, always, to any idea, no matter who they come from. Sometimes the most ridiculous suggestion might actually be the solution you need. It's important not to exclude that suggestion. If it's something that you don't like or you have a strong reaction to it, that means something. The second thing is that what I didn't realize is the editor's job is to try and take a lot of different inputs from people and channel it. I've seen a lot of people get into hot water because they can't take that input. It can be very political. I suppose it's hard, but you have to try and not be emotional about it.

TO: What are some personal film favorites?

CD: Oh, that's hard. Oh, God! I love the films of the '60's and the '70's.

I think there was a lot of freedom in filmmaking that I really like. I love (Sam) Peckinpah because of his way of moving things around. Nicholas Roeg's films: Performance and Don't Look Now—they have a freedom that I really like. Billy Wilder. Hitchcock because his films are so uniquely his movies. Oh, there are so many. I love Scorsese. I think Dan Hanley and Mike Hill are great. I like the French Wave in the '60's because of Truffaut and Goddard and how they broke rules and they were prepared to do anything—jump cuts and strange ideas. And I admire that kind of spirit.

TO: What do you love about your profession?

CD: What excites me is being able to use editing and the way it really helps you bring together images and music and sound. You have to cut around things and you often can find simple ways of solving problems. And as I said before, you have to have the courage to tear things apart and start again.

GLENN FARR

Photographed by Michael O'Farrell

LOS ANGELES, CA

Partial Credits: Akeelah and the Bee, Johnson County War, Norma Jean & Marilyn, Broken Trust, Shattered, Old Gringo, The Serpent and the Rainbow, Nothing in Common, Commando, Runaway, Gospel, The Right Stuff, This Is Elvis (co-editor), Fatso. Additional Editor: Brokedown Palace, Assistant Editor, Next Stop, Greenwich Village, W.W. and the Dixie Dancekings, Harry and Tonto. Television Series Editing: Nashville, The Mentalist, Rome.

Glenn is a terrifically articulate, knowledgeable craftsman who can evaluate a film with a very astute outlook. I learned so much from listening to him. And he is very grateful for his career. As he says, "Editing has been like a magic carpet for me. Because no matter what the project is, I'm learning something."

✂

TO: Glenn, you were a co-editor for The Right Stuff for which you received an Academy Award for Best Editing. How did you get your start?

GF: I loved going to the movies with my parents and my reaction was that it was magic. I was enchanted from a very early age. During the summers, we'd go to the Culver Drive-In in Culver City close to MGM Studios. We had a Ford station wagon and my sister and I would put our sleeping bags on the roof. It was a mystical, magic thing—going to the movies with my family.

TO: That's terrific. That you developed such a love for movies so early.

GF: In a certain regard, it may have been inevitable that I would be seduced by the movies to the extent that I would become involved professionally. A great uncle, Norris Baronian, was a staff film editor of the long running Christian TV series produced in Hollywood, This Is The Life. When I was about twelve years old, my grandmother made arrangements to for me to visit uncle Norris at work. Lights, camera, action. Uncle Norris gave me the full tour, including his editing room, how he worked with his Cutter Moviola, including the issues of working with separate picture and track. I was mesmerized by that experience.During my college years, I found a job working for an editor who made industrial and educational films. I became his sorcerer's apprentice—I swept the floors, did hot splicing—whatever had to be done.

TO: It's great that you were able to learn all the basics.

GF: My first feature experience was on a documentary feature called Indian and Keith Merrill, who has made a career with IMAX films primarily about USA national parks, made it. Prior to that, I was assisting on numerous rock and roll feature documentaries, working for various documentary producers including David L. Wolper Productions where I met Richard Halsey who landed a job cutting a feature at Fox for Paul Mazursky. Richard asked me to assist him on that one.

TO: Those were the films Harry and Tonto and Next Stop, Greenwich Village films.

GF: Yes, really excellent films. When Richard was chosen to cut the first Rocky feature, I had to make a decision having received an offer to cut Indian. I had been assisting for six years and while I could have assisted on Rocky, I cut this documentary which was never released. And it's a shame because it was gloriously shot in 35mm and I had a lot of fun doing it.Because of my positive experience working with Paul Mazursky, who was close to Mel Brooks, I was hired to cut a feature for Brooks Film which meant I had the opportunity to work for Anne Bancroft.

TO: On Fatso with Dom DeLuise.

GF: Yes, it was an amazing experience working for Bancroft. Because of her magnificent career as a consummate screen and stage actor, I learned so much from her about acting, acting technique, and the actor's process.

TO: Helped you to understand what to look for?

GF: Yes. Things like the intricacies of the art and techniques of shaping dialogue, the way the actors breathe as they deliver their lines is extremely important. And being aware of the actor's breathing pattern in any given scene can really make a huge impact on the way the editing is accomplished in the interest of emulating natural speech patterns in the situations where an actor is not breathing properly. It was extremely valuable information.

TO: That's pretty interesting.

GF: Yeah, the way the actor's breathing relates to the content and meaning of the scene and the way the breathing is related to scenes involving suspense or any number of emotions. And that was one of the most important things I took away from that experience. She had me come to the set and relied on me with certain questions of coverage and transitions. And Mel Brooks would come to my cutting room at 4:30 or 5:00 o'clock each day while Anne was with me during the director's cut. I was blessed with some excellent mentors along the way. In particular, Richard Halsey was an outstanding teacher.

TO: Only three years after you start working as a full editor, you find yourself working on The Right Stuff and you, along with your co-editors, each win an Academy Award for Best Editing. You were there from the very beginning.

GF: That was, indeed, an amazing journey that spanned a period two years. I had done a movie called This Is Elvis for Andrew Solt and Malcolm Leo. It was a biopic and we used a combination of found footage of Elvis' life and when we didn't have footage for an event it was recreated by the filmmakers. And I think what appealed to Phil Kaufman was the melding of found footage and the recreations using Elvis look-alike actors.

TO: Which makes a lot of sense considering how The Right Stuff was structured and ended up on screen.

GF: I believe that I was chosen for The Right Stuff because of that movie and because I was known at Warner Brothers and The Ladd Company.

TO: All those prior relationships helped of course.

GF: Yes, and what was exciting about the film is that the producers, Irwin Winkler and Robert Chartoff and the writer-director, Phil Kaufman, made the determination that if the footage in the National Archives that had been filmed by NASA contained all the necessary parts to flesh out the story-telling, then the feature film could go forward. Because it was really not a big budget film. I think the initial budget was $17 million.

TO: It looks and sounds incredible but that's not very much money for a film of that scope.

GF: It was an enormous challenge to develop a theatrical feature film hybrid by producing new sequences with a huge cast and believable sets and authentic life size aerospace props and their miniature scaled models interwoven with appropriate NASA footage. It was an epic, low-budget movie! (Both Laugh) Phil Kaufman had an extremely imaginative and clever vision. He created detailed storyboards with a very talented artist, Tim Boxell, with whom I became a good friend. Tim was working for Gary Gutierrez at Colossal Pictures which built all the scale models and produced all the flight scenes. Phil and Tim developed the storyboards for the action sequences as well as the ticker-tape parade in Washington when John Glenn achieved his incredible accomplishment of circling the Earth in that tiny Mercury 7

Space Capsule. There was beautiful multi-camera coverage that NASA shot in magnificent 35mm color. The studio and the producers knew that the footage was there.

TO: In the National Archives.

GF: Yes. But the footage had not been looked at it in detail based on the storyboards. I was sent to the National Archives months before filming began to do exhaustive research. The challenge was find the precise motion picture images to be used to create the sequences of space flight and launches, including John Glenn, Manhattan ticker-tape parade.

TO: What a great experience.

GF: It was amazing material—hundreds of thousands of feet of film in pristine condition. It was spectacular. I found what we needed and then some and we made the arduous arrangement to bring desired footage back to San Francisco. The production was really a Bay Area enterprise being shot there and in the Mojave Desert. It really was an Indy production made for a major motion picture studio.

TO: So, once you came back and had the NASA material what happened next?

GF: I would put sequences together using the footage and we would run it for the director, production designer, director of photography Caleb Deschanel and the visual effects people. And Phil would determine what was going to be shot by the first unit with the actors. The production designer was tracking Phil's work to figure out what sets would have to be built and how this footage could be used to save the production money by not having to build things. And that was an amazing experience working as an editor but thinking like a producer and a filmmaker.

TO: When did you hear about the nomination?

GF: I think I was working at Paramount.

TO: Surprised?

GF: Oh, yeah. It was like, 'What?' (Laughs) It was completely shocking. We knew we were working on a good movie and it was a hard movie to make. But it was a surprise and the film was a dark horse. They put those of us who were nominated at the back of the Dorothy Chandler Pavilion. It was in the nosebleed section. (Laughs) I think we were two rows back from the wall so we thought 'Okay, there's no way we're going to win!'

TO: Lisa Fruchtman said that she thought it was going to go to Terms of Endearment.

GF: I don't remember walking up there. I don't know how I got up there. (Both Laugh) It was completely shocking.And to be on a stage with Jack Nicholson and Angelica Huston who announced the category, was astonishing. The Right Stuff was an unbelievably fabulous experience and I was able to do all sorts of things as an editor.

TO: You had a freedom that today isn't in abundance.

GF: The symbolic pushing of the envelope in the movie is what Phil encouraged us to do and to have that mentality. Phil didn't want people who were just staying in the boundaries of the craft. We all loved him. The Right Stuff was the equivalent of a lifetime's worth of filmmaking experience over the course of two years of six day weeks. Phil challenged himself with adapting Tom Wolfe's satirical book into an epic feature film with two big endings. Halfway through the story which marked the end of the All-American Test Pilot era the NASA Space Exploration era begins. That's what made the shaping of The Right Stuff so challenging. In actuality the film is two epic heroic adventure stories told in part from a satirical POV inspired by the tone of the Tom Wolfe book.

Because of those storytelling challenges, the plan for having two to three film editors was expanded to include two more for various lengths of time in order to work out the weave of such a multilayered saga.

For me, the experience was amazing to be in the company of some of the top editors in the biz. Lisa Fruchtman had previously worked for Coppola. Tom Rolf was a legendary film editor. Steve Rotter after working for Dede Allen, had distinguished himself with many excellent feature films. And Doug Stewart cut several of Phil Kaufman's earlier features including White Dawn.

TO: I want to take you to Wolfgang Petersen's Shattered in 1991. Were there challenges in keeping the secret from the audience?

GF: That was a big shocker and we did our best to make it a surprise for the audience. And it was a thrill working for Petersen. Talk about a complete filmmaker—he was thoroughly prepared at all times. He would start the production day with his shot list and give them to the various heads of the production departments. And he'd say, 'This is what we are going to do today and when we're done, we're going home.' And that's what they did, every day. Petersen came in on schedule and under budget.

TO: What was your working relationship like?

GF: A real perfectionist. He already had an editor on it, Hannes Nikel, who had edited Das Boot. But it became evident with the schedule that they needed another editor to work as a co-editor with Hannes. Initially, I was assigned to the section where there's that amazing high-speed photography of the face crashing into the glass. Petersen had shot miles of gorgeous footage at different frame rates. It was shot by Laslo Kovacs, one of the great DPs. After dealing with those crash sequences, I was assigned to work on many other portions of the film because of the rigorous post-production schedule.

TO: What films have influenced you over the years and what editors do you admire?

GF: I think Jerry Greenberg is a wonderful editor and I've learned a lot from the films that he has edited. I quite like the films edited by Stuart Baird. He's done several for Richard Donner. And has become a notable feature director. I love the film editing style of Doane Harrison. He was Billy Wilder's editor. Wilder would have him on the set a lot because Wilder made no bones about the fact that he was a writer, and as a director, he was constantly learning. And he wanted his editor on the set with him to help him with various aspects of scene construction in terms of the angles and shots. And that impressed me. Robert Wise, before he became a wonderful director, worked at RKO as an editor. Wise was the editor of Citizen Kane. The editors of the Preston Sturges screwball comedies were masters. Bud Smith, who was Billy Friedkin's editor, was quite influential. He did The Exorcist and To Live and Die in L.A. He was one of my mentors. I didn't assist Bud but worked for editors who were his pals which provided access to the editorial departments of some of Bud's notable films.

TO: It's ironic that you were competing against Bud Smith in 1983 because he was up for Flashdance with his co-editor, Walt Mulconery.

GF: That was so crazy. He was a wonderful, solid influence on me and I really like his approach to editing and I learned a lot from his style and his way of putting scenes together. Film editor, Sidney Levin was also a very helpful mentor who made his mark editing many wonderful films for director Marty Ritt, including Norma Rae.Before he hooked up with Ritt, Sid was doing Rock and Roll feature documentaries on which I assisted him. I also like (Roman) Polanski's editor, Herve…

TO: De Luze.

GF: I like his editing a lot. And you know, Sylvie Landra, she cuts for Luc Besson. I was just watching The Fifth Element and the cutting style is terrific. That was a tremendous amount of work. She did a great job.

TO: What are some of the things you've learned during the course of your editing career that may not have been so apparent when you started?

GF: The ability to work with people and to be a good collaborator. We have to know how to relate to producers and the directors. It involves being a diplomat and a therapist in some ways. It's the ability to be nice and to be thoroughly honest about the footage and what the possibilities and limitations are. It's important to take an active role in the shaping and making of the movie. Editing is the last draft of the screenplay and, being so, it's imperative that the editor uses all of his or her talents and techniques and imagination in maximizing the story and the potential of what the director has given the editor. After the shooting stops, the focus is on you. You have to make it work. You're there to entertain, to be a storyteller and you need to use all of your skills to do that.

TO: When I listen to you it sounds like editing became the perfect profession for doing what you love.

GF: Editing has been like a magic carpet for me. Because no matter what the project is, I'm learning something. If it's a subject matter that I didn't know much about, through the process of doing the work, I am learning. I'm increasing my knowledge. It is a good thing to have an insatiable curiosity about life and people.I have found that one of the most satisfying aspects of being a Film Editor is actively mentoring those who work for me as Assistant Editors who demonstrate a true passion to learn the art and craft of editing. If one loves the work, it is a good thing to pay forward that passion.

LISA FRUCHTMAN, ACE

Photographed by Jane Wattenberg

LOS ANGELES, CA

Partial Credits: Love & Taxes, The Woodsman, My Best Friend's Wedding, Truman, The Godfather Part III, Children of a Lesser God, The Doctor, Captain EO, The Right Stuff, Heaven's Gate, Apocalypse Now, The Godfather Part II (Assistant Editor).

Would she go to law school? Into a science field? Imagine—you have zero feature film experience and yet, there you are, working on The Godfather Part II. What was so refreshing in Lisa's responses were her observations of how much joy and creativity filmmaking has given her but that you must be also ready for the sacrifices.

✂

TO: Lisa, you received an Academy Award for best editing for The Right Stuff. How did you get your start?

LF: I was at the University of Chicago and socially I got to know some people who were political documentarians. They had one of the first film collectives, called Kartemquin Films.

TO: I just looked them up. They had a very well-known documentary, Hoop Dreams.

LF: They're still around today, making great movies. After I graduated, I was unsure if I was going to go on to law school or into science. So I went by myself for a year to Europe and North Africa. And when I came back, I didn't want to do any of the academic things and began apprenticing at Kartemquin Films. They were editing a project and there was a woman editor there. I thought, 'Maybe I can be like her'.

TO: Inspiration!

LF: It was good seeing a role model. I was fascinated by the editing process. I just immediately took to it as a combination of an analytical skill and a creative skill. And it matched my brain in a way that I really wouldn't have anticipated. I moved to Montreal and I got a job at the National Film Board of Canada. I learned how to be an assistant there and it was really an amazing place to be.

TO: What a place to learn.

LF: It was great. I came to San Francisco and one of the places where I interviewed was at American Zoetrope. I had no feature film experience, but I was hired for a few weeks to redo the lined script on Godfather Part II. I had never seen a lined script before!

TO: That's terrific.

LF: I studied the lined script and I studied the footage and redid the notes and that was my introduction to feature films. It had been divided between Barry Malkin and Peter Zinner, who were working on opposite coasts while Francis was shooting. Francis decided to bring them to San Francisco and hire a third editor—Richie Marks. Richie needed an assistant and they had compiled a list of assistants and I actually wasn't on that list because I had just moved to town. But I got myself an interview and I got hired.

TO: That's an amazing beginning.

LF: It was an interesting time here—a very open time.

TO: You were working with some incredible editors.

LF: I learned everything from them. I got very captivated by the feature film world and working with Coppola and working on Godfather Part II, which was a fantastic editing job and which, of course I can't take any credit for.

TO: What a great experience to have worked on that film.

LF: It was a very creative editing process, full of discussions, controversies. It was a very rich, creative experience. There were huge expectations and at the beginning there was not a lot of appreciation for the risks and the direction that Francis took withthe back and forth threads. At screenings, it wasn't being so well received. But that turned out to be the film's greatest asset. That was really a great process and very playful.

TO: You were assisting Richie Marks. What was he editing on?

LF: He was a Moviola editor and I learned a tremendous amount from him. I would stand behind him and watch him with trims in hand. And there's not a better way to learn than that. Richie, Barry and Peter were different kinds of editors and it was a great immersive experience for me. For me the defining thing is the story. For me to accept a job the story has to resonate with me. Apocalypse Now was a film where I felt very strongly about the content.

TO: Right—it's a year or more of your life.

LF: And a lot of energy. It takes a lot of time and takes over your brain and your life. So, for me, the story is a crucial thing in choosing what movie to do.

TO: According to the literature, Apocalypse Now spent 238 days shooting and shot over a million feet of film.

LF: Apocalypse was an experience like none other! (Laughs) I was on the movie for two-and-a-half years. I came on as the first assistant to Richie Marks and editors came and went on that project. It was so long and arduous and I think Richie was the only person to have completed the whole timeframe.

TO: Richie said from beginning to end, he was on it for three-and-a-half-years.

LF: Yes, it took a huge chunk of his energy and life. It was an extremely difficult project both creatively and emotionally for everyone involved. But, for me, the major thing that came out of it is that I became an editor on that movie. I worked for eight or nine months as Richie's assistant. Richie would give me some scenes to edit and initially the scenes were not going to be in the movie but some of them did make it in.

TO: That's terrific.

LF: And I edited away at night and learned as I went along. I think after about a year, Jerry Greenberg left.

TO: Right. He left to edit Kramer vs. Kramer.

LF: And they needed another editor, so I asked to be considered. I was given the Playboy Bunny scene to edit. And I was on that scene for a long time—there were multiple cameras and a lot of coverage and it was very complicated. It started out as an eight-minute long dance sequence that was a parable about the Vietnam War and that's why they're dressed as Cowboys and Indians.

TO: I didn't know that.

LF: And I edited that scene and Francis saw the cut that I did and I was promoted. So, after about nine months as a first assistant, I became an editor on the film. And, of course, I was the junior editor but I had my own team and I had the benefit of having worked with Richie. And eventually Walter (Murch) came on.

TO: When you look back on this experience, what were some of the challenges and what did you learn?

LF: Beyond learning the craft on the job, I think the thing that was most amazing on Apocalypse is that it had such a hard time coming into being as a film. For such a long time it seemed that it wasn't going to come together. That it didn't make sense, it didn't work and yet in the end, as we all know, it did come together. And we plowed through some very dark periods of creative despair. It was a real lesson in how creative the editing process can be. People often talk about directors being out of control and movies going off the rails because they take so long. And the implications are that the directors didn't know what they were doing. But the other way of looking at it is that sometimes it really does take a long period of gestation to do really creative work and some projects demand that.

TO: You were also all under a lot of pressure financially and the release dates were changing.

LF: It was a very hard, hard job filled with a lot of angst and difficult times but at the end of the day, what an incredible gift to have that time until the film finally worked.

TO: From that experience, you took on another famous—some would say infamous—film, Heaven's Gate.

LF: It was a very different experience. I came to the film at a time when the movie was already in trouble and the relationship between the primary editor, Tom Rolf and Michael Cimino was already a bit rocky. I wasn't really involved in the same way with the film as I was on my other films. But my relationship with Michael was very good. And I thought it would be a different experience than my working with Francis. It was a fine experience. I was very surprised, actually, that the movie got the intense reactions that it did. During that time, Bill Reynolds came on the film.

TO: Really? I didn't know that. He was remarkable.

LF: Yes, and that was an interesting experience for me because Bill was older and much more experienced than I was. And Gerry Greenberg also came on to edit one of the main action sequences.

TO: That's right.

LF: We were all involved in it, but we weren't all working together as was my experience on the other big films I've worked on like Apocalypse and The Right Stuff.

TO: You were all more together on those films.

LF: We were all in the same place; we were all very much in a collaborative relationship. With all that that entails—the tensions, the rivalries, and also very great creative work. But we were very involved. On Heaven's Gate, it was different.

TO: And then, The Right Stuff.

LF: The Right Stuff was a really great experience. It's a movie I'm very proud of in terms of the editing. Glenn Farr, who had been the first editor, had been primarily a documentary editor. He was the one who did all the work getting the NASA footage that was in the movie as well as all the NASA footage that they needed to shoot to.

TO: How did you divide and conquer so much footage?

LF: Steve (Rotter) came on and Steve, Glenn, and I initially divided the project. There were sections of the film that involved plane flights and sections that involved rocket flights. So, there was the early flight stuff and then the early rocket stuff. And eventually we tossed things back and forth. Tom Rolf and Doug Stewart then came on at different times for about ten weeks each to work on specific scenes when we were up against the deadline. The real long-term collaboration was between Steve and me and Glenn.

TO: What other challenges did you have on the film?

LF: One scene which I think really demonstrates how creative the editing process can be is a scene that was entirely created in the editing room. The original opening of the movie—as it was scripted—had to do with moving through history through the use of documentary films up until the point of breaking the sound barrier. And that opening did not work and we were stuck trying to figure out what we could do differently. What we really needed was what the core of the movie was and I felt that was the experience of these test pilots as they took enormous risks with their lives.

TO: I really do think that feeling comes across in the final film.

LF: The opening that we created was totally invented and it used documentary footage of planes and a lot of clouds and blue skies that Caleb (Deschanel) had shot for later sequences in the movie. So I took that footage and made black and white dupes of it and did all kinds of things with it. I slowed it down, sped it up, twice, three times, played it backwards—all kinds of things. Remember, this was before computer editing, so all this was done in the optical house in several iterations.

TO: It had to be dramatic but you also had to be true to the facts of what really happened...

LF: You can't play with history. We knew that we had to have John Glenn orbiting the Earth three times and that he got into trouble. I found a piece of music that captured the feeling and started working with the NASA footage and started creating other footage with Jordan Belson and with Gary. And that's how the scene finally came into being.

TO: Did you expect to be nominated for the Academy Award?

LF: (Laughs) You know, I don't know! What we didn't expect was to win. When we went down to L.A. that weekend of the Academy Awards all of the newspapers were favoring Terms of Endearment.

TO: Terms was doing well that night.

LF: That's what I remember, and we were trying to be prepared if we might win but mostly we didn't think we would. So, that was really a big shock. That moment, as I'm sure you've heard from talking to other people is that all that crazy feeling is real. And all of a sudden, it's happening. But, I do remember, and it's pretty great.

TO: It's an amazing achievement for you and great work by you and your co-editors.

LF: Thank you.

TO: Children of a Lesser God introduced Marlee Matlin in her first feature film and who then went on to win the Academy Award for Best Actress. Can you recall getting the dailies and seeing that performance?

LF: I'm very, very proud of that film. The challenges of editing that film were enormous. The whole way of making that film had never been done before. Of the two main characters in the film, only one person spoke. Bill Hurt would say his line and he often would say her line. And then they both signed. I was essentially editing in two languages. The director (Randa Haines) and I had made a commitment that the signing had to be perfect and fluid so that a deaf person could watch the movie and understand it completely. I was very careful to edit the signing just the way I would edit any other language and never cut out words or do anything to stop the flow of the signing.

TO: That would really limit your ability to cut out of a shot.

LF: Right and it was very challenging to keep the flow of the signing and the flow of the spoken word—which was only one character—to keep going at the same time and to also keep the drama of the story. It was a very delicate balance. But the challenges were really very unique. And the fact that so many people responded to it as a love story without really being conscious of the fact that only one person was talking is something that I'm very proud of.

TO: What have you learned during the course of your editing career that may not have been apparent when you started?

LF: Gosh, that's such a great question. I've learned how fabulous and creative the work can be if you're given the time and space to do that work. I've learned how much it can give you in terms of creative life and how much it can take away from you in terms of the time out of your life. In some ways I think one of the reasons I was able to get into movies the way that I did was because I didn't know very much. And so it was all very fresh to me. And my responses were very visceral.

TO: What advice would you give to people considering editing as a profession?

LF: I think the real thing I would say to someone who is wondering whether or not they should become an editor is, number one, make sure that the craft itself really suits your personality and talents. You're in a dark room for hours and hours and days and days and months and months. And it's a very collaborative relationship with the director in those very tight and intimate conditions. You can get a lot of pleasure out of the process but you get a lot of pressures that come into the work that you can't control—pressure from the producers, pressure on the film to be done at a certain time and for a certain amount of money. And it has to be worth it to you.

MARK GOLDBLATT, ACE

Photograph courtesy of the American Cinema Editors and ACE Eddie Awards

LOS ANGELES, CA

Partial Credits: Death Wish, Chappie, Percy Jackson: Sea of Monsters, Rise of the Planet of the Apes, X-Men: The Last Stand, Pearl Harbor, Armageddon, Starship Troopers, True Lies, Terminator 2: Judgment Day, Rambo: First Blood Part II, The Terminator.

A kid from Brooklyn who grew up reading Variety? That's how much Mark was destined to work in the film industry. The incessant drive of The Terminator and the great comedic timing of the striptease in True Lies. He loves talking, working and being enthralled by films.

TO: Mark, you are an Academy Award and Eddie Award nominee for Best Editing. How did you get started?

MG: I've always loved films and growing up in New York we had lots of television stations showing lots of movies. Everything from King Kong to Citizen Kane. British films, Italian Neo-Realism. And every Saturday I'd see a double feature: Martin and Lewis, Science fiction and horror films, etc.

TO: Did some stand out?

MG: Hard to say, there were so many. There was The Apartment and I liked it so much I think I saw it five times in two weeks. There was Elmer Gantry. Horror movies like Black Sunday, La Dolce Vita, 8 1/2. When I saw my first Kurosawa film, Yojimbo, I went with my uncle to the Carnegie Hall Cinema. What a revelation. In stark black and white and Toho Scope, and Toshiro Mifune! I used to read Variety as a kid, to read reviews and see what films were coming out.

TO: That's so funny. A kid from Brooklyn reading Variety.

MG: Yeah, weekly Variety, published in N.Y.; they had all the reviews of the new films! But the directors I liked the most are the ones we revere most now. Orson Welles, Hitchcock—you knew you were seeing something special. At a certain point I was gifted with an inexpensive movie camera while I was in elementary school. Ultimately, I even got a set of rewinds and a viewer. And I made my own little 8mm movies with low cost visual effects. I went to the London Film School. It was a nuts and bolts school that taught you everything about filmmaking. You learned everything from taking a Mitchell camera apart, to editing on ancient machines called Acmeolas.

MG: I graduated, and Los Angeles was beckoning, and Don eventually put me in touch with Bill Hornbeck.

TO: Sure, he won the Academy Award for editing A Place in the Sun.

MG: Yes, and Bill was the head of post-production for Universal. I went to visit him and Rudi Fehr at Warner Bros. I got a job assisting an editor who was teaching a course on 35mm film editing. One time I was lucky enough to meet Sam Fuller, a great American director. Finally one day after watching Paul Bartel's Death Race 2000, I was inspired to walk into Roger Corman's office where I asked the lady at the desk, 'Who do I talk to about getting an editing job?'

TO: That's great.

MG: And she looked around the room and said, 'Talk to that guy over there.' And that was Jon Davison, who was head of advertising, and about to produce his first movie. He had told Roger that he could produce a movie for $100,000. And Roger told him he'd give him $60,000.

TO: What was the film?

MG: Hollywood Boulevard. It was the directorial debut of Joe Dante and Allan Arkush and was shot in ten days. I was a PA working for no pay, working seven days a week like everyone else. And after a few days I said they had to pay me something and I think it was $35 a week and it was great. I got into the trailer department and I became Joe's assistant editor. So, on Grand Theft Auto, I got to cut a few scenes.

TO: Grand Theft was directed by Ron Howard.

MG: Yes, and I got an associate editor credit. And then when Joe went on to make Piranha, that was the picture that I co-edited with him. I got a job at Warner Bros. as a staff television assistant. It was the first time I was assisting established studio editors. Some of them would paper clip their cuts and I would splice them together.

TO: And you had the time to watch other people edit.

MG: Yes, totally right. The early editors had to make the cut in their heads. They'd paper clip the edits. They didn't make the edit and run it through the Moviola to see it. Because they were using cement splices which take a while for the cement to dry; You couldn't instantly run such an edit so you'd make the cuts "in your head" by watching footage back and forth on the Moviola and marking where the cuts should be, paper clipping them, and then you'd move on.

TO: It's part of history now.

MG: Yes. So, I continued doing the low budget projects and those movies were making money. Pictures like Piranha and The Howling.

TO: And, in fact, those pictures led to The Terminator.

MG: Exactly. Terminator came out of the relationships I had made while I was at Corman. I had met Gale Hurd who introduced me to James Cameron. He liked my work and they hired me to do the film. It was a real turning point in my career, and great fun to edit.

TO: Did you have any idea it was going to be so well received?

MG: No. (Laughs). We all loved the movie and knew that Orion Pictures would provide a healthy marketing strategy. The budget was low for a picture of this magnitude, but Jim and Gale were incredibly inventive. The production looked much grander than the budget might have actually allowed.

TO: With Terminator, the editing keeps moving forward!

MG: Yes. I learned a lot from Joe Dante about pacing. He and Jon Davison used to do this thing called the Schlitz Movie Orgy.

TO: What was that?

MG: It was like a five-hour compilation of bits from films in the public domain that they spliced together, that would create its own subtext and story based on the montage and the juxtaposition of these images. The Russians would use a term, dialectical montage—for this. And with a movie like Piranha, you're able to create the illusion of much more happening. And that served me well—that basic concept—in my editing career, and it served Terminator very well. Jim was hip to that, along with his great filmmaking skills, brilliant screenplay, and terrific innovation.

TO: Seven years later, you're working with Conrad Buff and Richard Harris on Terminator 2.

MG: Jim Cameron is meticulously prepared, especially with effects sequences. They're really expensive. And he has something that really places him at the top of the filmmaking game. He'll even develop software to achieve his vision. And he's always breaking new ground on a technical basis.

TO: Your reaction to the first visual effect shot you saw?

MG: The first digital shot I saw was the morph when the T1000 morphs into the metal man and vice versa and they were so cool. The first time you see something that is new and hasn't been down before—it's pretty mind blowing.

TO: You worked with Conrad Buff on Rise of the Planet of the Apes and that had some very interesting visual effects.

MG: I can't remember how many months it was before we saw a finished shot. It must have been at least six months.

TO: That's a long time to go to see if things are working out.

MG: It is. But when we eventually saw a near final version, it really blew our minds. Performance capture is a terrific way to get a precise performance in creatures. And this is why the argument of Andy Serkis is valid—that it's important to acknowledge his acting performance. Because the performance of the "animated" ape Caesar is 100% Andy's performance.

TO: It is amazing to see how far this has come in a short amount of time.

MG: It really is. The fact that we can take a human performance and realize it in another non-human (in this case Simian) life form. And Rupert Wyatt, the director, just did such an amazing job with the film.

TO: Have there been films that should have done better that you worked on?

MG: I always thought that a film that was very underrated was Predator 2. And I think the reason that it didn't do as well as the first Predator is that Arnold wasn't in it.

TO: That whole section when they're in the subway is great.

MG: I love that. And that was a very intricate sequence. The director, Stephen Hopkins is very visual and economical. Throughout the film he conceived counter-moving master shots, which gives you a lot of different angles and different perspectives in a very utilitarian way. I think that Predator 2 works like gangbusters.

TO: Showgirls. (Both Laugh)

MG: I love Showgirls. A lot of people didn't. But I look at it from the aspect of its mis-en-scene. The moving camera shots were actually influenced by Fellini and it shows. I always say that if it had been in a foreign language with sub-titles, it would have been an art-house hit. It's an audacious journey through a distinctly American sub-culture.

TO: Detroit Rock City must have been a fun film to work on.

MG: Great fun. I loved the creative collaboration with Adam Rifkin and Peter Schink. It has a real cult following. I did another picture that is a personal favorite of mine. It's The Ambassador.

TO: Ah, that's with Robert Mitchum.

MG: Yes, I had done a bunch of film for Cannon Films. This movie was based on Elmore Leonard's 52-Pick Up, which was later remade by John Frankenheimer.

TO: That's right, with Roy Scheider.

MG: Yes, and in this one, all the action is transposed to the Middle East and Israel. It had a very good cast.

TO: I'll say. Mitchum, Rock Hudson, Ellen Burstyn, Donald Pleasence...

MG: And Fabio Testi. It was Rock Hudson's last movie and he gave a very energetic performance. It was directed by J. Lee Thompson.

TO: He was really a versatile director. He did Cape Fear, The Guns of Navarone...

MG: Yes, Cape Fear is just marvelous.

TO: And he did The Reincarnation of Peter Proud. It still bothers me.

MG: Yeah, that's a really scary movie.

TO: Yeah, that last shot just kills me.

MG: Also, Eye of The Devil, Tiger Bay, The White Buffalo, Return From The Ashes; You know, I honestly think he's a director ripe for rediscovery. I loved working with Thompson because he was a real craftsman. Terrific, motivated camera moves.

TO: What films do you like?

MG: You know, I loved Dede Allen—The Hustler, Bonnie and Clyde, Night Moves and more. Roger Spottiswoode when he was an editor did some great work like Straw Dogs. I think Conrad Buff—whom I've worked with a lot—is really excellent. His work is very humanistic. Action editing—what I call kinetic editing—is very easy to see and pinpoint. But getting the human performance and cutting performance is an art and Conrad is terrific at that.

TO: What have you learned that wasn't apparent when you started?

MG: Oh… Well, one thing is that if you get caught up in a scene and you think you've reached a dead end, walk away from it for a while. It's better to go on to another scene and come back to it. Sometimes these creative issues resolve themselves when you have a fresh start.

TO: True Lies is fun because it's a bit of everything—action, comedy, some perilous situations…

MG: And I got to do things in True Lies that is not the type of thing I usually do.

TO: An example?

MG: Sure. The striptease scene in the hotel room with Jaime. But I don't usually do sustained comedy and that scene is very comedic.

TO: You've worked with many directors who do big movies.

MG: Jim Cameron and even other top directors admire him. The words "no" and "can't" are not in his lexicon. He's inspiring. Paul

Verhoeven is a perfectionist and a great director. Michael Bay is tremendously talented. George Cosmatos was very visual and has been undervalued. Take a look at Tombstone.

TO: What is it about your profession that you like the most?

MG: I like telling a story and the unexpected alchemy that often results from the process. For example, sometimes you can achieve values in a scene that are over and above what you expected you'd get. I'm talking about the emotional reaction you get when characters are interacting. Sometimes the result is a conscious decision, and sometimes it's subconscious. Editing, like all filmmaking, is a collection of many, many, creative decisions and staying in tune with the material and what performance is right for that character. Often, you'll run a scene and you'll surprise yourself and often you'll surprise the director. And you'll think, 'Wow, that worked better than I thought'. And that's the magic—the magic of cinema.

WILLIAM GOLDENBERG, ACE

Photograph courtesy of the American Cinema Editors and ACE Eddie Awards

LOS ANGELES, CALIFORNIA

Partial Credits: Detroit, Live by Night, Concussion, Unbroken, The Imitation Game, Transformers: Age of Extinction, Zero Dark Thirty, Argo, Gone Baby Gone, National Treasure, Seabiscuit, Ali, The Insider, Pleasantville.

William—and he insisted I call him Billy—learned from the greats—Dede Allen, Michael Kahn, Donn Cambern, and Conrad Buff. And boy did he ratchet up the tension in Argo! But, by far, I think the most important piece of advice that you can get from an editor is his last sentence.

✂

TO: William, you are an Academy Award, A.C.E Eddie, and BAFTA recipient. How did you get your start in the business?

WG: I went to film school at Temple University in Philadelphia. I fell in love with editing and there was a professor who saw material that I edited and was really positive about it. I moved to LA and looked for work for about nine months. I found a production assistant job for a small production company. After working there for a while, I was asked if I wanted to be a set PA on a TV movie. I asked them if instead I could be the apprentice editor.

TO: That's asserting yourself!

WG: Yeah, and of course it still surprises me knowing what I know now. I was fortunate enough to work with John Wright, who went on to cut Speed and The Hunt for Red October and many other great films. I worked with John's assistant, Kathy Virkler and she taught me how to be an assistant. After that I worked a lot of apprentice and then assistant jobs, but eventually I got to work with Michael Kahn as his first assistant.

TO: What a great opportunity.

WG: I worked as his first assistant for four years and that was really my graduate school in terms of editing. He mentored me and taught me everything that I needed to know about being an editor—his methodology and his psychology of editing. After four years he said it was time for me to start cutting, so he moved me up to editor on Alive and gave me my first main title credit. That worked out well, so he continued to help me get other cutting jobs.

TO: That's a real compliment coming from someone so accomplished.

WG: It couldn't have been a bigger vote of confidence. It still means a lot to me. We've stayed close during the 20 years where I've been cutting on my own. When he was nominated for Lincoln, we got to spend a lot of time together and he was incredibly supportive and magnanimous when I won for Argo. He called me the next morning and it was fantastic. The whole thing came full circle and it was wonderful.

TO: That's a terrific story. You mentioned things that Michael helped you understand. What stands out?

WG: I'll be in a situation where there's an editorial problem that I can't figure out. I'll think to myself 'What would Mike do in this situation?' If I go back to what he taught me, I usually find the right answer. It's about taking a point of view on a scene and how to look for material that will help tell the story.

The best thing he ever taught me is when we were working together on Alive. He had to leave to cut Jurassic Park. I would cut scenes and he would suggest changes. On one of the scenes we went around five, six, seven times. I would show it to him and he'd give me notes and I'd make the changes and then show it to him and he'd give me more notes. I wasn't getting the scene right and then I started wondering whether or not I could do this. I said, 'Michael, I can't seem to get this the way you like it. Maybe I'm not cut out for this.' And he said, 'You don't understand. It's not about the editing, it's about you being able to take criticism.'

At the ACE Awards for Argo
Photograph courtesy the American Cinema Editors and ACE Eddie Awards

TO: He was getting you ready for working with others.

WG: Yes, he wanted me to understand that the notes I was getting from him had nothing to do with me. It had to do with the film and making it better, and that it wasn't personal. He would always say that you should make sure that the producers and the director and everyone else on the film know that you are always in control and part of that is being able to take criticism. It's one of the biggest lesson I've ever learned.

TO: You worked with Dede Allen on The Breakfast Club.

WG: The first time I saw the film, I knew it was going to be amazing. They shot the movie in Chicago and when they came back to Los Angeles, the movie was already in first cut except for a couple of sequences. I wasn't in the room with her a lot because I was reconstituting trims and finding things for her. Dede was incredible, she cut the film mostly on her own. John Hughes would come in now and then and comment on the film, but he trusted her, and she made all the right decisions.

She just would do what she wanted to do, and what her instincts told her to do, whatever she felt was right for the film. I remember once she made a cut that was 'against the rules of editing,' she just laughed and did it anyway because it worked. She told a story about an early screening of Bonnie and Clyde where the reaction wasn't great. A lot of changes were suggested, but Warren Beatty came over to her and quietly said 'make sure you save this cut.' And that's what eventually was released. Once I heard her say that she didn't ever give apprentices screen credit, so when she gave me one it really meant a lot to me. I worked as hard as I possibly could, and it really paid off. She was a force of nature and I loved her, she was so great to be around.

TO: Do you have a favorite genre?

WG: My favorite genre is dramatic films and doing Argo and Zero Dark Thirty in the same year was a standout. If I could do films of that ilk for the rest of my career, I would. I push myself to do films of different genres and to go from big tent pole movies to smaller movies because otherwise you get pigeonholed as only an action editor, or comedy or drama editor.

TO: You've edited many films that are based on true events and on real persons. Films such as Alive, The Insider, Ali, Seabiscuit, Domino, Argo, and Zero Dark Thirty. How much do you find out about the real background of these stories beforehand?

WG: I was already a big Ali fan, I had seen every fight and read a lot about him, but when I found out I'd be doing the movie, I went and did a lot more research. I was 13 years old and living in Philadelphia when he fought Joe Frazier, who was also from Philadelphia, so I was a huge Frazier fan. Only later did I understand the rift between the two of them and the politics involved. On The Insider, I learned as we were going along because there wasn't a lot of information. The Internet wasn't where it is now, so it was harder to look up material on Jeffrey Wigand. With Argo, I grew up during the Iranian hostage crisis, so I knew a lot about it.

With Zero Dark Thirty, it was particularly fascinating because events were constantly unfolding. From the time that Mark Boal finished the screenplay to the time we were editing, new information would come to light. While we were in post-production one of the Navy Seals who was on the raid on Bin Laden's compound wrote a book and did an interview on 60 Minutes.

TO: I kept wondering what you were all thinking because new information was appearing.

WG: We were just hoping that the information that we had was correct. According to his book, the information we had was accurate. His description of the events at the raid matched what was shot. We knew how politically controversial the film was going to be, and we were up against a release date. That pressure along with the secrecy involved and the potential political backlash was incredible. Working with Kathryn Bigalow is amazing, and it was one of the most rewarding experiences of my career. When I did Ali, I had one of the highlights of my life.

TO: How so?

WG: Ali came to my cutting room with his wife, a couple of his kids and his best friend and personal photographer Howard Bingham. He was so charming and funny. He took pictures will all of us and told jokes and made everyone feel completely at ease. We showed him about an hour of footage—the opening, a couple of early fights—and then we showed him the Foreman fight. That was an experience I'll never forget. It was just, the director, his family and me.

TO: What was his reaction to the footage?

WG: After we showed him the opening of the movie, he looked at the director, Michael Mann, and said, 'You're not as dumb as you look.'

TO: That's funny.

WG: When we were showing him the Foreman fight I hit play on the Avid and sat in the back of the room because I didn't want to block the screen. And just as Foreman was being knocked out, we had a 320 frame per second slow motion shot of him falling down to the canvas. Right in the middle of the shot, the Avid froze. Foreman is frozen in mid-air, halfway down to the canvas and it's in front of the real Ali. And everyone looks at me and yells, 'Billy!' as if I somehow had done something wrong.

TO: Of all the times… Domino is relentless in terms of the editing…

WG: Tony Scott was very involved, very hands on, and I can't say enough about him. He was just the greatest. I came onto the movie during post-production. A trailer / commercial editor who had cut a lot of Tony's television commercials had cut the film so the editing had that kind of feel to it. Tony had done a lot of the layering of images in camera, he used a hand-crank camera where he would shoot something and then roll the film back and then shoot over it, so we got these cool superimpositions. He also shot several different formats, black and white, 16mm, color reversal, etc. Then in post the layering continued using holdout mattes, and freeze frames that would then be superimposed over other images. It was really complicated. So, they brought me in to work with Tony to try and improve the clarity of the storytelling. The fact is that when you unravel the script and put the whole film in linear order it really didn't make complete sense.

TO: So, in a sense, you were brought in to uncut the movie?

WG: Right. The film has voice over so that was helpful in clarifying things. I love that movie and I'm very proud of it. It's more of a painting than a movie. It's really a work of art—the images, the colors, and the performances. Calling it a movie seems a lot less than what it really is.

TO: What was your working relationship like with Tony Scott?

WG: Tony was there every day, all day, and we worked together very closely. He was smart, instinctual and had a great work ethic. He had hip replacement surgery and he only missed a day and a half of work. Then he had back surgery and he missed only four days. Then he came in, put two pillows behind him on the reclining chair, and we worked. He was the coolest and toughest man I've ever been around. He was as brave as anyone I've ever met in terms of being a filmmaker and a person.

TO: Have there been a lot of challenges on Transformers: Age of Extinction?

WG: There are so many challenges. We were able to view the native 3D but had to cut the film in 2D. On this film, Michael Bay is shooting 3D IMAX, 2D IMAX, 2D RED, 3D RED, he's using GoPro cameras, he's shooting film. The hardest thing is managing the huge amount of film and having to imagine the VFX and 3D while cutting. With 3D you have to be careful not to overcut.

TO: Because you need to give the viewer time to adjust to new shots?

WG: Yes, your brain needs a certain amount of time to process 3D. So, when we get to the final version, in the scenes that are really cut up, we will make the shorter shots 2D. It's a real challenge on films like this because you're cutting with empty plates. Sometimes the sequences are so complicated that you really don't know if certain shots are a plate or if the camera is resetting. On Transformers 3, he would turn over plates and I couldn't figure out where the robots were going to be. What could possibly be going on in this shot? The camera's bouncing around and I'd have no clue. And then you get the shot back with the rough animation in it and you think 'That's genius.' I don't know how he does it.

TO: You won the Eddie, Bafta, and the Oscar for Argo. I love that the film opens up with the old Warner Brothers logo from the 1970's and subtly sets the time period.

WG: Right. We wanted the movie to feel like it was made in the 1970's, not that it was going to be a period movie. We had a lot of film references that we used: The Killing of a Chinese Bookie, All The President's Men, Three Days of the Condor, Sunday Bloody Sunday.

TO: Did you screen the movie?

WG: We did a lot of family and friends screenings. There was additional footage showing Tony's family life. Ben said, 'What do you think if we just take it all out?' They came out so easily that it seemed like a sign. We screened the movie that night for about 35 people, and at the end, Ben and I looked at each other and we knew that the movie had clicked in. We found the movie that day. We had a preview and the audience loved it and the score was huge. The Warner Brothers people were ecstatic, and Ben was speechless.

TO: People were squirming in their seats waiting to see if the plane would take off...

WG: That's part of the challenge. How do you keep the tension going when everyone knows the actual ending? We pretended that we didn't know the ending and we kept trying to ratchet up the tension as far as it would go.

TO: What films do you recommend students study?

WG: I think The Conversation, which Walter Murch edited, is magnificently done. Walter is a brilliant editor. I know that they were in post for an incredibly long time. It shows you how sensitive editing is. They put an incredible amount of work into it and it shows. It's brilliant. And the other film I think about all the time is Lenny, which Alan Heim edited. Another film that is more recent is Lincoln because it's about knowing when not to cut. One of the things that Michael (Kahn) said to me was that Daniel Day Lewis was brilliant in every single take and in every single angle.

TO: You don't hear that very often.

WG: I mean he was just flawless. There is always a great temptation of knowing that you have all this great stuff and that you're supposed to use it all. In that film, it was the integrity of the performance and great editing can be about not cutting. It's important to know that as an editor. You don't always have to make cuts just because you can.

JERRY GREENBERG, ACE

Photograph courtesy of the American Cinema Editors and ACE Eddie Awards

LOS ANGELES, CALIFORNIA

Partial Credits: Point Break, Invincible, Bringing Down the House, Get Carter, American History X, Awakenings, National Lampoon's Christmas Vacation, The Accused, The Untouchables, Wise Guys, Body Double, Scarface, Heaven's Gate, Dressed to Kill, Kramer vs. Kramer, Apocalypse Now, The Missouri Breaks, The Taking of Pelham One Two Three, Electra Glide in Blue, The French Connection, The Boys in the Band, The Subject Was Roses.

The rare occasion when an editor is nominated twice for an Academy Award during the same year. Apocalypse Now and Kramer vs. Kramer? How is that possible? It was so informative listening to Jerry explain how manipulating time in filmmaking has always intrigued him and how he has used it to such terrific results. His words show the real thinker behind this remarkable editor.

TO: Jerry, you are an Academy Award and BAFTA recipient for Best Editing for your extraordinary work on "The French Connection". How did you get your start?

JG: Actually, I was very much interested in theatre and growing up in New York City, one never thought about film as a career. I really had no thought about going into film. I kept trying to get into theatre.

TO: Did you see a lot of films growing up?

JG: Yes, movies were very much a part of my life ever since I was a little kid. I was a Marx Brothers devotee. I had a friend who was a soundman and he asked if I knew anybody who had a music background who would want to work for a supplier of music. I was desperate to get a toehold in anything remotely show business. I had no background in music, but boldly said yes.

TO: So many of your contemporaries in New York came up through sound or music.

JG: Alan Heim actually worked for a competing music and sound effects house and that's how I got to meet him. I used to get the actual film copies with all the actual edits—you saw them, felt them, and heard them—as they went through the very clackety Moviola that I worked on at the time.

TO: You heard the cadence of those cuts and as they went through...

JG: Sure—becoming so aware sensually of editing—I knew that I wanted to be a film editor. By the way, the noise of those things was not all that pleasant but it made me very aware of cuts. And more importantly, of the splices when the editor changed their mind. And you realized that it was also the non-splices that you were hearing as well. And decisions were being made. And you could literally see them, stop them, intuit why the editor made them, and I knew that was what I wanted to do.

TO: So, you decided that you wanted to be a film editor. What did you do next?

JG: (Laughs) Well, I had been working on a show called, 'Shell's Wonderful World of Golf' and I was responsible for all of those golf sound effects. I was getting very busy so the owners brought in Eddie Beyer, who was the reigning sound effects editor in New York City and he knew of my desire to get into picture editing. So, Dede Allen was working on America, America...

TO: Directed by Elia Kazan. I like the film.

JG: Yes. This was 1963 and the apprentice on that show was leaving to work on another film. Eddie asked me if I wanted to replace this apprentice and that's how I became Dede Allen's apprentice.

TO: What a fantastic break.

JG: Yes, and I worked on that for nine months. And because of my experience as a sound effects editor, Dede appreciated that and we became pretty chummy. Boy was I grateful! And that was my big opportunity. As it turned out, it was like hitting the mother lode!

TO: So, for five years, you worked with Dede.

JG: Yes, as an apprentice and eventually as an assistant. What could be better? When I was her assistant, she gave me an opportunity to cut. That's why people became assistants—you wanted to learn how to craft things. How to think. And it wasn't long before I was given an opportunity to edit scenes under her tutelage and it was wonderful.

TO: What did you learn during those five years working with her?

JG: (Laughs) A lot of people quote Dede because she says a lot of things: 'Make it sing.' 'If it doesn't work or you're having a hard time making it work, make it work!' In other words, there is no limit to choices and that is the thing that I took away from Dede. Always look to something else. There is always another way to do it. I always thought that the best cut that I ever did was sitting in the rolls of outtakes and trims hanging in the bin—that there was another way of doing it.

TO: That's a great outlook to have. When you were told that you were going to get your first picture editing credit on "Bye Bye Braverman" and work with Sidney Lumet, were you scared?

JG: Very. Very. Scared because it was Sidney Lumet. Holy shit! (Both Laugh) And I got the job because of a recommendation from Dede.

TO: Well, she thought you were ready.

JG: (Laughs) Yeah, she did.

TO: The films you've worked on have won 18 Academy Awards and earned 33 nominations.

JG: Luck played a big part of it. I love a good narrative. When you read a screenplay you get an inkling of what role the actual editing might play in assisting what has already been written.

TO: Within three years, you find yourself as the editor of The French Connection. It's a scant three years, Jerry. It happened very fast for you.

JG: Very fast.

TO: What did it bring out of you that you didn't know was there?

JG: I think unbridled enthusiasm that was encouraged by Friedkin and the producer, Phil D'Antoni. You were allowed to take your ideas and realize them in the film. But The French Connection, you couldn't tell, necessarily, from the script. "Gritty" was the word attached to those shows. Had to be shot in New York. Dark. Film noir. Sarcasm and hard-bitten characters and guns and drugs and all of that stuff. The Warner Brothers police dramas of the thirties were like that and we were all aware of that. And those were popular films. They made money.

TO: Paul Muni…

JG: Exactly, exactly. When I began to see the film that was being generated, going to dailies, you knew that something was there.

TO: When you were editing it, you saw how what was coming into your hands mirrored what they wanted to achieve—that feeling, that grittiness, as you said.

JG: Yes, it was enormous. Enormous. The fact that it was shot on locations, dark, the cinematography by Owen Roizman was spectacular.

TO: The chase sequence…it goes on for a long time…

JG: Hours. (Both Laugh)

TO: You had a lot of footage.

JG: Yes, it kept coming in. The gags—the stunts—by the way, were all multiple camera. That's not to say that everything was shot with multiple cameras. Billy Friedkin was savvy enough to know exactly what he wanted to do or exactly what he wanted to try to do. There was handheld footage, twelve cameras…

TO: Did you have fun cutting it?

JG: Oh, God yes! (Both Laugh)

TO: And when did you know you had it? That you had it right? When does the editor stop editing a chase scene like that?

JG: Well, you never stop editing something like that. I mean (Laughs) you're always going. I can't give you an answer. There is that point where things begin to congeal. Especially that chase sequence, which had multiple locales. Not only did you have to edit the particular locale, of which there may have been a lot of visual information, but you also had to get a sense of the timing of how those things were presented and also how the narrative within each one of those locales grabbed you, emotionally. And that's a big thing. This is not just an exciting chase sequence with all of these great angles and cars flying all over the place. This was about obsessiveness. This was Gene Hackman being obsessive and dangerous. As dangerous as a murderer might be. Gene Hackman is a superior actor. He can do that. He can make you think that just by how he contorts his face in a certain way.

TO: He's dangerous to himself and to everyone else on those streets, too.

JG: Exactly. That's exactly right. And of course you can't get that right, right away. It takes a lot of re-editing and rethinking and reorganizing and that was the most fun.

TO: Were you surprised at the reaction and reception of the film? When did you find out that you were nominated?

JG: (Laughs) Ah, that's a funny story. (Laughs) I was working on a film and I did not have a phone in my cutting room. The phone was a public phone out in the hall. Somebody had to answer the phone, and then call you. (Laughs) Oh, God! (Laughs) Usually it was an assistant who knew where everyone was working on the floor and they had to call you to the phone.

TO: No cell phones!

JG: Yeah, so, I got on the phone but I knew that I was nominated already. The Academy calls you when they announce the nominations. But this phone call was about a week after that. So, the man on the line says, 'Mr. Greenberg, I represent the Hollywood Reporter.' And he was very chatty. And he said, 'Would you like to take out an ad in the paper?' And I thought 'What kind of an ad?'

TO: (Laughs) He was trying to get you to take out an ad about yourself?

JG: (Laughs) Yeah! And he said, 'Well, you can take out a sixteenth of a page thanking the Academy. A quarter page, a half page...' And it was like, a sixteenth of a page was $250 or something like that. (Laughs) And of course I thought it very strange that you'd take out an ad thanking people for nominating you! So I said, 'Well, perhaps if I win I'll take out an ad...'

TO: How funny.

JG: When the actual event came, my wife and I went there. And it was so big and all the people attached to the film came—Gene Hackman, Roy Scheider, Phil D'Antoni, Billy Friedkin—and it was this big event. And nobody knew who the hell I was! And finally, I get the award and I didn't expect it.

TO: You had no idea that you were going to win?

JG: No, not really. I was in this daze. And then I had this ten-pound thing in my hand and I didn't know where to go and just behind the stage curtain there was this guy in his seventies, wearing these rimless glasses and he was perspiring. And he said, 'Mr. Greenberg, my name is O'Reilly, from the Hollywood Reporter. Would you like to take that ad out now?' (Both Laugh) He was the first person who greeted me!

In the Cutting Room
Photograph courtesy the American Cinema Editors and ACE Eddie Awards

TO: That's funny! 1979 was an incredible year for you. You were nominated twice in that year, for Apocalypse Now and Kramer vs. Kramer.

JG: Yes.

TO: How did Apocalypse come about?

JG: In the latter part of 1975, I went out to San Francisco to work on

Apocalypse. And I was there until April of 1978. I was there for a year-and-a-half working on Apocalypse and I was there with my family, my wife, my son who was twelve and my daughter who was nine. And it was scheduled to be six months. My kids went to school there and loved it. So, I remember being in a city that I adore, having a good time and working on the film.

TO: What part of the film did you work on?

JG: Well, everyone knows I did a lot of the helicopter stuff—the action stuff—but I also worked on the French Plantation scene, which I thought was amazing.

TO: It is amazing to see it in the restored version. We had to wait—what—some 20 years to see it? (Both Laugh)

JG: Yeah, you know, everyone was giving his opinion at the time that we were doing it as to whether it should stay or go. And I was one of the people who agreed that it stopped something in the film. But, no doubt—absolutely stunning. Storaro, I think, is a genius.

TO: You're a very modest person. You say, 'Everyone knows I did the helicopter stuff' and yet I don't think everyone knows that. Even Coppola when he was making it pretty much admitted that he didn't have anything past that and had to come up with something. I mean it's absolutely thrilling. The "Ride of the Valkyries" selection for the helicopter sequence...

JG: I put the Valkyries in there because it was actually written that way.

TO: The film went on for four years, from 1975 to 1979. In 1979, did you go back to New York to work on Kramer vs. Kramer?

JG: I went back in 1978. We bought a camper and went cross-country to do some camping and get the kids in school for September. Somebody was trying to reach me while I was in the Colorado

Rockies. I decided to call my Mother in the latter part of June or July 1978 and she herself was on a trip to Alaska, of all places! So, I called my sister and she said that someone was trying to reach me. And that person was Dave Golden and I called him and he said, 'We've been looking for you for weeks! We're starting a film in September. How can I get the script to you?'

TO: Talk about something that was meant to be!

JG: I said, 'Why don't you send it to the general post office in Denver?' I got to Denver, showed my ID, and got the script. I read it while we were camping out and the rest of my family read it. And I took a poll. I said, 'Should I do this film?' And they all said, 'Yes!' So, we got to New York in the first week of September and I had already hired an assistant and we got our usual cutting room in New York.

TO: You get the dailies. Did you see something special from the beginning?

JG: No, you have to wait and see. I knew Dustin somewhat. I certainly knew Benton.

TO: You're never, ever conscious of the editing in this film. And that's what's great about your work on this film. The film came out and did extremely well—five Academy Awards, including Best Picture. Your family had read the script. What did they think?

JG: My kids were very happy. It was different for me.

TO: You've worked with Brian DePalma on five features and a music video. One of the more famous montages is the Union Station shoot-out from "The Untouchables" which you edited.

JG: It was a big junction in my career. His editor, Paul Hirsch, who had edited all his movies up until Body Double—which is the first film that I did—had moved out to Los Angeles and Brian needed another editor. I read the script and I told him that I really wasn't interested. Well,

Brian DePalma really didn't want to take no for an answer.

TO: That's a great compliment to you.

JG: He kept calling me and said, 'Why don't you come down to my office and we'll talk about it?' His office at that time was an apartment on 5thAvenue and 11thStreet. I went and we sat down in a very small dining room that was six feet by ten feet and was mirrored to make the whole thing larger. The dining room table was basically his office. Everything was laid out and on the mirrors were all these three by five file cards. He had drawn these very primitive looking stick figures on the cards and had storyboarded a good part of the film. I was impressed as hell. I knew he was a visualist, but he thought like an editor. And I thought that it was great, it was terrific.

TO: Because you knew you'd really have something to work with?

JG: Not only that. It incorporates film editing. The editing isn't just an afterthought.

TO: He's designed it with editing in mind.

JG: It's filmmaking. That the editing is all part of one whole. I still turned it down.

TO: You're kidding...

JG: But he wouldn't take no for an answer. And finally he got me to do it. Now I have to tell you that over the lifetime of working with Brian and working with Bill Pankow, who was my assistant, and then my co-editor, it was a delight. It was fantastic. And the last film I did with him, he looked at the first cut I did and he said, 'Ship it!'

TO: That was "The Untouchables".

JG: Yes, "The Untouchables".

TO: And it was a big success.

JG: Yes, a big success. And it was nice—celebrating all of that. And working with Brian—he's a filmmaker.

TO: Did you enjoy cutting the Union Station sequence?

JG: Oh, I did. I mean, that was right in my wheelhouse!

TO: Multiple cameras, different speeds, slow motion…

JG: Right, all of that. You could play with time. And that was the idea. Manipulating time is an element in filmmaking that has always intrigued me. I got a lot of that from Dede. And it's not just stretching things out in slow motion, which is done ad nauseum.

TO: Right. It can be used to build tension…

JG: And it's longer. Or shorter. Without making you feel that it's either been telescoped and compressed or expanded. That is something that editors play with. The parameters of what happens in literal time shouldn't be your constraints. How much quicker or slower is it going to be? Are we talking about a microsecond or an hour? That has always intrigued me. You make the film plastic and elastic.

TO: I want to take you to "The Accused". It led to an Academy Award for Jodie Foster.

JG: I was not the first editor. Stanley Jaffe was the producer and he and I were friendly. He had issues with Jonathan Kaplan's version. And when I was asked to do it, the editor had already been dismissed. I looked at the film and I noticed that there were problems.

TO: So it was fully assembled when you were brought in…

JG: It was. I noticed that there was something out of whack. Not with the cut-to-cut editing, but with the narrative. There was something in the telling of the story that wasn't up to where I thought it could have been. It was only an inkling. And I told Stanley and Jonathan—who was involved—that I would only do it if I could do it as a page one recut, and to start cutting it all over again.

TO: That's really unusual—to be able to go right back to the beginning as if the first day's dailies were coming in.

JG: By starting all over again, I could cut in chronological order, which you can almost never do.

TO: Now you could really see how her performance had evolved.

JG: And that is a little bit better in the editing process because you can then tell the story straight through. So, they said okay. I hired Tara Capone, who was my assistant, and who is now an editor and we worked very hard, day and night, very long hours. And, again, it was working on film. So, we literally had to put everything back in dailies form.

TO: Is there a way that you can describe what was there in the first version and what you brought out in your version?

JG: I think the difference between the cut that I was doing and the cut that had existed was that the scenes became too perfunctorily edited as if they were normal scenes. Whereas with the scenes with Jodie, what you had to do is you had to stay with her a lot longer. That performance was so compelling that even though it broke every other rule of editing by what you did with her, you had to do it.

TO: You see what her lawyer is saying by staying with Jodie. You're hearing the lawyer's voice, but how it is affecting Jodie is what's important. Seeing Kelly McGillis—the lawyer—isn't.

JG: Yes.

TO: You're choosing to do something that's a bit unconventional editing-wise, but it's the right decision. Theory says, 'I should cut here because she stopped talking.'

JG: Precisely.

TO: And you stay with Jodie. And, obviously, the audience stays with her.

JG: I think they appreciated what was done.

TO: You've worked with a very diverse group of directors.

JG: I'll say.

TO: Sidney Lumet.

JG: The best living film director.

TO: William Friedkin.

JG: I'm waiting for all the harsh things that I've heard other people say about Friedkin to come to pass.

TO: Arthur Penn.

JG: "Bonnie and Clyde", arguably one of the best ten films made in my lifetime.

TO: Francis Coppola.

JG: Although I didn't think it when I was working for him, he is, in fact, a genius. I think a genius is somebody who jumps off a 500-foot cliff and just before they're about to hit the water or the ground, they soar. People that take tremendous chances. And I put Marty Scorsese in that category.

With Carol Littleton Receiving the ACE Career Achievement Award
Photograph courtesy the American Cinema Editors and ACE Eddie Awards

TO: What films do you like?

JG: Good films. I'm still a filmgoer. You know, actors entrust to me their characters and I work damn hard to not only deduce what they want, but if I think it's what the director wants or what the screenwriter is implying, I will endeavor to get that. So, they rely on me.

TO: Why do you keep doing this?

JG: Yeah, that's a good question. I don't believe in retirement, certainly not for me. Because I've always been preoccupied with my craft and I've always wanted to keep plying that. It's hard for me to think of anything else. I can't give you an intellectual answer. Maybe it's ego. I know I do it well.

TO: You bring a lot of experience to new directors.

JG: Tom, I say that things have not changed all that much. But, if you really think of what we do—and I include you in this—it's like writing a novel. We would never say that writing a novel is different today than it was a hundred years ago. The language and grammar have changed, as it is for film editors in making movies.

TO: You're still doing it. You're waiting for the next film.

JG: Precisely.

TO: You're itching to go. This is what you do.

JG: Yes. And I am very joyful about my career.

RICHARD HALSEY, ACE

Richard Halsey (L) with Scott Conrad
Photograph courtesy of the American Cinema Editors and ACE Eddie Awards

LOS ANGELES, CALIFORNIA

Partial Credits: The Little Mermaid, Spaceman, The Net, Sister Act, Edward Scissorhands, Beaches, Down and Out in Beverly Hills, Moscow on the Hudson, That Championship Season, American Gigolo, Rocky, Next Stop, Greenwich Village, W.W. and the Dixie Dancekings, Harry and Tonto, Pat Garrett & Billy The Kid.

Before Rocky, Richard had been steadily moving forward in the film industry, starting as a messenger boy at Warner Brothers. Rocky, Harry and Tonto, Beaches, Edward Scissorhands—characters who stay with you long after you've left the theater, and whose performances are honed by this marvelous editor.

TO: Richard, you are an Oscar winning motion picture editor. How did you get your start in the editing business?

RH: I was a messenger boy at Warner Brothers Studios delivering mail in 1959. I got into the music-editing department and then I moved to 20th Century Fox and worked in music editorial for some of the greatest music editors of all time: Kenny Wannberg, Ken Hall. I worked under Lionel Newman, who was the brother of the famous composer, Alfred Newman.

TO: Those guys were unbelievably prolific. I mean they literally had hundreds of credits—250, 300 films each.

RH: Right and that's where I got my music background. But I wanted to be a film editor. But then I got drafted! I went into the Army for 21 months and 16 days. I went back to Fox as an apprentice and then as an assistant editor on Peyton Place for television. Two years later I was editing the show. I assisted one editor, George J. Nicholson, and I sat behind George all day long asking questions and he taught me.

TO: What drew you to the business?

RH: My father was a literary agent at William Morris, so I was always around the film industry. My stepmother was born in Hungary, raised in France and spoke five languages. She would take me to foreign films. One of the earliest films I remember was Cocteau's Beauty and the Beast and that incredible shot in the mirror that he used.

TO: In 1974, you worked on Harry and Tonto and Art Carney won his best actor Oscar. Only two years later, you win an Academy Award for Rocky. It happened very quickly in your career.

RH: (Laughs) Well, I had a goal. Become a feature editor by 30, win the Oscar, and become a director by 35. Now, I didn't entirely succeed in that, but I certainly had early success. When I read the Rocky script, I remember saying to myself, 'I could be nominated for an Academy Award for film editing on this script.'

TO: It was just that clear to you?

RH: Yes, because it was very well written. I had just seen Stallone in The Lords of Flatbush, and I knew the director, John Avildsen. I had worked with him before on W.W. and the Dixie Dancekings.

TO: Whenever anyone thinks of Rocky, they almost always think of the music score.

RH: I hired Bill Conti and he came into the editing room and we did the montages. He was the composer on Harry and Tonto. He did temp music at his house and I cut it into the picture. Sylvester and John actually wanted to hire somebody else.

TO: The budget was a million dollars?

RH: Right, a million dollars.

TO: And it just became a huge phenomenon.

RH: I know, and Bill Conti got $13,000 for the score and that included the album!

TO: You were editing on film.

RH: There was quite a bit of film and we did pickups towards the end of editing because we didn't have the right ending on the film.

TO: Really?

RH: Yes, we did a one-day re-shoot to get the proper ending.

TO: What happened?

RH: Well, the ideas came out of the editing process. We had a kind of folklore ending where Rocky walks down the turnstile and then we had a hokey song—Rocky and his girl—but the movie had to end in the ring.

TO: Right, that's where all the power is. Him calling for Adrian.

RH: Absolutely, and we just did one day's worth of pickups with Adrian backstage and it made it into a simultaneous love story. Did he win the fight? Did he not win the fight?

TO: And with the ending that's there, it now doesn't matter, because he's given it his all.

RH: Right, the main thing was that he went the distance.

TO: From the first time that you read the script, it seems as if you really had a clear idea as to how to put the film together.

RH: I have to give John Avildsen a lot of credit. John went to Philadelphia and shot a lot of good stuff in six days.

TO: Only six days?

RH: Yes. Rocky running up the steps, running through a market...
Practically one of the first films to use Garrett Brown's Steadicam. John
is a terrific director and it was just the right vehicle for him. It was
good timing for everybody.

In the Cutting Room
Photograph courtesy the American Cinema Editors and ACE Eddie Awards

TO: You edit character-oriented, action, romantic drama.

RH: I've done comedies, dramas, romance, thriller, crime, action,
adventure, family, sport, fantasy, musical...

TO: It's unusual.

RH: I'm kind of proud of it because the worst thing in this business is
to get pigeonholed.

TO: From Rocky to Edward Scissorhands to Beaches…

RH: You know I did John Patrick Shanley's first picture.

TO: Joe Versus The Volcano.

RH: You know it's one of my favorite movies.

TO: The movie didn't do well when it came out but has since developed a nice following.

RH: It wasn't well received except by certain people. Probably because of the last act. But I love the picture to this day.

TO: You did six pictures with Paul Mazursky.

RH: He's my favorite director. Truly the greatest director I've worked with.

TO: He came from that period where the writing led to producing and then led to directing.

RH: Right, he was a writer, producer, director, and an actor. He did it all. I invited him to one of the first movies that I ever edited. And I'll never forget this. He sat in front of me and I sat behind him and after the screening he turned around and said, 'Richard, I liked it! I liked it!' And a couple of months later he hired me on Harry and Tonto.

TO: Edward Scissorhands has really developed quite a following. How did you get involved with the picture?

RH: I had just finished Joe Versus The Volcano and I got the call for the picture. You're not going to believe this, but Tim spent, I think, a maximum of 24 hours in the editing room.

TO: You're kidding.

RH: No. And, Colleen, my wife, co-edited the film with me. We went to Tampa, Florida, where they were shooting the picture. Tim said,

'Richard, I have to show the picture to the studio to see if they'll do a Christmas release. Colleen and I showed it to Tim I think a week after they finished shooting. And basically, the picture was finished. And then I introduced Tim to one of my old friends, the fantastic title designer, Bob Dawson. And Tim saw his reel and said, 'Oh my God, he did Re-animator. He's hired!'

TO: The titles really are beautiful and so evocative of what later became very intricate and stylized title sequences associated with Tim Burton films. He did an interesting thing with the studio logo.

RH: Yeah, Bob put the logo of Twentieth-Century Fox in Black and White with snow falling. I think it's one of the most terrific title sequences there is. There's a scene where Johnny Depp is trying to apply makeup.

TO: Yes, it's very funny.

RH: Right, and Colleen edited that scene and she sat down with Tim Burton and they did it in about an hour and a half. When we were viewing dailies, it was scripted that all the scenes with Vincent Price and young Edward were scripted in a block.

TO: All together.

RH: Right, one after another.

TO: I don't think they would have been as impactful like that.

RH: Right, and Tim saw that at dailies. He loved Vincent Price. And he said, 'Richard, this material with Vincent Price is too good to use all at once. I think we should split it up.' I said, 'Tim, you're absolutely right and I know exactly how to do it—how to space them out and how to do these transitions.'

TO: I think the transitions from the past to the present to the past really give the film a wonderful dimension and add to the fable-like quality of the film. It's very endearing.

RH: Yes. I did it, Tim loved it, and that was it! The movie was finished. I think it's one of his best pictures.

And Editing on Digital
Photograph courtesy the American Cinema Editors and ACE Eddie Awards

TO: When did you make the transition to editing digitally?

RH: I wanted to make the switch a lot earlier than I did. It was 1995 and that was The Net for Irwin Winkler. When you were editing on film you really, really, really had to study the film. You had to block it out and have a plan. You had to think at least three or four cuts in advance because you didn't want to cut the print into millions of pieces.

TO: How has the amount of time that you get to edit a film changed with the transition to digital editing?

RH: For me, what's changed is the amount of studio involvement. When I was working with Mazursky, we had one preview. That was it. And it was left up to Paul if he wanted to do anything. Now, three previews, if not more, are standard.

TO: You tend to work on very character-driven films.

RH: That's what I'm interested in—characters. That's what I like to do and that's what I do best.

TO: Are there films that you really admire how they are put together or other editors whose work you admire?

RH: There are so many different categories of film, what genre, etc. One of my favorite movies is The Thief of Baghdad. Did you ever see that film?

TO: There were a few.

RH: It's the one directed by Michael Powell. It was a masterpiece. The flying carpet...

TO: That's the one from 1940. The one that most people remember is the one with Douglas Fairbanks in 1924, directed by Raoul Walsh.

RH: Yeah, you know, you talk about directors—Raoul Walsh—what a director! I'm drawn to character-driven, inspirational films. The small film that makes it big. That's what I loved about Rocky.

TO: Are there other editors whose work you admire?

RH: Well, I've had two assistants that went on to win Academy Awards and I'm proud of that. Artie Schmidt and Glenn Farr. And Arthur Schmidt, what a guy. God bless him. He was struggling and once he hooked up with Bob Zemeckis, his career just blossomed. I'm a huge Paul Hirsch fan.

TO: It must give you great pleasure to know that you've entertained millions of people with the films you've edited.

RH: I have a few thoughts on this. One of the things that I think I most love about editing is the solitary aspect of it. Being totally by myself in the editing room at Twentieth-Century Fox, cutting Harry and Tonto. My assistant was long gone. Just being there, at one with the film. Or when I was doing Payday. Those are the moments that I relish. When there aren't all sorts of people around. Being alone, making those decisions. Trying to find some sort of magic.

TO: What keeps you going?

RH: A lot of it is a love of the craft. I'm still really looking for that perfect, character-driven film. That's what I'm still searching for.

GERRY HAMBLING, ACE

Photograph courtesy the American Cinema Editors and ACE Eddie Awards

LONDON, ENGLAND

Partial Credits: The Life of David Gale, Angela's Ashes, The Boxer, Evita, White Squall, In the Name of the Father, City of Joy, The Commitments, Come See the Paradise, Mississippi Burning, Angel Heart, Birdy, Pink Floyd The Wall, Fame, Midnight Express. As Sound Editor: Wuthering Heights, King & Country, Alexander the Great.

As I interviewed editors, Gerry's name kept coming up. He was nominated a staggering six times for the best editing Academy Award. Young editors and older editors remember and cite his work and that is what is truly special.

(Author's Note: Mr. Hambling was alive at the time of this interview, but unable to communicate directly with the author. His long-time editorial assistant, Carolyne Chauncey related the author questions to Mr. Hambling.)

✀

TO: Carolyne, you have a long relationship with Mr. Hambling and was his first assistant for a number of films. How did you come to work with him?

CC: I had seen Angel Heart and was raving about it. One of the assistant accountants, Isabel, came into the editing room and I asked her if she knew Gerry Hambling. She said that she did. So I said, 'Boy, if he ever needs an assistant who has an American passport, please tell him I'm a big fan.' One day the phone rang. And it was Gerry Hambling.

TO: Just like that.

CC: Just like that. I was going back to Paris, we had lunch, and we just got along beautifully.

TO: What year was that?

CC: 1989. The film we were talking about was Come See the Paradise.

TO: How did Gerry start in the business?

CC: He started as a production runner. They were shooting a film in Wales and they needed someone to take the rushes up to Wales and bring the negative back. Gerry took it and never looked back. Gerry absolutely loves music.

TO: What was his big break in the business?

CC: He credits his first break as a picture editor on a Ralph Kemplen film.

TO: Ralph Kemplen was a very accomplished editor. He cut The African Queen and Oliver.

CC: Yes. Gerry had been Ralph's assistant and Ralph had a conflict and turned to Gerry and said, 'Why don't you take this film?' and Gerry never looked back. He would tell you that every film is his big break. He never gets smug. Before he starts a film he says to me, 'I wonder if I can still do it, kid.' (Both Laugh) He never gets complacent even after cutting all those films.

TO: He won the BAFTA three times and was nominated five times. He was nominated for the Oscar six times. He also won an ACE Eddie for Mississippi Burning and received the career achievement award from the American Cinema Editors. Really a tremendous career.

CC: He's a very humble man. He takes great pride in his work—rightfully so—but he's the least arrogant man you'll ever meet.

TO: What is his working style and what did you observe on The Commitments?

CC: Some do a first assembly—an editor's cut. Then a director's cut and then the final cut. Gerry's approach has always been 'Let's get it right the first time.' So he tends to take more time, initially. If ever the director says, 'I'm not happy with that', Gerry's motto is 'You give the director what he or she wants even if you don't personally agree. You're working for the director.'

TO: Did he cut all of those films on film?

CC: Yes, all of the films on film.

TO: Are there films that Gerry feels should have gotten more recognition or that people should revisit?

CC: One that comes to mind is that Pink Floyd The Wall didn't get more recognition. And there was no script. Gerry literally created the script as he was cutting the movie. And Angel Heart should have gotten more recognition.

TO: What comes to mind in terms of really challenging experiences?

CC: Did you ever see Talk of Angels?

TO: No.

CC: Nick Hamm directed it and I think it's one of the first things that Penelope Cruz did that had an English-speaking role. There's a bullfight in the script and Gerry said, 'Don't shoot it.' Nick took two cameras into an actual bullfight. Gerry said, 'I don't want to see it and I don't want to cut it.' And I couldn't look at the rushes. Our assistant had to do it and he was a pretty hard-nosed assistant and he came out green around the gills. Finally, Gerry couldn't put it off and he said, 'Okay, bring the rushes in. I'll see what I can do but I'm pretty sure I can't do anything with this.' With Gerry, I'd usually hear him say that once or twice per film. And he turned that bullfight into a ballet. It was something else. It conveyed the horror without showing anything graphically. You won't see that scene in its original form.

TO: Why?

CC: We had to leave the film to go and work on White Squall and another editor took it over. So I asked Donna Gigliotti, the producer, about the bullfight. And she said, 'No, as far as Miramax is concerned, the bullfight is sacrosanct.'

TO: You mean that it was going to stay in?

CC: Yes. Years later, we were in New York on The Boxer. And I went to transfer some sound and there were piles and piles of mag (magnetic stock) and they were labeled "Talk of Angels". And I said, 'That's not still going on, is it?' And the man who was doing the sound transfers rolled his eyes and said, 'Oh, yes it is'. And when I finally saw the film on video, it bore no relation to what Gerry cut.

TO: That's too bad.

CC: It's a real shame, because it was some of his finest work. He's always learning on a film. And he said to me, 'Kid, once you think you've seen it all, you know you're a liar. You haven't.'

TO: Are there examples when you looked at dailies and broke them down for him where you thought, 'I don't know what he's going to make of these or how he's going to work this scene?'

CC: I have thought that so many times. I thought, 'Thank goodness it's him and not me!' (Both Laugh) The riot sequence is one. And yet, when he comes out with these scenes—whether it's the storm sequence in White Squall or the riot sequence—you think, 'Well, that's obvious!'—but I couldn't see it. And yet it's just right.

TO: Are you with him in the same room?

CC: No. He likes to work on his own. Once we were in someone's Avid editing room and he said, 'Kid, you know what the worst piece of equipment is in this room?' And I said no. And he turned around and pointed at the sofa!

Receiving the ACE Career Achievement Award
Photograph courtesy the American Cinema Editors and ACE Eddie Awards

TO: Can we talk about the Alan Parker – Gerry Hambling partnership?

CC: Alan Parker's never had another editor.

TO: How did they start their relationship?

CC: Commercials. There was a slump in feature filmmaking in England. Gerry went to work cutting commericals for Roger Cherrill, who owned a commercial editorial house. And the first man through the door was Alan Parker.

TO: Midnight Express is a harrowing film. Giorgio Moroder won an Oscar for his music score. There's that very recognizable pulsating beat that he has. Does Gerry work with temp music?

CC: Yes. He'll often say, 'Get me a copy of this or that.' And it really often starts with a temp track. And then the track will be handed over to the composer with notes about what he likes or what doesn't work.

TO: Why did you like Angel Heart so much?

CC: I think it was the first time in a long time where I was sitting on the edge of my seat. And the editing just took my breath away.

TO: Can you recall getting the dailies from some of the films and your reaction to them?

CC: One very definite example was on The Life of David Gale and it's in reference to Laura Linney. Gerry sat through the rushes and said, 'What am I going to do with that, kid? At best all I could do is mess it up.' It just knocked your socks off.

TO: It's interesting that Alan Parker and Gerry do both powerful dramas and musicals so well.

CC: We were on Angela's Ashes and Gerry cut something together musically and John Williams came on and did the score. John Williams had taken what Gerry had done and changed it slightly. And all three of them were sitting in the mix and Alan wasn't sure what music piece he liked—the one that Gerry had cut or the one that John Williams had changed. And John asked Alan, 'Are you sure that just because you're used to one you're not using the new one?' And Alan said, 'No, I don't think it's that.' And he turned to Gerry and said, 'The one you created is not musically correct.' And Gerry said, 'I know.' And they went with Gerry's cut.

TO: Are there Gerry Hambling films that you feel may have been missed by audiences and bear a second look?

CC: Certainly, Pink Floyd The Wall. Angel Heart.

TO: What have you learned by working with Gerry?

CC: Some of it is the emotional—the sheer integrity. The dignity. The way he approached things. The commitment to what he was doing.

DAN HANLEY, ACE

Photographs courtesy the American Cinema Editors and ACE Eddie Awards

MIKE HILL, ACE

GREENWICH, CT

Partial Credits: In the Heart of the Sea, Rush, Frost/Nixon, The DaVinci Code, Cinderella Man, A Beautiful Mind, The Missing, How the Grinch Stole Christmas, Ransom, Apollo 13, Backdraft, Parenthood, Gung Ho, Cocoon, Splash.

When I sat down with them in Connecticut, Dan and Mike couldn't have been more accommodating, despite the usual hectic schedule. Their list of credits is so varied in genre—from the hilarity of Grinch to that amazing reveal in A Beautiful Mind to the suspense and exhilaration of Apollo—all done with artistic perfection.

✄

TO: Dan and Mike. You both received your Oscars for Apollo 13. How did you both get started in the business?

DH: My Dad and Grandfather were in the business and I hung around the studios as a kid. It was fantastic hanging out at Paramount and a job came up in the shipping department. And Mike was there as well.

MH: Right. I started about a year before you.

TO: You were both in the shipping department at the same time?

DH: Yeah, we were both in shipping.

MH: Yeah, we met in the shipping department.

TO: That's such a cliché story that people won't believe it.

DH: And that's really how it started. I was a kid and they let me hack through black and white dupes, splicing things together, not knowing what I was doing. The Moviola and butt splicer were treacherous; I'd constantly cut my hands and cinch my fingers.

MH: I graduated from the University of Nebraska, Omaha, with a criminal justice degree. I ended up with a job at Chino State Prison.

TO: I had no idea.

MH: And I had to be a guard first, midnight to eight and the whole thing was horrible. After three months, I decided to quit and I couldn't go back to Omaha as a total failure! When I was in school in Omaha, I paid my way through college by working at the local T.V. station splicing 16mm film commercials together so that they could be aired. So that got me over to the Editors Guild and I filled out the forms to join. One day the phone rang and it was the Guild and they said to go to Paramount for apprentice interviews. And Dan came in about a year later and we worked together for a while.

TO: You both started working together in 1982 on Night Shift. What were you both doing when you moved from shipping to being apprentices?

MH: I was put on The Last Tycoon, Elia Kazan's last film. And Richard Marks was the editor but I never saw him because he was in New York and they were shooting at Paramount. I was just synching up the dailies and we'd ship them to New York. I was beside myself because Brando was my favorite actor and Kazan was one of my favorite directors. So, I couldn't even believe this was happening. And Kazan would only shoot two and a half, three reels a day.

DH: Three reels tops.

MH: So it was an easy job and by then Dan was synching dailies with me. I would run dailies for Kazan separately from the Producer, Sam Spiegel. And then I would run them for DeNiro. And this was almost too much to believe—Kazan said, 'I'm going to reshoot this scene. Why don't you cut it and we'll see?'

TO: Because it wasn't going to be shipped to New York.

MH: Yeah, and he said, 'It'd be good for you.' And I thought, 'Oh, my God', because I hadn't cut anything before! And it was a really simple scene, just two people in a car with a straight on and some side shots. And I butchered the hell out of it and cut on every line! (All Laugh) And I ran it for him and he was really nice. He was chuckling and said, 'Well, you don't need to cut quite so much...' (All Laugh)

TO: Night Shift, Splash, Cocoon, Gung Ho, Parenthood, EdTV, and The Dilemma are some of the comedies you have edited. Did you have to learn through experience how to pace the scenes?

MH: Well, yeah, that all comes with experience, but Ron had so much experience as an actor. He knew all about timing and performances. And you learn how to leave time for the audience to laugh so you don't step on the next line.

DH: To me, I just watched the footage and it really is a matter of what makes me smile, what makes me laugh, where do my eyes want to be and what do I want to see? That's how I approach comedy.

MH: A lot of this is instinct and experience.

DH: And when someone asks you why you made a cut at a certain point, you'll have a reason. Not because you had to make the cut at that point, but because that's where your eyes wanted to be and who or what you wanted to see.

MH: Your whole approach to a comedy is hinged on how you think the audience is going to respond to the material. Whereas with a drama, you have a story to tell and you don't have to worry about every single moment and how people are going to react.

TO: I'd like to take you to Apollo 13. Was there a lot of film shot for the film?

DH: Over a million feet.

MH: And we had three units going and we had endless footage of switches and dials…

DH: We were constantly going back to scenes and re-cutting them to put them in.

MH: We didn't know what these switches and dials were or where they went. We also had Dave Scott who was on Apollo 15 as a technical consultant. I remember thinking, 'How are we ever going to get this together?'

TO: Because you were editing on film.

MH: Yeah, it was our last one on film.

DH: Our first cut was about four hours and Ron did a small screening. And then we got it down to three hours.

TO: What was the point that you sat back and watched the entire film?

MH: I remember going home to Omaha over a weekend. And I took the film back on videotape and it was a very long version. And I ran it for my wife and she said, 'This is really good and this is really special.'

TO: I want to take you back to March 25, 1996. Apollo 13, Babe, Braveheart, Crimson Tide, and Seven.

DH: We were totally shocked.

MH: We were.

TO: I think it's because of the blend of the action, suspense, and the human drama. And that's a lot to accomplish well in one film.

DH: And how does a director, who has to balance all that, not get nominated?

MH: Some people said, 'You know the ending and what happened, but it's still suspenseful.'

TO: Ransom is a tricky film because you have to make sure not to reveal the surprise until the exact right time.

MH: I just remember really enjoying editing that movie. It was really fun. On the phone call, Dan only cut one side of it. Dan only cut Mel's side. And then Ron looked at that cut and shot Sinise based on that cut.

TO: That's an interesting thing to do.

DH: It started on video. And we played around for weeks on the Ediflex system and then the Montage. And then we looked at Lightworks. And then we looked at Avid. And we went in after they shot the scene and they shot it on video and there were all these videotapes.

TO: So the process was that you would cut just the video together and then that would be used as a guide.

DH: Yes, and Ron had already figured out the camera moves and how to integrate that back and forth...

TO: Between Gibson and Sinise...

DH: Yes, and we cut all of Mel's stuff and then left black between Mel's takes...

TO: To represent where Sinise's footage would go.

DH: Yes.

MH: There were several big scenes. And one that was kind of a tough one was when Mel goes on TV and talks to the kidnappers. And Ron shot a lot of footage and it was great that we were on the Avid because it would have been really tough on film. Ransom was unique to us in another way because the first cut was only two-and-a-half hours.

TO: So, it was already pretty tight in the first cut.

DH: Yeah, we had put some alternate versions aside just in case because it's easy to do in digital.

MH: But the film went together really well.

TO: Are there examples where a film didn't do as well as you expected?

MH: Well, the screenings of Cinderella Man did really well. It scored in the 90's. And they (the studio) thought it was going to be a huge hit.

TO: What do you think went wrong?

MH: They released it in June which was probably a big mistake and it didn't do anything.

DH: I think when it was released is a big reason and people were confused by the title.

MH: The Missing we didn't think would be a blockbuster, but it just didn't do well.

DH: All these editors that you're interviewing—have you found any commonalities in them?

TO: Well, I'd say that one of the things that comes to mind is that many of them like to watch people and they like to watch how people react to other people they're talking to. Another common thing is that many editors play some form of musical instrument—the drums came up a lot. Okay, did you have a lot of fun on How The Grinch Stole Christmas?

DH: (Both Laugh) Yeah!

MH: I did!

TO: It was an enormous hit. It appeals to so many different ages.

DH: We thought it would do well because Jim (Carrey) was really hot at the time. I love the fact that the movie has been playing during the Christmas season every year.

TO: Although one wouldn't expect it from the subject matter, "A Beautiful Mind" grossed over $313 million worldwide.

MH: That was a movie that went together like butter.

TO: Really?

MH: Yeah, from day one, it was all these great scenes. It wasn't difficult. I never thought it was going to be a giant picture, but to have it turn out that way was very satisfying.

TO: The shooting of the film was done in a very unconventional manner, in that it was shot in chronological order. As editors, where you able to see a benefit of that method?

DH & MH: (In Unison) Yeah, we loved that.

DH: Because we could really put things together and not have to make a lot of adjustments later on. We still had to adjust because of Russell's performances and how quirky he was and where he would end up.

TO: You mean the performance arc?

DH: Yes. (To Mike) Remember when we had the conversation about the degrees of quirkiness?

MH: Right because every scene Russell had degrees and we had to make sure they progressed correctly. We tended to go toward the middle ground and then adjust. For the actors, it must have been really great. It's a rare luxury.

TO: The scene of the reveal where Jennifer Connelly discovers the truth is simultaneously suspenseful and spooky. When she—and the audience—finally find out I can recall the loud gasp that came from the audience. When you were reading the script, how did you react?

DH: I remember saying to Ron, 'How are you going to make this work and be true so that when people see it they don't say that you cheated?' And we had a set of rules of what we could and could not do.

TO: The special edition DVD of the film is really great because it has a whole section on those rules.

DH: There are definitely clues.

TO: Like the pigeons don't move...

MH: Yeah, and these were things that we were discovering along the way.

TO: And it did very well worldwide.

MH: I never expected that. That was a big surprise. Not alone winning Best Picture.

TO: Why do you think it won Best Picture?

MH: Performances. And Ron did a great job.

DH: It was really the story and it didn't have all the other things such as lots of visual effects.

TO: As a viewer you don't get a lot of breaks. The school, the government agents, the human drama, and the bathtub... You're watching that with your fingers across your eyes...

DH: Yeah, that running water...because everyone's heard a story of a tragedy involving a child in a bathtub.

TO: Yeah, as soon as you hear the sound of the water in the bathtub, the dread starts.

DH: It's just like in Ransom—that kite flying away and the parents going through the crowd. And as a parent, you feel that immediately. Everyone's had their kid disappear for five seconds and that's what I think Ron did very well in both films.

MH: There are all these little flashbacks in the film and Ron told us just to try some things. And thanks to digital, I started doing things like freezing a frame or taking a frame and distorting it or doing a dissolve to a freeze frame. And if we were on film it would have been very time consuming.

TO: I was really happy that Frost / Nixon got nominated for editing. More or less challenging do you think?

DH: Very challenging. There's no place to hide. You have to be at the right spot at the right time.

MH: I agree. But it wasn't difficult—the actors were so great.

TO: What editors do you admire?

DH: Artie Schmidt for me. And I saw how he was in the cutting room and how he kept up with everything even though he was inundated with footage on Roger Rabbit. And then I saw him a few years later and he was working on The Birdcage. And he showed me a nine-minute sequence and he was really nervous. And I said, 'Artie, you've been doing this forever!' and he said, 'Yeah, that's the bad news; it's not going to go away'.

TO: After all that editing, he still got nervous showing a cut...

DH: Yeah, that first time you show someone a cut. So, for me, Artie, just because of the way he ran his cutting room. Chris Lebenzon on those Tony Scott movies.

MH: Lebenzon—how does he do it? How does he handle all that? I think back to Dede Allen—almost all of the films she edited.

TO: What films did you like when you were younger?

MH: To Kill a Mockingbird, for me, was always a standout. Midnight Cowboy, The Graduate, Bonnie and Clyde, M*A*S*H. Those were so amazing to me that I couldn't get enough of them.

DH: Cool Hand Luke, The French Connection, Bonnie and Clyde.

MH: When I was in the shipping department, the movie that everyone in editing circles talked about was The Wild Bunch. And we loved going to see it.

DH: Straw Dogs.

MH: I loved Peckinpah movies.

TO: What advice do you have for budding editors?

MH: To be an editor, you have to have patience. You can't have a big ego in the editing room—it's very counterproductive. You're in these rooms for hundreds of hours with people.

TO: What's the best part of your job and why do you keep doing it?

DH: For me, I just always loved the performances when I went to movies. To be able to see these performances every day and to showcase them and to perfect them. And because of the work environment that Ron creates is ideal, I know I am extremely fortunate.

MH: And your decisions actually create those moments. The freedom to be able to make a product that people will hopefully enjoy and that touches people. To know that you have the opportunity to do that. For me, it's the initial editing of the scenes, which I love the most. Just sitting in there and solving the problem and time is just flying by.

RICHARD A. HARRIS

Winning ACE Award for Titanic in 1998
Photograph courtesy of the American Cinema Editors and ACE Eddie Awards

SANTA YNEZ, CA

Partial Credits: Titanic, Indictment: The McMartin Trial, True Lies, The Bodyguard, Terminator 2: Judgment Day, Fletch, The Executioner's Song, Semi-Tough, The Bad News Bears, The Candidate, Downhill Racer.

Downhill Racer, The Candidate. The Executioner's Song. Semi-Tough? Uproarious laughter at the premiere. Then, the James Cameron films. Blending comedy and action in the Causeway sequence in True Lies shows Richard at his best. And on comedy: "There is a place to cut and you've got to know that point. It's inside you and you have to feel it."

TO: Richard, you are an Academy Award, Emmy Award, Eddie, and Golden Satellite Award recipient. How did you get your start in the film business?

RAH: I was born in Hollywood Presbyterian Hospital and went to Hollywood High School and didn't even consider this profession. I wanted to be a racecar driver! (Laughs). I wound up entering and graduating from the USC cinema school. You were lucky to get through a studio gate let alone get an interview. I went to work as an apprentice at Ziv and they were doing Sea Hunt.

TO: Synching…

RAH: Back then it was hot splicing, glue and acetone, all toxic.

TO: Were you editing by then?

RAH: Yes. Doing films for AT&T, Oldsmobile, and it was a great training ground. You did the music editing, the sound effects editing, the optical line-up, everything. One day Fairbanks was going to produce a feature and he had Hal Mohr, the famous cinematographer.

TO: He had a long career and was a two-time Academy Award recipient. He did A Midsummer Night's Dream, The Wild One, and Captain Blood.

RAH: And the film had Lois Nettleton and John Ericson and it was going to be a sci-fi picture.

TO: Was this The Bamboo Saucer?

RAH: You said the words! (Laughs)

TO: That was your first credit as a full picture editor.

RAH: Yes. So they shot this feature and it was full of these flying saucer special effects. And I had to do the optical line up and it would come out every color in the book! (Laughs) I got an opportunity to go to Paramount and work with a great editor, Frank Bracht. At Paramount, the head of editorial was Chuck West and I had opportunities to put little sequences together. And my first one was on The Odd Couple. It's those little opportunities that you get and that you have to take. One day Chuck asked me if I had worked with 16mm. I had done 16mm and 35mm and he said that there was a film being shot in Europe called Downhill Racer.

TO: Just like that.

RAH: Yeah, there it was. Downhill Racer. And it was all about the bits and the pieces because it was a very difficult film to shoot. And then I worked on Dusty and Sweets McGee and it was all about the little bits and pieces and what held them all together was the music that we picked. And that's the same music that George Lucas used for American Graffiti! We were way ahead of our time.

TO: There's a lot of comedy in your portfolio, including one of my favorites, Semi-Tough.

RAH: If it's comedy, I really want to do it. But there are serious films that I love and I see every submarine film and of course Das Boot is right at the top. Intolerance and, of course, The Godfather.

TO: You worked with Michael Ritchie on 13 features...

RAH: We were just of the same thoughts all the way and we had the same sense of humor. And you know there is a Michael Ritchie film that isn't mentioned very much but it is very near and dear to me.

TO: Which one?

RAH: It's Smile.

TO: That's about the beauty pageant.

RAH: It's a small-town beauty contest and I just had so much fun with that film. And I had fun with the music. I've always liked the music part of the films I've worked on, like with Semi-Tough, we decided to use Gene Autry and it worked.

TO: It really did.

RAH: With Bad News Bears, we decided to use Bizet.

TO: Toreador.

RAH: Yes. I edited that up at what became George Lucas's house in San Anselmo. And I remember trying to collect all the Toreador music from the smallest ensemble up to the operatic version. Comedy is probably my favorite thing to work on.

TO: Is it more challenging?

RAH: It's tough.

TO: Why?

RAH: It's frame perfect. Putting it together is tough. There is a place to cut and you've got to know that point. It's inside you and you have to feel it. You can't let a joke linger.

TO: You enjoyed great success with The Bad News Bears.

RAH: That was a really great Director-Editor experience because Michael would shoot these pieces and I'd put them together. And it was like sketching something out with a lot of blanks in there. And I would give him notes and say I need more of Vic Morrow looking at Walter Matthau—we need to build more tension there. And he'd shoot that and we'd get all those pieces.

TO: You edited two very acclaimed and controversial television films. The Executioner's Song was a first for television especially since the U.S. was in the midst of a large debate on the death penalty.

RAH: I got a call from the director, Larry Schiller and he asked me if I was interested in editing the film. So I went over and interviewed and that's where I met my wife, Pamela! (Both Laugh)

TO: Thank you, Larry.

RAH: (Laughs) And I read the script and I thought that it was pretty interesting. Putting it together, it was full of dark characters and locations and I found it very depressing. But I really enjoyed doing that type of film. I think an editor should be able to do comedy or action or any of the genres.

TO: Are you able to separate yourself from it?

RAH: I separate myself from it. Telling the story is the bottom line. That's what an editor does—we're storytellers. The writer writes the script. The director then takes it to the next creative level. And I think a good editor takes the director's material and takes that to another level. It's still telling the story.

TO: You received an Emmy award for your work on Indictment: The

McMartin Trial. Was it a difficult film to work on?

RAH: Yes. That was a very difficult film. I was ready to retire. And Mick Jackson the director asked me to do it. And I told him that I didn't think so, and he asked me to just read the script. And I read it and told him I'd do it. But it was very intense. Mick is a really wonderful director.

TO: He got great reviews for the film.

RAH: I've done three films with him: L.A. Story, The McMartin Trial and The Bodyguard. But it was intense because of the limited amount of time.

TO: And you won the Emmy.

RAH: That came as a real surprise! You don't do films because you're going to get awards for it. You do them because you're drawn to the project.

TO: You worked on Terminator 2, True, Lies, and Titanic, for which you won your Academy Award.

RAH: Well, the interesting thing is that I had never interviewed with Jim.

TO: Really? How did you come to work on Terminator 2?

RAH: They needed another editor and I just got a call from the producers. They told me that Jim was going to be looking at dailies as he wasn't looking at them every day because of the schedule and he let them go a week or even longer.

TO: That's a long time.

RAH: So, he had these marathon screenings. I went into the room and he said, 'Let's see the material in the Dyson house and the Cyberdyne scene'. And he said, 'Who's going to put that together?' And he looked at me with that intense stare and I said, 'Hi, I'm Richard' and he said,

'I'm Jim'. So, now I've met Jim Cameron.

TO: You were editing comedies and then get a call for that type of film...

RAH: I had just finished L.A. Story! We were watching dailies and every now and then Jim would lean over and say a few things about a take. But he never said, 'Use this, use that'. But you got the feeling of what he liked. I had a yellow legal pad in front of me and I wrote "Reel One" and that was all I had written after this marathon screening!

TO: That's funny.

RAH: But I remember everything visually and I was using three junior KEM's, one in front, one on my left and one on my right. You could interlock all the footage and move back and forth. And because Jim had used multiple cameras, it was a big help. I could go back and forth and constantly review the dailies. I also had a Moviola and a bench.

TO: This was a classic film editorial process.

RAH: All the film that I had to work with for the scene was in rolls on the floor. And I went through it at semi-high speed with the KEM and made my notes and pulled all the pieces that I wanted to use.

TO: For the Dyson house scene?

RAH: Yes. I put it together and Jim was totally blown away. He really liked it and he loved this one idea I had. When Linda Hamilton goes to the house, she sits down and prepares all her equipment and puts a clip in the rifle and she starts shooting. So, I started thinking about how many bullets these guns hold, they never seem to run out. I know nothing about guns and Jim knows everything about them. And I thought, 'Gee, there's a piece that I pulled', and I don't know why, but it turned out to be the piece where she was putting the clip in the gun and getting ready, hence more bullets and Jim really loved that. I made a lot of points with Jim with that one little cut! And it worked, and Jim and I were off to a really great start.

TO: The mix of humor and great action really hits stride in True Lies.

RAH: There is. But, I didn't start on that film. Pamela was on it.

TO: She was an Associate Producer on the film.

RAH: I was down in Key West with her while they were shooting. Jim would see me every now and then and say, 'You think you're escaping this. You're not.' (Both Laugh) Well, sure enough, when they came back to L.A., I got roped in and it was enjoyable.

TO: What did you work on?

RAH: My big sequence was the Causeway where Arnold is trying to get Jaime Lee out of the car. That was a lot of material. But all of the material he shoots is good.

TO: Did you have any idea of the impact that Titanic would have?

RAH: No idea whatsoever. We had moved from Hollywood to Santa Ynez, and we got the call. Pamela was asked for the visual effects and me to begin editing, and we said we weren't interested because we had just moved. And then came the script—or the manuscript—and we said this was going to be a huge thing. I was the first one hired because Jim wanted to edit the film himself. But it really was impossible for the amount of filming that was taking place.

TO: When you started getting the dailies for Titanic what did you start working on?

RAH: My first scene that I actually put together was the dinner sequence. And Jim shot it both ways. First, he shot it with Leonardo looking at Kate from one side and then from the other side. And I made the decision to cut the whole thing from Leonardo's point of view because that's where the love interest was. But all of the ship going down was difficult because I think Jim had eight cameras in place changing lens and position with each take, and that's a lot of film.

TO: Do you recall seeing the film with an audience?

RAH: That was pretty exciting. Pamela and I actually got the film up here in Santa Ynez for a private screening at our local theatre. We had about 50 people that we know, and they cried. That was my first experience where I got the WOW feeling. When it was over, Cheryl Ladd couldn't even talk—she was so full of tears. She was really moved. It all worked.

TO: The film moves so incredibly fast. You're not aware of how long it is.

RAH: It's true. It's pretty exciting.

TO: What was it like to hear your name announced at the Oscars?

RAH: I couldn't believe it.

TO: Do you remember the moment?

RAH: I do. I remember hugging Pamela.

TO: Was it one of the hardest you've worked on?

RAH: Yes, it was really difficult because of the amount of footage and the amount of visual effects. The scene down below deck with the dancing and the music was one where I spent a lot of time. I also spent a lot of time on getting the lifeboats down. My first cut was horrible. I love all the dialogue sequences, like the dinner sequences.

TO: Why?

RAH: I think the people looking at each other and challenging each other with those looks and the dialogue. So much can be said with looks and without words.

TO: What films do you admire?

RAH: Apocalypse, Gladiator, It Happened One Night, Intolerance, Das Boot.

TO: What are some of the things you've learned along the way?

RAH: Patience. Not to be rushed. Editing, especially with digital formats, is not a video game. I tell people that they should think about where they are going and what you want to happen with the next scene. It's a holdover from when I had to use a pair of scissors. And that's always been my thing—I know where I'm going. It's not about speed and editing fast, it's about story, and tomorrow.

ALAN HEIM, ACE

Photograph courtesy of the American Cinema Editors and ACE Eddie Awards

LOS ANGELES, CALIFORNIA

Partial Credits: Lenny, Network, Holocaust, Hair, All That Jazz, The Notebook, The Last Mimzy.

The boyish love he had for movies is still so very much alive. Beyond the awards—and there are many—Alan talks about having an instinct for editing and seems to be amazed (in a wonderful way) when I reminded him that he has been at the top of his game for more than 40 years. And, in the most marvelous way, when he was talking, what I really heard was the young boy who still loves movies.

✂

TO: Alan, you've won an Academy Award, three Eddy awards, a BAFTA, and an Emmy award. How did you get your start?

AH: I grew up in New York City, in the Bronx. And my first job was as a projectionist at my public school. My first paying job was at the Police Athletic League running movies in the summer, right across the street, at the 44thprecinct. It was known as Fort Apache. I went to a great deal of movies as a kid. When I went to school I really didn't imagine I'd be in the movie business. I was attending City College in New York and they had a very small film school and I decided to take courses there. The head of the school was a guy named George Stoney, a very fine documentary filmmaker. And he liked my work, as limited as it was. He recommended me for some summer jobs and I ended up carrying the camera in the woods for someone while he filmed his wife dancing. One of those movies…

TO: I take it you mean experimental and not one of those other movies!

AH: Yes. And that Fall I was asked by the cameraman if I wanted to come and work in an editing house in the evenings and on weekends. And that's how I started.

TO: What were you doing?

AH: I was a sound effects editor in the Army at the pictorial center in Queens, and I did some music editing. I learned how to cut music and make it all fit on one reel without mixing. And then I had been a sound editor for Sidney Lumet on three movies—The Group, The Pawnbroker, and Bye Bye Braverman. And Sidney asked me if I'd cut his next movie.

TO: What a break.

AH: Yes, and in those days, Sidney just stood over your shoulder and told you where to edit. And for me it was a great learning experience, absolutely wonderful. To learn about performance, about making quick decisions, and then I moved on.

TO: Which film was it?

AH: Well, the first film I did for Sidney was "The Seagull"—Chekhov's play.

TO: 1968.

AH: Yes. And it was not a very good movie! It was dull! But I learned some very interesting things from Sidney. My favorite being that he asked me to make a cut in a scene because we had to take some time out. So, he asked me to remove about three-and-a-half minutes of a scene, which I did. And it involved the actress's head turning around almost like the head in "The Exorcist"!

TO: Oh, no.

AH: Yeah, her head just whipped around. It was a complete crossing the line, stuff you're not supposed to do. It looks terrible. And he said,

'Alan, don't worry about it. It's a projectionist error!

TO: That's funny.

AH: And I looked at him blindly and said, 'What is a projectionist error?' And he said, 'You know, people go to a movie and they see it once and if there's a bad cut in the movie they figure the projectionist repaired the ripped film.' And what I learned from that was you can get away with a lot of stuff when you're editing a movie!

TO: That's amazing that he just had the confidence to do that.

AH: Well, if you do it more than a couple of times, they'll catch you.

TO: Michael Tronick is a big fan of yours and your work on All That Jazz. He said that you helped him make the transition to picture editing.

AH: Well, I remember the story a bit differently. Michael and I were having lunch one day and he was talking about how he wanted to move on from music editing to picture editing and I encouraged him and it worked out very nicely for him.

TO: What lessons have you picked up along the way?

AH: Well, it's very important to be able to work well with others. I always believe that when an editor comes into a production, he's really interposing himself between the director's vision and what the director really has. I'm just trying to make the best version of the movie that the director wanted—at least on the first cut. That's the psychological aspect of editing—you have to be willing to go in there and tell the director what's really on the film.

TO: Sometimes that's a tough conversation to have.

AH: It's rough, but you do have to do that.

TO: You become such a trusted partner of the director.

AH: I've got to live with that material for six, nine, fourteen months. And if I don't make my worries known—and I don't do it easily—but just jump in and attack the material, and I see a disaster brewing, I may be the one paying for that.

TO: New editors coming into the business have to figure out a way to do it diplomatically.

AH: Yeah, because six months down the line it may be a disaster and I'm going to be trying to explain why it's not playing and I like to try and correct that as much as I can.

TO: And as early as you can.

AH: A lot of editing is instinct. And I never knew that I had the talent to walk a narrow line like that. To be politically aware. But it seems to have worked out pretty well over 40 years.

TO: It sure has. What should people who go to movies realize about the filmmaking process?

AH: Editors work really behind the scenes, so to speak, invisibly. And, sometimes, the structure of the film is where you want to show the editing. "All That Jazz" warranted a structure right outside like a turtle's shell.

TO: You want to draw attention to it.

AH: Yes, and that was a wonderful mosaic, but most of the time, you just don't want to call much attention to the editing. You just want to tell the story. If you're calling attention to the editing a lot, you're not really doing your job. People say to me 'When you go to a movie do you look at the editing?' And I like to think that I don't unless it's not a very good movie.

TO: From editing on film, you've transitioned to editing digitally.

AH: When I started editing, the machine of choice in the United States was the Moviola. It was invented in approximately 1922 and lasted almost unchanged for 75 years. It was like a locomotive. All the parts were hand-machined to fit perfectly to each machine and anything that broke I could fix with a screwdriver or pair of pliers. I really liked the intimacy of working with film that way. Then I worked on editing tables—Steenbeck, KEM—but I never really felt comfortable working with those. But I did work on films for Milos Forman and Bob Fosse on the KEM and in Fosse's case it was because he really couldn't see on the Moviola screen. It was just too small for him. And Milos just worked that way. We did try the Ediflex, an electronic based editor which used videocassettes and one of the reasons it didn't catch on was that one day Milos said, 'Let's see what it really looks like, because you really couldn't see the image—it was terrible. I continued working on the Moviola, but I realized that at a certain point that if I didn't learn electronic editing, I'd be a dinosaur trainer—nothing good would come of it.

TO: That's funny.

AH: I like it now. I had an assistant who taught me the Lightworks. I don't think any of us had a concept that it would all go electronic.

TO: It only took about eight years—from 1992-2000.

AH: My next project was with Barbra Streisand, The Mirror Has Two Faces, and Columbia wanted me to do it on the Avid. They gave me a three-day cram course and I've ended up using that machine pretty much ever since.

TO: And how has it made the most impact for you?

AH: When you've finished a film on film, you have a test screening, if we changed the film twice, that would be a lot. If you were working with Lumet or with Fosse when the film left the cutting room, that was pretty much how it got into the theatre. Over the past 15 years, sometimes you have two test screenings in a week in a theatre.

TO: That frequently? I didn't realize that there were so many.

AH: And you couldn't have done that on film because of the mechanics of it. To move all those sound tracks around and to remix. It would just take too long physically. And now, if you want to, you can screen two, three times a week if you want to and make massive changes. And have copies of the old version. Which is not bad, given that test screenings mean so much both to the kind of release you get and how they market the movie.

TO: Tell me about "All That Jazz" and your work with Bob Fosse.

AH: Well, I worked with him on two projects before that, "Liza with a Z" which won him an Emmy and that was the year where he won the Emmy, the Tony, and the Oscar.

TO: Right, 1973. An amazing year for him.

AH: Yes, the Oscar for "Cabaret", the Tony for "Pippin", which was a really bad show that was superbly directed, and "Liza with a Z" for which I was nominated for an Emmy. And I've always felt a little unhappy that I didn't get it. (Laughs)

TO: You made up for it when you won your Emmy for "Holocaust" which is superb.

AH: Well, look, Fosse was brilliant. Absolutely brilliant. And he referred to me as his collaborator. And I think there can be no greater honor for an editor to be that close to the creative process.

TO: It's fantastic to be thought of in that way by someone like Bob Fosse.

AH: I did Liza with a Z and I interviewed with Bob the day before I was hired. And that night I went to see Cabaret which my late wife had seen. And she had said, 'You've got to go see this movie.' I didn't have that much of a stomach for movie musicals at that time.

TO: How ironic.

AH: Well, I went to see Cabaret and it's not a musical. It's an experience. And I came home and I said, 'Wow. My God. I really hope he hires me. I want to work with this guy!' Liza with a Z had nine cameras and it was a live, one-hour show. And no slates, which was my choice, and it was done in front of an audience. And we eventually put it together and it got tremendous response, critically. It got an Emmy nomination.

TO: It did pretty well on re-release. It's really good.

AH: Then I did "Lenny" with Bob and that was a tremendous creative experience. When we were working together, it was very, very exciting. That film was made in the cutting room.

TO: How so?

AH: The ending of the film was just not playing and we had to show it to David Picker, the producer, the next day. We just had big trouble with the ending. And my whole crew, along with Fosse, went out to dinner about 9 or 10 at night and came back to the cutting room, intending to really work all night. And in the elevator, I turned to Bob and I said, 'Why don't we just kill the son-of-a-bitch?'

TO: You're kidding!

AH: (Laughs) He said, 'What do you mean?' And I said, 'His life is over with as soon as he's dragged out of that courtroom. Why don't we just kill him?' And we went back to the cutting room and I took out two reels of film. It took no time at all and we looked at it and it's the kind of legendary story that you hear about from old-time moviemakers where they'd drop every other reel or something like that.

TO: I've heard stories like that and they always sort of shock me. Taking out 20 minutes isn't trivial.

AH: We realized we'd have to put back some of it and we had to figure out how to do it, but at that moment we suddenly had the ending of the movie. So that was a great moment for me personally.

TO: "All That Jazz". I remember seeing it on its first run and there were many little moments that just stood out.

AH: Well, it was a troubled project in one sense. Bob hired an actor and all of us said, 'Bob, you're making a mistake—this guy can't do it.' And Bob said, 'No, I think he can do it.' He was convinced he could get an actor to do anything. And this guy just did not work out. So, the first day I walked into the office and they had fired the actor. And it ended up being delayed for close to six months while they waited for Roy Scheider, who was an absolutely perfect choice for the role. Fosse would never admit it was his life. I trusted Bob a great deal—otherwise I wouldn't have played myself in the movie.

TO: The film took a long time to make.

AH: There was a hiatus over Thanksgiving while Bob was choreographing the big Erotica number and we closed for about a week. We had the six-month hiatus but Fosse wanted to keep his crew together so they paid us half our normal rate while we waited. It was a life-changing experience. Bob didn't want to take a break at the end of shooting—he wanted to go right into cutting which directors usually don't do. They like to take a little time to recuperate. Bob came into the cutting room but he was not comfortable. And I said to myself, 'I have to get back into the rhythm that we've always had before working together.'

TO: The starts and stops broke that rhythm and that relationship you and he had.

AH: Yes. And I said to my wife, 'I've got to figure out a way to break this pattern because it's not working between us. I want to make this a great movie.' There was a scene where Roy was sitting next to me at the KEM. And he was supposed to cough and I was supposed to look over because I was disapproving of his smoking and raise an eyebrow.

Bob said, 'Okay, I'm going to do the cue and you raise your eyebrow just a little bit.' And Bob's direction to actors was always, 'Stop acting. Just do it small.' So I did it and Bob kept the camera running and very quietly he said, 'Do it again…smaller.' I have very large eyebrows and I did five takes and by the last, my eyebrows were way up there like the villain in Charlie Chaplin movies!

TO: (Laughs) They're your signature features.

AH: Yeah, and they were up there—these enormous caterpillars near the top of my forehead. When I cut the scene, I had cut in my smallest version. And Bob said, 'How could I let you do that?' And I said, 'Bob, I'm not an actor.' And he said, 'But you're a human being. I should be able to get a better performance out of a human being.' And I laughed and I said, 'You know, Bob, that's the nicest thing you've said to me in two weeks.' And he absolutely broke up laughing and I had broken the tension. And it was an amazing stroke of luck because I was really at wit's end. And after that, we were fine.

TO: When you see the film in retrospectives, they always show the big dance scene at the end. But the other clip they show is the scene that, when I saw it on its first run, I thought 'Now that's really interesting what they've done there'. And that's the scene where he snaps the pencil.

AH: Yeah, yeah.

TO: Why did you do it?

AH: It's interesting. All the actors are laughing at this very bad play. And Bob really wanted to get the actors laughing fiercely. You know, when you have a panic attack, your senses change. Some people hear rushing water in their ears and some people hear other things. And we came up with that pencil—it's been a number of years, but I think it was mostly Bob. But the idea was that we would eliminate all but the loudest, sharpest noises. It was this desire to get into what was happening psychologically to this guy who thought he was connected to this disaster.

TO: I want to take you to 1976 and to "Network". It won four Academy Awards and the phrase "I'm mad as hell and I'm not going to take it anymore" is hugely popular—to this day. You were nominated. The editing buildup when everyone is looking out their apartment windows is still played in editing retrospectives.

AH: And if you look at it again, it's a prescient movie. I mean, for one thing, it came out a little early. Paddy Chayefsky, the screenwriter, was seeing things happening, and it's happening again. Paddy was an incredible writer.

TO: How did you get involved?

AH: Fosse was best friends with Paddy Chayefsky. And Sidney Lumet probably wanted to hire Dede Allen because Dede had done Serpico and Dog Day. And for those two films, Sidney did not stand over Dede's shoulder and tell her where to cut the movie.

TO: Yeah, I can't imagine she would ever put up with that.

AH: All of us were wondering how that would work. Dede being an immovable object and Sidney being an irresistible force. Or vice versa. She cut those movies and I think they are among his better-edited movies.

TO: I agree.

AH: But, she was not available, much to my good fortune. Fosse suggested that I work with Sidney. And I was terrified that Sidney was going to want to control the cut again. Fortunately, we stuck to the schedule and he didn't.

TO: Did you realize that the film was something special?

AH: Well, you have a great script, you have great performances. And Paddy, apart from being a terrific writer—he was also a poet. If you listen to the movie carefully, his words—nobody really talks like that. But the flow of it was remarkable—the rhythm. There was no music in the movie. There was just the theme to the TV show within the film. The music was in Paddy's words. And he sometimes made up words to make them fit right.

TO: I didn't know that. The performances are fantastic—Oscars for Peter Finch, Faye Dunaway, and Beatrice Straight.

AH: When Bill Holden comes into Faye Dunaway's kitchen—chases her in and talks about feeling that he loves her and wants another chance, I go to Faye only twice in this very long scene. And I did it once because Bill flubbed his line and we had to pick it up in another take. And I stole the piece that I used of her at that moment when she sort of bites her lip. And it's a moment of hesitation on her part, but that's not what she was actually doing at that section. And then I cut to her again at the end and then the phone rings and breaks the moment and she goes to take the call.

TO: You would never guess that because what she does then is a perfect reaction.

AH: But, Beatrice Straight...she gave that performance and it was a stunning performance.

TO: She doesn't have much actual screen time, but you would never think that.

AH: It's a tiny performance... She was in the film for that scene and a couple of other walk-ons, really.

TO: The scene with Holden.

AH: Yes, and the whole scene is three minutes long, maybe. And she won an Academy Award for it. And as we were cutting the movie, the scene as scripted was in the wrong place and it was very clear to me that it was in the wrong place. And I suggested to Sidney and to Paddy and to the producer, Howard Gottfried that we take the scene and move it after the scene with Faye Dunaway when they go on their beach vacation. It used to be before that. And they said, 'No, no, no. It's not gonna work, we have to drop the scene.' I said, 'You can't drop the scene. It's a spectacular performance. You just can't drop it.'

TO: That's stunning. To think that they'd be that close to dropping her performance. You viscerally feel the pain she feels being Holden's wife.

AH: I said to Sidney, 'Let me just move it around.' And Sidney sometimes just had no patience and he said, 'No, no, we're gonna get rid of it, but leave it for now.'

TO: In its original location.

AH: Yes. So, our producer, Dan Melnick, flew in. And we showed the film to him the way the scenes were, with Holden breaking up with his wife before going away with Faye Dunaway and I got a call Monday morning from Howard Gottfried. And he said, 'Alan..." and he sort of sang my name. (Laughs) And I know that when people sing your name that they have something a little embarrassing to say or they want something from you. And he said, 'You know, Dan Melnick came up with this great idea.' And the idea, of course, was the idea to turn the two scenes around, just flip them. And I said, 'You know, Howard, I've been after you to make that change for most of the past week and you guys haven't wanted to do it.' And he said, 'You know, boychick' (Laughs)—which means a little boy in Yiddish—he said, 'It doesn't matter where a good idea comes from.' And when he said that, he's absolutely right. It was another valuable lesson.

TO: And an Academy Award nomination.

AH: You know, I never thought I would get a nomination for that.

TO: Really?

AH: Really. I mean it's not false modesty. I knew it was a good movie.

I figured it would be nominated for best picture, best writer, a couple of performances, but I never thought I'd be nominated because I thought it was so simple. I was finished with my cut in about five days. Sidney cut the 'Mad as hell sequence' himself. And I wanted to make it better, but I felt it was so good that I was just going to leave it the way it was.

TO: It says a lot about you to give credit where it is due.

AH: Sidney watched over me and said, 'I want this and this and this.' And I did it. But at the same time, for the end of the movie, Sidney had shot a lot of stuff. I didn't know what he was reaching for. He came up one day at lunchtime and gave me a bunch of notes that made no sense. I knocked it together in ten minutes and he said, 'Oh. That doesn't make any sense. Do it your way.' And he left. (Laughs) That was a very thrilling movie to work on.

TO: What are some favorite films?

AH: You know, there's a lot. Taxi Driver, Lawrence of Arabia, Cabaret. I think it's just a perfect movie. I always regarded film as a plastic medium, like a piece of wire. And you can bend it and form it. But if you keep bending it back and forth, it's going to break. And that's the same for the strand of a story, too. You can only push the story a certain distance and then it will start pushing back and it's not good then. You just have to stay with the story and trust the material.

PAUL HIRSCH, ACE

Photograph courtesy of the American Cinema Editors and ACE Eddie Awards

LOS ANGELES, CA

Partial Credits: The Mummy, Warcraft: The Beginning, Mission Impossible: Ghost Protocol, Ray,Mission Impossible, Planes, Trains & Automobiles, Ferris Bueller's Day Off, Star Wars: Episode V - The Empire Strikes Back, Star Wars: Episode IV - A New Hope, Carrie.

What diversity! The end of Carrie. The exuberance of Ferris. The propulsion of Star Wars: Episode IV. The hilarity from Planes, Trains, and Automobiles. And on it goes. So generous is Paul's desire to answer—really answer—your questions that while I was interviewing him, he was teaching me.

✂

TO: Paul, you received an Academy Award for Star Wars: Episode IV and an ACE Eddie award for Ray.How did you get started?

PH: After graduating from Columbia, I attended the School of Architecture briefly, but dropped out early in the first year. I got a job as a shipping room guy for an industrial films company in NY called Dynamic Films. I worked as a neg cutter for six months, then segued to a job as an assistant editor at a trailer house assisting a young editor named Chuck Workman. He taught me his approach to cutting trailers, which I used on a trailer for a film entitled Greetings, directed by Brian De Palma. On the strength of that, I was hired to cut his next picture, Hi, Mom! which starred Robert DeNiro. I cut four more pictures for Brian before he recommended me to his pal George Lucas who needed help on Star Wars.

TO: Was that the big break?

PH: Well, each break was big at the time. Getting my first picture; working with and befriending Bernard Herrmann on my second, Sisters; cutting Phantom of the Paradise, which brought me to the attention of the Lucases; Carrie, which was my first studio picture; and of course, Star Wars, which changed my life for good.

TO: How many films did you edit for Brian DePalma?

PH: Eleven, over 31 years. My relationship with Brian was like a film running in reverse: we began as brothers, then became friends, then colleagues, then acquaintances, and now strangers.

TO: You edited Carrie. It certainly scared audiences! Were you surprised at its success?

PH: Hi, Mom! premiered at the Loews State theater on 45thstreet in NY, and the room held about 1,000 seats. I think there were 30 of us there, all of whom had worked on the picture. So that first experience was a bit of a reality check. I thought Sisters would make a splash, with Bernard Herrmann's first American score in many years. I thought Phantom of the Paradise would be big, after all, it was the most any studio had ever paid for a negative pickup deal up to that point. I thought Obsession was a terrific film. Herrmann himself thought it superior to Vertigo, to which it bears a great resemblance. He claimed that Genevieve Bujold's performance was better than Kim Novak's. And I thought Carrie was great, too. By the time it opened, I was in Marin County, working on Star Wars, so I didn't really experience its success. George Lucas, who habitually went to bed early, stayed up to accompany me to the midnight screening of Carrie on Halloween, a gesture which was very touching to me.

TO: The film features multiple split-screens to impart multiple, simultaneous action.

PH: Brian was always enamored of split screens. Brian was determined to have the prom and the destruction of the gym in split screens, and shot it that way, framing the action in one half of the frame or the other. Brian cut it himself, on a multi-headed Moviola. When he showed it to the studio, they freaked out and hated it, so he turned it over to me at that point and told me to do what I could to satisfy the studio. I used full frame shots wherever possible, and the split screens only where it was absolutely necessary, due to the way the original footage had been framed. I think the end result works well.

TO: The audience reaction at the end of the film was quite spectacular—people literally jumped out of their seats.

PH: We screened the picture in the MGM building on 55thSt. in NY. The room had upholstered blue velour seats with reclining backs. Brian and I would sit in the back of the room, and every time we got to the moment of Carrie's hand shooting out of the grave, every seat in the theater would jolt violently backward, as each and every person there would stiffen in fright. We found it hilarious. Brian got the idea for the ending from watching Deliverance. We saw the film together, and Brian, a big admirer of John Boorman, told me he loved the hand coming out of the river at the end, but "I could do that much better." The key to the effectiveness of the scare is the music. I used Albinoni's Adagio for Organ and Strings to lull the audience into thinking the picture was over. Then, at an arrhythmic moment in the music, I cut to the murder cue from Sisters by Bernard Herrmann, which begins with an anvil strike. The sudden, loud metallic sound does the trick. Pino Donaggio faithfully executed the plan in the final score.

TO: The Heist scene from Mission Impossible has high angle shots, slow motion, intensified sounds, lack of identifiable sound, etc. How did all these decisions come about?

PH: The scene in question is when Ethan Hunt, played by Tom Cruise, breaks into the CIA super-secure vault housing the computer terminal containing the NOC list (the Maguffin of the film.) The sequence was "inspired" by the iconic heist at the center of Jules Dassin's Topkapi, during which the thieves lower one of their number by rope from the ceiling of the museum to steal a jeweled dagger from the central exhibit, set in a room where the slightest weight on the floor would set off the alarm. When Dassin saw Mission: Impossible, he asked, "Can they do that?" The silence was a technique Dasin had used in his classic Rififi, in which the heist is pulled off in a twenty or thirty-minute sequence without dialog or music. Brian did storyboard all of his set pieces. He used to do crude drawings himself, which I never found very helpful, because they were a bit hard to decipher, and the key to these sequences, for me at least, had to do with the timing, which is absent from storyboards.

TO: You have worked with many accomplished film composers, such as Bernard Herrmann, John Williams, Georges Delerue, Ennio Morricone, and Pino Donaggio. What did you learn from Bernard Herrmann?

PH: Benny taught me two invaluable lessons. The first is that the best film music is psychologically expressive of the character's interior life, rather than merely descriptive of the action. He described film music as providing the emotional link between the audience and the events on the screen. The second has to do with when not to play music. His choices of when to introduce music in a scene were brilliant. Everyone remembers the famous crop duster scene in North By Northwest. The scene has no music at all until it is virtually over.

TO: Did you think Star Wars would be received so enthusiastically?

PH: No. I certainly liked it. I thought it was great. But no one could have predicted that the picture would become such a cultural phenomenon. In his mind, Star Wars was to be like one of Disney's films, made for children, re-released every seven years for a new generation of kids. "This picture will gross $16 million. That's what every Disney pictures grosses." He was off by a factor of ten, at least during the original release.

TO: Star Wars and The Empire Strikes Back had some startling sound effects. Can you recall some examples where you first saw the addition of sound effects?

PH: I was the last editor hired on Star Wars, and by the time I joined the team, work had been well under way for a while. Ben Burtt had an encyclopedic memory for sound effects and could say that a particular sound effect in a film we would be watching was a pre-1952 Warner Bros gunshot. Ben and George had been working together for months, using a synthesizer to create R2D2's voice, with George specifying the emotion he was hoping to express. He combined several different animal vocals to create Chewbacca's voice, the main component of which was a bear cub, I believe. I remember one of the first scenes I saw was the interior of the sand crawler, where R2 and C3PO are reunited.

TO: During the editing of The Empire Strikes Back film, were you under pressure that may not have existed during Star Wars?

PH: George had decided to finance the film himself, so he was feeling the pressure intensely. Irvin Kershner, the director, had been given a 16-week production schedule, but he soon fell behind, and every passing week, even further behind. We finally finished principal photography after 29 weeks. I did the first cut on a 4 plate Steenbeck (one picture head, one sound head). I am proud that we locked the film one month later, and despite the 13 weeks that we lost from the post-production schedule, we made the deadline without an extension.

TO: Certainly, there was a collective gasp came from audiences who learned of the relationship between Luke and Vader.

PH: The secret was held very closely by George, and I didn't find out until very late. He never revealed to me the identity of the person Yoda was talking about when he said "No, there is another." I found out with everyone else, when I saw Jedi.

TO: The editing of the Twist and Shout segment in Ferris is fantastic.

PH: The choreographer for that sequence was Kenny Ortega, who has directed the High School Musical films. The point of the scene was that Ferris infects all of downtown Chicago with his energy, and the audience can tell the real from the fake. One of the cameramen shooting the crowd noticed a workman on an upper floor of nearby building under construction. The man had stopped to watch the filming on the street and started spontaneously dancing to the music. In other words, what the script intended was actually happening, and at screenings, the instant I cut to that man, the audience would erupt in a roar of appreciation. They could feel the genuineness of the action.

TO: The end credit sequence is noteworthy in that it is among the first examples of using end credits to continue the storyline.

PH: I thought of this in the shower one morning. John and Matthew had been fooling around on the set the day they shot the scene of Ferris's opening monologue to the audience. Matthew walked up to the lens, looked out at the audience, and improvised a number of lines, or John fed them to him, We decided to use "You're still here? It's over. Go home!" That morning, as I am showering, I think to myself, the audience is going to be gone by the time we get to the end of the credits, and nobody is going to see that. Then I remembered the scene of Rooney having to get home on the school bus because his car had been towed. We had cut the scene, despite it being funny, because it stopped the story dead at a point in the film when we needed to keep moving forward. It occurred to me that we could restore the scene at the end of the movie by playing it alongside the credits and get the audience to stay until the very end, when they would then see the tag. At the preview, as soon as credits started to roll, many in the audience got up to leave, as they do, but then started to turn back in the aisles to face the screen as they backed out, and then stopped, to watch the scene.

TO: You've worked with a diverse group of directors. Among them: Brian DePalma, George Lucas, Herbert Ross, John Hughes and Taylor Hackford.

PH: I learned something from every director I worked with. Brian is unparalleled when it comes to moving the camera, and he relies heavily on point-of-view shots. This insight greatly influenced my work, even when working with other directors. Herbert Ross was the best at working with actors. George Lucas is the best when it comes to production design and sound. The worlds he created through the six Star Wars films are unmatched in their originality. Hughes was a writer and his focus was less on filmmaking technique and more on the characters. Taylor is also great with actors, knows how to cover every moment he is going to need in the editing, and has the patience to get all the angles.

TO: You have edited enormously successful films that are being watched from generation to generation.

PH: My most gratifying films are the ones that connected with the greatest number of people. The whole point of what we do is communication, and to be involved in a project that touches millions of lives is what it is all about.

TO: What films and editors do you admire?

PH: I was always a big fan of Alan Parker's editor, Gerry Hambling. All his films have a great, graceful style, as well as terrific pace. I am very proud of the work of the cohort alongside whom I worked throughout my career. Fellow New Yorkers like Walter Murch, Richard Marks, Jerry Greenberg, Lynzee Klingman, Robert Dalva, the aforementioned Thelma Schoonmaker as well as Michael Kahn, Billy Weber, Mark Goldblatt, and a bit younger editors like Chris Lebenzon, Joe Hutshing, and David Brenner. I was thrilled to meet Cecile Decugis who edited Godard's Breathless, and broke new ground with her jump cuts. Donn Cambern, who cut, among other well-known films, Easy Rider. The great thing about editing is that it is an international language, and you can see stylistic innovations from American editors picked up in foreign films, and vice versa. As we discover new ways to tell stories, these innovations become standard means of communicating, and part of a gradual and global evolution in the language of cinema.

CHRIS INNIS, ACE

Chris Innis and Bob Murawski
Photograph courtesy of the American Cinema Editors and ACE Eddie Awards

LOS ANGELES, CA

Partial Credits: The Black Tulip, The Hurt Locker, The Boy with The X-Ray Eyes. As Assistant Editor: Spiderman 3, G.I. Jane, The Quick and The Dead. As Apprentice Editor: Indecent Proposal, J.F.K.

Listening to Chris describe the way that she and Bob Murawski approached the editing of The Hurt Locker was fascinating—the concept of nothing happening to actually create tension. Wonderfully articulate and to read how she describes Oscar night shows that not only do we have a brilliant editor here, but—perhaps—there's a writing Oscar in her future!

TO: Chris, how did you get your start in the industry?

CI: From the age of fifteen, I started working as an usher and concession salesperson in several San Diego movie theaters. There were a lot of fringe benefits – one of which was being able to watch a lot of free movies. I moved to the Bay Area where I attended U.C. Berkeley, majoring in film studies. Director David Rathod was cutting his first independent film and brought me on as a part time assistant editor on the indie film, West is West. He was cutting 35mm film on a flatbed, and that was where I learned the basics of how a film cutting room operates. I fell in love with the works of the "rule-breakers," filmmakers such as Luis Bunuel, Michelangelo Antonioni, Roman Polanski, and especially Federico Fellini.

I graduated from U.C. Berkeley with a Bachelor of Arts in film studies and then moved to Los Angeles to attend California Institute of the Arts (CalArts) to finish my Master of Fine Arts in filmmaking. While at

CalArts, I worked as a production coordinator on the first season of the hit ABC series "America's Funniest Home Videos." After that, I worked as an apprentice editor on

JFK alongside film editors Joe Hutshing and Pietro Scalia. I would work during the day on JFK and then drive a half hour from Santa Monica to CalArts in Valencia and labor until 3 or 4 in the morning editing my own thesis film. I would grab a bowl of soup at an all-night diner, go back home and sleep for a couple hours and then get up and do the whole thing over again.

I continued to assist Pietro Scalia and Joe Hutshing. Pietro and I were a team for almost six years on projects such as the pilot of American Gothic, and Ridley Scott's G.I. Jane which we edited in London at Shepperton Studios. At one point I also assisted Dann Cahn Sr., the editor of the successful hit series, I Love Lucy, and mentor to Steven Spielberg's editor, Michael Kahn. I learned a lot of tricks and techniques by looking over these master editors' shoulders.

Pietro Scalia called and said he had been offered the job as editor on The Quick and the Dead and asked if I wanted to assist. I was initially hired as the 2nd assistant editor, but during production I was promoted to first assistant editor. It was a full year-and-a-half in post-production hell, with the studio tinkering and previewing the movie to death. During that time, I learned a lot from director Sam Raimi.

Sam then hired me for my first shot as picture editor on the TV series American Gothic, which he was executive producing. It's also where I met my husband, Bob Murawski. Bob and I became friends and co-workers then and about a year later, when we weren't working together, we started dating.

TO: JFK must have been a very interesting experience given the subject matter, the amount of footage, and the use of videotape editing.

CI: I have fond memories of working on JFK as an apprentice/assistant editor. JFK was very ambitious in its scope, with its use of images from multiple sources, and Oliver Stone had a great editing team to manage the creativity and scope of the project. It was a perfect storm of talent on that film – the right people, the right time, the right director, the right film. Sometimes that just happens – all the chips are in a row. It's like a great rock band making a great album. Oliver Stone is a character – a smart and misunderstood film director. He is part macho, part intellectual over-thinker, part caveman and part devious little boy – a bigger than life personality.

Oliver would frequently walk into my room and he would nearly always have a famous person in tow, and maybe a few others chasing after him. There were people measuring him for suits, or burnt-out Vietnam Vets pitching projects, or a "Doctor Feel-Good" chasing him with a long needle – a B12 vitamin shot, or strange Italian spray paint artists trying to make him custom leather jackets. You never knew what it would be. Each time, Oliver would ask me (as if it was the first time he was asking) the same question he always asked in front of his guests, "Just exactly *how* much footage do we have?" and I would always have to respond the obligatory, "Over a million feet, Oliver." He would smile mischievously. There was probably more footage than that, if you count the hours and hours of stock and archival footage.

It was a daunting film for everyone. I was pulling double duty, toiling at nights at film school editing my own thesis film. I got no sleep, but neither did the others. The film was predominantly edited on ¾" tape decks, augmented by 35mm film conformation. The editors would cut in a linear fashion on offline ¾" decks. The tapes would then be hand conformed (eye matched) to a 35mm film print. So the film cut was always just behind the offline ¾" picture cut. But that was all in a linear world, long before the Avid, so if there were major changes it was a real challenge for everybody. There was also a secondary team of yet another ten to twelve assistant editors in another room, all conforming the dupe picture and making change notes for the sound editors. It was a massive project from an editorial standpoint. I've labored on a lot of major films since then, and none have held a candle to how many people were employed in post-production and how massive and complicated that project was, because it was before non-linear computer systems had been universally implemented. The editors had experimented with the EditDroid on the previous Stone film, and it had been so problematic with cuts being off by frames here and there, that they decided to ditch it. The 3/4" offline editing deck system also had its drawbacks, especially when it came to conforming sound.

Part of my job was to sit next to the editors and watch them cutting on ¾" and then fine tuning the cut on 35mm Kem flatbeds. My job was largely to run and locate 35mm film trims for them, as well as to reconstitute and manage all those dailies and small film trims in the library. There were four editors counting the two main editors and the associate and additional editor, so there was a lot of running from room-to-room. It was the beginning of the end of the film era, of cutting on film. I learned a lot by watching and talking with the editors about their choices during that film. Sure, I had previously learned how to edit on my own, making shorts and attending film school – but nothing beats learning the tips, nips and tucks from Academy Award winning professional editors.

One of the things that I like best about the film JFK was that it was self-reflexive of how editing can be used to manipulate an audience. Within the film there is a news documentary that has jump cuts and there are "missing frames" out of the famous Zapruder super-8 film as well. So the jump cuts in JFK are totally an ingrained component of the concept and methodology of the film, as a piece of the conspiracy, and not just used as a "lazy" filmmaking choice the way jump cuts are used in many films today. With the jump cuts the editors and director Oliver Stone are saying to the audience, "Something is missing. Something is being left out. Why is this being manipulated? Ask questions. Don't just believe the cover story." It's an acknowledgement of the power of editing itself. With documentaries and news segments, someone – an editor, a producer, or a director – is picking and choosing what you get to see or not see on the news, trying to shape your opinion of reality. This is what is ingenious about the film JFK. Not that it is telling who shot Kennedy, because that may never be known or understood. Questioning the media and its methods is healthy in a democracy that frequently is so "free" that it delivers us a non-relenting barrage of info-pinions which shape how we digest and respond to historical events. It's up to the all of us to fill in the gaps and to question historical accounts when the stakes are so high.

Photograph courtesy the American Cinema Editors and ACE Eddie Awards

TO: How did you become involved with "The Hurt Locker"?

CI: My now husband, Bob Murawski, was approached to cut The Hurt Locker but he was still on Spiderman 3 and couldn't take the job. They came back to him and said, "What if someone else starts editing the picture in Jordan and then you come on later?" So he and I discussed it and we decided that we would do it as a team—that I would start it and he would come on later. The production had already started filming and the exposed film was already piling up. I was willing and able to go. It was a case of being "at the right place at the right time" but then having the ability, the experience, the preparation to do something about it.

Amman, Jordan turned out to be a great place and I enjoyed it. It was interesting being a woman head of a department working on an American film being shot in a Middle Eastern country – that doesn't happen every day. We were only the second or third film that had ever shot in Jordan, the first being Lawrence of Arabia (and that was filmed way back in the 1960s). I was on location in Jordan for a total of nine weeks. Bob later joined us when we got back to Los Angeles. We then both finished the picture together, as a team, for the following final eight months or so until everybody was happy with it and the picture was locked.

TO: I recall first seeing The Hurt Locker on an overnight flight from Australia to the U.S. I thought, 'This is the film that is going to win Best Editing' this year.

CI: Bob and I had decided in advance how we would approach the editing on The Hurt Locker. We knew that the director, Kathryn Bigelow, and the cinematographer, Barry Ackroyd, were going for that shaky, handheld, docu look popular in dogma and Paul Greengrass films. We felt like that style had been pretty much played out from an editing standpoint, so we secretly decided to go in the opposite direction a "yin" to their "yang," to give the film a formal balance and to make sure the audience didn't need to be issued vomit bags to deal with motion sickness. We decided to take their informal docu style raw footage (almost 200 hours of it, or a 100:1 shooting ratio, more than Apocalypse Now) and turn it into something a little cleaner, more focused from a suspense, story and character point of view.

If I had to choose, I would say that my favorite scenes were the ones where the characters get into a kind of "Bermuda triangle" of existential tension, which is analogous for the feeling we get when editing, that sensation of intense concentration when your mind and your hands have to be perfectly coordinated. In the case of the bomb technicians, this is life or death. I think the analogy of "what wire do I cut?" can be made to both the editing on this film and the dismantling of bomb threats depicted in it. That's why I love the Italian poster of the movie. It is a big tangle of red wires with the quote "Cut the red one." We had so much footage we could have made it into almost anything. Cut the red one? *Which* red one?

With 200 hours of raw dailies for "The Hurt Locker," by cutting out 198 of them, we cut out a lot of information, tons of dialogue, and any scenes that didn't propel the tension and story forward, all to narrow the film down to its essence.

Our approach was formal in that we were very aware that we were giving information to the audience or withholding it, and we had to do it in just the right way to make the audience think a bomb was going to go off or not. There was a lot of "negative action" which is counterintuitive to Hollywood filmmaking and pacing. It's when nothing happens and nothing is going to happen. The challenge was to make "nothing happening" seem tense and suspenseful as if something could happen at any time. While formal in concept, we still kept the editing flowy, poetic, character-based, realistic and dynamic, trying to give the audience the feeling that they were there experiencing war right along with the characters.

We also allowed the audience a certain freedom of interpretation that is rare in most films, through the power of juxtaposition. We cut dialogue that was too "on the money" and instead we relied more heavily on images and sounds to tell the story. People will draw their own conclusions as to what the images mean. We used point and counterpoint to keep all the subplots and characters present and conflicting juxtapositions to break up the rhythm. If you expected the guys to ride off into a beautiful sunset, we would instead cut to something more disturbing. If you expected something awful to happen, we would break it up with an improvised piece of humor or with a beauty shot. Giving the audience leads and false leads, was the way we kept the audience clenched to their arm rests.

TO: Avatar, District 9, Inglorious Basterds, Precious, and The Hurt Locker were all nominated. What was it like to hear your names announced?

CI: It meant a lot to have been nominated alongside Sally Menke, whose editing we had admired on Pulp Fiction and other Quentin Tarantino films. I feel fortunate that we got a chance to get to know her and hang out with her. We were just becoming friends when that sad and tragic accident happened up at Griffith Park where she lost her life, just a few months after the Oscars. It's a loss for everyone, for Quentin Tarantino and Sally's friends and family, and for film audiences.

When people ask what winning an Oscar was like, I tell them that it's one of the few experiences in life that I don't think could be easily recreated in a narrative film. It's just so big, so bizarre and so surreal. They name the nominees and show clips. Your heart is beating through your chest so hard you think it is going to rip a hole through it; it's the only sound you hear. You wipe the sweat from your palms. Then your name is called! You get up there. You have about twenty seconds, so you try to spit out a coherent sentence or two. You look out into the audience and the person who catches your eyes is Matt Damon – you don't know why but that's who it is – and you are thinking that he is thinking about when he won. You go back stage and it is a circus. People are pouring champagne out of gargantuan magna bottles, you are signing posters, and famous people are nodding and congratulating you. Sean Penn walks by, then Tim Robbins, on their way to present more awards. Tarantino bum rushes us and gives us big hugs, ever the good sport. Then we have to give another speech, to the online backstage camera and I've left my cheat sheet in my purse back at the seat. We are pushed into a room with a wall of photographers.

"Stand here," "Stand there!" "Look here," "Over here." Flash! Pop! Flash! We are husband and wife so they yell, "Make your Oscars kiss! Make your Oscars kiss!"

Then we are lead away from the lines through Wolfgang Puck's back kitchen, as all the workers congratulate us – it's like a long Steadicam shot in a Scorsese film. We pass heads of lettuce and pots and pans and steaming food and waiters bringing delicacies out on trays, and then we are led into the grand Governor's Ballroom which is decorated like a dream.

You ask yourself – did all of that really happen? Yes, it did! Your bathtub dreams of speeches don't even come close to what it feels like. It is rewarding to be acknowledged as the best, especially when it hasn't happened overnight – when you have spent so many years in film school, more than a decade working your way up, for other talented editors who you have also watched win these awards, as well as after having been put through the ringer on a very difficult indie film shot in the Middle East during a war.

TO: What have you learned during your career that wasn't so apparent when you started in the industry?

CI: I've learned that you can fight for the films you work on, for what you believe in, but you can't fight or change the system. It's a system that tends to be managed by people who often take advantage of the fact that they are running it, with little or no regard for the working guy or gal making the "product." But the fact is that it's a feast or famine world, especially in Hollywood. You have producers living in $20 million-dollar mansions in Beverly Hills and assistants scrambling to pay for their laundry at a coin op on East Sunset Boulevard. It's been like this for decades and the only thing that keeps it going, is the big dream – the hope for that kid that they can study films, work hard, show some talent and maybe get lucky one day and win an Oscar.

The cookie jar is also shrinking, as revenues from ancillary markets are flattening to almost zero—with bootlegging, downloading and free streaming becoming so common and taking away precious profit margins. If content is all free, then nobody can get paid and there is no incentive for artists to participate. If producers don't get paid, they can't hire anybody else. Film audiences need to know that downloading movies for free off of illegal web sites doesn't just hurt corporations, but that it hurts the artists and filmmakers who they love. They need to know that they have to pay for content for there to continue to be a consistent pipeline of movies. If they love films, it may just be their own future jobs that they are saving.

MICHAEL KAHN, ACE

Photograph courtesy of the American Cinema Editors and ACE Eddie Awards

LOS ANGELES, CALIFORNIA

Partial Credits: The Post, Ready Player One, The BFG, Bridge of Spies, Lincoln, War Horse, Munich, Minority Report, Saving Private Ryan, Schindler's List, Jurassic Park, Raiders of the Lost Ark, Close Encounters of the Third Kind.

Editors kept saying I wouldn't get Michael to agree to an interview. He'd be too busy, doesn't like doing interviews. But he answered straightaway and it's interesting that when he's done with a film, he's done. No looking back. The next film comes and it's all brand new. Michael: "I'm just a kid from Brooklyn!" A kid who has certainly left his mark on Hollywood.

TO: Michael, how did you get your start in the motion picture industry?

MK: I was working for an advertising agency in New York called the Milton Biow Company. And I was just a kid in the film department who ran the projection room for the executives. One of the executives liked me and told me I should come out to the west coast. I met with Desilu Productions, because advertisers like Phillip Morris sponsored I Love Lucy. And I wound up as a young apprentice in the editorial office at Desilu.

TO: You worked on Hogan's Heroes.

MK: That's right. I was doing Hogan's Heroes and one of the writers liked me very much and he recommended me to George C. Scott. He was going to act in and direct his first feature.

TO: Okay. That was Rage in 1972.

MK: Right. Before that it was all television. And after that, it was all features. I worked six to eight years in television and it was the greatest experience for me because I learned everything and that made me ready for the feature field. You only had three or four days per episode and I did about 140 episodes of Hogan's and it was on for six years. People got to know me a little more. And eventually I was asked to go over and meet a guy named Steven Spielberg.

TO: And?

MK: And I had a very nice conversation with him that lasted about five minutes. And then I got a call a while later to meet him at Devils Tower in Wyoming.

TO: And this was for Close Encounters of the Third Kind.

MK: Yes.

With Steven Spielberg during Close Encounters of the Third Kind
Photograph courtesy the American Cinema Editors and ACE Eddie Awards

TO: A 30-plus year relationship was over a five-minute conversation?

MK: Yeah, we just talked and he probably spoke to every editor in town. Maybe he was tired of talking to people! (Both laugh)

TO: What do you think he learned in those five minutes that had him entrust his next film to you?

MK: You know something? I don't know. All I know is that I felt comfortable with him. He asked me an interesting question.

TO: Which was?

MK: He said to me, 'Are you very good at what you do? Are you a good editor?'

TO: (Both laugh) How did you answer that?

MK: I told him that all I know is that everyone who hires me wants me back.

TO: Great answer!

MK: It was just a really short conversation. Sometimes there's a chemistry that happens between director and editor. Even today, Steven and I are very comfortable with each other and it doesn't seem like we've been working together that long. It's always new and fresh each time we work. It's quite exciting and he's quite a visionary. Why he liked me I don't know. I'm a boy from Brooklyn! I think television made me ready for him.

TO: In what way?

MK: It gave me the mechanics and the creativity needed to fulfill what's in the director's mind's eye. Take Hogan's Heroes. Almost every show, you had a new director. So you learned how to work with all these different kinds of directors. They shoot differently. They react differently. And by the time I got to Steven, I was very well versed on how film worked.

TO: It must be rewarding to know how many people have been affected and entertained by the films you've edited.

MK: I think it's very nice that people feel that way. People may have a higher opinion of me than is deserved.

TO: Do you find yourself affected by these films as you're editing them?

MK: Oh, very much so. My God, if you don't get into the spirit of the film, I don't know how you can edit it. On Schindler's List, that took a lot out of me. It was just emotionally draining. We were right in Poland. We went to the camps. And you look down at the streets and you realize the Jews that were walking there. And we were there—on the same spot. So, it really works on your emotions. And, of course, when I'm working on a film, I'm in all the way. I put all my feelings into it.

TO: It's the reason you're able to keep doing what you're doing.

MK: There's a passion to it. An excitement to it. I don't usually get too involved with the films after they're edited. I don't carry the challenges of the films with me. When I start a new film, it's like the first time I'm doing a film.

TO: That sounds impossible coming from someone who has done so many films as you have and so many huge films.

MK: But that's what I do. I come in fresh with each new film and it's very exciting that way. I want to be completely free to give my passion over to that film.

TO: What have you learned during the course of your career that you feel students should be aware of?

MK: It's not the techniques, but it's the relationships and the mental outlook that you have to have with different directors.

TO: You edited Saving Private Ryan on a Moviola. Do you ever find yourself overwhelmed with the amount of material you get?

MK: It doesn't matter how much film comes in. And it doesn't matter what modality you're working in—whether it's an Avid or a Moviola. It's one cut at a time, one piece of film at a time. You look at it. You study it. I think about the totality of everything. To use a big word—the macrocosmic view! (Both laugh) The only reality when I'm cutting a scene is how much footage I have for it and it's only those pieces of film.

TO: Never been overwhelmed with all the footage and multiple cameras?

MK: No, no! Multiple cameras are wonderful! It's great! I don't have to worry about matches. There are a lot of benefits. And of course, you have to remember that editors don't work alone. You work with the director and the director has ideas about what pieces and performances should be used.

TO: Is it difficult to avoid using all the coverage that may exist?

MK: Well, that's a choice the editor has to make. If one piece of film works better than using all the different coverage, that's a decision the editor has to make. Just because there is a lot of coverage doesn't mean you have to use it all. And, again, I have to stress that you are working with the director—you are not alone. You're a team. You collaborate. A lot of editors think we make the film. But we don't make the film.

TO: You play a role in the filmmaking process.

MK: Right. And I'm proud to be a film editor. I enjoy it and I love to be the right arm to a director. I've always been very comfortable with editing. There is something in my head that enables me to take various pieces of film and adjust them in a certain order. I just feel comfortable that the order feels right—this order feels better than that order.

TO: Are there scenes you've edited that stand out for you in your work?

MK: Oh, I can't single anything out. I have an excellent memory for footage and that's why I have to leave the film behind. Because I remember every little thing that happened in that scene. Why we did it this way. Why we did it that way. I have a good memory, but Steven has a better memory! So, I always have to be prepared to answer his questions.

TO: You grew up in New York. Did you go to the movies a lot?

MK: I lived in the movies! And you know something? The best thing students who are coming up through colleges can do is to see as many movies as they can. Good ones. Bad ones. If they see bad ones, they can think about how they'd fix it. The best way that editors are going to make something work is to edit. They have to get comfortable with changes in angles. Why you change an angle. You don't just edit a scene without a point of view on the scene. That's how you help a director.

TO: What films were they showing?

MK: I was a young kid and I loved the Charlie Chan movies. I loved the Sherlock Holmes movies. I loved They Died With Their Boots On. The Searchers. Classic films. I'd go every weekend. Whoever thought I'd be in Hollywood? I mean I was from Sheepshead Bay in Brooklyn!

TO: Are there films you edited that you feel audiences should revisit?

MK: There's one film I did that was based on a famous book. It was called, The Spook Who Sat By The Door.

TO: You did that in 1973 after Rage.

MK: Right. They didn't have an editor.

TO: Ah… Ivan Dixon directed that.

MK: That's right. And I knew Ivan because of Hogan's Heroes.

TO: Were you surprised at your first Academy Award nomination and your first win?

MK: Oh, absolutely. I was scared to death!

TO: Really?

MK: The first time I got nominated was for Close Encounters. And there are billions of people on TV. And I'm not used to talking in front of people. And I was so relieved when Star Wars won instead of us because I didn't have to get on the stage! (Laughs)

TO: But four years later you won for Raiders of the Lost Ark.

MK: The second time, I had to face the music! All the nominated editors were sitting together in the same row. And it's sort of corny, but we were all sort of new and we were holding hands. And they mentioned my name and all I knew from then on out was that I walked up and I was scared to death.

TO: Really?

MK: Yeah, I walked up on the stage and I saw all these people who were looking at me. And I was shaking like a leaf.

TO: Did that happen on the next one?

MK: Every time I went up since, I was shaking like a leaf.

TO: Still?

MK: Yes, because you're in front of billions of people!

TO: What editors do you admire?

MK: Ralph Winters. I really liked him. He was terrific. He was such a gentleman. In those days, all the editors wore suits and ties. They wouldn't spend time with the assistants. There was a whole dichotomy there. It was a very different culture than today. Editors were respected and they were really important people. And the other editor I really liked did The Sound of Music.

TO: That's William Reynolds.

MK: Bill Reynolds. Oh, he was so good. He was such a smooth editor. He wasn't afraid of all the footage and neither was Ralph Winters. Of course, those days, directing was different.

TO: In what way?

MK: Directors would shoot long takes and then they'd move the camera and the actors and you just had less physical editing in the early days. So, when they made a cut, it was a proper cut and it was right for those days. And then television came in and you got younger directors who wanted a lot of coverage so that they could change the performance and make changes in pace and rhythm. Today it's much more difficult.

TO: How so?

MK: Well, today there are some films that couldn't be accomplished without the editor. The editor is now in a much more important position than before.

TO: Are there films that you find yourself watching if they're on?

MK: Oh, I love the Godfather films. I could watch them anytime.

TO: You've had an incredible career and I wish you continued success.

MK: When I first came into the business, I didn't know a thing. But by osmosis, it just sort of worked out. There were editors who were good to me and gave me scenes to cut and to try things. And, all of a sudden, you discover you have a talent for something.

LYNZEE KLINGMAN, ACE

Photo courtesy of Lynzee Klingman

LOS ANGELES, CA

Partial Credits: Hearts and Minds, One Flew Over the Cuckoo's Nest, Hair, True Confessions, Baby Boom, The War of the Roses, Little Man Tate, A River Runs Through It, Outbreak, Matilda, City of Angels, Man on The Moon, Ali.

Lynzee has an infectious enthusiasm that instantly conveys the energy that she brings to films. She didn't even know what a film editor did! She just 'kept pounding the pavement' until she got hired. She's an absolute delight and the love she has for the characters in the films is so evident when you speak with her. A true gem.

✂

TO: Lynzee, you are an Academy Award and Eddie nominee, and a BAFTA recipient for Best Editing. How did you get your start?

LK: I was a history major in college at Columbia and the day before I was going to graduate I met someone at a party who was a film editor. And I said, 'You mean you work in film and you make money?' I had no idea what a film editor did.

TO: Just like that.

LK: Yes, just like that. I looked in the yellow pages in New York. Sometimes I would just go knock on doors even though that was hard for me, because I was terrified. All the editors I came across were men and they didn't want to hire women because they'd have to watch their language and women couldn't carry a lot of film cans! The more they told me that, the more I wanted to do it!

TO: Okay, what happened next?

LK: I just kept pounding the pavement and I finally found someone who wanted to hire a girl to cut negative, read soundtracks, and answer the phone. I didn't know anything—like even what a film splice meant!

TO: By 1968, you were cutting the Vietnam War documentary, The Year of the Pig.

LK: My fantasy about getting into film was ultimately to work on documentaries like the Russian Revolution or The New Deal. I had seen the brilliant "Point of Order", which was one of the greatest documentaries ever. That director, Emile de Antonio, was looking for someone who would work long hours for very little money because they were passionate about ending the war in Vietnam. That was me! I had been very much against the war so it was natural match.

TO: Were you under any political pressure while you were editing?

LK: Sure. Of course. The F.B.I. used to come around all the time. They would wear suits and had crew cuts and told me they were working on a student newspaper at some college in New Jersey. Yeah, sure! They came often. By the way, they knew I knew they were FBI and I knew they knew; we all just played along…

TO: Really?

LK: Yes, of course. They wanted to know how we had gotten the North Vietnamese footage and I would tell them the truth— that this North Vietnamese footage was sent from, say, Sweden, or Paris, etc. It was really a very divisive time in America and we hoped that the film would be helpful in educating the American public and that would ultimately stop the war; it certainly did not!

TO: You worked on different films until you worked on the Academy Award winning best documentary, Hearts and Minds which was released in 1974.

LK: I worked on films about the civil rights movement, a TV version of the Army-McCarthy hearings and I even did multimedia projects with multiple screens.

TO: I want to take you back to April 8th, 1975 and the Academy Awards. And the film was Hearts and Minds. Michael Moore rates it as the best documentary ever made. Did you ever have any idea as to what was going to happen with this film while you were editing it?

LK: You always hope, and sometimes even secretly believe, that any film you work on will win an Academy Award! But on Hearts and Minds, we were in adeeper fantasy: we hoped it would helpto end the war—Ha! —or, more realistically at least, we hoped the film might have an impact on public discussions leading to its end. And that crazy thinking gave us a sense ofmission. It's those dreams that help your head at ten o'clock at night when you are still in the cutting room, exhausted, re-cutting a sequence you have reworked a thousand times trying to make it really sing.My friend Susan Martin was co-editor on the film and Heartsand Minds is how sadly relevant it still is today.

TO: Tough footage to watch?

LK: Oh, it was just heartbreaking to witness,day after day, what my country was doing to this small nation so many thousands of miles away. So many of the people in the film touched me deeply and they are still in my head—like the Vietnamese carpenter who was making coffins for little children—lots of them. The bereaved father yelling at Richard Nixon for killing his little girl and his wife. The Medal of Honor veterans of the war angrily dropping their medals into a garbage can in NYC's Central Park. And, by the way, John Kerry was one of them.

TO: The film includes two of the most famous pieces of media. The picture of the young girl whose skin is falling off from the napalm blast and the point-blank execution of the kneeling Viet Cong captive. Audiences had never seen this before.

LK: Those two incidents were completely shocking—very compelling. They were shot by news cameramen who were so courageously documenting the war. They knew it was important to film this stuff—someone had to—and show it to U.S. citizens. The footage was shot by Peter Davis and his crew. They shot for a year and then we spent a year cutting it.

TO: The Westmoreland comments are unbelievable and there were three takes of it. He said, "The Oriental doesn't put the same high price on life as does a Westerner. Life is plentiful. Life is cheap in the Orient."

LK: Yes, shocking and racist. Westmoreland was the Commanding General of the U.S.

Armed Forces in Vietnam and that was what he said; It was clearly what he believed.

TO: Roger Ebert wrote that he felt he was being manipulated because of the juxtaposition of images but that what you were seeing was still the truth.

LK: He was absolutely right—that cut was a choice. By choosing where to point the camera, what to film, and if and where you use it in a film, you are making a political choice. But, in fact, what Westmoreland said—that the Oriental has less regard for human life than the Westerner— that was not taken out of any context. In fact, he repeated it because the camera ran out of film the first time he said it and so, when the camera was reloaded, he went back and said it again. Unbelievably, the camera somehow malfunctioned a second time and he said it a third time—he wanted to be absolutely crystal clear! What you see is the third and final take. This is what he wanted the American public to know! And yes, it was shocking to then cut to a hysterically crying mother and child at a Vietnamese soldier's funeral, but that is what went on and so it is the truth. We had a lot of discussions and thought about morals and morality and whether it was fair to juxtapose that child crying with Westmoreland, but, finally, we did that to make that shocking statement have the most impact.

TO: When you wanted to break into Hollywood features, were you typecast because of all the documentary work?

LK: Absolutely! People didn't want to hire me because they didn't understand that documentaries were also storytelling.

TO: One Flew Over The Cuckoo's Nest. How did that come about?

LK: I got a job interview on the film and I knew Richard Chew from working in San Francisco and I had seen Milos Forman's films and was just so thrilled to meet him. I knew at the time that I was very lucky. I was working with a director who I idolized and Richard and ultimately Shelly Khan. I was grateful, and I was happy.

TO: Did you have a special feeling about the film while you were editing it?

LK: Yes, I loved the book and I knew the film had everything going for it - the script, director, and Jack Nicholson as McMurphy so, yes, I felt it was going to be very special. I didn't know it was going to hit the way it did. But, yes, I was thrilled with it. That film is an editor's dream.

TO: In what way?

LK: There was so much wonderful footage to work with. Milos loved the editing process and felt the cutting room was where the film was made. He would cover from every angle and in many different ways so that there are endless possibilities to explore. He was completely involved in the editing of the film, loved to try everything, and was open to his editor's ideas. He's talented and charming and was easily the most influential person onmy editing. Even today, going over a cut, I hear his voice in my head.

TO: How did you go about dividing up the scenes?

LK: We each had our own scenes, but Richard was the first editor and Milos would mostly hang out with him.My first assignment was to cut the improv stuff with the doctors, which really was kind of like a documentary.

TO: That material is hilarious.

LK: Oh, I was completely charmed by the footage, just delighted with it. I was so thrilled that I would pinch myself to make sure it was true!

TO: The War of the Roses is a dark comedy and when dark comedies are done properly, the audience often finds itself never knowing whether to laugh or to gasp. Did you ever think it went too far?

LK:That was the point. These are two not particularly likable but very compelling people in a fascinating and ever escalating tango of one upmanship. Michael Douglas was absolutely brilliant playing a completely obsessive and obnoxious guy who is trying to get back at his wife who doesn't want to be married to him anymore and that is something he can't believe. Itis very disturbing but I thought it was ironic and mischievous. And grimlyhilarious!

TO: You've edited films concerning very public figures: Jimmy Hoffa, Andy Kaufman, and Muhammad Ali.

LK: Man on the Moon is a very interesting film because the audience only knew Andy Kaufman's life through his various personalities. I think that's what makes his illness all the moreprofound when you see it on-screen. At the same time, the last sequence where Tony Clifton appears and you see Zmuda, now you're not so sure if he's having the last laugh on you or not. It's really a marvelous blend of acting and directing. Here is a crazy thing about me working on Man in the Moon. I knew Andy because he was close friends with both of my brothers. They were all crazy creative and talented guys, even in third grade. My brother Moogy could never believe that Andy died. He went to the funeral and to the tenth anniversary of his death convinced that Andy would show up; Moog kept thinking it was one of his bits.

TO: That's pretty remarkable. I really like Hoffa and I think it should have done better than it did with audiences.

LK: One thing that happened on Hoffa was that we were not aware of how few people knew who Hoffa was. Everyone in our generation had certainly followed his dramas but we never realized that most younger people had never learned about the Teamsters and the labor movement. That was a problem for us because we didn't have previews on that film so we didn't know. We probably should have intercut some newsreel footage so people would know why he became so legendary. He was a really tough combative guy who negotiated salaries for the Teamsters that were way above what people who did equivalent work got. There simply wasn't any explanation of that in the film.

TO: Ali is a very interesting film. How did that come about?

LK: Well, first of all, the subject was just irresistible and the footage was fantastic. It was fun for me in so many different ways.

TO: How so?

LK: Well, first of all, of course Muhammad Ali was a major hero of the 20th Century, certainly to me and my generation—a great man whose life story was unbelievably rich, touching so many of the major issues, events and movements of his time. And in the film, he seemed to inhabit Will Smith—who played Ali— it was a stunning performance and it was exciting because Michael Mann's vision and style are quite unique. In the scene where Martin Luther King has been shot, there was a montage of people in the street. And we were going over it and Michaelgot a phone call. When he got off the phone, we looked again at the sequence and he said, 'What did you do?' So, I said, 'I added a few frames to the outgoing cut to smooth it out'. It turns out he had no interest in smooth cutting. He liked it more jarring. That's his style. I got it!

TO: You were an additional editor onStarting Over with Burt Reynolds and Jill Clayburgh. It's really funny.

LK: Both Jill and Candice Bergen were nominated for Academy Awards.

TO: There's an unbelievably funny scene in that movie where Candice Bergen sings to Burt Reynolds and the look on his face is really indescribable.

LK: You know they had taken that scene out. And, when I first came on the film, I looked through earlier versions of the film and there was that scene! Candice was so adorable singing that song with all her heart and completely off key and so terrible that it was hilarious. I was completely captivated and so I showed it to Alan Pakula and he put it back in and she was nominated for an Academy Award for Supporting Actress. I believe it was because of that scene!

TO: And after all these years, that song "Better than ever" is still in my head.

LK: Mine too!

TO: You made the transition from film to digital nonlinear on Outbreak.

LK: I don't see any downside to digital; it's all good! With film, you needed a lot of knowledge and dexterity; it was very physical and very complicated. But, while you were doing all this, it is true that you were doing a lot of thinking and planning.

TO: There are conscious decisions being made during that process.

LK: Absolutely. Ultimately, every cut is a conscious decision even when you made it unconsciously! There is a reason you decided to start with this particular shot and then cut to that one. And so, finally, there is a reason for every frame you cut on and to. It's surprising to some people but there's a reason for everything you see and hear on the screen.

TO: What films do you really like?

LK: Dog Day Afternoon. It's brilliantly edited and brilliantly put together. I never pass by a Cary Grant / Hitchcock movie, Jaws, Goodfellas, Breathless, The Godfather, The Conversation, The Fifth Element. Everything by Milos Forman, Fellini, William Wyler.

SYLVIE LANDRA

Photo courtesy of Sylvie Landra

PARIS, FRANCE

Partial Credits: Lucky Day, Cézanne et Moi, It Happened in Saint-Tropez, The Dandelions, Hideaways, Secrets of State, Orchestra Seats, Viva Cuba, A Sound of Thunder, Catwoman, The Dancer, The Messenger: The Story of Joan of Arc, The Fifth Element, Léon: The Professional.

I was in the audience in Paris during the cast premiere for Léon—The Professional. Action, suspense, comedy, all blended so well by the cast and director, but brought together by the marvelous editor, Sylvie Landra. She says, "I am still like a kid in the editing room." A "kid" whose work shows the wisdom of a seasoned professional.

✂

TO: Sylvie, you are a four-time César nominee, a member ACE and AMPAS. How did you get your start in the film business?

SL: I got a job in a small TV studio and I learned the trade. Writing short scripts to camera operating, sound operator… One day, I sat down in the editing room and cut my first piece, which was a play and I loved it. I stuck with editing and since then I haven't done anything else! I started to do a lot of documentaries. Documentaries teach you how to build a story out of the footage. It teaches you also to be instinctive. Editing is a lot about instinct.

TO: You have to find the story.

SL: Exactly and track down unscripted emotions to steal moments creating a story, a journey to invite people to follow. I started cutting promos, commercials and short films. Technically I was in a very good position because I started with video and then I went to film and then I went to nonlinear with Avid.

TO: How did you break into features?

SL: I met Luc Besson while I was doing commercials. One day, he asked me if I'd cut his next movie. And that was my golden opportunity and the big break. He left a message on my answering machine and I first thought it was a joke a friend was doing to me! Of course I said yes! No one had used digital nonlinear in Europe before on a feature film.

TO: You were using the Film Composer.

SL: Yes, and it was very challenging. We had to design the workflow with the sound people and test it and foresee what problems there might be. And it was really exciting to do that. We felt like pioneers!

TO: And this was not a small picture. This was Léon. The English title was The Professional.

SL: Yes, this was my first feature.

TO: It was a huge international hit.

SL: It was. It was an amazing movie to work on, Natalie Portman was amazing, Gary Oldman a genius actor. It is an enormous honor, and gift for an editor to cut a film with such amazing actors, with a director like Luc. This movie has a special place in my heart for all those reasons.

TO: The relationship, his fated history, incredible action scenes—it has all those things which are a lot for a first-time feature editor.

SL: My heart was beating very fast! And still is! (Both Laugh). Technically it was a challenge, we had to invent a workflow, find workarounds. Storage wasn't big enough to store all the footage, so we had to cut the first part, delete the unused medias and load the rest. I remember the day I put together the two parts of the movie together, watch it, close the bin. Came back the next morning. I couldn't open the bin. Imagine you have your movie cut in the machine but you can't open the bin! I rushed in the nearest supplier and bought some ram memory. At that time, we didn't know if it was going to work.

TO: You mean conform the negative?

SL: Yes, and the sound and it was all a question mark. It was the first time I went to America, I was in LA for three months cutting it. There was so much excitement.

TO: It kicked off a great collaboration with Luc Besson…

SL: I did three films with Luc— Léon, The Fifth Element, and Joan of Arc, and a lot of commercials. You have a collaboration, a friendship, and you're nearly one mind. You know what he wants and that's an incredible, amazing creative experience to have. You are spending a long time in a small room with only that person and it's a very unique relationship.

TO: About a year of your life.

SL: For the longer ones, yes. Everything is dedicated to that film and to find what that film needs. Creativity brings something very special to relationships. I think that's very true in the film business. It's an amazing thing I experienced in working with Luc. The duty of an editor is to take care of the characters and to take care of the story. And that is something that I really love in my job. You are actually building characters in the editing room. You are taking care of them. You are nurturing them.

TO: Do you recall getting the dailies?

SL: Léon was brilliantly shot and so well acted. Natalie Portman was amazing. And Gary Oldman was more than amazing. I remember watching his dailies and forgetting to choose which one was the best one because they were great from the first to the last! Everything was at the top level and you felt that you were not allowed to fail. Shooting, acting, everything. The scene when she is changing, I just compare it to being like a kid in a candy shop—you just have to choose which one you want to eat.

TO: They were all that good?

SL: Yes. Everything.

TO: The Fifth Element had so many visual effects. What kind of challenge did that represent?

SL: It was the first film that I had done with visual effects like that. Set design and visual effects were really at a high level. I was working very close with Mark Stetson from Digital Domain cutting previz and editing them in the film. We went from cars that looked like squares and then became more refined. So we had a constant evolution. The challenge was really to be able to work with the team doing the visual effects and to keep up with them and to keep everything in sync. That was a huge, huge challenge.

TO: Some editors don't want to go to the set because they don't want to know what was involved in getting the shots. Do you have a preference?

SL: I'm more on the side of not visiting the set. I want to work on the movie and not know what went into making the material.

TO: What have you learned along the way that you didn't know at the beginning?

SL: The main thing that I really didn't know is that the editor really needs to become the best friend for the director. I wasn't expecting that of the relationship. And you have to be instinctive. That's the real thing about being an editor. I didn't really think of it that way at the beginning.

TO: What do you mean?

SL: Sometimes you cut a scene by instinct and you just get it right. And sometimes you can try it 20 different ways and it's just not right. Some people say, 'Well, why did you do it this way?' And the only answer would be 'Because it felt right.'

TO: You've worked on films with a lot of footage...

SL: When you have tons and tons of footage for things like battle scenes, it's a little like going back to documentaries. When I did A Matador's Mistress with Penelope Cruz and Adrien Brody, there's a bullfight scene. They shot for 20 days with three cameras. I ended up with 13 hours of dailies for one scene. It took me 15 days to look at everything, sort it out, and cut it. When you finish something like that, you really feel like you accomplished something because it's really raw material.

TO: What should students do to prepare for a career in the editing profession?

SL: I can tell them what worked for me. Always be ready to challenge yourself. Keep the freshness of what you're doing. Never forget that you are telling stories.

TO: What films do you admire?

SL: There are plenty of them. I loved The Reader. I cried. It's just an amazing movie. All That Jazz was amazing. J.F.K. is incredible. Raging Bull. Blade Runner. Magnolia. Brazil. There is a very old movie, Man With a Movie Camera...

TO: Yes, that's used in a lot of film schools. It was done in 1929.

SL: And every modern film editing convention is used in that film. It's an incredible film.

TO: If you weren't an editor what do you think you'd be doing?

SL: I think I would be a funambule.

TO: Okay, I can figure out that ambule has to do with walking or ambulate. What's a funambule?

SL: You know—people who walk on strings...

TO: Oh, a tightrope walker?

SL: Yes. (Both Laugh) Like Man on Wire.

TO: Because?

SL: Because it is freedom and unique moments and I can't do it! (Laughs) I've always been excited about editing. I am still like a kid in the editing room—a bit scared and excited at the same time. It's one of the best jobs in the world.

CAROL LITTLETON, ACE

Receiving the ACE Career Achievement Award
Photograph courtesy of the American Cinema Editors and ACE Eddie Awards

LOS ANGELES, CA

Partial Credits: All the Way, A Walk in the Woods, The Other Boleyn Girl, Margot at the Wedding, The Manchurian Candidate, Dreamcatcher, Tuesdays with Morrie, Mumford, Beloved, Wyatt Earp, Benny & Joon, Grand Canyon, The Accidental Tourist, Swimming to Cambodia, Brighton Beach Memoirs, Silverado, Places in the Heart, The Big Chill, E.T. the Extra-Terrestrial, Body Heat, French Postcards.

She is still amazed every time she sits down anew to edit a film. You would think, given all her experience, that some of the luster would naturally have worn off—but that's not the case. I can imagine her—ageless—in that cutting room. She best described it— "My work nourishes me."

TO: Carol, you are an Emmy award recipient for your editing of Tuesdays with Morrie and an Oscar nominee for the world-renowned film, E.T. the Extra Terrestrial. How did you get your start in the film industry?

CL: At the end of my junior year abroad in Paris, I was travelling in Europe with a girlfriend before returning home. We were staying in Florence, Italy where I met a young fellow, who introduced me to the idea of working in film. That young fellow is now my husband.

TO: That's John Bailey, the cinematographer.

CL: Yes. John said he was going to finish his undergraduate studies at Loyola in Los Angeles and then attend USC Cinema School. This was back in the '60s and I didn't know there was such a thing as a cinema school. After several years of a long-distance romance, John asked me to move to Los Angeles in 1970. John said, 'Let's make a go of it!' We've been married ever since. I caught the movie bug from John.

TO: Cinema in France in the '60's was a pretty unique experience.

CL: When I was in Paris, I was a serious student, but I spent all my free time going to concerts, plays or films. A fellow student suggested we go to the Cinematheque. I acquired the unusual habit of looking at films two or three times as a way to learn idiomatic French more quickly. And the more I looked at the movies, the more I realized, 'There's something happening here that's different from the way movies are made in the States.' And this was during the height of La Nouvelle Vague, and yes, the French films of the 60's were very different.

TO: The New Wave... What happened next?

CL: The more that I hung out with John and his cinema friends at USC, the more I realized I wasn't that interested in pursuing an academic career. The first entry-level job I got was at Grey Advertising where I worked for an agency producer. Well, it meant that I was a glorified gofer, really! (Both Laugh)

TO: Commercials are a great training ground.

CL: And after a couple of years at Grey Advertising I got another entry-level job at Richard Einfeld Productions, which was a small, boutique sound facility. My first job at REP was to organize the sound library. I worked for almost three years doing sound transfers, organizing Richard's library and acquiring film editing skills.

TO: Many editors started in the sound department.

CL: About halfway through my first year working at REP, Richard had a documentary on the shelf that he was supposed to cut, but the people who gave him the project weren't able to pay him. He said, 'Carol, if you're interested in cutting a documentary for practice, in your free time, why don't you do it?'

TO: That was a great training opportunity.

CL: I'd start in the morning doing sound. In the afternoon, I'd cut the documentary and then I'd be in Richard's editing room at the end of the day. And my days got longer and longer, and I loved it.

TO: Full immersion! (Both Laugh)

CL: That's really how I learned. Richard was an extraordinary teacher. If you got into a bind, he'd explain what you needed to do and push you back in the cutting room. I started doing a number of small projects—which also included my sweeping the floors and cleaning the toilets! (Both Laugh)

TO: Your first break as a picture editor was on Legacy.

CL: Legacy was Karen Arthur's project for the AFI Women Directors Workshop. Karen was the director and Joan Hotchkis was the writer/actor. I think they scraped together thirty thousand dollars for the budget. John was the DP and we used short ends for the shoot.

TO: Those are the short end leftovers of unexposed film.

CL: Yes. And sometimes they weren't so short at 400 feet. Film came in 1000-foot loads, (about 11 minutes of film) so a 400-foot short end was a gift.

TO: A lot of films have been made with those short ends.

CL: And that was the first narrative film that I cut. Karen was a terrific director—she was very inspirational. Karen and Joan wanted to create a cinematic, artful film that explored a women's emerging consciousness. It was just a lovely first feature film experience for the three of us.

TO: When you look back on it, what did you learn that you carried with you to the next film?

CL: We had such a small budget. Karen was not only the director but also worked as my assistant. I realized right away that film is truly collaborative. We worked as a tight, creative unit. We took responsibility for each other. I realized that collaboration was essential to feed the creative process. Those are the things that the textbooks don't tell you—that you don't work alone, ever.

TO: Do you find yourself naturally gravitating towards dramatic, people-driven stories?

CL: I think so. The scripts that I gravitate towards are the ones about the human experience, stories that are rooted in everyday life. I'm amazed at what actors can do and I love working with their performances. It's what I enjoy most of all—being the last person to honor and to preserve their performances. It's a responsibility that I take very seriously and, of course, it's fun as well.

TO: If you look at 1981 and the next ten years—Body Heat, E.T., The Big Chill, Places in the Heart, Silverado, Brighton Beach Memoirs, Swimming to Cambodia, Vibes, The Accidental Tourist, White Palace, Grand Canyon. How did it feel to you, living it?

CL: Oh, I was so excited. I couldn't stand it. I was popping with enthusiasm. I like a film that has a mixture of tone—that's what I'm drawn to more than anything. Even if you look at something like Body Heat or The Big Chill, there's a mixture of tone. Body Heat is a film noir, but there's also a lot of humor.

TO: There is.

CL: I'm drawn to films that have a mixture of humor and drama, unpredictability, films that have rich narratives, and challenging performances. I had already done Body Heat with Larry and on The Big Chill he wanted to do something that he couldn't do on Body Heat. And that was to have a rehearsal period.

In the Cutting Room
Photograph courtesy the American Cinema Editors and ACE Eddie Awards

TO: That makes a lot of sense given the ensemble cast and the story.

CL: And the rehearsals were going to be done in the actual location where we were going to be shooting. So we went to Beaufort, South Carolina for a couple of weeks ahead of the actual shooting. The actors would rehearse with Larry in the morning. In the afternoon, we'd all get together, including the cinematographer who was John, my husband, and me. It gave us an extraordinary preview of the overall dramatic emphasis that Larry wanted to have for the film.

TO: So many people lament the fact that there's no rehearsal period.

CL: I fell in love with the process and the notion of working with Larry. And we all wanted to bring our unique skills and talents to the project, in a true collaborative spirit.

TO: You've worked with Lawrence Kasdan on eight films, more than any other editor he's worked with.

CL: I love the combination of writer-director. What makes working with Larry so special for me is that not only are we very good friends, but I am drawn to his humanism and the humanity with which he infuses all of his projects.

TO: What is your usual working style with him?

CL: He's very particular with the spoken word. He wants it to be like a play—verbatim from the book. And the actors will tell you that as well. As an editor, he wants you to preserve the script. But he's flexible enough to know that if there's something that comes out of a rehearsal or on the day of shooting, he will change it, especially if revisions help the narrative or the actor. He wants the first cut to be pretty much as written. But after that, he realizes that the next creative step is the editing which means we do whatever is necessary—changing the words, changing the script, changing the structure—whatever needs to be done.

TO: Are there times when you see dailies where you are flabbergasted by what you're seeing?

CL: Oh, God, I'm surprised every day. I'm just amazed at how extraordinary this whole thing called 'making a movie' is. You read the scenario and then you see dailies with what the director, the actors and the other collaborators bring to the written word, and then through the editing, the film comes to life on the screen. Making a film is extremely plastic—film is like a piece of sculpture. You can change it in all kinds of ways. I'm always overwhelmed with what everyone is able to accomplish. It's just amazing!

TO: Benton, Demme, Kasdan, and Spielberg, Jay Roach is a sampling of the directors you've worked with.

CL: What all of them have in common is that they are very aligned with the artistic process. And I think the greatness of each of them has to do with being in touch with film as a collaborative process. They aren't dictatorial, and they don't say 'This is my vision and you'll do what I say.' They are extremely inclusive, alive and willing to accept what each of us brings to their creative process. What makes them great is that they appreciate what each of us has to offer, incorporate it and make it their own. They keep their own view very strong and very alive but allow everyone to contribute.

TO: When I know that I'm going to see a Carol Littleton edited film, I know the actors are going to be very well taken care of, and actors seem to be well watched after by you.

CL: Why thank you very much. I think that's an observation that can be made for many editors because that's really what we do— we are custodians of the actors' performances—that is our main job. Everything else—action sequences, montages, and visual effects—are relatively easy in my mind. The real challenge is to make sure that what the director and the actor wanted to achieve is being achieved. And that the scene contributes in the way it is supposed to in the narrative. Artful performances within a moving narrative—that is our principal work, that is editing.

TO: It must be difficult when there is a lot of material shot and a lot of line readings.

CL: Making choices is the real challenge but that's the fun of it, too. That's the crux of it. That is the lively part of the art as far as I'm concerned. It's extremely enjoyable when you have the time and the resources to explore a variety of choices to see what works best.

TO: And technology has helped and impaired you as well.

CL: True, we don't have as much time anymore. People ask me 'Well, don't you miss touching film?' And, no, I don't miss the tactical sensation of celluloid. What I do miss was the time it took to handle film: viewing on a Moviola or a KEM, making splices, rewinding reels. During that time, I was able to think about what I was going to edit, weighing choices in my mind.

TO: Sure, you were planning it all out in your head.

CL: Yes! And now, in digital editing, you can just click and it's done. I don't even have time to think about it! (Laughs)

TO: When I was talking with Walter Murch, he said that when he was rewinding film, he'd see things that weren't obvious when he was watching the film in normal motion.

CL: That's right. I miss that step, too. I have a routine approach to my work initially. After the dailies are in the Avid, the assistants will arrange them the way that I like to have them, which is essentially in the same way I asked scenes to be ordered on KEM rolls when we worked on film. Then I'll read the scene again and watch the dailies and make some notes. Once I've looked at everything, I'll sit for a few moments and think about the scene. Then I'll start cutting it and once I'm done I won't look at it. Instead, I'll move on to the next scene that's ready to cut. The next morning, I will review the scene that I didn't review the previous day with fresh eyes, make some revisions and move on to a new scene. This approach mimics how I worked on film.

TO: Instead of refining one scene before moving on…

CL: Yes, and I find it's very fluid that way. But later on in the editorial process, once scenes and sequences are edited or semi-locked, I go back and look at all the dailies again. And on that second dailies viewing, I'll very carefully evaluate things that I overlooked. Each step in the editing process becomes an enrichment by accretion of detail.

TO: What about the preview process?

CL: We previewed ET with an answer print, with no focus group. Can you imagine! So the filmmakers had an opportunity to make a very personalized film that didn't fit into a mold. The way we preview movies now, the movie becomes less and less a personal film and they become more generic.

TO: What do people who go to see films not know about your profession that you wish they had a little bit more understanding about?

CL: Editing is really the last line of storytelling. It's not so much putting pieces of film together as it is putting together a narrative that works, performances that work. I think people outside of the process think that we hang out with the actors and that it's a glamorous life. But my work is work and it's not social—I don't see the actors during the shoot, except during rehearsals and if there is a problem on the set. If you want to enter into this as a career, it can take a toll on your psyche and your physical state of being. You have to know how to accomplish a lot every day and not burn out. And you have to learn how to still be cheerful, healthy, alert and optimistic. It's a stressful job, but the rewards are worth it.

TO: Are there any films and editors you admire?

CL: This is a very hard question to answer. I think the matriarch of all editors is Dede Allen. I can look at any of her films and I'm amazed at how she is able to take performances and make them instantly understood, emotionally and artfully. There are very few people who have had her talent or who ever will. I think you can take anything she's cut—say Bonnie and Clyde. Today it looks somewhat dated, but in the context of movies at that time, it was totally revolutionary in every conceivable way. She's number one on my list. Then, coming to a contemporary of mine whose work I find to beextraordinary on every film I've seen him do edit is Tim Squyres.

TO: That's lovely. He will be amazed at that, I'm sure.

CL: I just think he's an extraordinary talent. He's bright, he's smart, and he has a way with performances. They're clean, honest, extremely accessible, simple, and straightforward. Simplicity is very hard to achieve in film.

TO: You mean achieving something without clobbering it over the audience's head?

CL: Yes, it's very, very hard to achieve, believe me. It's a lot easier to cut an action sequence than it is to cut a clean, clear, unadorned performance. Tim can do both.

TO: He's a very genuine, nice person.

CL: And I greatly admire Craig McKay's work and he's a protégé of Dede's. He's a master of documentary, of action, and of narrative. I would also add to my editing Pantheon Jerry Greenberg, Tom Rolf, Peter Zinner and for comedy, Stephen Rotter. Other contemporary editors are Jay Cassidy, Susan Morse, Alan Baumgarten, Billy Goldenberg, Dylan Tichenor, and Joan Sobel. In addition, there are so many young, talented editors, too many to name.

TO: Did you have any inkling that E.T. the Extra-Terrestrial would turn out to be such a hit?

CL: I would say no and yes. I had no idea it would be a crossover film that would appeal to both children and adults. Melissa Mathison's script was impeccable. Steven said, 'If people can accept this rubber puppet as a real character, then we've done our work well.' And that's what we spent a great deal of time doing—getting E.T. to be real and believable. Both Ben Burtt and Charles Campbell worked miracles with the ET's body movement and voice. So when we took it to our first audience screening, which was the preview in Houston, Steven said 'Well, if we get past the first reveal of E.T. and people don't get up and start to walk out, we're okay.' That preview was extraordinary. The house went crazy. Amazing. I've never had a preview like that since. Steven looked over at me and joined his index finger and thumb together and made a sign that we were okay. It was very exciting. So, yes, I was surprised, but I wasn't totally surprised. (Both Laugh)

TO: What keeps you going?

CL: My work nourishes me. Editing is a very lively art. Every day is a discovery—about myself, about others, about the film, about what makes a film work or not work. Editing has so many rewards. I've spent a lifetime in film and it's been very exciting and that's what keeps me going.

MARCIA LUCAS

Photo courtesy of Marcia Lucas

HAWAII

Partial Credits: Star Wars Episode VI: Return of the Jedi, Star Wars: Episode V: The Empire Strikes Back (not credited), More American Graffiti (not credited), Star Wars, Episode IV: A New Hope, Alice Doesn't Live Here Anymore, American Graffiti, Taxi Driver (Supervising Editor), The Candidate (Assistant Editor), THX 1138 (Assistant Editor), The Rain People (Assistant Editor).

I wondered why I hadn't seen more interviews with Marcia and I was determined to hear more about her career. Without any pre-notice from me, she could outline very specific details of each film even though 30 years had passed. You don't hear enough about her film contributions and I hope you will get a much better understanding of her amazing talent.

TO: Marcia, you received, along with your co-editors Richard Chew and Paul Hirsch, an Academy Award for Star Wars. How did you get started?

ML: About 1964, I was working as a global phone operator. My boyfriend got a job in Hollywood and the County of Los Angeles had plans to build a Hollywood museum for the public. He said that I had to go to the State Hiring Employment Office to formally apply for a librarian job! And so the lady said, 'Film Librarian: No Experience Necessary. Light typing.'

TO: That's funny.

ML: And I walk out knowing that this isn't the job my boyfriend was talking about, but I go to the interview anyway at this placed called

Sandler Film Library in Hollywood. And we walk past the rewind desk and a Moviola and film vaults and old film cans. I took the job and this young man, Steve, showed me how to work the Moviola, how to take down key numbers, and how the card file worked for all the shots they had.

TO: The fundamentals…

ML: Whenever the library was slow, they started training me to be an assistant editor. They were teaching me how to handle dailies, coding the film, breaking it down, and learning all the mechanical post-production work. I got into the union and was hired to be the assistant editor. I started working on television commercials. I ordered the opticals, reviewed all the answer prints, and sometimes I'd supervise the sound mixes. And I even would cut negative. But I wasn't even being paid scale. So, I left and there was a woman in the San Fernando Valley who liked to hire female assistants. And it was Verna Fields.

TO: She, of course, won the Oscar in 1975, for editing Jaws.

ML: Right. And I interviewed with Verna and she had a documentary contract for the USIA—the United States Information Agency. The documentary was about Lyndon Johnson going to Southeast Asia during the Vietnam War. I was working as an assistant to Verna and I was getting all the footage broken down and coded. Verna had hired a bunch of film students from USC to look at the footage and identify it. The Moviolas were going all day!

TO: And one of those students…

ML: Was George Lucas. Verna asked a couple of the students if they could cut some sequences because we had so much to do. Since I had more experience, I was helping George when he was cutting a scene. And that's how we got to know each other. When the film was finished, George went back to film school and I went back to television commercials. George and I started dating and then George got a Warner Brothers Scholarship while he was at USC. Francis Coppola was shooting Finian's Rainbow and then he was going to shoot The Rain People. Francis asked George to make a behind-the-scenes documentary. And George shot it, recorded the sound, and edited it—he did it all.

TO: Okay, that was Filmmaker.

ML: Right. I went to work at another commercial house that was co-owned by Haskell Wexler, who was going off to direct his movie, Medium Cool. Meanwhile, George was on location with Francis and their editor was Barry Malkin, who had his editing room set up in a trailer. They finally got to Ogalala, Nebraska to shoot for five weeks. Barry told Francis that if they could rent a space, he could get an assistant and could get a lot more done. George said, 'Well, my girlfriend's an assistant editor.'

TO: (Both Laugh) That's great.

ML: And Francis said, 'Let's hire her and get her out here.' Meanwhile, Haskell asks me to go to Chicago to be an assistant editor on Medium Cool. I was interested in working in movies so I made the decision with my heart and went to Ogalala. I met Barry and there was another assistant, Richie, who Barry had worked with in New York.

TO: And this must have been Richie Marks, right?

ML: Right and we all got along famously, and we got all the work done.

TO: It's pretty amazing to think of Lucas, Malkin, and Marks all in the same cutting room. Talk about talent.

ML: It was funny the way it worked out. I went to work as an assistant on Medium Cool working for Paul Golding, the editor. George and I got married in February of 1969. I finished Medium Cool and George and I moved to Mill Valley, California. Meanwhile, Francis had moved all his operations into a warehouse.

TO: Was that American Zoetrope?

ML: Yes. And Francis was encouraging George to write a script, and that was THX. And it was extremely low budget and George was directing. George set up a small production area and was editing and I was the assistant editor.

TO: When did you meet Walter Murch who did the sound design on THX?

ML: I had met Walter earlier while George and I were dating. There was a whole group of people who hung out together—Matthew Robbins, John Milius, Brian DePalma...

TO: You were all a pretty amazing cast of characters...

ML: I fell in love with Marty and Brian because they were so damn funny. They had that whole New York sense of humor. George would edit during the day with me assisting. Walter was out all day recording sounds and at night he'd come in and build all the sound tracks.

TO: It must have been interesting to come in the next day and hear Walter's work.

ML: It was very cool. George was working on a Steenbeck and could listen to two tracks—one picture track, one dialogue track and one sound effects track. So, Walter was building sound, George was editing, and I was doing everything that an assistant has to do. The film came out and it didn't do well and George always wanted to make a movie about his teenage cruising days in Modesto. George had finished his story treatment for Graffiti and had gotten a ten thousand dollar advance to write the script and then he got the go-ahead.

TO: And you moved on to edit Graffiti...

ML: Yes. Francis had bought a house in Mill Valley and we edited Graffiti over the garage in Francis's house. George had two cameras going the whole time he was shooting. Every single take had an A camera and a B camera, and you can shoot fast when you're getting a close-up and a medium close-up. When you're making a low budget feature you have to move fast.

TO: I didn't know that Graffiti was shot that way.

ML: George shot THX, Graffiti, and Star Wars with two cameras and asked Verna Fields to edit Graffiti. Verna had cut Paper Moon for Peter Bogdanovich. Verna came on board and I had told George that I liked editing and that when shooting was over I wanted to be the second editor.

TO: It was time to assert yourself.

ML: Yes. So they wrapped shooting and Verna was keeping up pretty well. But there was still about 25% of the movie that hadn't been cut. So, I started cutting scenes and we finally had a rough cut which was three-and-a-half to four hours long. Verna had already made a commitment to cut Peter's next movie.

TO: Daisy Miller.

ML: That's right. George and I had to cut down the film. But as the film got shorter, all the scenes got very abrupt. George had written the script around four key characters. And the script went 1,2,3,4,1,2,3,4 following those characters. So a scene with Curt would be followed by one with Steve, then John, and then Terry. But it didn't work.

TO: Why?

ML: I was constantly being yanked away from the story before I was feeling the intention of the scene.

TO: So what did you do?

ML: I made a lot of index cards and worked on a new structure. And I said, 'If we combine these three scenes, that will create a complete structure and then we can cut to Steve. And maybe we could combine two of Steve's scenes and then cut away.' And George said, 'No, no, no. The movie has to go 1,2,3,4,1,2,3,4.' (Laughs) And these weren't heated arguments—these were just the normal discussions between a director and an editor. Finally, George let me restructure things and then we took a look at it. How the characters intertwined during the course of the night necessitated that approach. We finally got all the scenes and the transitions working and down to two hours and then we started laying in the music. The source music is almost 90 minutes in total.

TO: Were scenes conceived with particular music in mind?

ML: No, but George had a list of songs he wanted. Remember, in everyone's scene, anytime they're in a car, there's music. There's music at the sock hop, the live band, background music and the radio is a character because Curt goes to find Wolfman Jack.

TO: How were the previews?

ML: We had 300 people in the theatre and people were laughing and the audience just loved it. And the Universal studio executive said, 'This is a nightmare. This is un-releasable.' Francis said to the studio exec, 'I will write you a check today. I will buy this film. It's a great film and it's going to be popular.' The exec went away with his tail between his legs and then went to Verna Fields and asked her to re-cut the movie.

TO: I didn't know that.

ML: All they really did was to take out two scenes, one that was about a minute and a half and another that was about 30 seconds.

TO: And thenyou were nominated—with Verna Fields—for an Academy Award. Were you surprised?

ML: The nomination shocked me. They opened it in something like ten theatres and then every weekend it got bigger and bigger.

TO: A personal favorite of mine is Alice Doesn't Live Here Anymore.

ML: Once Graffiti was a big hit, Marty called me and said Alice was going to be his first studio movie for Warner Brothers. And really, to establish myself as a feature film editor, I had to start working with other directors.

TO: Right. You felt you couldn't just cut George's films.

ML: Absolutely. And George felt it was a good idea. I went to Tucson, Arizona where they were shooting. We took over a motel room to be the editing room. When I got a scene finished, Marty would come in and although he thought he was going to be cutting, he liked what I was doing, and came in less frequently.

TO: There are pretty amazing performances in that film.

ML: Oh, absolutely. And you know what else I remember about that film? The camera is moving almost all the time. Dollying, panning... And I can remember being nervous seeing the dailies and wondering if I could make a clean cut. And it worked. Eventually we wrapped and moved the cutting room back to Los Angeles. We got to our first cut and we screened it. And it was so apparent that we really needed to get her on the road with her son and we couldn't spend that much time on Ellen and her husband, Harvey Keitel.

TO: He's scary in the movie. He's got the scorpion in his belt buckle...

ML: It's very high energy. Alice gets the job in the diner with Flo. And eventually they become friends. And when Kris Kristofferson comes into the diner, he really didn't get there fast enough to keep the momentum going.

TO: What do you mean?

ML: We restructured the film so that when Kris comes into the diner, Alice and Flo haven't become friends yet. That way, we had to keep Alice and Flo apart from each other and eventually we resolved that relationship into a friendship.

TO: What's your take on digital editing?

ML: I think there's a temptation to try too many things. To me, a movie is a two-hour experience where you sit in the dark and you watch a story. And from frame one to the end, the movie has to work—it can't get bogged down, it can't get confusing, it can't get boring. Scenes are written for a reason—to tell a story and to develop characters. I will go back and work on a scene until I know that scene is as good as it can possibly be. And my perspective as a motion picture editor is that the film has to work from the beginning to the end credits.

TO: I didn't realize you were the supervising editor on Taxi Driver.

ML: After Alice, Marty told me about his next movie and I signed up to do it. Marty was shooting in New York and the movie was primarily shot at night. After Marty wrapped production, he came out to Los Angeles and we started cutting. We were cutting and cutting and it was going slowly. And there was over 100,000 feet of second unit footage on the streets of New York at night. I told Marty that I didn't think that we could get through everything in time and he agreed. So, we brought in Tom Rolf and we were both cutting. We were working long hours and then we brought in one more editor.

TO: Melvin Shapiro.

ML: Right. Finally we got everything assembled and we saw it from beginning to end. It became apparent to me that the entire story of DeNiro and Foster had to be started earlier and integrated throughout the film. The most famous scene—the 'You talkin' to me?' scene—was one where Marty shot literally ten-minute takes. He shot a whole roll of film in one take and then he ended up printing 25 takes.

TO: That's about 250 minutes or over six hours of footage just for that scene.

ML: Marty came in and we were ready to cut the scene. And I said, 'Why don't we give this scene to Tom?' And we were all laughing and we said, jokingly, 'Okay, Tom, we'll see you in a few weeks!' And I swear, two days later, Tom had the scene cut and we all went in to look at it. And it was just perfection and not one frame was changed.

TO: That's a great story.

ML: And that's the scene that everyone remembers. Tom was a great film editor. He did a magnificent job. Another challenge for me is that the movie ends five times.

TO: How do you mean?

ML: It could end when he sits down on the sofa and puts his finger to his head. The camera tracks down the stairs and then there's the reading of the letter from the parents and it could end there. Then there's the montage of newspaper clippings, and then he's on the street with his taxi buddies and then Travis takes the passenger who ends up being Cybill Shepherd. And he looks at her in the rearview mirror and things are very abstract and the visuals are distorted. And he flips the mirror back and she's gone. And he drives off and the movie ends. And it could have ended at any one of those junctions.

TO: What did you think of all those endings?

ML: I really felt that we needed every one of them. I needed to know that he was a hero and that he wasn't going to jail. And I needed to know that Jodie Foster had changed her life and went back to her parents. The little end tag with Cybill Shepherd was abstract enough so that it left you thinking 'Was that real or was that imagined?' To me, it was all just the right note.

TO: I never actually thought of it that way.

ML: Those were threads of the story that needed to get resolved. It would have been horrible to get up from the theatre and not know what happened to him or what happened to the little girl.

TO: And then you move on to Star Wars.

ML: I wasn't planning on editing Star Wars. I wanted to start a family by then and George had hired an editor in England. George wanted me to come out to Elstree Studios, where they were doing all the set shooting. And I'd drive to the studio, look at some dailies, and then drive George home and cook dinner. Eventually, there were some cut scenes and we went to look at them. And my heart just sank.

TO: What happened?

ML: I had seen the dailies and I had an image in my mind of how a scene would go together. And it just wasn't working. It was as if the editor had an interpretation that Star Wars was a comic book and he was using performances that were very broad. And I told George that he had to go into the cutting room when he wasn't shooting and talk to the editor. As the production wound down, George made a decision to make a change. And he asked me if I'd cut it and I said sure because I knew all the dailies by then.

TO: What did you do?

ML: The first thing I had to cut was the end battle sequence when the rebel ships attack the Death Star. Because those scenes had hundreds of visual effects.

TO: Because you had to turn them over to visual effects, you had to have them cut sooner.

ML: Right. Industrial Light and Magic (ILM) needed the cut of the scene so that they could time the shot. And what George had done because he's such a talented filmmaker is that while he was writing Star Wars we had a Betamax machine. While he was writing Graffiti, he would tape all the World War II movies that had aerial battles in them. And he took all those battle scenes, sent them to the lab, and made 16mm black and white prints. That meant that you could use them as live action storyboards with planes flying right to left, and left to right, and planes exploding and POV shots of a pilot shooting at a plane in front of him in a dogfight.

TO: So they formed a template to follow.

ML: Yes. We had the 16mm material blown up to 35mm so that I could start cutting with it. I was using the old dogfight footage to time the action. One day, George came into the cutting room and said, 'I can't believe this. They've spent over one million dollars and they are not even remotely close to one shot that I could use.'

TO: I thought things went well from the get go.

ML: No. By that time, I'm working on the end battle in San Anselmo and George is at ILM helping them build the models and telling them how to light them. On the weekends, he'd come home and one day I had to tell him that there was no way that we could get everything done. I told George that we needed another editor. I liked Paul Hirsch's work because he was cutting for Brian DePalma. We called Paul and it turned out that a lot of the material that was cut in England wasn't so easy to correct. We ended up pulling everything apart and reconstituting the dailies.

TO: You went right back to the starting point.

ML: We had to. And still there was no end in sight in getting to the completion date. Finally, Paul and I talked, and we hired Richard Chew. I'm in the end battle forever and we finally got everything to a point where we felt it was working and we sat down and watched it all assembled.

TO: At what point did you feel you had something special?

ML: I knew after we got the film cut down to two hours that the structure, timing, and flow was right. The characters were working, and the shots were working even though about 30% of them weren't final. And then I got a call from Marty Scorsese.

TO: This was for New York, New York?

ML: Yes, Marty had shot it in New York and was editing in Los Angeles. Marty brought Tom Rolf in and then asked me if I could come in and troubleshoot for a couple of weeks because the film was running three to four hours. And at that point I felt comfortable leaving Star Wars because the only thing left to do was to replace the temporary shots with the finished shots.

TO: But you were on New York, New York for more than two weeks…

ML: It turned into months and months and grueling work. Marty likes improvisation and he loves to give his actors that freedom. So a lot of the work is finding ways to integrate improvisational material with the scripted material. One weekend, George had a screening of Star Wars and he invited Marty, Brian DePalma, and Steven Spielberg.

TO: So how did it go?

ML: Well, we had the screening at the house and we went into the kitchen and Brian DePalma said, 'George, what the F*** have you done? What is The Force? Get that out of the picture!' (Both Laugh) And I thought Brian had lost his mind because the whole idea was the Jedi aspect is critical to the film. John Williams hadn't finished the score so that wasn't there, but everything was working very well. I went back to work on New York, New York and after a while 95% of the shots for Star Wars were done and we had another screening. And guess what?

TO: What?

ML: The saying, "May The Force Be With You" was in the movie maybe seven or eight times. All of a sudden, four or five of those had been cut out of the movie.

TO: Really?

ML: So guess who hit the roof on that one?

TO: You.

ML: Me! And I said, 'George, what are you doing? You can't take those out.' And we put them back in.

TO: Gee, that's amazing given how that phrase became part of world culture. You must be very proud of your impact on filmmaking.

ML: All I want to do when I go to work on a movie as a film editor is to make it work and be as best as it possibly can be. That's my job. But it's the director's movie and I'll always respect the director. On New York, New York, I went round and round with Marty on how to end the movie because he shot three different endings. And you have to defer to the director. Steven, Marty, and George were born with the talent to make films. I feel I had a gift for that and a lot of luck, too.

RICHARD MARKS, ACE

Photograph courtesy of the American Cinema Editors and ACE Eddie Awards

LOS ANGELES, CALIFORNIA

Partial Credits: How Do You Know, Julie & Julia, Spanglish, You've Got Mail, As Good as It Gets, Father Of The Bride, Dick Tracy, Say Anything, Broadcast News, Pretty In Pink, St. Elmo's Fire, Terms of Endearment, Pennies From Heaven, The Last Tycoon, The Godfather Part II, Serpico, Apocalypse Now (supervising editing), Little Big Man (associate editor), Alice's Restaurant (assistant editor), The Rain People (assistant editor).

Think about this—three years of Richie's life were spent on Apocalypse Now. The Godfather Part II, Serpico, Broadcast News. Great work and an amazing career. And what I loved the most? What keeps you going? "I love it! I love the process. It just envelops me. I just tune out the world."

TO: Richard, you are a four-time Academy Award, four-time Eddy, three-time BAFTA award and one-time Emmy award nominee. You are entering your fifth decade in the motion picture industry...

RM: (Laughs) This is beginning to sound like a eulogy...

TO: How did you get your start?

RM: Very serendipitously. I graduated with a degree in English literature back in the sixties when it was fashionable not to really have a goal! There I was with an English lit degree not knowing what I wanted to do, no way to earn a living and my savings running out. I was having a drink with a friend and he said, 'Why don't you get into movies?' And I said, 'Yeah, but what would I do?' I wound up getting a job as a runner in a release print house. It was the same company that Craig McKay worked at. As I was exposed to film editing, it seemed a perfect fit for my rather compulsive anal personality! (Both Laugh)

TO: Perhaps you're just a perfectionist…

RM: Maybe, but I sometimes think that it's a pre-requisite for this job! After a year, there was an apprentice job opening in this commercial editorial company and I realized that I wanted to work on feature films. I got a break on a film that Alan Heim was the supervising sound editor on. I was hired as an apprentice sound editor. Dede Allen was the film editor.

TO: This was Rachel, Rachel?

RM: Right, directed by Paul Newman. Fortunately for me, her assistant and her apprentice decided not to go on to the next film with her and I made a bid for the job.

TO: What was the film?

RM: Arthur Penn's Alice's Restaurant.

TO: 1969.

RM: Yes, and I was Dede's firstassistant on that.

TO: And you continued being an assistant to Dede on Little Big Man.

RM: It was very interesting working with Dede. I learned just how endless her energy was. I mean she could just bury me in the hours she could put in, in the cutting room. Most importantly, the key things I learned, was her approach to editing and her belief that editing is ultimately about story, character and performance. It's not about anything else but helping to tell a story. I think this was a very important lesson for someone like myself who came from a background in literature. It was an amazing learning period for me. Dede was someone who liked to talk while she was editing and invited you into both the experience and her thought process. She encouraged you to try things. She gave you scenes to cut. On Little Big Man, they needed a second editor and she got Arthur Penn to agree to give me a try—she offered me the job. That's where I got my break in editing features.

TO: Were you scared?

RM: Oh yes! I remember how really terrified I was. I was scared of failure. I was scared that if I screwed up, I'd never get another chance. Arthur Penn shot a lot of film and the first scene Dede gave me to cut had close to 30,000 feet of printed film.

TO: About five and a half hours…

RM: Yes. It was the scene where Wild Bill Hickok gets shot. When you're first starting to edit you want to use everything—every angle of every performance. And the decision-making is much harder than the physical cutting. A lot of the approach to editing has to do with the editor making decisions and a commitment—at least initially—to follow a certain character or storyline. It's really difficult to do when you are first learning to edit because you're terrified that you're going to make the wrong decisions.

TO: That you may be going down the wrong path.

RM: But in truth, there are no wrong paths, as long as you're open to change. You just have to commit to start to follow a path and then be willing to constantly alter that path as you make new discoveries along the way. You have to try to make the scene work as it was intended and remember that as the scene changes, the scene's overall role in the story may also change.

TO: The films you've worked on have won 16 Academy Awards and have received 33 nominations.

RM: Really?

TO: Yes.

RM: (Laughs) I had no idea of that.

TO: It's a pretty impressive number.

RM: Thank you. That's very interesting.

With Cast and Crew of The Rain People
Photograph courtesy the American Cinema Editors and ACE Eddie Awards

TO: 1974 to 1979. You work on two of the most recognizable films in film history, The Godfather Part II and Apocalypse Now.

RM: I never go into a film expecting I'm going to be involved in making a landmark movie. I thought there was something intriguing about the script and intriguing about the fact that it was a sequel at a time when there were few sequels. I remember reading the script and realizing it was about so much more than the original Godfather.

TO: In what way?

RM: Well, in terms of content and character. Godfather II wasn't as much an "action" film as the first one was although there certainly was a significant amount of violence in it. GF II seemed to be the intellectual justification for the Godfather saga. Francis is a great writer, who created these amazing interlaced stories that take you from the present to the past. Our job was to find the balance of those stories. There were three editors on GFII (and four primary editors on Apocalypse Now) and the thing about working with Francis is that we all worked on almost everything.

TO: You shared scenes back and forth.

RM: Yes, we juggled and traded sequences and over the course of the film, we all worked on almost everything. So, to take ownership of any particular part of a multi-editor film is too much ego. It was a cooperative effort.

TO: The Godfather Part I and Part II rank very high in the opinion of other editors.

RM: I think it's because they are editorially complicated films. In Godfather II there was a balancing act between two stories that had very different internal rhythms. There is a legato pace to the old story and a much faster pace to the modern story. Those rhythms and the contrast to those rhythms are the interesting part of the structure of the film—and the most difficult part.

TO: Why?

RM: Because you're watching a film or a part of a film that has a very strong, fast-paced forward movement and all of a sudden you hit a wall by jumping to the old story, which has a much slower, almost romantic, pace. It's like a piece of music that keeps speeding up and slowing down, speeding up and slowing down.

TO: If you don't get it right, the uncomfortable feeling builds up...

RM: Right and how long is an audience willing to sit through a certain rhythm and how long can you maintain their interest?

TO: The Godfather Part II is three hours and twenty minutes and when you're watching it you are not at all conscious of the time.

RM: It moves along.

TO: You were the supervising editor on Apocalypse Now and you worked on it for a long time.

RM: Almost three years.

TO: Three years of your life!

RM: It was a logistical nightmare. Everything that could possibly go wrong did go wrong. It was an unfinished piece of work in a way. I mean the end of Apocalypse Now was something we created in the editing room. It was a shoot that was never really completed and the Kurtz character—the Marlon Brando character—was never a really completed character. The film was shot in such a way that the action and dramatic sequences were photographed, but most of the connective tissue of the narration and the traveling material to support the narration wasn't shot during the original, principal photography. It was something that over the years—and I mean that literally—was slowly reconceived and shot and shot again.

TO: It must have been extraordinarily difficult for you to spend so much time on it, especially as other editors were coming and going.

RM: Maddening. I think in some ways we were all the Martin Sheen character. We went up river into the heart of darkness.

TO: You became the film.

RM: We became the film. (Laughs)

TO: Why did you stay?

RM: I can't really explain why I stayed on the film for almost three years. I mean this in all seriousness. I think I was at a point in my life where I just bought into this madness—as we all did. It was a strange experience that I can't begin to describe. I signed onto that film for six months and I was there for three years. Which, in essence, is the story of the film.

TO: Life imitated art to its fullest extent.

RM: Yes, to the fullest extent. I mean it was a film with problems. I guess most editors find great joy in helping solve problems. I found it hard to even consider abandoning the process.

TO: You wanted to solve as many of those problems.

RM: Yeah. (Pauses) Oh, God. The dark time. (Both laugh). You have to remember that we had well over a million feet of film back in 1977.

TO: That's over 183 hours!

RM: Right. And you were dealing with KEM rolls and Moviola rolls.

TO: You were limited in how much you could roll through at any one time.

RM: Yes. It was a lot of material to go through and absorb without having the super structure of the narrative voice. You could edit separate scenes but how they fit into the larger story was another issue. There was nothing, physically as an editor, to be able to hang it on until we started to create the material that was Willard's journey up the river.

TO: Did you think Terms of Endearment was going to get such a great reaction?

RM: Oh, no, no. I was sent the script, cold. I didn't know Jim Brooks. His producer sent it to me. I read the script and I remember that it made me cry. And this wasn't a usual reaction for me. It really brought tears to my eyes. I remember saying to my wife, 'Either I'm emotionally unstable (Laughs) or this is really good. Would you read it?' She read the script and she thought the same. And I went in to meet Jim. It's very difficult to hire an editor.

TO: You think so?

RM: In the cutting room, it's like a marriage. So, when you go to meet someone that you don't know, it's like going on a blind date. Only you're committing your film—and a lot of money—to someone you don't know. And the blind date could turn out to be a real bust. It worked out with Jim. I loved the film. I loved the work. It was hard work. We had some wonderful previews and I knew audiences liked it but I didn't have any idea it was going to be as successful as it was. But ultimately a film is about the script and the casting...

TO: And the execution of it...

RM: Well, a lot of time what you read is not how it winds up being executed. A script takes on a life of its own once it is in production. Directing, casting, acting, photography, production design, costumes, editing and all the things that go into making a film makes it a very different entity than the script. What you hope is that you can help make that film into what the script intended to be. You want, in the process, to take advantage of the things that you never imagined could be in the script—the subtext, what's not on the written page. And that's always the fascinating part—that's the challenge of it—how films change during the process. How a gesture or a look can be substituted for a page of dialogue. I mean it's a fascinating process of how we understand things from images and not just from what the characters say or how they say it. It's an image, a look, set design, a camera angle, or lighting on a person—they can change what's on the written page.

TO: You worked in television. How was the experience?

RM: I worked on a TV series for a couple of episodes. The producer said, 'There are certain rules. We don't overlap dialogue. We just don't.' I started to work on this episode (Laughs) and I'm cutting, and I turn to my assistant and say, 'This is bullshit! I'm gonna cut it the way it needs to be cut! If they don't like it, they'll fire me!' And (Laughs), they loved it! They loved the episode.

TO: With As Good As It Gets did you realize you had something special?

RM: You wait to get the dailies and you hope that they're great. As Good As It Gets has great performances in it. I loved the script. The actors were all really solid. The truth is that you have to take pleasure in the work and in the process. That's what makes it all worthwhile. If you start to think beyond that, you're on thin ice.

In the Cutting Room
Photograph courtesy the American Cinema Editors and ACE Eddie Awards

TO: How have you had to adapt to audience screenings?

RM: I have an example from Pennies From Heaven. This is a film that has a very dark story. And in choosing Steve Martin to be the lead, you've chosen someone who brings a specific public persona to the screen—that of a stand-up comic.

TO: Right. It was done in 1981.

RM: Yes, and in those days, films were marketed differently. And that evening there were thousands of people outside the theatre waiting to see the wild and crazy guy with the arrow through his head. The screening was an unmitigated disaster. I remember walking out of the theatre, sitting in the lobby holding my head, nauseous with the failure of the screening. People were walking out in droves. We had reshoots and re-cuts and kept cutting and cutting the film, trying to make audiences like it. In the end, the director, Herbert Ross, did a really brave thing and said, 'I can't do this anymore. We're butchering the film. It's not going to make people like it one percent better. I'm going back to what I started to make.' And I think that was an incredibly brave thing to do.

TO: What have you learned along the way?

RM: Just to keep trying. Apocalypse Now taught me that in spades. There's always a solution. You have to keep trying to make the film better. And to be a little philosophical about one's career. There are always times when you say to yourself, 'Why did I turn down that film? Look at how successful it turned out to be!' You make the choice and that's it and you live with it. Beating yourself up with hindsight, in an attempt to give some order to the chaos of life is very different than editing film.

TO: In what way?

RM: Editing film allows us to believe that we actually can give order to the chaos. (Laughs)

TO: Okay. Lumet. Coppola. Kazan. Ross. Brooks. Crowe. Beatty. Ephron. Nichols. Marshall. Donner. A pretty impressive list.

RM: They're all different people. They all have different approaches. They all have a different list of priorities when they work.

TO: How about a director versus a writer-director? A big difference?

RM: Oh, you bet. A huge, huge difference. I believe it's important for a director to own the material in terms of their personal investment in characters they have created. They've lived with them and they've thought them through. It's not just a job.

TO: Is your interaction different?

RM: Yes, a writer-director never wants to lose anything! I remember that Francis was always willing to throw out anything and would often rewrite a scene the night before. And Jim Brooks is that way, too. He's always willing to try something—to drop a shot or a scene or to change them in some way. A lot of people aren't willing to do that.

TO: Your films are so nicely paced and have a flow to them.

RM: I think films have an internal pace to them and as an editor you have to discover that pace. That pace is in the writing, that pace is in the performance and I think if you're a good editor, you're able to tap into that pace. So, when I look at films, it's like listening to a piece of music. If you feel like someone's cut out a quarter note, it gives you a start. If it has a flow to it or lack of a flow because it's cut in a staccato rhythm because that's what the story requires, you, as the editor need to tap into that intention and try to use it.

TO: What keeps you going?

RM: (Laughs) I love it! I love it. I love the process. It just envelops me. Just ask my wife. She'll tell you that I just tune out the world.

CRAIG MCKAY, ACE

Photograph courtesy of the American Cinema Editors and ACE Eddie Awards

NEW YORK CITY, NY

Partial Credits: The Conspirator, The Manchurian Candidate, Philadelphia, The Silence of the Lambs, Something Wild, Reds, Melvin and Howard.

What I think is most remarkable about The Silence of The Lambs is what's overlooked—Craig's editing of the dialogue scenes between Lecter and Starling. That work is so seamless, and it accomplishes so much and on so many levels. He can recite the history of filmmaking and as he talks about film, it's that ten-year-old boy who still delights with every new film he's on.

✂

TO: Craig, you are an Emmy award recipient and a two-time Academy Award nominee for Best Editing, for The Silence of the Lambs and Reds. What got you started?

CM: From a very early age, I've had a fascination with film. I was very fortunate because my parents could afford to buy me a 16mm Bolex when I was ten years old. A friend of my father's knew someone in the film business. He ran a commercial editorial house called Cinemetric in New York and he asked me if I wanted to come and work for him and it took me about a tenth of a second to say yes.

TO: What was your first job?

CM: I got hired as a messenger! They had a business that distributed film prints of commercials to all the stations across the nation. There were two of us who got jobs as messengers—the other was Richard Marks. I remember one of the first commercials we did was for the DNC (Democratic National Convention) for the Lyndon Johnson campaign and it was called Daisy. And the camera zooms into her eye and an atomic bomb blows up. And I think it was only on the air for one day.

TO: That's the famous ad used during the 1964 campaign—Johnson calling out Barry Goldwater who had said that he wouldn't rule out using an A-bomb in Vietnam.

CM: I had some experience on Woody Allen's Take the Money and Run and The Way We Were and then I got my first full-time assistant-ship with Alan Heim on a Sidney Lumet film. I couldn't have had a better entrée into feature film cutting than with Alan Heim. I worked with Evan Lottman and Barry Malkin and I had done some work with Dede (Allen) but that was mostly sound work. There were a few top assistant editors—Steve Rotter was one, Richie Marks, and I was fortunate enough to have a good reputation to fall into that category so I got offered a lot of stuff. So those people—Alan Heim, Evan Lottman, Dede Allen, and Barry Malkin were my mentors.

TO: So, at some point, you felt you were ready to move from assistant editing to editing.

CM: And I told everyone in town that I wasn't going to do anything until I got an editor job. And then I was out of work for ten months! And then finally I got a call from Dede Allen (Dog Day Afternoon, Serpico, Reds, Bonnie and Clyde) and she said that there was a film being done at ABC television and that led to Free To Be You and Me with Marlo Thomas and it was a huge success. I was brought in to work with Herb Gardner on a segment he directed with Dustin Hoffman and it was a great piece. I read in the trade magazines that Herb was going to do a film called Thieves. So I called him and said 'I heard that you're doing a feature. How could you do it without me?' And he said, 'You're right.' And I got my first feature!

TO: Just like that?

CM: Yes, but I learned that the most important thing is that you have to ask. No matter who it is—even if it's your best friend—you still have to ask.

TO: I was speaking with Alan Heim and his comment was that regardless of who you are or what you've done, "everyone has to interview!"

CM: Then I got a call from Steve Rotter who was the supervising editor on Holocaust and he had an opening for show number three. Because we all came up as assistants, we were like family, and so he hired me. And it was a very powerful film and although I didn't know much about the Holocaust it really resonated with me. There was something about it that—still to this day I can't explain—really touched me. I just felt this extraordinary responsibility to treat the subject as best as I could and to work as hard as I could to make the show work.

TO: And you, Alan Heim, Bob Reitano, Steve Rotter, and Brian Aston received Emmy awards for your work. You also received an American Cinema Editors Eddie award, which you shared with Steve Rotter.

CM: It was very exciting and then I got a call from Jonathan Demme who was doing a movie called Melvin and Howard. He said he'd like to get together for lunch and that Barry Malkin had recommended me. I am still deeply grateful to him.

TO: And this begins your long-term collaboration with Jonathan Demme—eight films and counting.

CM: And there I was, off on a Demme run!

TO: Let's move on to Reds. It lasted two years. How did you get involved?

CM: It was totally unexpected. I got a call from Dede. She had already started but she knew it was an enormous job and that she needed some help. She described the film and that it was about the Russian

Revolution and John Reed and asked me if I'd be interested and of course I said yes. I met with her, we shook hands and she said, 'We're partners in this.' It was very difficult. We did, in fact, have 64 people in post-production and we actually created a mini-studio with departments for coding and dailies and trims and video.

TO: Video?

CM: Yes, Reds used a video setup that was developed by Stanley Kubrick's editor. And we actually brought that setup from Kubrick. He made a film chain out of a Moviola using two cameras, one on the footage counter and one on the image and that all got transferred to Beta (max) tape. And Dede and I both had Beta decks.

TO: That was perhaps Ray Lovejoy.

CM: Every line of dialogue had a footage count and we had huge volumes of books with the numbers. We were able to get through all the footage because we had the beta decks and we could just zip down to each line reading. While we may have had 80 line readings, we could only use one (laughs)!

TO: How much was there?

CM: Enough for three movies!

TO: That works out to about 450 hours for a film that is just over three hours long.

CM: We were working six and seven days a week for two years. And what was it like? Well, it was great with Dede who was somebody who I had tremendous respect for and who is a giant in the film editing world. When we talked about a scene it was very strange because we sort of understood what it needed and we didn't have a dialogue about it.

TO: You were both on the same wavelength.

CM: Yes, there was this mutuality of what a scene needed—what to go after. And Warren would come in and he'd make his comments. These are all extremely bright people—they know story and they know performance—and it was absolutely great to be in the company of all that and to learn. I mean we had people coming in the cutting room like Mike Nichols, Elaine May, Robert Towne, Stephen Sondheim…

TO: No shortage of experience in that group.

CM: The place was wild. It was an amazing experience on so many levels. Now at that point I had a strong sense of performance and a strong sense of story and I learned more of that from Dede but what I learned from Dede was how to be a general and how to run the ship. It was such a huge film and it was a struggle—it was a difficult film to do on many levels. When we saw the first cut of "Reds" which was longer than four hours, when the lights went up, everyone was just dumbfounded about how powerful it was.

TO: Some editors say that they know how to put a scene together immediately after they watch the dailies while others simply say that they cannot do that and need to find their way through the footage.

CM: Well, let me say that all of this can be learned. I don't think it's exclusive or you have to be gifted. I had always wanted to do some writing.

TO: Editing is the final rewrite…

CM: Well, editing is very much like writing. I was at dinner once with Herb Gardner and Paddy Chayefsky (Network, The Hospital, Marty) and I said to Paddy that someday I wanted to do some writing. And he used to talk like a New York cab driver and he says, 'Kid, there's only three things you gotta know: Who's the main character? What does he want? What's preventing him from getting it? That's all you gotta know.' I started to study writing and storytelling which made the biggest impact on my editing. And you start to learn about clarity and narrative movement and so the real thing that helped me become an editor was learning about storytelling.

TO: In Something Wild, the story starts in one direction and then goes to an entirely different place.

CM: Well, we got a lot of people upset with that movie because of the sharp left turn we took. There's always a promise in storytelling about who the story's about and what it's to be. And that film totally betrayed (laughs) the promise! And it made a lot of people angry but also a lot of people enjoyed it because it wasn't conventional. But making that turn—I owe all that to Demme and to his skill and to Ray Liotta.

TO: Who is incredibly scary in the film...

CM: Oh, my God. I can remember getting the dailies and there's one shot in which Ray shows up at the dance and sees her (Melanie Griffith) and him (Jeff Daniels) and from that point on, it's a different movie.

TO: Right, that's the moment that the viewer just stops.

CM: The whole transition happens just by seeing this guy. He was just magnificent in it. Absolutely brilliant. But the comedy wasn't lost in it, either, even though it was dark comedy.

TO: But what's interesting is that whether audiences loved it or hated it, the film gained a lot of attention.

CM: Yes, it garnered a lot of attention because of the left turn but it was also a hard movie to do because we didn't have a lot of time. From the first day of shooting to the final answer print was six-and-a-half months. And it was done on a Moviola! I was there around the clock.

TO: How did The Silence of the Lambs come about?

CM: I was in a mix with Jonathan Demme for Miami Blues and he said, 'Orion just gave me this book and I read it last night and it's unbelievable.' And he hands me the book and says, 'Tell me what you think.' And I went home that night and read it and the next day I told him 'I want to do it.'

TO: It was a huge commercial success. Now, it's been reported that Anthony Hopkins has only 16 minutes of screen time.

CM: Really?

TO: Yes.

CM: Well, certainly, he commands a bigger presence in the film than sixteen minutes.

TO: Suspense, drama, it has to be one of your finest achievements. Did you know you had something special?

CM: Well, we start shooting and I get the first day's dailies and my assistant and all of us are wondering what Hopkins is going to do. Silence of the Lambs was cut on a Steenbeck. So, we put the first roll of dailies up and we're running and it's Lecter. And he turns to the camera and he says, 'Hello, Clarice.' And we all went, 'Holy shit!'

TO: The very first day?

CM: Yes, we really said that! We said, 'He's got it! Oh, my God, what do we have here?' And from that day we knew, we knew every moment and every day that we had an extraordinarily powerful film. And it kept coming in that way.

TO: What did you keep in mind when you were editing the film? Was it the notion of suspense? Of drama? Or something else?

CM: Jonathan and I had talked about it and after I read the book I said, 'John, give me something that I can key off of when we're not together—something that I can just keep with me when we're not together, when I'm doing the assembly. And he thought for a moment and he said something really brilliant. He said, 'You know, this is a very sad story.' And I got it. It's a very human story. This is not a supernatural, vampire kind of movie. It's a movie about the darkest part of our own beings and he nailed it there. And I keyed off of that all the time.

TO: The feeling of melancholy that Clarice Starling has—her backstory...

CM: Right and even though Hannibal is a monster, he is one of us.

TO: Which makes it all the more frightening.

CM: Yes, that was key. The other thing we discussed was a style thing and we both agreed that the audience should never get ahead of the story for even a tenth of a second. You never knew where you were going, unless you read the book and even then, we were really good at that. And the other thing we did was not to explain everything.

TO: How so?

CM: For example, there's a lot of jumping where you don't see the in-between steps. Hannibal Lecter's in a cell, looking at a pen. And the next time you see him, he's got it. Of course he could get it! He's so smart. Or they find a cop dead on the gymnasium floor and then you're in the ambulance and it's Hannibal. But you never see how all that's done.

TO: But the audience has no problem accepting it.

CM: Right, and in a way that film has a literary sense to it because with film, everything is usually up front. But we were asking the audience to fill stuff in, which is more likely to happen in a book.

TO: You and Demme left no time for the audience to breathe.

CM: That film was an intense cutting experience. That thing is razor sharp to the frame. I think, in terms of my career and how I feel about some of my editing, that film and Philadelphia, are some of my best examples, both for very different reasons. I knew I had great performances. But something interesting about the film was that in building those performances and putting them together; most of Tony Hopkins's performances are his first take. Between set-ups he would prepare himself and he gave pretty much everything on the first take. The other takes were absolutely fine but they didn't get to the place that he got to on the first take. It was just extraordinary.

TO: What was the reaction to the first screening?

CM: We knew right away that it was special. There's an interesting story about the scene with the crosscutting between Crawford going to a house and Clarice going into Jame Gumb's house. When I got the dailies, it wasn't really delineated in the script and so I felt that this was a perfect thing to be parallel cut. So, I talked to the script supervisor and asked if Demme wanted it parallel cut or linear. And she said that she wasn't sure and that there were no notes and that they shot it linear. So I did it linear and about a week or two later we were looking at the cut and that scene comes up and Demme's looking at it and he leans over and whispers in my ear, 'Why don't you parallel cut that?' (laughs). I went back and parallel cut it and it took about three days and I was getting it to work really well except that I needed one piece. I was really close but I needed something and I'm sitting there and I'm looking at Colleen Sharp (first assistant editor) and I can't get it to work. And I look across the room at the film bin and there's one piece of film hanging on the bin.

TO: You're kidding.

CM: No, and I look at it and it's a shot of Crawford. And it's the one shot I needed. I don't know what it was doing there. How it happened. I put it in and that was the scene!

TO: And all the while the audience is thinking, "Get there, get there, get there!"

CM: Right, it was amazing.

TO: What are some of the films that have influenced you?

CM: When I was fairly young I had the ability to see a lot of films from 1949-1961. I liked Kurosawa's The Seven Samurai, Citizen Kane. I liked Rene Clement's Forbidden Games, The Apu Trilogy by Satyajit Ray. Definitely Bunuel, Exterminating Angel and Viridiana. DeSica (Vittorio). I got to see all of those when I was young and it had a profound influence on me.

TO: What keeps you going? Why do you keep doing it?

CM: I love the craft. I love building the story. And I love making it work and I love making performances and building those. What I really learned to do and that I enjoy the most is building an emotional moment that works. The ebb and flow of it—that's the real challenge. I like all of it. But it's all about successfully conveying the emotion of a moment.

STEPHEN MIRRIONE, ACE

Photograph courtesy the American Cinema Editors and ACE Eddie Awards

LOS ANGELES, CA

Partial Credits: Suburbicon, The Revenant, Birdman: Or The Unexpected Virtue of Ignorance, The Monuments Men, The Hunger Games, Contagion, The Ides of March, Biutiful, The Informant!, Leatherheads, Ocean's Thirteen, Babel, Good Night and Good Luck, Ocean's Twelve, 21 Grams, Confessions of a Dangerous Mind, Ocean's Eleven, Traffic, Swingers.

He was almost going to stop pursuing editing and take a different job. And the next call led to the start of Stephen's amazing career. How inspiring to hear him say that he reached an understanding of the importance of never giving up—that he had to do everything possible to make a scene as great as it could possibly be.

TO: Stephen, you are an Academy Award recipient for Traffic. How did you get your start?

SM: While I was at U.C. Santa Cruz I figured out I wanted to be an editor. In 1991, I moved to Los Angeles and immediately started volunteering, trying to get work on graduate student thesis films at USC and UCLA. There was a flyer of a film that was shot in 35mm and they had arranged cutting rooms on the Disney lot. I called, and it happened to be the thesis film of Doug Liman.

TO: That's great.

SM: He had an editor and I was working as an assistant and after a few weeks she was done with her cut. Doug asked me to take over editing picture and to do some sound design. We worked through that summer and right around the time we were finishing, he got an offer to direct a fairly low budget feature with Andrew McCarthy and Kristy Swanson.

TO: This would have been Getting In, right?

SM: Yes, and they agreed to hire me and that was our first film together.

TO: What were you cutting on?

SM: 35mm on a KEM. It was seven days a week, long, long hours, and we were both essentially learning in terms of dealing with something at that scale. And it's a bit of a rollercoaster, which is somewhat typical in the industry. You wait a year expecting a film to get distribution and it may or may not.

TO: Okay, what happened next?

SM: A few months passed, and I got a call from Doug Liman. He said he was going to do a low budget film. And I really was seriously considering turning it down because I started to think that I was being irresponsible.

TO: In what way?

SM: I was thinking that I was being greedy in just wanting to cut instead of paying my dues as an assistant.

TO: And you do have to choose wisely because it's a 9-12-month commitment.

SM: That's exactly right and when I worked on this movie or that, it could be a year of my life. And, financially, I was living month to month already. At that point, I was 24 years old and I felt that if it didn't happen by the time I was 30…

TO: Being a full editor and making a good living…

SM: Yeah, I mean I was already a few years out of college and barely scraping by. And you really start to question what you're doing. I had a friend who was working on The Real World. They had a job opening for a post-production supervisor. It paid well, I went in for an interview.

TO: But you'd be off the editing path…

SM: Yes, and they hadn't yet offered the job. But if they had, who knows what choice I would have made. I ultimately ended up doing Doug's movie and that was Swingers. There was something that happened on that movie—a do or die moment. And that's what was going on in the movie—that you're going to make it or you're going to give up on your dream.

TO: Pretty amazing that you came that close to walking away.

SM: I think everyone involved in that movie was kind of experiencing that same moment in life. But on Swingers, something happened.

TO: What do you mean?

SM: I realized that if I had just given it that extra ten minutes or that extra hour on those movies it may have made a difference. I realized that what we do lives on forever. There's no going back and changing that. And it was while I was cutting Swingers that I got into the mode of 'I can never give up on a scene and making a scene work.' The movie has to be great and every moment has to be great.

TO: To think that you came so close to not pursuing editing.

SM: I owe so much to Jon Favreau and Vince Vaughn and the whole cast really, for giving me such honest material to work with. To me, that was the moment, where everything really changed. And every movie I did after that were movies I wanted to do rather than doing them for work.

TO: What attracts you to a project?

SM: The most important thing is the script. If I read it and I don't understand it or don't relate to it, I know I'm not going to add as much to that project. After the script, the most important thing is the director. And is that a director whose movies I respond to?

TO: You do a lot of L-cuts. You bring a lot of sound into scenes that are upcoming. I watched Babel again last night and you can enjoy the film just by listening to it.

SM: Yeah, exactly.

TO: Do you think you'd like to direct?

SM: I don't think so. I don't have that thing that I'm trying to say to the world. I look at what I do as having a sensitivity to emotion, to rhythm, and being able to accomplish a goal with the given material as an artist with my own life experiences. I read the script and then I try to forget it. And this is where it becomes difficult to describe the process. Sometimes you build the entire scene based on a single line or a single expression. Sometimes it really is going through frame one, line by line, and watching it grow as you put it together.

TO: I think Babel is a more complex film to put together than Traffic. That wonderful shot where the two kids being blown by the wind at the top of the mountain.

SM: Well, I want to respond a bit. To me, editing is about point of view. Helping the audience understand a scene—whose head you're in—whose eyes are you seeing the scene through? That's what an editor has the most control over—creating that point of view and altering that. A lot of people give me praise for specific moments that occur within a movie. Those things are all scripted.

With the kids, Alejandro wanted to have a few shots of the kids and he knew that there weren't going to be a lot of times where you'd see them happy. They got up there on the top of the mountain and they did the shot of them peeing—no big deal. And then suddenly this huge wind came up from nowhere. Alejandro saw that moment and told the kids to lean into the wind. And he was able to capture this magical thing and the spirit of what they were feeling up there. And it was such an emotionally charged shot that we couldn't just put it anywhere. We got to the end and we were actually mixing the movie and we still had no place to put this shot.

TO: I had no idea.

SM: Alejandro would say, 'Can you think of someplace to put that?' And I looked through the movie and the brother had already been killed. And one day, for whatever reason, I remember seeing the shot of the boy's face and finding a spot to put it in. I wouldn't have even have tried it except every day Alejandro would come to me and say, 'You have to find a spot for it.' I put it in and he loved it and of course he was right—that moment said emotionally, without having continuity to anything—it said what you wanted the audience to feel.

TO: Because of where it is in the film, that moment will never happen again.

SM: Exactly. In that moment, he has this heightened awareness of what he's lost. And that's one of the great things about working with Alejandro. He's able to keep pushing and recognize that, deep down, there's still something missing.

TO: In 2000 it was Almost Famous, Gladiator, Wonder Boys, Crouching Tiger Hidden Dragon. And any one of those films could have won.

SM: I'm a fan of all of those movies where the editing was just exceptional in ways that weren't completely obvious. There was a subtly to all the work that year that was really impressive.

TO: Did you have any idea you'd be nominated?

SM: (Laughs) Well, first, I have to go back a couple of years. I was at home and Steven called me and said he had a small movie he was going to do called Traffic, he liked Go, and he thought I would be perfect to edit it. I thought this was going to be a small movie. The script was so good and so powerful. The characters were so well drawn. And that was the last time I talked to Steven because they were shooting all over the world.

TO: Were you cutting electronically?

SM: I was cutting on Avid, but we were printing film. We would watch the film every day and then I would put the scenes together. I worked really hard and he came back for a day and we watched some of the scenes with Benicio del Toro where he's in the car with Manolo. The scene is in Spanish. Steven turns to me, 'So, do you speak Spanish?' And I said, 'No'. And he said, 'Oops, neither do I!' And that was the last time I spoke with him until I put the first cut together. Eventually we worked for a couple of weeks. And then he said, 'Well, I feel we're ready to screen this.' And I said, 'Really, are you serious? And he said, 'You've already done a tremendous amount of very hard work and you did a good job. So if it's easy, let it be easy.'

TO: That's great.

SM: Yeah, and that for me, was a real specific moment in terms of my life where I was very happy. I think that what I brought to that movie was a sense of urgency and pace and a new way of dealing with jump cuts and shifting place in an expressive way. I had seen The Limey that he had done and saw the way that he had used jump cuts. But with Traffic, any time that happened it had to feel smooth—it had to be expressive—it had to feel like a documentary.

TO: It really does, though. You definitely achieved that feeling. It was too real at some moments. Michael Douglas's daughter's scenes—I had trouble watching them. They were so realistic.

SM: I do think that, regarding the editorial style, which I didn't know if he'd respond to at first, was the right thing and he responded to it.

Every now and then he'd say, 'Let's do that thing where you pre-lap and then do a jump cut.'

TO: You mean bring the audio from the other shot into the current shot and then jump to it.

SM: Right and to me, that's a very simple trick. And when you're cutting a dialogue scene and the cut feels unmotivated or is bumping, if you prelap the other person who's talking, naturally the audience wants to see who's talking.

TO: Right.

SM: And it smooths out the cut in a way because you're manipulating the audience into wanting to see the cut. I certainly thought Benicio's performance was exceptional and Don Cheadle's performance was Oscar worthy. But I also had very low expectations.

TO: Why?

SM: Steven knew that Erin Brockovich was being received very well and the chances of both movies being nominated—well, who knew? So, when the nominations actually happened, it was absolutely incredible. And meeting Dede Allen and shaking her hand was a great honor. Going into that award ceremony, I did not expect to win and didn't want to.

TO: Really, why not?

SM: It's a weird thing to say, but I thought, 'This is all happening too fast.' And I thought, 'What happens if I do achieve this? What happens next?' And it really blew me away when I actually won and it definitely gave me a different perspective coming out of that.

TO: You had a cut that was three hours and ten minutes and the final film was two hours and twenty minutes. Was it difficult getting it down to that time?

SM: You want to make sure that you know what an audience is thinking from frame one to the end. You're controlling all the information. You're controlling everything that they know from the beginning to the end. And you have to make sure that they don't go on some tangent that they can't come back from. We pretty quickly got from three hours down to about two and a half hours by removing things that were redundancies. And then from the 30 minutes down to 2:20, we had pressure from the studio to get it shorter.

TO: There was a collective gasp from the audience of the POV shot of Erika Christensen when she's lying on the bed.

SM: Right. I want to talk about one of the strategies that I had to adopt because we had so much footage on Traffic. One of the things that you're trying to do as an editor is limit your choices because your choices are infinite. On Traffic I decided that I was going to think of this as a documentary and that there could only be one camera at any time.

TO: That's really smart.

SM: And so I was always going to cut a scene as if there was only one camera even though there were two cameras and they were shooting multiple setups. And it really helped me to create an authenticity with those scenes. The other thing is to try and never repeat a setup within a scene.

TO: Ah, that's really interesting.

SM: And if the director has been able to cover a scene with a number of setups and I don't have to repeat one that means that with every cut I can reveal something new. And if I only had two shots to work with, I tried to hold them for as long as possible to make it seem as if I had only one cut in the scene. And so a scene like that—that point of view—I knew how powerful it was and that there was a real power in that image. And I knew that the shots that came before and after it were really important.

TO: You're flipping through television channels. What films are on that you'd stop and watch?

SM: A Hard Day's Night because for me, more than any other movie, it was a movie that I watched in the middle of cutting Swingers. And I had this epiphany of freedom of style and the freedom of using shots. Up until that point, I was using the rules of editing. But then after that, I gave myself permission to be looser with things.

TO: Who knew you could do that stuff until you saw it in that movie?

SM: Yeah. Dazed and Confused. That movie is amazing in terms of the reality of the dialogue and the pace of pulling you through that night. The music, the locations… I just think it's flawless. I loved the editing in that movie. A movie that is just so good and where I'm not even aware of the editing is Dog Day Afternoon. That movie starts and it's over and you just lived through it and it's really astonishing the work done on that movie.

TO: What else?

SM: Oh, there's this movie that whenever it's on I have to watch it from beginning to end. Do you know Blood In, Blood Out? It's directed by Taylor Hackford.

TO: No, I don't know it. Wait, let me look it up.

SM: I can't remember who edited it.

TO: Okay, it shows Fred Steinkamp and Karl Steinkamp.

SM: There you go. I don't want to offend anyone and it's a tiny bit cheesy. But, the moment it starts—and it's the editing—there's just something about that movie from the first lines of dialogue that just pulls me through to the end.

WALTER MURCH, ACE

Photograph courtesy the American Cinema Editors and ACE Eddie Awards

NEW YORK CITY, NEW YORK

Partial Credits: Tomorrowland, Particle Fever, Jarhead, Cold Mountain, The Talented Mr. Ripley, The English Patient, The Godfather Trilogy: 1901-1980, The Godfather: Part III, Ghost, The Unbearable Lightness of Being, Captain EO, Apocalypse Now, Julia, The Conversation.

Picture and sound editor, sound designer and mixer, author, and known to editors around the world. With The English Patient, he received Academy Awards for both film editing and sound mixing. Walter will say there is a reason for a picture edit and a reason for the presence or lack of a sound. This is the talented Mr. Walter Murch.

TO: Walter, you are a three-time Academy Award recipient for your work on Apocalypse Now and The English Patient. What have you learned about filmmaking that wasn't so apparent when you started?

WM: Well, I guess it depends on what you mean by 'started'. I fell in love with the tape recorder when I was 10 or 11. And the surprising thing, I think, is that recording and editing sound—which is essentially what I'm doing now given a few changes of technology—is something which I had no way of knowing would turn into a career. In fact, I was the only person I knew who was interested in this kind of stuff.

TO: Recording sounds.

WM: Recording sound and then cutting them up into pieces and rearranging them. Playing them backwards, which is something I was doing this morning. (Laughs) So the big surprise is that I'm still doing it and that I've been able to make a living out of it and to have had such enjoyment in it.

TO: It reminds me of the notion that your optimum job is to be able to do something that you loved doing between the ages of eight and eleven. You bring that up in the Ondaatje book, "Conversations: Walter Murch and the Art of Editing Film". The thought that 'they're paying me to do this?'

WM: I guess that's it. And the other big surprise—and this is strange even to me—is that in my mid-teens, I put the tape recorder away.

TO: You outgrew it?

WM: Well, I was a kid then and the recorder was like my bug collection. As an adolescent, I didn't see how a career could emerge out of it. What was I going to do with my life? I wound up spending a year in Paris at the Sorbonne in 1963. This was right at the height of the French New Wave - Godard, Truffaut, etc. – and I started thinking about film as a result. Later, I found out that there were such things as film schools. I got accepted to USC with a fellowship. And it was like you were saying earlier—'they're paying me to do this?' But, despite my earlier "bug collection" I had absolutely no idea how sound was done for motion pictures.

TO: Really?

WM: But I found that we do with film sound exactly what I was doing with my little recordings. And editing picture is pretty much the same: chop the dailies into little bits and then rearrange them. This realization really cemented the love affair that had begun when I was ten: the unity of film construction, whether it is picture or sound.

TO: You've written about this but to learn about how you started on this journey is interesting.

WM: The word "editing" is really awkward, because it implies a connection with journalistic editing or book editing. And film is something completely different, more like music or dance.

TO: Whereas, as you said earlier, constructing seems to be a really good word to use. When you were growing up, what films did you go to see?

WM: I grew up in Manhattan. I used to go to the Thalia Theater on 95thStreet and Broadway. I remember going to The Seventh Seal—the Bergman film – probably in 1958. I wasn't thinking anything about the mechanics or the construction of the film. I just was overwhelmed that somebody decided that they could make a film about this subject matter. Totally unlike Hollywood films of the time.

TO: Which is about Death coming to take Max Von Sydow's life.

WM: And that you could show a half-decayed corpse on the screen the way he did. But the thing that struck me most was that I got something out of it that I had never gotten out of a film before.

TO: Which was?

WM: That it had been made by a human being—"somebody" had made this film. I was far from being an obsessed filmgoer. I saw the usual amount of films that a kid growing up would see. But films, before I saw The Seventh Seal, were a little like landscapes or mountain ranges: kind of natural phenomena that just existed. I never thought about the people who made those films. Whereas with The Seventh Seal – it was so strong that I suddenly understood it must have been made by a person—Ingmar Bergman, as it turned out.

TO: So, perhaps it was clear that a book is written by someone and that a film is made by someone.

WM: Yes. His personality came through so strongly and I guess creative personalities had not come through in the other films that I had seen up to that point.

TO: Were you also aware of the set of conscious decisions and the amount of people who are involved in making the film?

WM: I didn't take it quite that far. I walked two miles home from the theater still in a daze from having seen the film. And I began a kind of iterative, logical sequence:

1. A person made a film.
2. I am a person.
3. Therefore (dot, dot, dot)...

But I never completed it because I wasn't in a film world and nobody I knew had anything to do with films. So, the idea that I could ever work on a film didn't seem possible. But, looking back on it, that's where the crack opened up. I went to a lot of films in the late '50's and early 60's. Fellini. 400 Blows. Breathless. Kurosawa's Yojimbo. Other Bergman films. Because I wanted to recapture that feeling. I intuitively felt that I was only going to get that from World Cinema and not American films, which had a bland corporate feel.

TO: Editors told me they wanted a different way of looking at a story.

WM: It was certainly true of our generation who were all going to film school in the mid to late '60's. That was a great commonality in those years.

TO: Have you edited films that didn't do well with audiences but that you feel should be revisited?

WM: Sure—K19, Cold Mountain, Jarhead, The Talented Mr. Ripley.

TO: It's amazing to me, because each of those films offers something really unique.

WM: For each of them, there was a certain amount of expectation. And in each case, the general consensus was that they had fallen short for some reason. Now, what that reason is I leave to the viewers. I had a great deal of joy and hopes for them. I think the common thread in all of them, which is what attracted me to the stories in the first place, is also what made it difficult for them to be accepted.

TO: Which is?

WM: With the exception of Talented Mr. Ripley, the United States was at war and all of those films have a slightly skewed view of the military experience.

TO: There is often a "war weariness" syndrome and they just don't go to films when they have war themes.

WM: With K19, it asks you to sympathize with the Soviet military. Cold Mountain asks you to sympathize with a Confederate deserter. And Jarhead asks you to sympathize with the frustration and boredom of war and the frustration of the foot soldier who is relatively helpless trying to compete with massive air power.

TO: How do you find previews?

WM: The most powerful preview experiences were American Graffiti and Ghost. With both of them, the audiences were very vocal.

TO: You mean those two films struck an immediate chord…

WM: Yes, audiences may be affected by The English Patient or Apocalypse Now, but those films don't ask you to be vocal as you are watching them. The American Graffiti preview was one where the audience rocked from the very first second and never let up. Ned Tanen, who was the Universal executive, came out shaking his head saying that this film was an embarrassment to the studio. But, that discontinuity between the experience that you have in the audience and whatever you're going to get from the studio are sometimes wildly divergent.

TO: Films you have worked on are known throughout the world and several are preserved by the Library of Congress.

WM: I'm very happy that that's the case.

TO: Today's films have a lot of very sophisticated visual effects. Audiences can understand the use of constructs such as flashbacks and flash forwards. But do you think audiences can follow films that are told in a nonlinear way with parallel or converging storylines as opposed to the normal timeline?

WM: Godfather II has a converging structure, and Julia has many flashbacks, and both of those films were made in the early to mid 1970's. English Patient, made in the 1990's, is clearly a film with a parallel time structure. I think if you could go back in time and show Godfather II to an audience in the 1920's, maybe they would be confused. That, certainly, was the bone of contention between Orson Welles and Universal on Touch of Evil. Welles had two stories told in parallel and the studio just didn't like that, didn't think audiences were ready for that.

It's true that an audience has to work harder when the storyline is time-shifted in some way. That's one of the things that's interesting to me as a filmmaker but I also acknowledge that it does require extra mental gearing when you're watching those films.

But I think in the 40 years that I've been working in film, I don't detect a greater sophistication in this department. I would say that audiences are less willing to put in that extra effort now than they were. But, it's also true what you said—that there is a greater degree of sophistication about the image itself. So those two things are slightly contradictory. But that's the world we find ourselves in – a world where many of the film heroes are wearing skintight outfits and masks.

TO: And yet, I think that if the audiences encounter films that are told in this methodology—if they're good films, if they're well told, if the audience is led through and not left in a confused state—then audiences will go to see those films and some of them tend to do quite well.

WM: Yes, I absolutely agree.

TO: If you weren't working in the film industry, what would you be doing?

WM: (Laughs) Hmm… Astronomer, maybe. That's my default mode in reading—not only Astronomy but also Physics and Biology. It's very dramatic what's happening in those fields these days. Particle Fever is about the Large Hadron Collider and the search for the Higgs boson. The fact that I get to spend time with physicists while making a film about it is a very nice dovetailing of my two interests: film and physics.

THOM NOBLE

Photo courtesy of Thom Noble

LOS ANGELES, CA

Partial Credits: The Headhunter's Calling, Point Break, Alex Cross, RED, The Time Traveler's Wife, Flightplan, Reign of Fire, Vertical Limit, The Mask of Zorro, The Hudsucker Proxy, Thelma & Louise, The Mosquito Coast, Witness, Red Dawn, The Apprenticeship of Duddy Kravitz, And Now for Something Completely Different, Fahrenheit 451.

You don't speak French and your first feature is Fahrenheit 451 for Francois Truffaut. That's Thom Noble. I would often ruin the recordings because he'd have me laughing—especially from his impression of Otto Preminger. He's fast, precise, doesn't second guess his cuts, and doesn't live in the cutting room. He's a terrific man and a remarkable editor.

✄

TO: Thom, you are an Academy Award and ACE Eddie recipient for Witness. You've been editing for six decades!

TN: It's amazing isn't it? And you know something? As soon as it starts to be boring, I'm not going to do it anymore! (Both Laugh)

TO: How did you get your start?

TN: I started off not editing movies but editing books. I did that after I got out of military service. Eventually a friend of mine, John Bloom, was responsible for getting me into film editing.

TO: John is the Academy Award winner for Gandhi.

TN: I had known John since I was nine. After John had done his military service in the RAF, as did I, he started working for the story department at Pinewood Studios. John moved across to the cutting rooms for a TV series and asked me to come over and see how I felt in the cutting room. For dailies, they'd say, 'See where the clapperboard comes down? You mark an X on that. And when you hear the sound, put a line on either side and when we have a moment we'll try to show you how to sync it all together.' I did three or four films as a first and then I got the big break with Truffaut.

TO: Which is really amazing. Your first full editing credit was on Fahrenheit 451. How did that happen?

TN: I was the first on a film directed by Terence Young, who had done Dr. No and From Russia With Love. It was The Amorous Adventures of Moll Flanders. About a year after that, his producer, Mickey Dalamar, called me. And he said, 'Oh, Thom, I'm here with this French director and he's going to make his first English language film. And he's looking for an editor, but it has to be a woman because he's only worked with women editors in France. He then goes on to tell me it's Francois Truffaut.

TO: You're kidding...

TN: Mickey was amazed that I had heard of him and that I had read the book they were planning to film - Fahrenheit 451! (Laughs) Five or six weeks go by and I was working on Stanley Donen's Arabesque.

TO: You were an assistant on that, right?

TN: Yes. And I get this call from Mickey, 'I'm with Francois and I've told him about you. Would you like to meet him?' And I said, 'Of course!' And he said, 'Don't forget. He doesn't speak a word of English.' And I said, 'Mickey, don't worry, it's not a problem.'

TO: Okay, what happened next?

TN: I went to meet him and I realized that I couldn't form a single sentence in French! (Both Laugh) I understood everything he said and I could say, "D'accord" or "Entendu" or all of those fillers.

TO: You must have been dying.

TN: I was and I thought, 'This is so stupid. This is my big opportunity and I've screwed it up!' The interview ground to a halt pretty quickly. (Laughs) And as I walked out the door, all the French came flooding back to me! Too late to go back in. On New Year's Eve, the phone rang late at night, something like ten to twelve. It was Mickey: 'Happy New Year! Francois wants you to do the movie' And I said, 'Wow! How? Why?' And he said, 'Just get your crew together. We start shooting in 14 days at Pinewood. Just practice your French.

TO: Amazing.

TN: While we were shooting, at the end of the day Francois would invite me to watch Hitchcock films. Eventually I asked him, 'You know that first interview? Why did you choose me?' And he said, 'I interviewed all these people and they all told me how they loved Jules et Jim and my other films. But you were so shy and so nice that I had total confidence in you and so I decided to hire you.'

TO: That's great.

TN: Isn't that crazy? I would say to Truffaut, 'I think we need a shot here' and it was no problem—it was that kind of budget.

TO: Bernard Herrmann did the music...

TN: We had a problem. We had given him all the revisions for the cues and he never took any notice of them. So when we came onto the scoring stage, one cue was a minute and a half too long. And he said that he had never gotten any of the changes. At which point I blew up and called him a liar in front of the whole orchestra. Then out from the control room came the mixer, an irate Scotsman in a kilt and told Benny I was absolutely right and that he should shut up and fix his mistake. After that Truffaut always referred to Benny as "your friend'.

TO: You did a lot of movies with Ted Kotcheff…

TN: Working with Ted was always a blast. I got a call from Ted's wife and she said that he was doing a film in Canada, but they had absolutely no money.

TO: The Apprenticeship of Duddy Kravetz with Richard Dreyfuss.

TN: Yes. His wife said, 'There's no editor. The stuff is piling up and he's just too embarrassed to ask you to come and help him.' I went to Montreal and it was a mess. They were six weeks into a ten-week schedule and the thing is that by the ninth week, I had caught up.

TO: That's amazing.

TN: Then, out of the blue, I got a call from Otto Preminger's office. He had a film that they had shot in Israel. They had an editor already on it, but they needed help to keep on schedule.

TO: Which film was that?

TN: It was called Rosebud.

TO: Oh, okay, so you have Peter O'Toole, Richard Attenborough, Raf Vallone, Isabelle Huppert in Rosebud.

TN: And the first thing is that you'd go into the production office and everyone was scared shitless of Otto. I mean the terror that this man caused… (Laughs) So they said to me, 'Look, before you even go in to meet Otto, there are 54 people that Otto has already fired from the picture!'

TO: That's ridiculous.

TN: Right. And then they said, 'Good luck with your interview!' I went in and Preminger is sitting at his desk and he says (imitates with thick accent) 'What have you done recently?' And I told him I'd just done this film in Canada, The Apprenticeship of Duddy Kravetz. And he says, 'I have never heard of this. What else have you done?' I said that I had done Billy Two Hats with Gregory Peck. And he says, 'Why did you make him so fat?' (Both Laugh) And I said, 'I cut him as lean as I possibly could, I assure you!' And he said, 'Gregory Peck lives next to me in the South of France and he is not this fat.' (Both Laugh) So I said, 'Can I be forgiven?' And he looked at me and said, 'Go and fix your money.'

TO: That's really funny.

TN: Actually, before Peter O'Toole came on the film, they had cast Bob Mitchum. And I asked whether there was any footage of him. I saw this Rififi style scene where Mitchum was just drunk out of his mind and swaying from side to side. (Both Laugh) And now I know why they replaced him! Then the phone rings and Otto wants to see me. I go in and he says, 'You will edit the last ten reels of the film.' And I said, 'Great, that's fantastic!' And he said, 'Oh, you think the first ten reels aren't good?' And I said, 'No, no. It's an action film and obviously there's going to be a big shoot out at the end!' And he says, 'We shall see. Come back at four o'clock and we will screen the ten reels.' So there's this small theatre in London and in the front there are two huge armchairs and Otto and I are sitting in them.

TO: This is when you're first seeing what the other editor had done?

TN: Yes. And sitting behind us are the associate producer, the first A.D., and a whole bunch of other people. It was only an assembly. It was just that—after 'Action', the editor had cut and just before Otto said cut, the editor had cut there. And Otto said to me, 'You could maybe take something off the front of this shot.' (Both Laugh) Then he looks at me and says, 'You're not taking notes.' And I said, 'No, I never take notes.' And I hear this urgent whispering from behind. So I've survived to the end of the screening and Otto says to me, 'Mr. Noble, how long will it take you to do these cuts?' And I said, 'Lunchtime tomorrow?' And he said, 'You will be working through the night?' And I said, 'No, I'm going home now and I'll be in tomorrow around nine o'clock and it will be done.' And he said, 'Do not lie to me.' (Both

Laugh) And I said, 'I promise you. It'll be done.' So I went in that next morning and it was really and truly easy and I was done by half past twelve. I went down to the washroom to wash my hands because they were covered in china marker. And strolling down the hall coming towards me is Otto.

TO: Okay…

TN: Otto says, 'What are you doing out of your cutting room?' And I told him I'd finished. And he said, 'Finished? We can see it now?' And I said, 'We could.' And he said, 'No. I will take you and your wife to lunch and then we will see what you have done.'

TO: You edited First Blood. That movie is marvelously edited. It's got an amazing Jerry Goldsmith score…

TN: It does.

TO: Wasn't it frustrating for you to see the great response the film had but not being able to take credit for it?

TN: It was frustrating. But I couldn't get into the Union. I had a green card, but I couldn't get into the Guild.

TO: Okay, so that's why your credit on First Blood is Visual Consultant? Because you couldn't get the editor credit.

TN: Right. I could never take credit for stuff. On Uncommon Valor I got Editorial Consultant. On North Dallas Forty I had a weird credit as well. Three pictures in a row. When I first came to America it was for Who's Killing The Great Chefs of Europe? That had been shot in London, Munich, and Paris and by the time we brought it to America, I had cut all of it and I was allowed to take credit.

TO: And then you moved on to Red Dawn.

TN: By then the Guild had figured out that I wasn't going to go away, and we reached an agreement. So that was my Christmas present.

TO: So, there you are working on Red Dawn with John Milius.

TN: I read an article that when Quentin Tarantino was planning Inglorious Basterds, he used Red Dawn as a model of people fighting back.

TO: Any favorite genres?

TN: No, not really. It's the script. I was interviewed by Ridley (Scott) for Black Rain because Claire Simpson had put me up for it. And I said, 'That part of the barmaid is really interesting. Who are you thinking of casting?' And they said, 'Well, we haven't cast it yet.' And I never heard another word from Ridley. I called Claire and said, 'What happened?' And she said, 'You worried them. Normally, when editors come in they say anything to get the job, but you were discussing casting!'

TO: So what happened?

TN: About a year later, Phil Gersh, my agent, sent me the script to Thelma & Louise. And I told my him that I had to do the movie, no matter what, and I said, 'Just tell Ridley that I want to do this picture more than any other picture I've ever done. I would kill to do this picture.' (Laughs) And I wound up doing it and I guess that was the force of wanting.

TO: What made you want to do the movie so badly?

TN: It was just a great script. They were great female characters. And there was no question about it—that was a film that was going to make a difference. You know, at the time, no one had ever thought of two women in a road movie. It was like, 'Wow!'

TO: Even though The Time Traveler's Wife changes time periods, it's crafted in such a way that an audience can follow it.

TN: We would get the material into my machine by 10:30 in the morning. By lunchtime, I'd cut everything that had to be cut.

TO: That's amazing.

TN: And that happened every day.

TO: You know when you're done.

TN: Exactly. You have to know when to stop messing with it. I mean, I was lightning fast on the Moviola, but now, with the Avid—and thanks to you, of course—your amazing half-day training—(Laughs)

TO: You didn't need any more time. You picked it up so quickly.

TN: The first rule in my cutting room is that we never have food sent it. We always break for lunch. We get out of the cutting room and always go for a good meal and then come back and work. The second thing is that I, of course, do the first cut. When I'm done, I pass it over to my assistant who works on the sound effects and I do the music. Then, when we have the director's cut, I never touch the film after that or very rarely.

TO: You're that familiar with the material by then...

TN: I know every take because I've been through them all.

TO: What about previewing films?

TN: With Truffaut, the studio kept away and no one messed with him. I had worked with Stanley Donen who did exactly what he wanted to do as did Anthony Asquith. And you realize that no matter how powerful the director is, he's not really. Because the people making the film are the people paying for it. Unless you're in the Spielberg arena, you're running around doing what the studio says and it really doesn't matter what department you're in.

TO: What drew you to Witness?

TN: The Amish stuff is so majestic at the start and slow and dreamlike whereas the city stuff is much faster. The barn-raising scene is more dreamlike as opposed to the shoot-out at the end. So, you always had that balance between the two. The original editor had been fired because he had tried to cut the Amish stuff at the same pace of the city stuff. And it didn't work.

TO: I never knew that.

TN: Yeah, and I had never had the luxury before where a film had been completely shot and then being able to go from the start and right through in continuity.

TO: Right, it's rare when that happens.

TN: I had this meeting with Peter by the pool at the Bel Air and he was on the phone to Maurice Jarre…

TO: The composer…

TN: Right and he was saying to Maurice that the Amish don't have music and that it was going to be tricky. I said to Peter that there's a guy named David Hykes. David does this thing called Overtone Chanting, which is a group of people who sing one note. And if you do it, what happens is that behind you, you can hear this absolutely extraordinary, almost like a high clarinet note that develops. And it's caused by the vibration in the air, like a musical instrument. Peter was fascinated by that.

TO: I've never heard about that.

TN: I got a call from Peter and he said, 'Oh, Thom, I'm just about to get on a plane. I know you're perfect for this film. Just come out to Australia and we'll go from there.'

TO: Talk about a vote of confidence.

TN: So now I'm in Australia and Peter said, 'How long do you need?' And I said, 'Oh, I don't know. I've never done this before.'

TO: Meaning starting from the very beginning?

TN: Yes, so I said, 'Well, I'm not sure how long it's going to take to cut the first third of the picture, but I can't imagine more than ten days.' I called him and said I was on schedule and we sat down to watch what I had cut. The assistant was running the KEM and I was sitting on a rattan couch. And I was really, really nervous. But I knew that I had gotten it right and had achieved that dreamlike quality all the way through the train ride with the little boy and the scene in the bathroom where the boy sees the killing. And that was about the end of the first third.

TO: The bathroom scene is pivotal...

TN: I wanted to make the scene almost like a nightmare dream and I cut it like it was that. It's slow and you see half images of the character without really seeing what's going on. I tried to keep everything inside the little boy's head from the time he got on the train. And I thought, 'This is the finest work I've ever done. If he doesn't like it, I'm going to kill myself!' (Laughs) And really nothing was ever changed from the time I cut it and Peter looked at it and it went out to the theatres.

TO: What did he think of that first third?

TN: I'm sitting on one end of this couch and Peter is sitting on the other end. And I'm starting to get really nervous and I'm starting to shake a little and it's making the rattan make a creaking sound. (Both Laugh) I was nailing my feet to the ground so that my legs wouldn't move. Finally, he turned to me and said, 'I love it. I love it. It's so European.' (Laughs) Then I did the next third in ten days and the last third, which was the tricky part, because it has the barn raising and the shootout. Then I did the notes on that one and we were done!

TO: That's amazing. You did the whole thing in a month or so. It's Witness, A Chorus Line, Out of Africa, Prizzi's Honor, and Runaway Train. Did you think you had a chance?

TN: I was on Mosquito Coast in Belize and I thought, 'Witness is too subtly nuanced for anyone to get an Academy Award for it.'

Eventually, they announced the award and I was just amazed. I truly was. It was the last name I expected.

TO: You made the transition from editing on film to editing on digital. That's when I first met you, when I spent a few hours showing you the Avid. You picked it up, really, after less than two hours.

TN: What gave me the confidence was you saying to me, 'This is just a tool. You know how to cut already. This is just to help you go faster and smoother.' It's not an enemy, it's a friend.

TO: What have been some other career challenges?

TN: It was really difficult to cut three cameras running consecutively on a KEM—it's not the easiest thing to do. With digital, it's insanely easy. On Thelma and Louise, you had to be really careful.

TO: There were a lot of multiple cameras?

TN: Yes, usually three: one for Geena, one for Susan and the last for a two shot of them both. When I showed Ridley my first cut, he said, 'I know what you've done. You've cut it for performance. But there's just one thing.' He has an absolutely photographic memory of every shot that he's done. And he said, 'There's an exterior scene where she comes out of a phone booth and in the background there's a firefly that just goes by. It's not the best take but if you could just put that in.' And that was practically the only note on the first cut.

TO: That's really a great testament to your skills. I'd like to shoot out some names to you, okay?

TN: Okay.

TO: Truffaut.

TN: I think I learned everything about cutting from Truffaut. I had never cut two pieces of film together before I started on that film. It was a complete learning experience and also conducted in French. So you can imagine, you're speaking another language and you're cutting scenes together for the first time. I had done trims before and alterations before but not actual editing.

TO: Ted Kotcheff.

TN: A person who put his genius into his life. He's done some amazing movies.

TO: Preminger.

TN: Well it was at the end of his career, so it's difficult to judge. But I admire many of his earlier films—extraordinary films.

TO: Milius.

TN: (Laughs) Oh, that was a riot! He found a cameraman who was willing to shoot most scenes with six cameras so that he didn't have to be there at the start of the day. He figured everything would get covered (Both Laugh) A brilliant writer, brilliant mind, brilliant man. He chose to direct, but his heart and soul is into writing, not really directing. When it comes to cutting, it's insane. I did my cut and when it came time for the Director's Cut, I didn't see him for a couple of weeks. Finally, he came in and we started with the shootout with the boys. Not at the beginning of the movie as one normally would. We ran that and a few other scenes and he said, 'Great, great. I'll see you next week.' Then when he came back he brought Spielberg with him. And I showed him the same three reels and more. And Spielberg said, 'John, this is the best thing you've ever done.' So, John thought he could completely relax and he went away again!

TO: That's great.

TN: We were on the MGM lot as it was then, and we were waiting, and he finally came in around half past two. He had a big cigar and said, 'Okay, if we have to do this, let's do it.' We started running the film and after five minutes, the curtains part and this very small woman who's blinded by the light starts to find her way up where we are. She finally finds John and grabs hold of him and he's a big guy. And she drags him out of the theatre, screaming at him. (Both Laugh) And I said to the producer, 'Who's that?' And he said, 'Oh, you haven't met her. That's John's wife. We call her The Warden.' (Both Laugh)

TO: That's hilarious.

TO: Ridley Scott

TN: An amazing photographic memory. Shoots absolutely beautifully. There's no wasted stuff with Ridley. Towards the end of the film, he loses interest, because he has the next film lined up. I think they destroyed the real ending of Thelma & Louise because he wasn't around to fight for it.

TO: And yet now it's an iconic ending.

TN: It is an iconic ending, but there is a better one. It wasn't in the Director's Cut. There's a C-camera and the hubcap comes off the car as it travels vertically down after they make the jump. It flashes to the bottom of the canyon. Harvey Keitel feels something at his feet and it's the Polaroid that the girls took when they first set out. He holds it up and the camera over his shoulder moves closer and the image reverses and becomes nothing and that's the end of the movie.

TO: That's great.

TN: It was great, but I don't know where it is or how anyone would ever get to see it.

TO: You did two pictures with Martin Campbell.

TN: I think that Martin Campbell shoots better than any director I've ever worked with. His material is beautiful to put together. It's just so easy.

TO: On The Island of Dr. Moreau, did you work with Frankenheimer at all?

TN: Not at all. Frankenheimer walked away after the preview and didn't want to touch a frame of it. New Line called me in and said that the preview audience hated David Thewlis. They thought he was spineless and he was also a lawyer so they hated him for that! (Laughs) Val Kilmer and David Thewlis have a scene at the beginning of the film. And somebody asked David Thewlis 'What do you do?' And I managed to get him to say, by dubbing lines over his back and shoulder, 'I'm a lawyer, working for Amnesty International'! (Both Laughs)

TO: That's great!

TN: And that clears the whole lawyer thing for you and you're okay. And then there's a scene where the audience said that they had no idea what Dr. Moreau is actually trying to do. It's never explained what he's trying to do. So I said, 'Is there any footage whatsoever?' And they said, 'There is a scene, where they're on a veranda and it's a long shot of the two of them. Brando is drunk out of his mind and Val Kilmer is totally incoherent and no one can understand what they're saying.' (Both Laugh) And I said, 'Okay, but it's shot at a wide angle. And it looks like Val Kilmer is chewing the whole time and it looks like Brando is just spouting.

TO: Right.

TN: So I thought I would write some dialogue that would fit in with the chews from Kilmer. Something like 'You have to tell me... what's going on here?' (Laughs) And then Brando can rant and rave and I'll try to put words in Brando's mouth. I found an Australian actor who could do both a Val Kilmer voice and a Brando voice.

TO: This is incredible.

TN: And I put the words in their mouths and it worked like a dream. (Laughs)

TO: Amazing.

TN: And then I wrote a voiceover at the end for Thewlis to wrap everything up and then my work was done. I never saw the final film to see what they kept of mine or what they kept from Frankenheimer. But I did my bit.

TO: Any advice for students?

TN: People always make this mystique out of editing, but when you finally come down to it, you're joining two bits of film together and when it works, you know it. And if you don't know it, get out of the business! You have to know how to tell a story and gracefully edit out unnecessary dialogue. It's the final re-write.

TO: What keeps you going?

TN: The sheer pleasure of doing it.

BILL PANKOW, ACE

Photograph courtesy of the American Cinema Editors and ACE Eddie Awards

NEW YORK CITY, NY

Partial Credits: Gifted, American Ultra, Trespass, Letters to Juliet, Redacted, The Black Dahlia, Assault on Precinct 13, Mr. 3000, Drumline, Femme Fatale, Snake Eyes, The Funeral, Money Train, Carlito's Way, The Bonfire of the Vanities, Casualties of War, Body Double, Still of the Night. As Associate Editor: Wise Guys, Scarface, Dressed to Kill.

Assistant Editor: Kramer vs. Kramer.

What great versatility Bill has as an editor—romantic comedy, action, suspense thrillers, dramas. He is just genuinely appreciative—blessed is the word he'll use—to have the opportunity to do what he does for a living. He's an unassuming, modest, and extremely talented editor.

TO: Bill, you started your editing career in the mid 1970's and have worked almost without a significant break since then, which is a remarkable achievement. How did you get your start in the film business?

BP: I had just come out of NYU Film School and while I was there I met Bob Colesberry, who became a successful producer. He had gotten a job for no pay on a film. They needed someone to work in the editing room for free. I was offered the position and went into the editing room and there was an assistant, Hanna Wajshonig. Hanna taught me the ins and outs of a film editing room. I learned how to log and code and when that film was over, she referred me to someone who needed an apprentice sound editor on The Missouri Breaks. At that point I had gotten into the union and I started working in sound editing. Later on, I got promoted to a second assistant editor on Equus, edited by John Victor-Smith.

TO: I didn't realize you had worked on The Missouri Breaks and Equus.

BP: Yes. Sometime after that Jerry Greenberg, who had just finished working on Apocalypse Now, was driving back to NY. He called Dede Allen and said that when he arrived he would need an assistant to work with him on Kramer vs. Kramer. I had been working on the sound crew of The Wiz and Dede recommended me and I went to work with Jerry. We became good friends and he has been a mentor to me. I worked with him for a while and kept going from there.

TO: You worked with some amazing editors very early on. Was Still of the Night your first feature?

BP: Well, when I was working with Jerry as his assistant, he let me cut scenes as much as possible. He was always very generous. Still of the Night and Body Double were both films where I got an editor credit but I did all the assistant's work and then cut some scenes. But I really truly wasn't a co-editor until we got to The Untouchables.

TO: How did that come about?

BP: Jerry was hired to do the film but he was busy on another project and he wouldn't be available until the shooting of The Untouchables was finished. So he recommended to Brian (DePalma) that I edit while they were shooting and he'd join me when he was finished and that's how it worked out.

TO: You've worked with Brian DePalma on 11 films, two as assistant editor and nine as editor, more than any other editor he's worked with. And with DePalma, his collaboration went from Paul Hirsch to Jerry Greenberg to Bill Pankow and you've handled many of his films.

BP: Yes. I am extremely fortunate that Brian chose me to collaborate with him. It was a bit daunting at first to try and follow in the footsteps of such accomplished editors.

TO: You've edited his last nine films. What's your usual working style with him?

BP: He is a really great filmmaker and a great guy to work with. It's clear that he knows exactly what he wants to do in every film and that's how he shoots it. He's very respectful of every craft, especially editing. For the last few films, I'm editing as he's shooting, and as you know, directors are very busy while they're shooting. So, on the weekends, he'll come in and review what I've been editing. I'll make notes of what he wants to do and how he wants to change things. Then he'll go away until I'm ready for him. And that time away gets shorter and shorter as we refine the cut. And eventually it will get to the point where he'll stay for the day and we'll fine-tune everything.

TO: One of the things you always remember from Brian DePalma films is that there is always one amazing set piece that has this great editorial showcase. Sometimes there are more than one.

BP: It's one of the great things that sets Brian apart from other directors. In Bonfire of the Vanities, there is of course the whole opening, and at the end there was a wonderfully choreographed set piece where Tom Hanks' character takes the sword from the statue of justice and swings it around trying to make his escape. Unfortunately, it didn't make it into the final cut. Casualties of War also has a great opening scene when Michael J. Fox's character is saved by the character Meserve played by Sean Penn. Later in the film is the killing of the woman Oanh set against the battle on the bridge. Snake Eyes has an extremely complicated opening and later there is a classic De Palma split screen scene. Carlito's Way has a beautifully executed scene in the back of the barbershop and then at the end the train station scene which I suppose was presaged a bit by the train station scene in The Untouchables.

TO: I think when you look at The Untouchables it was a big break out film for DePalma. Carrie was huge but in a different genre. Untouchables did extremely well at the box office. And it's also quite famous for the Union Station sequence.

BP: Right. I was glad that it was so successful. I remember going to a preview in Boston and I was so happy when the audience loved the film. As far as the Union Station sequence, beautifully choreographed and executed all around.

TO: I think what's fun about the DePalma-Pankow collaboration is that you have angles, you have coverage and you have speed—the speed at which footage is shot or manipulated. It must have been pretty exhilarating to work on the film.

BP: Untouchables was my first big movie so I was a bit nervous. And we were working on the Moviola as well.

TO: Ah…I had forgotten that it was edited on film!

BP: Yes, and physically when you have a big scene with a lot of footage, we'd break them down into individual takes. So you'd have ten or twenty or more small rolls on the table and it was a challenge to keep track of everything in your head that's in the scene. You used the word exhilarating and for me what's exhilarating is when I look at the dailies. I refer to that as "reading the dailies". That is, I look at the dailies and try to ascertain what exactly is the director's intention is—the way they shot it and the angles and such. I try to achieve that intention by putting the film together that way. And when any director—and certainly Brian DePalma—looks at the scene and says, 'Yes, that's what I wanted', it's a very exhilarating and satisfying feeling to know that you've been able to assemble and edit the dailies in a way that the director intended.

TO: Did you have any inclination that The Untouchables would be the success it turned out to be? The shoot-out in Union Station has, of course, been compared to the Odessa steps sequence in The Battleship Potemkin.

BP: Jerry Greenberg cut that sequence. While we were editing, there was so much footage coming in from Chicago. That was a big set piece and I thought I would just leave it to the end. When Jerry finally finished his other job, he came on and he tackled that scene. And he did a beautiful job on that.

TO: I had long been waiting for the return of the "classic Brian DePalma treatment" and was really thrilled when Femme Fatale came out. It simply had a little of everything we've come to know and expect from him as a director. I think you did an amazing job and you received the Seattle Film Critics award for Best Editing.

BP: One of the challenges of Femme Fatale was that after the opening shot, we start out on the red carpet outside the Cannes film festival. And then there's the whole intercutting between getting the girl into the toilet, getting the jewels off and switching the fake jewels, the security guys on the TV monitors, and the bodyguards who are guarding the jewels. Intercutting all of that was quite challenging and a lot of fun when we got it right.

TO: Everything really works in that film. The execution, the editing, the music. It was entertaining and you weren't sure what was going to happen.

BP: Brian is a master at filmmaking, maximizing every part of the process and manipulating the audience so that he keeps everyone in suspense as long as possible.

TO: But that's hard to do if you don't have that relationship with a director like that.

BP: Femme Fatale was a lot of fun. As you say, it has that long opening shot for several minutes. It has the intercutting. It has split screen sequences. It has the idea of the double, which occurs a lot in his movies. It has the dream and the water symbolism. It has clues, where, once she's in the tub and falls asleep, the clock shows 3:33. And then every other scene you see if there's a clock in it, the time is 3:33. In the airport, or in the police station when Antonio Banderas is being interrogated, it's always 3:33. It's a lot of fun to play with those things.

TO: Are there films that stand out where you were particularly challenged at making something work or that are noteworthy in what you personally accomplished?

BP: There's a big scene in Casualties of War when all these soldiers are out on a ridge. There are enemy troops coming with the gun boats below them. The girl who had been raped is dragged into that picture and is going to be killed. That was a very challenging scene. There was a lot of footage and there was also quite a bit of helicopter footage of other troops coming in. We tried to incorporate that, but every time we did, it seemed to take away from the drama of the patrol on the ridge. So we eliminated the helicopter footage and the other troops. We did it on film and it took whatever time it took. You put your thought process into it and that was that.

TO: You've edited across many different genres. Crime, drama, suspense, comedy. Any favorite categories?

BP: Because I've done so many films with Brian DePalma, I'm known for the suspense-thriller genre. But I wouldn't say I gravitate towards that. I make myself available to all types of films because I don't want to be pigeonholed into one particular genre. It really comes down to something that I learned along the way and experience I got from working with Jerry Greenberg and Brian DePalma. And that is visual storytelling.

TO: What do you mean?

BP: Visual storytelling applies to any type of imagery where the audience has to understand what is happening, and they want to be entertained, and they want to be involved in the drama and the characters' lives. And your ability to tell that story and achieve those goals is part of what makes editing such a special craft.

TO: What are some of the things you've learned during the course of your editing career that may not have been so apparent when you started?

BP: You realize what a unique situation it is for the editor and the director to be working together. So you have to be able to, A. get along with them on a social level and B. to be able to remind yourself that you're achieving the director's vision. You can't get caught up in your own ideas and not be open to other ideas. Otherwise, it can be very difficult. Another thing is that you get so involved in your choices when you're editing—you go inside the scene so deeply. Once the film is put together and you're watching it, you need to be able to go outside of the film and look at the film as objectively as you possibly can. And once you've done that, you have to be able to go back to the dailies and reconsider your choices.

TO: With the DePalma films, you know you're going to get incredible set pieces with a lot of footage and angles and slow motion. They require expert assembly and that drawing out of suspense. That's why I think Femme Fatale is so beautifully put together, in every aspect. I wish it had done more in terms of box office. And I think you did a brilliant job on it.

BP: Thank you.

TO: Drumline was a great surprise. It did well with audiences and I think it was great for you as well. It's back to story and back to conflict. Nicely done and nicely told. I think the expert Pankow hand was at work there.

BP: Well, it was a lot of fun and Charles Stone (Director) is a wonderful filmmaker. We first collaborated on Paid in Full, which was more in the action genre that I had been known for and we got along very well. When he asked me to do Drumline, I was very happy, because as you say, it was a different style of movie for me and something that I hadn't done a lot of before. Charles is a great filmmaker and he got involved in the editing too. When we got to the end sequence, Charles was shooting on location and we were editing here in New York. We wanted to have a first cut for when he came back to New York but we didn't have time. So I said to my assistant, 'you edit one band and I'll edit the other band'.

TO: What do you mean?

BP: That I would cut one side and my assistant would cut the other side.

TO: Okay.

BP: And this would be the battle of the bands and we'd put them together and we'll see which one of us wins. Trissy (Patricia) Bowers was my assistant and co-editor.

TO: That's a pretty interesting idea.

BP: And that's how we approached that scene. And then Charles came in and got involved. So the three of us worked really very hard to massage that ending to the point where I think it's one of the most extraordinary set pieces in the movie and it works so well. Also, it's a good tale of camaraderie, competition, and has some good lessons.

TO: You made the transition from editing on film to digital nonlinear. Any drawbacks from your point of view.

BP: The thing that we have to remember is that the thought process in editing takes the same amount of time. You cannot short circuit the time it takes to view the film, think about the film, think about the director's intentions, and execute it and then use your own judgment of what to try. Every film's post-production process seems to be getting squeezed and there are fewer weeks.

TO: With respect to what you have to do every day, what should people know about your craft?

BP: I think it's obvious to a lot of people what the directors do and what the writers do and what the actors do. But when it comes to the film editing part, I think people have a simplified notion of what happens. You want it to be invisible, but at the same time, if people knew about the process, it might help them understand editing more. I think that's important because it's good to have any art and craft respected by the people who are enjoying it.

TO: I'd like to go back to The Untouchables for a moment…

BP: One scene that I had a lot of fun with is when the guy comes to kill Sean Connery. His character Malone is doing something in the kitchen and he goes and pretends to put the phonograph record on. Then he grabs his gun and a guy is revealed to be in his apartment and lures him into an alley. It was a bloody scene in the alleyway where he gets shot. I was sort of having fun with it because this was one of my first big Brian DePalma shoot out scenes. The first time I cut it, I think I put in every single squib. Every shot that exploded on Malone's body—his shoulder, his neck, or wherever he was getting shot—I used. (Both Laugh) I kept going back to the gun, and him crawling, wherever I could to highlight all that. It was fun for me to show it to Brian. He sort of chuckled and was enjoying it. And then he said, 'Okay, come on now, let's make it more realistic!' (Both Laugh) He obviously enjoyed the fun of it.

TO: That's funny. Are there any films that come to mind where you really admire how they were put together?

BP: French Connection is one, with Jerry Greenberg's Academy Award (editing). It's a wonderfully done film as is Bonnie and Clyde. Apocalypse Now I admired very much as well as Slumdog Millionaire. I thought that the way that they moved around with time was very, very, well done. I have a lot of respect for that film and how it was edited as soon as I saw it. Some of the Hitchcock films—especially Psycho and North by Northwest—excellent examples of visual storytelling, very well put together, great acting, good music. Zelig was a very interesting film on different levels because of all the different elements they incorporated. High Noon, because for me, it was a great editing breakthrough with the clock and the tension and the intercutting. Hervé Schneid's work on Amelie, which I thought was beautifully executed in every way.

TO: What keeps you going?

BP: I really enjoy editing. You hear a lot of actors accept an award and say how blessed they are in being able to make a living doing what they love. And I feel that way myself. I enjoy doing what I do very much and the fact that I can make a living and support my family is a blessing and a wonderful situation to be in. That's what keeps me going—the enjoyment of it. It's a challenge to go from one film to another. Even if you're working with the same director or a film in the same genre, it's always a new and exciting challenge. And eight to ten months later, you start all over.

TOM ROLF, ACE

Photograph courtesy of the American Cinema Editors and ACE Eddie Awards

LONDON, ENGLAND

Partial Credits: Windtalkers, The Horse Whisperer, Heat, The Pelican Brief, Sneakers, Jacob's Ladder, Black Rain, Nine 1/2 Weeks, The Right Stuff, WarGames, The Executioner's Song, Heaven's Gate, New York, New York, Black Sunday, Taxi Driver, French Connection II.

Every decade of Tom's work is filled with films recognized all over the world. 19 pictures alone in the 1970s. The Right Stuff. WarGames. Taxi Driver. As he said, "It was a great way to spend a career. The only important thing in filmmaking is story. If the story works, that's what really makes a movie."

TO: Tom, you are an Academy Award and an A.C.E Eddie recipient for The Right Stuff and WarGames. What led you to becoming an editor?

TR: My stepfather was a contract director at MGM and when I got discharged from the Marine Corps in 1952—Good God! —I had no idea what I wanted to do with the rest of my life. I asked him, 'If I want to do what you do, how would I get a start?' And he said the film editor is the first person that sees what was done the previous day and through osmosis you'd see what is good and what is bad. And you'd learn about filmmaking. You had to be an apprentice and then an assistant and then an editor and that process took eight years. It took longer than becoming a doctor!

TO: Your first feature was in Sweden.

TR: It turned out to be the last film by the legendary American director

King Vidor. Unfortunately, he died in the middle of production and Yul Brynner was brought in to finish the movie.

TO: That was Solomon and Sheba. Tyrone Power is in that movie. So, Yul Brynner was acting in it and then he directed it to finish the film?

TR: Yes. And that gave me about a year in Madrid.

TO: In the 1970's you worked on 19 pictures! The Mackenzie Break. Hardcore. New York, New York. Black Sunday. The French Connection II. Taxi Driver. It's an extremely astounding decade's worth of work.

TR: I said to myself, 'Never work for the same director more than three times'. It wasn't easy to go from project to project, but I never accepted a job where I didn't like the script. If I liked the script, that was half the battle.

TO: You worked with Lamont Johnson, John Frankenheimer, Stanley Donen, Paul Schrader, and Martin Scorsese. What did you learn from them?

TR: It really depended on the experience levels of each director. I did three pictures with Schrader. Blue Collar, which was a pretty good little picture. Then Hardcore, and finally the prequel to the Exorcist, which didn't work. He was very receptive to what I wanted to do, and it was fun working with him. Lamont Johnson was one of the great guys of all time. When I saw Vanishing Point that Dick Sarafian did, I knew that was someone I wanted to work with.

TO: How did The Right Stuff come about? You were one of five editors.

TR: It was a lucky break. I came to the film late and was one of the last editors hired. Phillip Kaufman was a wonderful man, a lovely person. It was a very nice experience. By the time we were finished, there were just two of us left. And the two of us ended up on the dubbing stage to finalize the job.

TO: Did you have an inkling that you were going to win?

TR: Oh, no! (Laughs) Not even close. The fact that there were five of us—it was a whole basketball team! (Both laugh)

TO: You won the ACE for WarGames.

TR: I had a great time on that film, but I didn't think I would win with WarGames because it wasn't that high profile of a picture. But some people just love that movie. I was happy to win and then with The Right Stuff, I couldn't believe it. It was a great evening.

TO: Can you describe how you approached a film?

TR: When I'm working on a picture, I can't wait to get my hands on a scene. If a scene is shot over three days—let's say it's Scene 25—I put it together and then I'll go back and refine it. Once I think it's ready, I'll put it up on the shelf and eventually I'd have to go back to Scene 25 and put it in the continuity of the other scenes I've edited. Then I'd run it and see it in context with Scene 24 and Scene 26 and say, 'What the hell was I thinking?' (Both laugh) It doesn't fit. It's the wrong timing, the wrong pacing.

TO: The editing approach had evolved since you cut Scene 25 so early in the process.

TR: Yes. I had to go back and make it fit the overall story. But I did love editing on film. It would be all over the place and in my pockets and taped to my forehead! (Both laugh) But, of course, with electronic editing we don't have those problems!

TO: When did you make the transition from film to electronic editing?

TR: In 1992, on The Pelican Brief. Somebody showed me what the Lightworks could do. I was a convert within 15 minutes. And I never looked back.

TO: Are there films that didn't do as well as they should have?

TR: One of my favorite pictures is Jacob's Ladder.

TO: It's a great film. The six and eight frames per second footage where the head is shaking back and forth is frightening. It must have been a thrill to work on that.

TR: It really was, and I really respect the director, Adrian Lyne. He took a chance by doing that script. The script had been around for many years and nobody knew how to make it. I liked every minute of that movie. The marketing of the film killed it. They marketed it as horror movie.

TO: I agree.

TR: It wasn't a horror movie. It was a psychological thriller. And they used the face of Tim Robbins painted like Munch's "The Scream" and it sent the wrong message. People just didn't go. It was a tough movie for many people to watch and it did scare a lot of people because, as you said, the shaking head and the dancing with the snake. But it was incredibly inventive on Lyne's part. That's one of my favorites.

TO: Black Rain has a wonderful look to it.

TR: Ridley Scott has a signature with his use of lighting and color and I'd say the same for Adrian Lyne. It's a glossy, very attention-getting look and Ridley operates the camera himself. And let's say he did six takes on the master. Well, you wouldn't really have six takes on the master because he used a 1:10 zoom most of the time and each of the takes would end up in a different place on the set. He would never repeat the same action exactly the same way.

TO: A real matching nightmare.

TR: Right, so you'd have ten variations of the master. At one point I joked with him and told him I wanted to break his knuckles, so he couldn't operate the camera anymore! (Both laugh)

TO: There was an enormous amount of footage on Heaven's Gate and multiple editors.

TR: Heaven's Gate was a disaster from day one. Not that the script was bad. Everyone knew it was lengthy and Cimino admitted he was making a much longer movie than everyone thought he was going to make. I might say that I thought a shot was a little too long. And he'd have me add ten feet to it, which was exactly the opposite of what should be done. I didn't finish the picture and I left early. And the film came out and generated no box office at all.

TO: Here are the directors you worked with in that decade: Phil Robinson, Mike Figgis, Alan J. Pakula, Michael Mann, Robert Redford. Another new batch of directors—different from the '80's, different from the '70's.

TR: Well, again, I liked moving around to different directors.

TO: What films and editors do you like?

TR: Bill Reynolds I really admired, and he was a real gentleman.

TO: When you think about the films he edited. From The Sound of Music to The Sting…

TR: The Sand Pebbles—big sweeping things—and his career lasted a long time. He had a feeling for film. Oh, Wages of Fear—I loved that film and how it generates suspense. Up until that time, I had never seen anything like that. After a while, I couldn't watch the screen because I was so terrified of what might happen.

TO: Yeah, it really turns the screws on you.

TR: For Whom the Bell Tolls with Gary Cooper and Ingrid Bergman and High Noon, of course. But I didn't look at them in terms of editing, just as films that could transport me.

TO: Now that you are officially retired, what did you love about editing?

TR: I loved sitting in my little room and I loved the initial editor's cut where it was strictly my interpretation and feeling about what worked. But when I made an editor's cut, I never left anything out even if it didn't fit because I felt if it was shot, it was worth including.

TO: I found your Oscar acceptance speech. First of all, the presenter was Robert Wise, which must have been quite special.

TR: It was.

TO: You said: 'I just want to say I'm deeply grateful and if I could ever do anything for anyone here, let me know!'

TR: I had forgotten. I know it brought a giggle to the house. I've had a great time as an editor. It was a great way to spend my career. The only really important thing in filmmaking is story. If the story works, that's what really makes a movie.

STEPHEN ROTTER

Photograph courtesy of the American Cinema Editors and ACE Eddie Awards

WESTBROOK, CT

Partial Credits: Enchanted, What Women Want, My Blue Heaven, Dirty Rotten Scoundrels, The Right Stuff, The World According to Garp, Holocaust.

Three hours by car brought me to Westbrook, Connecticut where Stephen and his wife Janet welcomed me into their lovely home. Early in his career, he was with Dede Allen, Jerry Greenberg, and Richard Marks. Holocaust. Garp. The Right Stuff. His impeccable editorial timing in comedy. A wonderfully talented editor and warm and generous host.

TO: Stephen, you are the recipient of an Academy Award, an ACE Eddie, and an Emmy award for your editorial work on The Right Stuff and Holocaust. How did you get your start?

SR: I had met my wife who happened to be working at NBC as a guide. I got into NYU Film School, which was part of the education department—it wasn't a true film school. And I got a job as an apprentice in the news film department at NBC News covering local news and Huntley/Brinkley and that sort of escalated. And I married my wife who launched me into the business just by being cute!

TO: (Both Laugh) The best inspiration!

SR: After about three years, I discovered that if I'm going to be in editing, why don't I do something that has some meaning to it. I left and worked on independent documentaries on the same floor and building as Dede Allen who was working on Alice's Restaurant. And she had left a little note on my synchronizer. I was working for a friend of hers. Would I please see her? And she offered me a job as Jerry Greenberg's assistant.

TO: Talk about the right place at the right time.

SR: Jerry was her second editor and I jumped at it. And I pretty much stayed with her for a while and she launched me on my editorial career.

TO: What a break. This was 1969. You were working with Dede, Jerry Greenberg, and Richard Marks.

SR: Richard Marks was the first assistant. The best university you could go to for film editing!

TO: From 1969 to 1972, you worked on Alice's Restaurant, Little Big Man, and Slaughterhouse Five with Arthur Penn and George Roy Hill. Cream of the crop...

SR: Exactly. The nice thing was that we were all pretty close and very protective of one another. And the workload in those non-digital days was horrendous because it required a lot of physical activity as well as knowing what you were doing. A few years later some other guys came in, like Billy Pankow.

TO: What did you learn from Dede?

SR: Well, she never gave up. Nothing would stand in the way of making something better and making the director happy. She had sort of an intense devotion to getting things done the way she wanted them. And also just a terrific teacher. We all just never wanted to let her down in any fashion at all. In watching her, it sort of gave you a methodology, which you, yourself, could apply to your own work. In many instances, I would copy her methods. And in others I thought 'Boy, that's a waste of time.'

TO: After a while, you created your own style of working.

SR: Exactly. It just did give you a total understanding of the hows and whys of making films. Not just editing, but from cutting negative and doing opticals, all the way through.

TO: Did you have any idea of how lasting the films that you were making were going to be?

SR: I don't think we actually did. These films were never financially that successful. Films were coming out of Hollywood that were doing business that we never even dreamed of. For instance, Little Big Man is just the most brilliant film. It opened to some scathing reviews and it had a premiere in Los Angeles in which people were shocked that this was a film—a film about genocide—that they were showing for a charity benefit.

TO: In 1973, you edited The Seven Ups for Philip D'Antoni who has said that he wanted to create a car chase to outdo The French Connection.

SR: That's a funny story. Jerry Greenberg, who I was working with at the time, hired me to be his second editor. And then right after shooting, they fired me. And so I went home and my mother, who was living at the time said, 'What happened? Those sons of bitches!' (Both Laugh) And then I got a phone call and would I be willing to come to California to be the assistant.

TO: On The Seven Ups?

SR: Yeah. And my mother said, 'You tell those so and so's, if you're not good enough, you're not going to work on their film!'

TO: We all need mothers like that, pushing us on!

SR: (Laughs) I went and finished it out as an assistant. The truth of it is that when you're first starting out, I had no idea what I was doing. I mean every cut was like agony. I would spend hours agonizing on 30 seconds of film. It was quite humbling. And the next time I got the chance, I was okay.

TO: Are you still nervous when you show your first cut?

SR: Yes. It's the tensest moment of all. When you're preparing the first cut while they're still shooting, you're hanging out there a little bit. That's the most nerve-wracking part. It's a delicate, feeling-around process. But the important thing is that you shouldn't do something because you think someone else wants it this way. It's the relationship between the director and the editor that's really, really important. If you don't have a good relationship, no matter how good the work, you're liable not to make it through the film.

TO: You like comedic and dramatic.

SR: Right. In fact, more comedic lately—in the past 15 years—ever since Dirty Rotten Scoundrels. The one film type that I haven't done since The Right Stuff is action-adventure.

TO: Don't you think it takes a special skill to edit comedy?

SR: Right. You just don't want to force the performances by being in the wrong place at the wrong time. It's all instinctive really. I can't explain to you how I do what I do but I can say that I can make things the funniest that they can be. Sometimes you just laugh out loud during the dailies. The best one is in Dirty Rotten Scoundrels, the whipping scene.

TO: It's hilarious. Steve Martin's expression after Michael Caine comes running at him with the whip is priceless.

SR: Right.

TO: What Women Want was phenomenally successfully with audiences.

SR: Nancy Meyers has the best instinct for comedic situations. It's so great to have the situation be funny and the onus isn't on the performance because the situation is just so unusual that you have to laugh at what's going on. The actor has a built-in head start. Another situation that I laugh out loud about is one that has really been reviled in history is Ishtar. And the buzzard scene is absolutely hysterical.

TO: Yeah, it's really funny.

SR: It's one of the funniest things in a movie that I've ever seen. One, Dustin is really funny in it and two, who would have thought that a buzzard could land on cue? I mean it's just unreal. The buzzard trainer made those buzzards land.

TO: Before CGI, it was real!

SR: Yeah, it was real! And in Garp, the airplane flying into the house was real.

TO: Have you been surprised at audience reactions to films you edited?

SR: I will tell you a funny story about a film we previewed. You couldn't hear a line of dialogue. The audience was so raucous that I thought to myself 'This is the hugest hit in the history of mankind' and that was Ishtar.

TO: I didn't know it had previewed that well.

SR: I thought from this particular screening that it was gangbusters. It was unbelievable. And then when we previewed My Blue Heaven, I thought it was funny and many people agree with me. But the preview scores were pitifully low. They were in the 30's, which is considered an unmitigated disaster.

TO: Steve Martin is great. That scene with him and Carol Kane in the supermarket is really funny.

SR: We previewed it in Richmond, Virginia. I was amazingly depressed. So, we went back to the drawing board and I started making changes and sending them to the director who was in Richmond. And I went to the next preview without him and it did a 65. But the studio immediately lost confidence in the film and dumped it. And today it's considered a very funny movie.

TO: Did digital help you with Enchanted's animation?

SR: On Enchanted, you put in sketches but the actual animation that goes in takes months so you don't have it. But you have a pretty good idea. And of course we worked with the music all the way along. I feel my work is as good as it's ever been if not better. And I think that digital editing can extend a career by physically not being so exhausting.

TO: 1973. A lot of things were happening in the world. It was a very tumultuous time. You worked as an assistant on Visions of Eight, a documentary about the 1972 Olympics. In 1978, you worked on Holocaust and won an Emmy. Which segment did you work on in Visions and since you were doing this after the games were finished, did it take on a different context?

SR: Our particular segment was the pole vault. The tragedy of Munich happened but all of these things had already been planned. I think there was one segment that dealt with the tragedy. That segment was not quite as dramatic and hard-hitting as I think it could have and should have been. With Holocaust, that did have a big effect on me because it was something I grew up with and had been hearing my whole life. I know people who are children of survivors. I know survivors. The acting was superb. Of course, my Dad was over the moon.

TO: 1983. The Right Stuff. It's a big film.

SR: Huge.

TO: How did you get the job?

SR: I got a call to come out to San Francisco and work on Never Cry Wolf directed by Caroll Ballard. And he said, 'I thought we were doing pretty well and then we went to a preview in San Diego and we got a six!' And I almost collapsed. I mean no one had ever gotten a six.

TO: For the reader, can you put that into context?

SR: It would be as if you were in college and your average was 20.

TO: Ouch.

SR: And it was a pretty good film. I worked on it for three weeks and the earliest I left was three in the morning and I think I worked seven days a week. Carroll ran into Phil (Kaufman) and said, 'I have this great guy' and Phil hired me. My wife and child stayed in New York. I was out there for eight or nine months. The film had already been shot when I came on it and it was the greatest job I ever had. It was fantastic. Because all I did was cut film. They just kept throwing stuff in and I kept cutting it. And Phil and I became really close. The film was five hours long and we worked like crazy. And Phil was great. It was one of the greatest experiences I had.

TO: It only did about $21 million.

SR: Right, which is nothing. And, of course, he who deserved the most reward of all got nothing.

TO: Philip Kaufman.

SR: Right and I ended up working with him again and he's got it all, plus being a really nice man. He wrote it, he directed it. He did everything. He deserves everybody's award as far as I'm concerned.

TO: Are there scenes that you're particular proud of?

SR: The flying scenes. Breaking the sound barrier—the Chuck Yeager stuff. And that was just going through tons and tons of footage. They shot special effects footage for months and months. Throwing planes out windows. Sailing them across the room. Putting CO_2 cartridges in them. When we were finished mixing, we took it to the Northpoint theatre and it was like magic. I mean it was just great. But it was made by the Ladd Company for Warner Brothers. And I have a feeling that there was a Warner Brothers movie that they paid more attention to than The Right Stuff.

TO: It came out three weeks after Never Say Never Again with Sean Connery as 007. About five weeks later Warner Brothers released Sudden Impact. It was sort of squeezed. They should have released it later.

SR: Plus the fact of its length and they didn't sink a lot of money into the advertising. It really didn't get a fair shake.

TO: Tell me about that night. Still clear in your mind?

SR: Yes, it is. The thing about that year is that Richie (Marks) was nominated for Terms of Endearment and at the time I was sure he was going to win.

TO: That was definitely the year that Terms was winning everything.

SR: You have to walk up there, which is knee shaking. Then you have to say something and you're already ready to faint. And my wife, Janet, was with me and it was incredible. And my daughter, who was then eight, they woke her up in New York to look at it and she was nonplussed—'Oh, that's nice.'—And then went back to bed. (Laughs)

TO: What have you learned along the way?

SR: How important it is to get along with people. You must learn to accommodate other people. There's a hierarchy. You're not your own boss. If the director or the studio says 'We want to see this tomorrow', that's it.

TO: What do audiences not know about the craft of editing?

SR: Maybe it's just the amount of time and effort that goes into it.

TO: What are some of your favorite films and editors whose work you admire?

SR: One of the great films of all time is The Godfather, which I'm just crazy about. I love Richie's (Marks) work. Pietro's (Scalia) work is unbelievable. Alan Heim, Craig McKay. Paul Hirsch. The luck end of this business is so important because there are pretty talented people who just didn't get the chance to work on a really great film. I thought Slumdog Millionaire was great. I though Benjamin Button was really well done and David Fincher is fantastic. I thought Frost / Nixon was unbelievable. I thought the performances of those actors were great and the editing was great.

TO: Others?

SR: He Who Must Die by Jules Dassin. The Champion or In Cold Blood. Or The Apartment. At the time I wasn't even aware that there was such a thing as a film editor. Alan Parker's editor, Gerry Hambling is phenomenal. John Bloom is great. Dede Allen, Thelma Schoonmaker, Tim Squyres, Jay Rabinowitz. And, of course, Walter Murch, who I know pretty well.

TO: What's the first film you saw where you were conscious of the fact that an editor was orchestrating what you were seeing?

SR: Probably Godfather. Oh, Midnight Cowboy—an unbelievable experience. That film just wrenched your heart out. Papillon.

TO: Enchanted did really well. It made $340 million!

SR: I read the script, and right from the script it was phenomenal. Amy Adams was great and Patrick Dempsey was fantastic. I mean it all just came together. And the director, Kevin Lima, is really, really gifted. I mean he did the voice of the chipmunk. He can do anything.

TO: Arthur Penn.

SR: Unbelievably gifted. The nicest man. Has a fundamental grasp of acting unlike anybody. Arthur didn't even have to think about it before he got to the set. He could rap off twenty shots and then say, 'Oh, we gotta go back, I forgot to do this one.' That's how good he was at it. More responsible than any director for my getting a good start in this industry.

TO: George Roy Hill.

SR: Phenomenal. Maybe the best overall technical director of them all. He had all the skills in the world. He had story sense, actors loved him. He was truly unique and was very entertaining.

TO: Even as great as that David S. Ward script is for The Sting, the wrong director could have really messed that up.

SR: Right. And don't forget—he's directing two of his closest friends. It just must have been a camaraderie that you wished you could have partaken of. And his sense of enjoyment of the process bled through to people's enjoyment of the film. In a way, the films were so enjoyable because he loved doing it so much. And I think it came fairly easy to him.

TO: Philip Kaufman.

SR: A true intellectual. Very democratic thinking. Unbelievably gifted writer. Tremendously imaginative director. He's his own man when it comes to decisions on how a film should be done.

TO: Elaine May.

SR: She is so brilliant. She once said to me, 'What do I know? I never graduated from high school!' And that's when I came to find out that's because she went to the University of Chicago when she was 14 or some insane thing like that!

TO: Why do you keep doing it?

SR: First, you like doing something you're good at. It gives you satisfaction. Second, I'm still competitive and I think that in my heart I can do it as well as anybody. And I've been doing it so long that it would seem like a crime not to be able to do it anymore.

TO: If you weren't an editor, what would you be doing?

SR: I have no idea. There's nothing I'm qualified to do besides this!

CHRISTOPHER ROUSE, ACE

Photograph courtesy the American Cinema Editors and ACE Eddie Awards

LOS ANGELES, CALIFORNIA

Partial Credits: Jason Bourne, Captain Phillips, Green Zone, The Bourne Ultimatum, United 93, The Bourne Supremacy, The Italian Job.

He learned through a classic film apprenticeship with some of the greats and is thoughtful, perceptive, and has terrific insights into how films are made. The Bourne Ultimatum—and that ticking Waterloo station sequence—is a marvel. But it is the emotional connection he has to films like Anne Frank or Captain Phillips. These are stories about people and they truly touch Chris.

TO: Chris, you have been awarded the BAFTA, ACE, and Academy Award for your work on the films United 93 and The Bourne Ultimatum. How did you get your start?

CR: My father was a writer/director, my mother an actress, so I grew up around the business. That said, my dad hoped I wouldn't pursue a career anywhere in the entertainment industry, since he didn't want me to face the financial and emotional uncertainty he experienced. When I got out of high school, my father was prepping a film he was directing and I hounded him for a job. Finally, he gave in and hired me—with the caveat that he would open a door—but whatever I did after that was up to me.

The editor of the film, Bud Isaacs and his wonderful assistant Bernie Balmuth took me under their wings. They were fantastic first teachers. Bud helped me get into the union and took me with him on his next job, and so I worked at Fox as an apprentice editor on the TV movie "Raid on Entebbe". I left U.C.L.A. before being graduated, and I was fortunate to land a job as an assistant editor on a Hal Ashby film. I worked for Hal for three years in my early 20's. It was a tremendous learning experience about film and more importantly—about life.

TO: You were also an assistant to Richard Harris on "The Golden Child". Richard is very proud of your success.

CR: I was incredibly lucky to have worked with people like Richard, who apart from being an extremely talented editor is a true gentleman besides. I ultimately learned so much by working with people like Richard, Bud, Robert C. Jones, Hal, Bob Ferretti, Chuck McClelland, and many others. Each of them helped me to become the editor I am today, and I am very, very grateful to them.

TO: You've also done quite a bit of work for television and cable.

CR: I'm a much better editor as a result of having spent time cutting television shows, both episodic and long form. In TV, you've got to be fast and trust your instincts, or you're lost. The speed of the process will swallow you up and before you know it, you'll be looking for a job.

TO: Your first full editor credit was "Desperate Hours", directed by Michael Cimino. It was a remake of the 1955 film directed by William Wyler and starred Humphrey Bogart. How did you get involved and had you seen the original?

CR: I had seen the original, but it had little bearing on Michael's piece. And for the record, the screen credit I received on "Desperate Hours" was as an Associate Editor— but I did ultimately function as a full editor on that film. I got a call to work on "Hours" after Michael had fired most of the editorial department. I came on as an assistant then was moved up after Peter Hunt left the show. In the end it was another assistant who had been promoted, Erica Shaevitz, and myself cutting the film. I had a good working relationship with Michael during "Desperate Hours" and he hired me to cut his next film, Sunchaser. He and I had some differences on that project, and I finally told him I thought it would be better for him and the film if I left.

TO: You worked on The Pennsylvania Miners' Story and Anne Frank: The Whole Story. Are you ever affected by the subject matter or can you separate yourself from the material you are editing?

CR: I'm affected by every project I'm involved with, and working with material that contains profound human suffering can be very difficult emotionally. Certainly, that was the case with Pennsylvania Miners, Anne Frank, and of course United 93. Anne Frank was shot in Prague during the winter, and the company built a concentration camp set that was eerily real. During scenes actors were often wearing rags, shivering in sub-freezing temperatures. The material from our director Robert Dornhelm was highly charged emotionally- from time to time I had to walk away from the Avid in order to clear my head. Similarly, there were occasions during United 93 where (usually without warning) tears would come to my eyes. The overwhelming nature of that footage coupled with the ongoing realization that our world had been changed forever as a result of 9/11, would often hit me like a tidal wave.

TO: United 93 was directed by Paul Greengrass. How are scenes divided up?

CR: I had cut Bourne Supremacy for Paul and he asked me to do 93, but I was finishing Eight Below when they started shooting. Paul hired Clare Douglas, with whom he'd worked on Bloody Sunday to start the film, with the understanding that I would jump in as soon as I was free. 93 was an insane schedule—a November shoot for and end of April release. I arrived in London at the beginning of January, and poor Clare was swimming in footage. Because of the nature and amount of material, I immediately asked Universal post-production for additional assets, a slew of assistants and most importantly, for my friend and co-editor of Bourne Supremacy, Rick Pearson. Luckily Rick had a small window before his next gig, and so he was able to come over for a bit to help with some very heavy lifting. For example, the cockpit charge at the end is all Rick's work; he did a brilliant, brilliant job.

TO: Your next film, The Bourne Ultimatum is an amazing achievement of your ability to move along a story at a pace that never stops. The Waterloo Station sequence is thrilling but it is the coordination of all the elements that I think really showcases your talents in this section of the movie.

CR: "Challenging" and "fun" often go hand-in-hand. I loved cutting the Waterloo sequence for the reasons you mentioned. Multiple characters converging at a busy train station monitored by another group, with huge stakes on the line. Move and countermove, forward motion and building tension... Paul's material bursting at the seams with energy. In sequences like Waterloo I try to inject as much specificity as I can editorially, so that the audience is led in a sure-handed way and they're able to assimilate details of plot and character while the camera is continuously moving and probing. I also try to be aware of where the action is taking the viewer's eye from cut to cut, so that shorter cuts and aggressive camera moves can be registered better.

The Tangier sequence culminating in Bourne's roof run and the apartment fight was also rather formidable—another long series of episodes clocking parallel action, culminating in an intense climax.

TO: Green Zone was a very realistic depiction in all areas of production and had an amazing cast of actors. You stop production, assemble the movie, and then go back to shoot additional material as you continue to refine the film. Could you talk a bit about that process for Green Zone?

CR: The process of shooting additional material is not uncommon, and on Paul's films we've dealt with different scenarios requiring different types of supplemental photography. Often with Paul it's a matter of grabbing just a few key pieces that will make a scene really sing. The situation on Green Zone was a bit different. We were hit with a writers' strike before we began filming, and so many of the issues that might have been solved on page were instead left for us to puzzle-out during production. It wasn't the optimal way to sort things out.

With Paul Greengrass
Photograph courtesy the American Cinema Editors and ACE Eddie Awards

TO: What was it like to hear your name announced during the Oscar ceremonies?

CR: It was a totally surreal experience. I was a nervous wreck. I don't enjoy speaking in front of crowds (unless it's work related), and so while I hoped to win, I dreaded having to make the speech. I have vague memories of kissing my wife and shaking hands with my friend James Newton Howard, who congratulated me as I walked to the stage. I wanted to acknowledge my late father, who had won an Oscar for writing, and the rest of my family, and I began to get choked up during my speech. That fact, coupled with the huge digital clock directly in my eye-line that counted down the 45 seconds I had to complete my speech... I'm just glad I got through it reasonably well.

At the ACE Awards for The Bourne Ultimatum
Photograph courtesy the American Cinema Editors and ACE Eddie Awards

TO: Are there examples where you were surprised at the audience reception for a film you edited?

CR: I was a bit surprised at the "friends and family" screening we had for Ultimatum. I waited outside the theater after the screening and when the film was over, my son Anno ran up to me wide-eyed saying, "It's great! It's the best of the three!" I can be pretty skeptical about praise, but his was such an honest, emotional response that it confirmed for me we had something pretty darn good.

TO: Are there any films that come to mind where you really admire how they were put together as well as other editors whose work you admire?

CR: There are so many films and editors I could cite that are absolutely brilliant, and any list I give will be woefully incomplete. I'm an enormous fan of David Lean—in my mind he is the consummate editor turned director. Kwai, Lawrence, and Brief Encounter are three very different types of stories, all brilliantly constructed. So many sequences in Welles' films are genius—every time I watch Kane, or Touch of Evil I discover something new. Kurosawa's work, Peckinpah's earlier films I've watched over and over. Some of the giants of editing—artists like Dede Allen, Ralph Winters, Sam O'Steen, Thelma Schoonmaker, Michael Kahn, Alan Heim, and Walter Murch, are editors whose work I constantly return to. I love Gerry Hambling's films—the guy is so spot on. Guys like Pietro Scalia and Chris Lebenzon are truly superb. Daniel Rezende's work on City of God dropped my jaw. And then there's the excellent work in television and documentaries—I could go on and on...

PIETRO SCALIA, ACE

Photograph courtesy the American Cinema Editors and ACE Eddie Awards

LOS ANGELES, CA

Partial Credits: Solo: A Star Wars Story, Alien: Covenant, 13 Hours, The Martian, The Sea of Trees, Child 44, Amazing Spiderman II, The Counselor, Amazing Spiderman, Prometheus, Body of Lies, American Gangster, Memoirs of a Geisha, Black Hawk Down, Hannibal, Gladiator, JFK.

I first met Pietro in Tuscany while he was editing Bertolucci's Stealing Beauty. And I was surprised that this co-winner for J.F.K. went to Blackhawk Down and started the film in total fear. I think he best sums up his dedication to a film when he says, "as the material becomes part of you, you feel more comfortable with it".

TO: Pietro, you are a two-time Oscar winner. After graduating from UCLA in Los Angeles, you were able to work with Oliver Stone as an assistant editor on Wall Street and Talk Radio. How did it come about?

PS: At UCLA, I wanted to be an editor, but I also wanted to direct, and I thought the best thing to do was to be as close to a director as possible and learn how to become a filmmaker. I wanted to work with a director/writer like Oliver Stone. The opportunity to start on Wall Street, to learn from Claire Simpson, to work alongside David Brenner and Joe Hutshing is what started my mentorship with Oliver that lasted almost six years. The culmination was the Academy Award for JFK and it's thanks to the experiences and opportunity that Oliver gave me.

TO: JFK is remarkable.

PS: We were working six, seven days a week, twelve to fourteen hours a day. Just add up the hours that we put in there—it was literally non-stop. It was an amazing period. We had the freedom and the guidance from Oliver during those years. He had final cut and we were making movies and we were working with great collaborators. People like Bob Richardson, the cinematographer, Mike Minkler, Sound Mixer and Wylie Stateman our Sound Designer. We were working with 35mm film Steenbecks, with laserdiscs and ¾ inch videotape on EditDroid. JFK was cut on ¾ inch tape and film.

TO: JFK and Black Hawk Down are part of the US consciousness for vastly different reasons.

PS: I love history. I learned a lot from Oliver with JFK and Born on the Fourth of July. JFK was a great opportunity to research the documentary footage, to work with different film formats and the layering of stories and structure. It was pure cinema. But it was also scary—having this huge responsibility to work on the film whose subject was part of the American psyche and for the sheer size of it.

TO: And yet the film moves along so quickly despite the density of the material. You're never conscious of the length of the film.

PS: The first cut was over four hours long. There was a lot of material, a lot of juggling, and many story elements. But we had Oliver as a guide. At the beginning, it was very scary because we had so much material and it was overwhelming. But as the material becomes part of you, you feel more comfortable with it. There are things in there that are the pure enjoyment of editing because we worked on the rhythm of the narrative. We also felt that people might get lost because there was so much material—because it was too dense. But people were able to follow it because the eye and the brain both work on so many different levels at the same time.

We had every imaginable format—from Super-8 to 16mm to black and white, color, 1.85 aspect ratio, Cinemascope aspect ratio, stock footage, and videotape. We transferred the various film formats to ¾ inch video and we had to create our own logging system to later conform the picture. We had to do everything in a very short amount of time. Everything happening at the same time and at the last possible moment. They finished shooting in August and we were out in December.

TO: I was listening to Stone's commentary on Born on the Fourth of July and he said that he thought the John Williams score for that film was great until he heard the JFK score.

PS: John Williams came to visit us in New Orleans where we were shooting and saw 45 minutes of scenes that Joe Hutshing and I had done. He said 'I'm going to go away, and I'm going to send you some themes.' A couple of months later, he sent us a "conspirator's" theme, a "JFK" theme, together with other musical ideas. During the editing process, we took these themes and combined and layered them with other musical elements.

TO: How did the prologue come about? It's an incredible amount of information that the viewer has to absorb in a very short amount of time.

PS: We struggled for a very long time to get this opening down to size as a prologue to JFK's background up to the day of when he was in Dallas. We really had to condense it and I finally managed to get that compression down to about seven minutes, but the whole sequence didn't come together until I finally put this piece of music which was the "Drummers Salute", a snare drum track from The Royal Scots Dragoon Guards, and the reason I was listening to this was because JFK was a fan of this Scottish marching band. I thought maybe it would be an interesting idea to use it, which also tied in with Oliver's concept of a planned execution, that this was a coup d'état, because the snare drums sounded like machine gunfire. It was a perfect fit and the rhythm worked well for building up tension.

TO: I found it gut-wrenching. The inevitability of what you know is going to happen...

PS: If you look at the last section of JFK when they get off the plane and how the drums are played, it really builds up to that moment when he gets shot. When we were mixing that segment, the sound supervisor, Wylie Stateman, combined the roar of the Harley Davidson motorcycle sounds from the motorcade. So you had this beautiful interaction of sounds. The snare drums with the low roar, the motorcycles coming by, the inside of the limousine, the outside with the public, the tension building up, almost like a machine gun, an execution. When I put the snare drums in, I got goose bumps, so I knew we had something really powerful.

TO: You hear isolated for a moment the sound of Zapruder's Super-8 camera and it takes over everything.

PS: The sound of the super-8 camera was an organic outgrowth from the work we were doing. The movie editing process is always in a state of flux, changing and growing as you weave together images and sound. When I finally showed the prologue with the snare drums to Oliver, after months and months of working, he jumped with joy. He literally jumped and did something that I still remember to this day. He came over and he hugged me. I was completely shocked, and he said to me, 'We have a maestro.'

TO: What a compliment. How difficult was the Black Hawk Down experience?

PS: It was labor intensive, simply because it is based on historical facts, but also for me as an editor to really understand the minutia of what happened that day. I basically had to create a picture in my mind in order to know exactly where everyone was. I was moved by the book. I loved it. The struggle was to keep all the thirty or so characters in the action.

TO: Did you have some kind of map or index cards showing you where characters were fighting that you could use to keep things clear?

PS: I had pictures of the map of Mogadishu, I would visit the art department, and I would see how they reconstructed the locations in the city of Rabat and Salé and which streets were where. It was my way of researching so that I could understand it as well. Because if I couldn't understand it, how could I expect the audience to understand?

TO: The sound design and mix in Black Hawk Down is frightening in its intensity.

PS: The incursion of the helicopters made me think that it was almost like a science fiction film. You had these great helicopters that look like insect machines landing on a foreign planet. Going from that idea, I built the sequence in silence, as just images of helicopters shot by the aerial unit. I tried to create a visual ballet in a way, inherent in the musicality of it. I thought about what it would feel like being a soldier at that moment.

TO: You hear things that are terrible—screaming, helicopters, bullets whizzing by your ears—you're hearing as if you are the soldiers.

PS: In Black Hawk Down, it had to be very specific. It had to consist of specific visuals and sounds to make the viewer go through that sense of a realism and experience.

TO: You had a lot of footage. Was it ever overwhelming?

PS: I started off in total fear. Even though I had a good relationship with everyone, there was fear. It was a big task. After almost ten years of working with Ridley Scott and having done movies like Gladiator and Hannibal, Black Hawk Down was still a big task. We had just seen an amazing war film, Saving Private Ryan, which was brilliant both visually and audibly. I just remember Ridley saying, 'Saving Private Ryan raised the bar dramatically in terms of visuals and sound design and music, but we have to raise that bar again with our war movie.'

I remember my experience working on Black Hawk Down, being painful and exhaustive, the hardest thing I've ever done. I thought that

JFK was hard, and that you had to go through hell only once, metaphorically, but with BHD I had to do it a second time.

TO: What reactions stand out?

PS: I have to tell you, one of the most surprising reactions was that I was invited to this fundraiser in New York for Global Green because I was working with Leonardo DiCaprio on a documentary called The 11th Hour, and the guest of honor was Mikhail Gorbachev.

It turns out that Gorbachev's favorite film is Gladiator, and I was stunned, asking, 'Wait, Really?' During the break, I was told that I should just go and say hi to Gorbachev. I was taken over and introduced as the editor of Gladiator. At a table of about 12 people vying for his attention, he grabbed my hand and pulled me over to him so that I was literally kneeling at his side, with his interpreter right there. The translator was telling me that Gorbachev was saying, 'Gladiator is my absolute favorite film. The number one movie on my shelf. I see it all the time, I go home and watch Gladiator.' He just went on and on like that.

TO: That's terrific. There are economists, environmentalists, and politicians all around waiting for his attention and he wants to talk to you about Gladiator. How about films that you admire and whose editing style you like?

PS: I admired the editing in City of God and Memento. Their approach was fresh, and innovative, and reflected the aesthetic honesty of form to the subject matter. I liked the editing in Master and Commander as well. You can see the control and the calm with which Peter Weir stages the action and builds character and how meticulously the editor constructs the scenes for maximum effect. I also like Apocalypse Now, Clockwork Orange, Silence of the Lambs, Missing, The Right Stuff, Citizen Kane, A Place in the Sun, Once Upon a Time in the West—and my all-time favorite Raging Bull—that's great editing. There are a lot of films that move you in a certain way and sometimes it's hard to know why. Any well told story that transports you to a different place I think is well edited.

ARTHUR SCHMIDT, ACE

Photograph courtesy the American Cinema Editors and ACE Eddie Awards

SANTA BARBARA, CA

Partial Credits: Pirates of the Caribbean: The Curse of the Black Pearl, Cast Away, What Lies Beneath, Primary Colors, Contact, The Birdcage, Forrest Gump, The Last of the Mohicans, Death Becomes Her, The Rocketeer, Back to the Future Part III, Back to the Future Part II, Who Framed Roger Rabbit, Back to the Future, Coal Miner's Daughter, Jaws 2. As Additional Editor: Flight, Congo, Beaches, Marathon Man, The Fortune.

An incredibly soft-spoken, humble man who always wanted to be as true to the material as possible— "I just had such respect for the film". I loved hearing Artie describe how he wanted the audience to squirm while they were watching the bathtub scene from What Lies Beneath. Watch the scene and you'll see for yourself.

✂

TO: Arthur, you are a two-time Oscar recipient for best film editing, for Forrest Gump and for Who Framed Roger Rabbit. You are an Emmy recipient for Outstanding Film Editing for The Jericho Mile and a three-time recipient of the ACE Eddie award. How did you get your start in the film industry?

AS: My father was a staff film editor in the early '30's and '40's for RKO and then at Paramount Studios. My father would show me what he did in the editing room but I found it sterile and technical and complicated with the optical tracks and nitrate film he was working with. And my father always advised me not to get into the business. He said it was too tough and he told me to go and do something sane like sell insurance! (Both Laugh)

TO: You're not alone. I've talked to a lot of editors who had no plan on pursuing editing.

AS: When I went to the University of Santa Clara, I wasn't sure what I wanted to do. I knew business bored me and so out of desperation I became a Liberal Arts and English major. After I graduated, I worked the summer at a Coca-Cola plant in downtown LA and made enough money to finance my first trip to Europe. Then I applied to the Peace Corps to get a little more adventure in my life and to try and do something worthwhile.

TO: So what happened?

AS: I went to Madrid and one day I got a telegram telling me that my father had died. I went home to my father's funeral and about 10 days later, two of his former assistants called me and said that there was a job as an apprentice at Paramount. I was flat broke and I jumped at the chance. I thought that I'd try it for a year and if I liked it I'd stay. Obviously, I liked it, and that was the beginning of my career.

TO: And your dad was very accomplished.

AS: He edited some great films. He worked with Billy Wilder on Sunset Boulevard, Spirit of St. Louis, Some Like It Hot...

TO: Sayonara, Ace in the Hole, incredible... He was never really recognized for those films in each of the years, but they've stood the test of time and are classics now.

AS: Yeah, some great films. Especially Sunset Boulevard and Some Like It Hot. Sabrina is a delightful film. He was nominated for an Oscar for Sunset Boulevard and Sayonara. At Paramount, some very nice assistants taught me how to sync dailies. After about a year at Paramount as an apprentice, the second in command of the editorial department called me into his office and said that they were going to promote me to the film library.

TO: Stock footage?

AS: Right and most of the people who worked in the library were 60 or 70 years old. To me, it was like being buried alive! Never seeing anybody! I just quit.

TO: Hmm…

AS: I had a girlfriend in Spain but it didn't work out. I was running out of money and came back to Hollywood. Flat broke, I went to the Union and they got me a job at Twentieth Century Fox as an apprentice. I was starting all over again. An assistant called me and said that he was working on a film that was in trouble at the Sam Goldwyn Studio. I went to work the next day and worked at Goldwyn for the next four years going from one independent project to the next. After two or three years, Dede Allen came to the studio to do the sound mix on Little Big Man and I asked the head sound effects editor if Dede needed a standby editor/assistant while she was in Hollywood. He put me on the phone with Dede, we had a nice conversation and I got the job. And I worked the next six or seven months as Dede's assistant which, of course, was a fantastic experience.

TO: A tremendous experience.

AS: It really was. It turned out to be enough just to be near her, hoping some of the magic would rub off. She didn't talk a lot about her process but it was enough to be in the room with her to see how bold and creative she was and how she made the film often do things it wasn't meant to do. "Cut from the gut" was Dede's motto.

AS: I got a call from Stu Linder, who had been Mike Nichols's assistant editor to the great editor Sam O'Steen. Stu said that he was moved up to editor on Mike's next film, The Fortune and wanted me to be his assistant. I was in my ninth or tenth year as an assistant and I was just dying to edit. After a sleepless night or two, I called Stu and told him I wanted to be his assistant. Stu is a great guy and it was a Mike Nichols movie, The Fortune with Jack Nicholson and Warren Beatty.

TO: You were an Associate Editor to Jim Clark on Marathon Man. Jim went on to win the Academy Award for editing The Killing Fields. How did you make the jump to work with him?

TO: Okay, what happened?

AS: I called Paul Haggar, the post production supervisor at Paramount and Jim agreed to have me as his assistant / standby editor. Jim was finishing editing Sherlock Holmes's Smarter Brother with Gene Wilder. Meanwhile, John Schlesinger was still shooting and film was piling up unedited. So, there I was, watching all this film come in and it would just sit on the shelf waiting for Jim. Jim finally arrived, at least a month late, and started cutting scenes. He eventually realized how far behind he was and he started giving me scenes to cut.

TO: That's great.

AS: He gave me scenes that he had cut and tell me to try and make them better. And that was very, very intimidating. Fortunately, he liked whatever changes I made. It was a great experience working with Jim because he was such a great guy. We became great friends during the film, had a lot of fun, a lot of laughs, and worked really hard and a lot of weekends. When the end of the film came, Paramount wanted to give me a coediting credit. I went to Jim and told him that I knew that I worked really hard on the film but that I didn't feel that I had cut enough scenes to warrant a co-editor credit. And he and John Schlesinger agreed and they decided to give me the Associate Editor credit. I had no idea that it was going to be the first credit that came up in the end credit crawl, so I was thrilled.

TO: You were on Jaws 2. That must have been an interesting experience…

AS: I had known Neil Travis, who was the main editor, from my days at Paramount. They had fired the first director. The film was a chaotic mess, in total disarray. They hired a new director, Jeannot Swarcz. When I was done with my scenes, I left and Neil finished the movie. And, obviously, it was never as big a success as the first movie. But it was one of those lessons where you were thrown into the fire and you had to produce.

TO: Your career was in high gear because you did The Jericho Mile, for which you won an Emmy award.

AS: It was full of running sequences and someone had told ABC that I had done all the running sequences in Marathon Man. I met Michael Mann at Sony Studios, he gave me the script, and I went and parked in the Culver City Library parking lot in the pouring rain, read the script, and an hour and a half later I went back and said that I'd do it.

TO: That's great.

AS: They turned the movie's opening and running sequences over to me. The opening sequence was a montage that set up our lead character and the fact that he was a runner and had a black running mate; that there was a White Supremacist group, a Chicano group, and a Black Power group. And it was a big jumble of film. And that's the first scene that Michael had asked me to put together. I spent about three days looking at all the material and thinking about how to construct the scene. I had a piece of music from The Rolling Stones, Sympathy for the Devil, which is a great piece of music to cut to. By the third day, still struggling to find a shape for the montage, I had only edited about 30-40 seconds of film. From time to time I would go into Michael's office and tell him that I didn't quite know what to do with a particular scene, that I didn't really "get" why he shot it in the way that he did. He told me to just go and do whatever I wanted. So then I felt I was really free. I asked myself what would Dede Allen or Jim Clark do with this or that scene. So, with them as my inspiration, I did a lot of unconventional things (or so I thought) with a lot of sequences. Michael would come into the cutting room, look at the scene I had just done and said he thought what I had done was great. And leave me to go on to the next scene.

TO: That's great. Especially coming from someone who has a

reputation of being very demanding of his editorial staff.

AS: Oh, absolutely.

TO: And you won the Emmy award.

AS: Yes, and Michael was nominated for best directing and writing and won for best writing. It was a great thrill but by the time the movie was shown on television, I was already on Coal Miner's Daughter and on location in Kentucky. My wife and I had Sunday off and we were driving around doing some sight-seeing. When we got back to our hotel, it was on television.

TO: Okay, on to Coal Miner's Daughter. Not only did Sissy Spacek win an Academy Award for Best Actress, but you received a nomination for Best Film Editing. I think this was a turbo thrust in your career. How did Coal Miner's Daughter come about?

AS: It never would have happened without my wonderful friend and mentor, Jim Clark. He was working in London with Michael Apted on Agatha with Dustin Hoffman and Vanessa Redgrave. Michael said to Jim that he was going to Hollywood to do Coal Miner's Daughter, and asked Jim for a recommendation, and Jim, thank God, recommended me.

TO: Can you recall getting the dailies on the film?

AS: Yes. I was editing in a rather rundown motel room in a West Virginia coal mining town. Every morning when I came to work, I found cockroaches running all over the film and under the synchronizer! My introduction to Appalachia.

TO: That's disgusting... (Both Laugh)

AS: After two weeks, it was pretty clear that this was really special material. And it required me to be as good as everyone else on the film. The performances were terrific, Michael was doing a wonderful job directing, and Ralf Bode, the cinematographer, was doing fantastic work, as was everyone else. And it was kind of scary to me, a bit intimidating.

TO: What do you mean?

AS: It made me sit up and hope that I could be as good as the rest of the cast and crew. I really was in awe of the excellent material and performances that I was getting. Pure gold. The challenge was to edit the film in as real and honest a way as possible. I didn't want to draw any attention to the editing or make the musical sequences cool or flashy. I just had such respect for the film I was getting and wanted my work to be has real and honest as everyone else's. As my father used to say - "Keep it simple".

TO: At the Academy Awards in 1980, you were in some pretty amazing company— Raging Bull, The Coal Miner's Daughter, The Competition, The Elephant Man, and Fame.

AS: I can remember going to the Oscars for the first time and sitting in the row with all those wonderful editors. I was sitting next to Thelma Schoonmaker. I didn't know any of those people at the time and no one was really talking. Everyone was nervous. Thelma's name was called for Raging Bull. It was enough to be nominated for something that was not very showy editorially.

TO: We then enter a pretty amazing ten-year period in your career, from 1985 to 1995. There are quite a number of ground-breaking movies in that time. The first, of course, is Back to the Future. How were you introduced to Robert Zemeckis? Did you have any idea that it would be so successful?

AS: No, we didn't have a clue about what we had on our hands. I met Bob by a complete fluke. I was working for Michael Apted on a film called First Born. In the film were two teenage boys, and Bob Zemeckis was looking at every actor in Hollywood to cast as Marty in Back to the Future. He called Michael and asked if he could look at some of the sequences that our two boys were in. I ran four or five sequences and at the end, there was absolutely dead silence. And Bob said he thought that neither one of the boys was right for the role but that he really liked the way the scenes were edited. And I turned about six shades of red because I was asking for what he thought about the boys, not about the editing. About two weeks later he called me up and asked me if I'd come over to his office at Universal to talk about editing Back to the Future.

TO: That's great.

AS: I went for the interview and he gave me the script and a copy of Used Cars. A couple of days later I went back to talk to him about the script and he gave me the job. I don't know how you explain it— it's just one of those things that was just fate. Meeting Bob was obviously a major turning point in my career.

TO: I'm sure you hadn't read anything like that before. Were you beyond intrigued?

AS: It was mostly how we were going to pull this off - science fiction, comedy and a lot of special effects. And a very tight post-production schedule. You know, in those days, it seemed to be a heavy special effects film and I hadn't had any experience with special effects. It was kind of intimidating. I didn't know we were going to make this fantastic movie that everyone was going to fall in love with. It was a major challenge to get the film out for the release date and that led to us hiring another editor, Harry Keramidas.

TO: The film comes out and you see this wave of interest and then it goes through the roof.

AS: Right. It was tremendously exhilarating and that started with our first preview. You know that the film started out with Eric Stoltz in the lead?

TO: Yes.

AS: We shot for five weeks with him.

TO: I didn't know it was that long. What happened? It must be pretty difficult to go through that.

AS: I happened to be in a pre-production meeting about three weeks before we were going to start filming. And it's not usually a meeting I go to. It's mostly for the production crew to sort out logistics and any anticipated problems during filming. We were starting filming in the last week of November and we had a release date for the middle of June. And with all the special effects, it was a very tight schedule. I thought that Bob Zemeckis was going to have to come into the cutting room at the end of each day's shooting and give me notes. But, that didn't happen until the end of the fifth week of shooting.

TO: Okay, so you were cutting for five weeks and then he came in. What happened?

AS: We ran all the cut sequences for him and at the end, nobody said anything about Eric. The studio wanted him. But there was all this drama going on the shooting stage that we in the editing room knew nothing about. Bob Zemeckis never said anything to me. And on that Sunday, someone in the room said that we had a very big hole in the screen—referring to Eric. And Bob asked me what we were going to do.

TO: That's a tough question to answer. What did you do?

AS: I said that if we really have a problem, that he should show these cut sequences tomorrow morning to our producers, Bob Gale and Neil Canton, and if they agreed, then he should show it to our executive producer, Steven Spielberg, and if Steven agrees, show it to the studio heads. Meanwhile, Bob Zemeckis said he wasn't 100% happy with how the scenes were edited. I told him that we didn't have enough time to recut those scenes and I would take full responsibility. I told him to tell them that he was unhappy with the editing but that he just wanted to get the film in front of the producers and studio so that they could see what Eric was doing. And by Wednesday, everyone was in agreement that Eric should go.

TO: A pretty critical discussion that could have backfired on you...

AS: Absolutely. I could have been out as the editor.

TO: So, they made the change to Michael J. Fox...

AS: We had to start shooting the whole movie over again because Bob doesn't shoot a lot of isolated close-ups that we could have saved from Doc Brown. 100% of the movie was reshot and we had this release date breathing down our necks and scaring the hell out of us. Universal moved the date from the middle of June until I the Fourth of July weekend. So, we had three weeks extra but from the end of shooting, we had only three weeks until the first preview. We were working night and day, seven days a week, and also doing a sound mix simultaneously to get ready for the preview.

TO: So was it obvious when you started getting the dailies with Michael J. Fox?

AS: Oh, absolutely. Michael was just Marty. The movie came to life once Michael came on board and you also had that incredible chemistry between Marty and Doc Brown. We were just working so fast and hard to put it together and to get it ready for preview and make the release date.

TO: You recently attended some of the festivities from the 30th anniversary for the film. What was it like? It was a worldwide celebration.

AS: I know! It was crazy because all of those Back to the Future fans were kind of going nuts! (Both Laugh) It started off for us with a concert at The Hollywood Bowl where they showed the first Back to the Future and the score was played live by the L.A. Philharmonic. Then we and other cast and crew members were called to the stage to and introduced. And you know that doesn't happen that often to film editors! (Both Laugh)

TO: That's great.

AS: A lot of the audience came dressed in their '50's clothes or as characters from the film. Christopher Lloyd was there and afterwards we were invited backstage to celebrate and have a glass of wine with Alan Silvestri (Composer), and the other members of the cast and crew.

TO: It's really great to see something you made be so loved and bring so much entertainment to people.

AS: And people came from all over the country and the world that week of October 21st, which was the date on the dashboard of Doc's DeLorean. There was a reenactment of the Enchantment Under the Sea dance at the church hall where the original scene was filmed. Harry Keramidas and I were there and we actually signed autographs for people who lined up and most of them brought a poster of the movie to be signed. So I saw Italian, Japanese posters, BTTF posters from all over the world.

TO: Who Framed Roger Rabbit? won three Academy Awards—for sound editing, visual effects, and your first Oscar for film editing. These were the days before computer animation and digital compositing, with everything being accomplished through cel-based animation and optical compositing.

AS: It was a real surprise to me that I was nominated. I think maybe word got around about how complicated a process it was and how difficult it was to edit the movie without the animation. I only had the live action and the dialogue of the animated characters. We had six previews and we made editorial changes after each preview.

Back in the Cutting Room
Photograph courtesy the American Cinema Editors and ACE Eddie Awards

TO: Were they significant?

AS: No, little tweaks here and there. One day while Bob and I were making changes, he asked me what I would like to see happen at the end of the movie. I guess he felt something was lacking. I said - off the top of my head - that I would like to see Eddie give Roger a kiss, echoing back to Roger giving Eddie a kiss at the beginning of the movie, which Eddie found quite disgusting. But now Eddie and Roger were good friends. And Bob went and filmed that shot and we put it in the movie at the last minute.

TO: What was Oscar night like for you?

AS: Oh you know, I was obviously panicked and nervous as hell. It was a big surprise to me that I won. And I felt, a little bit, that I got the nomination and Oscar that should have gone to Bob.

TO: There are lot of interesting pictures between Back to the Future and Forest Gump. There were the other Back to the Futures, The Rocketeer, and then Death Becomes Her with that set of visual effects. And then you work again with Michael Mann on The Last of the Mohicans. Were there films during that period that you think maybe bear another look from audiences?

AS: Well, I always thought Last of the Mohicans had become kind of a classic film. Michael was absolutely wonderful to me on that film. I had quit the film about four or five weeks into shooting because Michael is very tough on getting everything right in the Michael Mann way.

TO: It still generates a loyal following. What do you mean about the Michael Mann way?

AS: He was extremely demanding of all of the crew, many of whom were very vocal about their discontent. Michael was never that way with me—he was absolutely terrific with me but after a while, I had this previsualization that pretty soon it was just going to be Michael and me in the cutting room. I had seen my father have three heart attacks working on difficult films in the cutting room and I just thought that I didn't want that to happen to me. So, I wrote my letter of resignation and quit the film three or four weeks into shooting.

TO: I didn't know that.

AS: Michael asked me not to leave and I said that I'd stay on until they got another editor to come in. I was trying to be completely professional about it. So I just kept working on the film, but in the meantime, I had gotten a call from Bob Zemeckis who asked me to do Death Becomes Her which I agreed to do because I had already resigned from "Mohicans" before I got the call from Bob. When I left, I heard that as many as four or five editors came and went.

TO: There were a lot of editors on that…

AS: Michael is very demanding in his search for perfection. He has a specific way he makes his movies and many of his movies are wonderful.

TO: Okay, on Death Becomes Her, it's a pretty dark movie and always a balance between the satire, comedy, black comedy with some very interesting visual effects. Was this similar to Roger Rabbit where you were just getting the live action?

AS: Yes, we were getting the live action plates and the shots with the hole in Goldie's stomach or Meryl's head turned around backwards—all of that came later.

TO: I'm always curious as to what your reaction is when you get back the visual effect…

AS: I'm always surprised and happy when we get a finished VFX shot back and the work is invisible. The same was true of getting the scenes back on Roger Rabbit with the final animation.

TO: You won your second Oscar for Forrest Gump. When did you know you had something special?

AS: As I was getting the dailies. The quality of the material, Tom's performance and everyone else's work was so good that all of us in the editing room—fell in love with the movie. We felt it was something very special, and kind of delicate. I didn't want to make any false moves or do any kind of manipulative editing to milk the emotions in any of the scenes. It was a bit tricky. I hope I don't sound too hokey, but maybe I was taking my editing cues from Forrest—to be direct, simple and honest and not embellish anything or milk emotions with extra cuts.

TO: Were there particular scenes that were meaningful to you?

AS: Well, young Forrest losing the braces and running. The whole section in Vietnam was a challenge. Again, a little bit tricky to not overemphasize things or make any false moves, emotionally, especially when Bubba dies. And any scene between Forrest and Jenny.

With the Oscar for Forrest Gump
Photograph courtesy the American Cinema Editors and ACE Eddie Awards

TO: What was your working style with Zemeckis?

AS: Bob and I really didn't sit down together until the movie was finished shooting. When Bob finished filming, we moved the editing room to Santa Barbara where both Bob and I live.

TO: You had some pretty interesting competition that year at the Academy Awards. It was Forrest, Hoop Dreams, Pulp Fiction, The Shawshank Redemption, and Speed. During the editing segment, they showed the scene where young Forrest loses the braces. Were you more prepared this time?

AS: No, it was very surprising. You just mentioned the competition and there were a lot of people who were very high on Pulp Fiction and Shawshank and Speed. And those were all beautifully edited. Hoop Dreams as well. I was surprised.

TO: The film was a phenomenon. On a worldwide basis, it just kept becoming bigger and bigger. How much time did you spend on the film?

AS: I think I spent about nine months. The film was released in July and we had a reasonable post-production schedule.

TO: They called the budget at $55 million and at $678 million worldwide box office.

AS: That's pretty good.

TO: Slightly profitable. (Both Laugh) Did you preview it?

AS: Yes. We went back to San Jose to preview it at the same cinema where we previewed the Back to the Future movies because that was our good luck cinema. We had a fantastic preview. The audience loved the movie.

TO: Were you concerned at the running time? It's about two hours and twenty minutes.

AS: You're always trying to tighten things up and make it as long as it needs to be. The first cut was about three hours and from there it was just a matter of getting it down to what worked and what played.

TO: You must have had a lot of fun getting the dailies for The Birdcage.

AS: Oh, it was a lot of fun, but it was also intimidating.

TO: In what way?

AS: I had worked for Mike Nichols as an assistant on The Fortune and he had called Dede Allen to edit The Birdcage. Dede was busy on another film and she said, 'Well, why don't you call Artie? He just won an Oscar for Forrest Gump.' I was thrilled to edit the film for him because he is such a great director. There was a bit of time between the end of Forrest and the beginning of The Birdcage and I went and helped out Anne Coates on Congo and for about three months. It was great to work with Anne, one of my idols. And there I was, having just won an Oscar, in awe of working with Anne. The other intimidating thing for me in editing with Mike Nichols was his longtime editor, Sam O'Steen, who edited all of Mike's movies until The Fortune. I was in such awe of Sam's work, such as Who's Afraid of Virginia Woolf?, Carnal Knowledge, The Graduate and all the rest. He was one of the best editors out there.

TO: How did you handle that anxiety?

AS: One of the first things I did to find out whether or not I was in synch with Mike, was that as soon as I got the footage for the very first scene, I put it together. When I got home that evening my wife met me at the door and said, 'Quick. Mike Nichols is on the phone for you.' And he said, 'I just wanted to tell you how much I loved what you did. You got it absolutely right.' He couldn't have been more complimentary. And I breathed a big sigh of relief.

TO: Contact is a very ambitious film and has a very large number of visual effects. What a long way from Roger Rabbit! What kind of challenges did it represent for you as an editor?

AS: The scene somewhere in outer space between Jodie Foster and her deceased father was a wonderfully acted scene but when I got it, it was just green screen and the two actors. And I just edited it as honestly and delicately as I possibly could. When I got it back from special effects, I couldn't believe it. The beauty of the background scenery added to the drama emotion of the scene.

TO: What else stood out for you?

AS: The climax of the movie where she goes into outer space (or did she) and the inquiry scene with Jodie Foster being asked if it actually happened, were really challenging. The interrogation scene had multiple angles and a huge amount of coverage.

TO: You worked on Cast Away and then took a break to edit What Lies Beneath before going back to Cast Away. Let's talk about What Lies Beneath. This is a very suspenseful film and the bathtub sequence is always showcased in studies about editing.

AS: You know, you're the first person who told me that. I did have a lot of fun doing that scene but I had no idea that it was shown in editing classes.

TO: It's true.

AS: I wanted this scene to do for bathtubs what Psycho did for showers. (Both Laugh) Even though the shower scene is something like 47 seconds long and the bathtub scene is 10, 12 minutes. That's really what was going on in my head.

TO: You achieved it. It's excruciating...

AS: One of the funny things about the scene was that Bob shot all of the material on Michelle and then the second unit shot for maybe four weeks on the tweaking of her foot with the faucet and her hand, etc., with a body double. I was putting together the scene as they were shooting it and after about a week or so, Michelle's foot looked different than it did in the dailies the day before. The feet didn't match and the toenails didn't match. (Both Laugh) And I went to the second unit director and asked what happened. The first foot double got another job so they got someone else. And, of course, we discovered that one foot and one toe is not like another! (Both Laugh)

TO: That's funny...

AS: So the second unit had to go back and reshoot everything with the new replacement foot! I had tons and tons of film to play around with...

TO: You know, the film did very well. It made almost $300 million.

AS: Oh, I had no idea! That's great. I thought maybe the film was a bit of a box office disappointment...

TO: No. It made $291 million...

AS: It was a lot of fun to edit the movie because it was all about the creepiness of what was going on in the house or whether it was all in her head. And really just trying to create suspense. Psycho, Hitchcock and his long-time editor, George Tommasini, a good friend of my Dad's in their days of working together at Paramount, were the inspiration for the editing in WLB.

TO: Okay, that was the film between the Castaway shoots. And Castaway was also a big success. It's around the same running time as Forrest Gump, made almost $430 million...

AS: It made that kind of money?

TO: Yeah.

AS: Wow. When I read the original script, I thought that Bob was now going to do a manual on how to survive on a desert island. But, of course, it wasn't that because Bob is such a brilliant director. But it was a challenge. Once the plane crash happened, and once Tom is on the island by himself, that was a big challenge to keep it moving and keep it interesting.

TO: You do some amazing work in that movie. There's some very exciting stuff, certainly, for the plane crash. And the emotional part when he loses Wilson. I think that was a year where you should have been nominated, too, not to take away anything from the films that were nominated that year...

AS: Oh, well, thank you very much. Castaway was a lot of work. The two escape attempts from the island were difficult to do. Tom making fire and just about everything on the movie was a unique challenge.

TO: The fire making scenes are terrific because you want to say, 'Come on, catch, catch!', and you want the audience to be saying that.

AS: Yes. Absolutely. And Bob always gave me complete freedom to do whatever I wanted with those montage scenes. And what I did was to take bits and pieces out, making jump cuts, going quickly to the next stage, and just keeping the really active moments. That's what my gut instincts were telling me to do. And I had no idea that the death of Wilson...

TO: It's really emotional...

AS: I've seen that scene recently and I remembered trying to go for the most emotional parts of the multitude of dailies on Wilson. And it all sounds so silly because it's just a ball bobbing in the surf. A lot of it was about picking the right pieces where he just kept drifting further and further away.

TO: That's what your skill and the art and craft of editing is all about. Yes, dramatically he is the companion and losing him is something that you easily could have messed up. You maximized that loss. I don't think that's mechanically easy to do. I think it was done brilliantly.

AS: Oh, well, thank you. Having seen it fairly recently, what really makes the scene work, even though I did work hard on what was 'Wilson's performance', is that Tom's performance in that scene is wonderful. Tom was losing his best friend.

TO: What films and filmmakers influenced you as you were growing up?

AS: Because of my Dad, certainly Billy Wilder, also George Stevens, and, of course David Lean. After I saw Lawrence of Arabia I was blown away and thought that I would love to be in the business even though I originally tried to avoid it. Seeing my first foreign films had a big effect - Fellini, Truffaut, Bergman, Renoir opened up a whole new world of cinema for me.

TO: You edited eight films for Robert Zemeckis. What kept you together?

AS: I think it's because we were very relaxed and compatible with each other, being on the same wave length. Bob is a huge talent. The film he gives you to work with is a gift. He's a master film maker and story teller.

TO: Did you ever get nervous with a new director? I mean, did the butterflies ever go away?

AS: I don't think the butterflies and a bit of insecurity ever went away. I was always concerned as to whether I'd be up to the task on the next one. Every movie is different from the one that came before it. The thought of whether I'd be as good on this one as I was on the last one—that was always there. Every film presents new and different challenges—new story, new actors, often a new director—it forces you to be on your toes all the time.

TO: Mike Nichols, Michael Mann, Michael Apted, Taylor Hackford, and Robert Zemeckis are some of the directors you have worked with. What did you learn from each of them?

AS: From all of them I learned to tell the story in the most honest, direct, and simple way as possible.

TO: Of all the films that you edited, if you were flipping through the channels and one of them was on, is there a particular one you'd stop and watch?

AS: I would watch Back to the Future, Forrest Gump, Coal Miner's Daughter, Last of the Mohicans. You know, when I'm flipping through the channels and I see a movie that I've worked on, I stop and admit that most of the time I get nervous because I start looking at the cuts to see if there's something I could have done to make the movie better.

TO: While you are retired now, what was the most satisfying aspect of your craft and profession?

AS: I think what comes to mind, mostly, is that I was extremely lucky to have become a film editor when my father tried his darnedest to put me off the business because he thought it was too hard and too crazy. Despite what he said, it was quite apparent that he loved what he did. The most satisfying thing that I loved is that I worked at something that was absolutely right for me. I loved what I did. I never had a passion to be a producer or a director. I was quite content to be a film editor and hopefully work with good directors on good films which I was fortunate enough to have done. I was just happy to be on the receiving end of other peoples' good work and to make them and all of us look as good as possible.

JAMIE SELKIRK

Photograph courtesy the American Cinema Editors and ACE Eddie Awards

NEW ZEALAND

Partial Credits: King Kong, The Lord of the Rings: The Return of the King, The Lord of the Rings: The Two Towers (Co-Producer), The Lord of the Rings: The Fellowship of the Ring (Co-Producer), The Frighteners, Heavenly Creatures, Dead Alive.

The Lord of the Rings Trilogy shot five million feet of film—926 hours—over 400 days. Jamie started as a studio cabler for New Zealand Broadcasting and literally fell into editing…by being hit by a car. As the films became more complex and ambitious, Jamie's skills grew and flourished. He is still surprised at the amazing journey his career had taken.

✂

TO: Jamie, you are an Academy Award and Eddie Award recipient for best editing for the The Lord of The Rings: The Return of The King. How did you get your start in the film business?

JS: After leaving College in 1966 I joined up with the NZBC, the New Zealand Broadcasting Corporation. I started as a studio cabler. I had no concept of what film editing was. And I started cutting news on film and then moved into current affairs editing. Finally, I moved on to drama editing and that seemed to suit me—it gave me a chance to really make a contribution.

TO: All the content was shot on film, especially that day's news.

JS: Yeah, that's right. For news you'd have to scramble to get it on the air for 6 or 630 at night. And really, that's where my ability to quickly cut was born.

TO: You did some work in London as well, right?

JS: Yes. I went over to work at the BBC for about a year doing documentaries. Then I came back to Wellington and really got into editing fairly big dramas. But what was interesting about my experience in TV, Tom, was that we did everything. We did the editing, the sound laying, and negative cutting.

TO: It seems you were pretty isolated, too, so you had to develop those skills, right?

JS: Right. We didn't have a lot of other companies around who we could go to, so we ended up developing all those skills ourselves.

TO: You have had the ability to go from the most basic way a film is made from your television days to moving to digital editing and then experiencing the incredible leaps in computer graphic imaging (CGI) and ground-breaking character creation and performance capture.

JS: Filmmaking has become a lot more complex. We moved from editing on film to doing it on U-matic videotapes and it was so cumbersome on video. Then we moved on to digital. The whole process has become a lot easier for people to get into editing but they don't tend to concentrate on the pacing and the story and the rhythm.

TO: There was very little time to complete The Return of The King due to the amount of footage, visual effects, and schedule. Could you provide a little background?

JS: The Lord of the Rings was a huge project for us to undertake. None of us really realized the span of it; perhaps Peter did. But we didn't realize the amount of footage we'd be shooting and it was really a learning curve.

TO: When did you make the move from editing on film to digital?

JS: The real move was on The Lord of the Rings. And film three was always going to be the big one and I also thought the script was really fantastic. I had already done a version of the cut on film three while

Peter was finishing film two. And we did that because the following year would be spent doing any pickups we needed.

TO: Were those extensive pickups?

JS: Yeah, usually the pickups involved two months of shooting. And having the first cut, which was very rough, would give us a good idea of what we needed to make the story better. We shot the three films together and obviously Peter can't be editing while he's shooting and so we have to get everything together for him so he can concentrate entirely on film one, and so forth. And then, while he's fine cutting film one, film two will be in a rough cut. And then while he's fine cutting film two, I'd be doing the rough cut for film three. And that gave us the opportunity to do pickups for anything we needed.

TO: You have worked with Peter Jackson on seven films, starting with Dead Alive.

JS: On Dead Alive, that was a film that was entirely storyboarded and Peter shot it almost exactly as storyboarded. And I could have cut the entire thing just following those storyboards. From then on, Peter and I got along quite well and it was fun.

TO: And then you moved on to do Heavenly Creatures with him.

JS: It was a really interesting experience and we looked at all the footage and it's still one of my most favorite films that I've done with Peter. And it was the first time that we had gotten into visual effects—we had bought our first film scanner and recorder. We didn't have any idea on how we were going to do these visual effects. And we really had to experiment. Remember, you couldn't really see what you had until you filmed it out.

TO: Meaning you recorded it back out to film and then could project it.

JS: Right. So, we recorded out at night and then sent it out to the lab and we'd come in and see that we had some black frames or problems and we'd have to start again.

TO: What a long way it's come today from those early days.

JS: Yeah, you just couldn't see what you were going to get until you got it processed and it was quite scary, really.

TO: Especially given the pressure that puts on budgets.

JS: Yet we managed to do it and that put us on the road to getting more fantasy type movies. Then it became Weta Digital and we went from eight visual effects people to about 34 for Heavenly Creatures and then 100 or so for the first Lord of The Rings. And for the last one we had over 1,000 people working for us.

TO: It must have been quite thrilling to see the creatures come to life via performance capture and animation.

JS: It was so exciting. Because you're cutting with blue screen and green screen footage and there's nothing in the background, just actors on the stage. And Peter is saying, 'There's this here and that there and there's going to be a wall there...' And so that means you have to make sure you hold a shot long enough because there's going to be something there eventually that you can't see. So, it's challenging.

TO: And then you'd refine it again as you started to get the temp and finished shots coming back in to you?

JS: Yeah, you never knew how it was really going to work until we got the shots back and we'd cut them in. And often we'd get shots and cut them in and say 'Oh, that's not quite how we imagined it', and that would change the pace of some of the elements.

TO: February 29, 2004. City of God, Cold Mountain, Master and Commander: The Far Side of the World, Seabiscuit, and Lord of the Rings: The Return of The King.

JS: The film had 11 nominations and we were getting many of the craft awards and I kept thinking 'Oh, this can't go on'... I can hardly remember my name being called out, really. I remember going up and I had written something, but I didn't even remember to take it out of my pocket! It was pretty amazing and something certainly where I never expected to be, Tom. Really, for all of us involved in The Lord of the Rings films, we never imagined we'd be going to the Oscar ceremonies.

TO: You've got New Zealand influencing the whole filmmaking world in terms of what you accomplished down there.

JS: I'm very fortunate to have hooked up with Peter and it's been great to be able to stick with him and do all the films. The technology now is that we don't have to be in Hollywood, we can be anywhere and you feel like you're in the office next door.

TO: And to see the improvements that digital color correction enables you to do now as part of the digital intermediate process.

JS: That's really something that has come into its own. It doesn't matter how you shot it on the day—you can change things to suit your desire.

TO: All in, how much film did you shoot on the Lord of the Rings trilogy?

JS: Something like five million feet.

TO: You rolled right into King Kong.

JS: We had just come out of the Lord films, which had taken six years and we then went straight into King Kong, which was another complex film. And it was a film that I really enjoyed doing. A lot of stuff came out of that movie that we just couldn't fit in. The dinosaur chase scene was originally twice as long and we cut it down.

TO: What are some of your favorite films?

JS: I've always loved westerns and Clint Eastwood films. Love Steve McQueen films. I wasn't really a big movie guy, and it's weird that I ended up in films.

TO: What do you like most about your profession?

JS: Seeing the audience reaction. You spend a year or more in the cutting room and you think you're making a good movie—an exciting movie. But you're never quite sure until it goes to the audience. And I always love to see a movie on the opening night and I think when the movie's working it's one of the most satisfying things.

TIM SQUYRES, ACE

Photo courtesy of Peter Sorel

NEW YORK CITY, NY

Partial Credits: Billy Lynn's Long Halftime Walk, Unbroken, The Armstrong Lie, Life of Pi, Rachel Getting Married, Lust, Caution, Syriana, Hulk, Gosford Park, Crouching Tiger, Hidden Dragon, Ride With The Devil, Lulu On The Bridge, The Ice Storm, Sense and Sensibility, Eat Drink Man Woman, The Wedding Banquet.

Read Carol Littleton's comments about Tim and it's a better summary than I could ever write. His editing methodology is so unique, and it makes so much sense. Watch his films from the earliest to the most recent and you will see precision, versatility, and enormous talent.

TO: Tim, you are a multiple Academy Award, BAFTA, and ACE Eddie nominee for Best Editing. You were the recipient of the Golden Horse, Taiwan's version of the Oscar, for Crouching Tiger, Hidden Dragon. How did you get your start?

TS: I went to college, not initially for film, but took a film class and got hooked. I had a friend who was going to film school at NYU, so I worked on a bunch of films for NYU students, doing production sound as well as editing. And I quickly realized that I liked editing and started doing more of it.

TO: You have a lot of experience in terms of sound editing. Was the transition to picture editing easy?

TS: I had always gone back and forth between sound and picture editing. I did a lot of television documentaries, industrials, and commercials. And on those things, you almost always end up doing both picture and sound. I was fortunate because my second feature as editor was with Ang Lee on his first film, and we continued to work together from then on.

TO: What was that film?

TS: Pushing Hands, in the spring and summer of 1991. We started working together by chance. It turned out that we could collaborate well. The things that interest him thematically and his approach to filmmaking are very similar to mine. I learned to edit with his footage. And he learned to direct with me editing his footage. Our careers came up together. We developed our filmmaking abilities together on the same footage, so we have a lot in common in figuring out how to make a movie.

TO: What's the working style?

TS: He's off shooting, and I get the footage and get scenes cut and turned around as quickly as I can so that he can see them. We don't watch dailies together. He has never been interested in giving me instructions about what to do with a scene. He's more interested in having me do what I think is best. Crouching Tiger was a 128-day shoot. He was in China and I was in New York, and we only spoke to each other twice during that entire time. My job during production is to make sure everything's okay. First, if there's a problem and I also have to show him what he's doing so that he can decide if it's going well or not.

TO: Meaning if there's something you need that's not in the footage?

TS: If he feels he's got the scene, he doesn't want to think about it again until we're together in editing. At the end of production, we'll have a screening within a couple of days or a couple of weeks.

TO: Of your first cut?

TS: Yes, a full assembly. Then we sit in a room, all day, every day, until we lock picture. He's not really one to give notes and go away. He's a hard worker and we work until we're done.

TO: What is that give and take like?

TS: It depends on what we have to do. But, the way I prepare scenes is that I have already tried a lot of things. I never do one version of a scene and move on. So, I have lots of variations ready. During production, I don't just send him one version of a scene—I'll usually send him two to four.

TO: You have an unusual editing method that I haven't encountered before. It's pretty fascinating. If a scene is covered in wide shots, medium shots and close-ups, you'll actually assemble that scene three different ways—one assembly with only the wide shots, a second assembly with only the medium shots, and a third assembly with just the close-ups.

TS: I started doing that on The Ice Storm. There was a particular scene with Katie Holmes and Tobey Maguire. When you edit a scene, you're taking an hour's worth of footage and turning it into a one-minute scene. So you're eliminating a lot of material. The first thing I do is find the pieces that I'm going to use to construct the scene. For most of this scene we had the two of them sitting and talking, covered in medium shots and close-ups in each direction, with no 2-shot or master. On Tobey's side I has four takes of each size. The problem I was having was that practically every reading of practically every line was good and interesting and different. Once I'd pulled everything I liked I had hardly eliminated anything. And I thought, 'Okay, what am I going to do now? I've left myself with too many choices!' I decided to just completely ignore the medium shots and cut the scene in only the close-ups. And then I did the scene again using the medium shots and ignoring the close-ups.

TO: I like it.

TS: It was a way for me to artificially limit my options and force myself to work with only a subset of the footage I had. What I discovered was that the whole scene played much better in the close-ups. The other great thing is very often you cut a scene and you do it in the master up until a certain point and then you go in to the coverage. When you finally sit down with the director and he says he imagined that earlier section in the close ups, you've already done it, and you don't have to go back into assembly mode while the director is sitting there.

TO: Right.

TS: On a big complicated scene, or a scene that wasn't covered with normal coverage—Gosford Park and Rachel Got Married are examples—is that I'll cut the scene once, then just do it again. The way I work is that I initially have a sequence of pulls—all of the things that I want to use to make the scene—in rough script order. For a two-minute scene that sequence might be 15-20 minutes long. So after cutting version one, I duplicate the pull sequence and stick the version one cut on the end of that. If you enable dupe detection in the Avid, you can see what you've already used. Then I'll cut another version, trying not to repeat myself.

TO: You see all the variations.

TS: And I may have made a great edit in version one, but I'll be careful not to repeat it in version two, but rather go look for something else. Sometimes version one is better than version two but often not. I view my job as not just cutting the scene during the assembly—it's to explore the footage and find out the possibilities and to get myself ready to work with the director. My job is to find out what's there.

TO: You got your first nomination for Crouching Tiger, Hidden Dragon.

TS: I'm very proud of Crouching Tiger, but it wasn't as hard as some other films, like Gosford Park or Sense and Sensibility. I think it was nominated for editing partly because the film was so well received, and partly because of the martial arts. And the martial arts was the easiest part of that film.

TO: Really?

TS: I don't want to imply that it was easy—it was challenging and difficult—but if you ask any editor what scenes they're most proud of, most will tell you it's the dialogue scenes. The hard part of doing action is making sure to keep the characters and the emotions involved. I'm happy that people appreciated the editing of the action scenes, but the dialogue scenes were harder and took more work.

TO: Are there films where you were particularly challenged on a scene?

TS: Sense and Sensibility was a very interesting film and very challenging for an editor. There are a lot of scenes with a lot of people and a lot going on. And there are a lot of secrets being kept, so when someone says something, it means one thing to one person and another thing to a different person. So, this person knows something that the person sitting next to them does not know. And what they're dealing with is very important, emotionally, to them. It's very rich emotionally and intellectually and those are the best kinds of scenes for an editor.

TO: Why?

TS: Because the situations are so complex and rich and dense. There are some scenes that are remarkable for how much is going on and how many balls you're trying to juggle emotionally. There are some dialogue scenes where, just over a minute or two, they're cut faster than some of the fight scenes in Crouching Tiger.

TO: Really?

TS: Yes, the number of shots per minute is more but it doesn't feel like it because every cut is motivated. When the density of the ideas flying around is high, the speed of the cutting can be high without drawing attention to itself. The preview scores were among the highest they'd ever seen. At the time the picture was about two-and-a-half hours. We eventually released it at 2:16:04.

TO: You remember it down to the second. (Both Laugh)

TS: Crouching Tiger is really not a martial arts film. It's a big, sweeping, romantic drama that has martial arts scenes in it—and pretty good martial arts scenes. Some of the fight scenes I'm very happy with. There's a 20-minute flashback in the western desert that takes place two years earlier and that whole section is just wonderful. Just the beauty and the sweep of it are terrific. Those are my favorite things in the film.

TO: What don't people know about your profession?

TS: What you really do is take away 99% of what they shot. So, you're not really taking away. You're building up the 1% that's going to make it.

TO: You have a daunting number of choices in most cases.

TS: Yes. For example, the two lead performances in Sense and Sensibility from Emma Thompson and Kate Winslett. Emma wrote the script, so she had been saying those lines in her head for five years. Her performance was wonderful, but there wasn't a lot of variety. She gave a coherent performance and of course Ang coached her in his way. Kate, on the other hand, came into it later. She was young, it was an exciting part, and she is a wonderful actress. But her performance was all over the place.

TO: Meaning that it varied greatly from take to take?

TS: Yes, in a good way. It was consistent, but there was a very wide range of things that she was doing. So that's a performance that was a bit more under my control in terms of how it turned out because I could have taken it in a number of different ways.

TO: Have you had to take out things from any of the films that you wished you hadn't?

TS: We took out a couple of things from Sense and Sensibility that I maybe wish we hadn't. There's a scene towards the end where Marianne is sick and lying in what we think might wind up as her deathbed. She wakes up out of her daze momentarily and sees her father who had died at the very beginning of the film. And she speaks to him. It's wonderful and really chilling. She's looking off into a dark corner in the room and it's completely black back there. Emma, knowing perfectly well that he wasn't there, turned and looked anyway. And in the hands of a less-experienced actor, that could have been silly. And she did such a wonderful job of putting so much emotion into that simple look back.

TO: What else?

TS: There's a scene towards the end of the film after Edward comes back and proposes and before the wedding scene. It was a scene where Edward and Elinor are walking along and they tie up some narrative loose ends and kiss. Now, it's a romantic movie in which nobody kisses. And we immediately took that scene out. The scene where Edward—Hugh Grant's character—comes back and proposes—there's this big emotional uplift there, and we wanted to carry that emotion into the wedding and then straight out into the credits. So putting in this scene where they're walking and talking just destroyed that emotional flow, even though it ended with a kiss.

TO: How do you go about trimming a movie to reduce its time?

TS: You go back and reexamine every cut. Ang and I talked about this after we finished Sense and Sensibility. We were under such pressure to shorten the film that there are a bunch of cuts that are just a little bit too tight.

TO: Gosford Park was for Robert Altman. How was that relationship?

TS: During production we didn't talk but I did cut scenes and send them to him. The way that film was shot was very interesting. The coverage was really minimal. They had a couple of cameras that would dolly back and forth and they weren't really worried about traditional coverage at all. And this was all done without a plan of how it was going to cut.

TO: I didn't know that.

TS: In some instances, there were characters who spoke scripted lines and they were never on camera. I had to play character lines off other people because they were never shot. And I don't think they knew that on set—it was a very relaxed, casual way to shoot which I think for that movie was absolutely right.

TO: I know but it's pretty unusual…

TS: I was really tearing my hair out at the beginning because I had never seen coverage like this. Most of what I thought I knew about editing didn't apply to this material. And it was only after really diving into it and trying a lot of things that I got a feeling of what the best way to edit the footage was. I was cutting in New York and they were shooting in England. We rarely got into re-cutting the scenes themselves—Altman never really wanted to do that. What we did, though, is, say there was a sequence of three scenes—things that were going on simultaneously in different parts of the house. We'd cut each scene in half and scramble the pieces.

TO: Really?

TS: Yes. That's the kind of thing we did in that film.

TO: It all works.

TS: Yes, and it was very pleasant. And we locked picture two weeks early! All the above stairs stuff was shot first and all the below stairs stuff was shot later. But in the script, they were completely intercut. So, the film was like a checkerboard, and halfway through the shoot I only had the black squares—every other scene. I could never really get any sense of rhythm.

TO: What films do you like or what films inspired you?

TS: Well, one of the films that got me started thinking about a career in film was Days of Heaven. It's just a remarkable accomplishment in taking something big and structuring it in a way that's so beautiful and flows so well. It's such a coherent feeling all the way through. It's really a wonderful and remarkable film. I thought it was so well planned. And only years later did I find out that it wasn't the case at all—it was a mess. They invented voiceovers and it was a huge amount of work to change and restructure that in the editing room. But it's just a stunning film. Little Big Man, the Dustin Hoffman film that Dede Allen did such a wonderful job editing. It's really interesting how she was able to modulate the pace of the film and take it up and energetically move it through certain sections and then pause and create these powerful moments when she had to. Apocalypse Now is, of course, editorially breathtaking in how they were able to create moods in places.

TO: If you weren't an editor, what would you be doing?

TS: I had been planning on being a scientist of some sort. And I think that's certainly an area that I could very well have gone into.

ZACH STAENBERG, ACE

Photograph courtesy the American Cinema Editors and ACE Eddie Awards

LOS ANGELES, CA

Partial Credits: Pacific Rim: Uprising, Good Kill, Ender's Game, Lord of War, The Matrix Revolutions, The Matrix Reloaded, Antitrust, The Crossing, The Matrix, Bound, Gotti, The Cisco Kid, Police Academy, Once Upon a Time in America (uncredited).

While Zach became known because of the three Matrix films, his work on Lord of War is extraordinarily good. And the freeway chase in Reloaded? Sit back and enjoy that very hard to achieve blend of action and humor. It's a real education of how this one-time PA has become a truly talented motion picture editor.

✄

TO: Zach, you are an Academy Award and two-time ACE Eddie award recipient. How did you get your start?

ZS: I think it started when I attended the University of Wisconsin, Madison. There were all these student film societies, so you could see all these great movies. After I graduated I found my way down to Chicago and started getting freelance work as a PA or camera assistant. About six months into that, 20thCentury Fox did a movie directed by Brian DePalma called The Fury.

TO: That's with Kirk Douglas and John Cassavetes.

ZS: Yes, and I got a job on that as a PA and I loved it. Brian DePalma had closed dailies because he didn't want everyone to see them. I wasn't allowed to see them. But one day I was in the PA office late. The editor was Paul Hirsch and they were editing in New York and his assistant called and said, 'Listen, Paul's not getting any notes from Brian. Is there anyone who can take notes from Brian for us?'

TO: Opportunity knocks.

ZS: And I leaped at that. The assistant told me what they needed and we devised a little form and I sent it to Paul and Brian for approval. Then Brian said, 'Okay, you're coming to dailies.' So, I went and sat between Richard Kline, who was the DP, and Brian. I took notes from both of them and sent them to Paul's editing team in New York.

TO: That's great.

ZS: Some days I'd be a PA. Some days I'd be a third A.D. And when I went to dailies, I realized that all the work these hundreds of people were doing was all going to filter down to these two individuals—Paul and Brian. And I realized that short of directing, editing was the thing to do.

TO: Okay, what happened next?

ZS: Eventually, I moved myself out to L.A. and started working as an assistant editor.

Robert Brown hired me to be his assistant on Police Academy. Bob ended up leaving the film and I became co-editor. And that's really what I'd call my big break.

TO: The film that I think really bears another look is "Bound". Also, it was your first experience working with The Wachowskis and it was their directorial debut.

ZS: I would say that Bound is one of my favorite films that I've done. They sent me the script and when I finished reading it, you could just tell that they knew what they were doing and that they were going to have a very clear vision and the talent to back it up.

TO: There was a lot of controversy over the film.

ZS: We had a big argument with the MPAA about getting an NC-17. There is a moment in the seduction scene and the camera pans down and you can see Gina Gershon's arm. You can see all the tendons flexing but nothing else. And although you couldn't see what she was doing, it was clear as a bell. So, we used a different take of that.

TO: Did you preview it?

ZS: Yes. It was at the Castro theatre in San Francisco. When the film was over, people were stamping the floor in appreciation. The place was shaking. It was one of the best screenings I've ever been experienced.

TO: Can you recall your first reaction and thoughts when you were presented with the idea or the script for "The Matrix"?

ZS: What I loved about it is what I'm always looking for in a movie—where there are some really great ideas, a great theme, and trying to be truly artistic. And when you can wrap that all into an established genre—in this case, action—it can really work well, which in the case of Matrix, it did. It has this pyramid structure, where the broad base contains a great genre action film upon which you can build multiple layers of sophisticated ideas.

TO: What particular challenges did the film represent to you?

ZS: Well, the first thing is that with a movie with so many visual effects, it totally affects how you go about the editing. Because, remember, they don't usually get finished—by and large—until you start mixing the movie. At the most extreme end, the process of creating visual effects is such that you can continue to create and refine them until the very possible last minute. And that changes the editing process. You're no longer editing with shots that are finite. In fact, they're plastic—you can change them and work them into a different shot.

TO: Were there a lot of shots you had to wait for?

ZS: The first Matrix didn't have, relative to current films, that many visual effects. I think Matrix had between 350-400 shots, Reloaded had about 1100 shots, and Revolutions had about 800 shots. The only really unusual thing that was hard to understand how it was going to work was what became known as 'Bullet Time'.

TO: It must have been fun to see the versions as they were coming in.

ZS: The action was shot with a circle of continuously firing field cameras. And they just got it all stitched together and that happened pretty quickly. It was clear—early on—that it was going to work. And you could feel that it was going to be exciting.

TO: What I love is how the film starts—it's a juggernaut of a start and you're right in this new world, but it's part of the old world or it seems to be.

ZS: The opening of the movie, if you break it down, is really not different from other movies.

TO: It's very film-noirish.

ZS: Exactly. And part of the story telling in that is the editing. Editing is the one thing that is unique to movies. Cinematography or production design exist in other art forms. But, how images are juxtaposed to emphasize a point, or to underscore something, is what makes a movie a movie. That is the essence of editing. There is certainly no major technological invention in the opening of the film—it's a lot of wire work and a lot of cuts.

TO: Yes, but those cuts are fast and just get that story going right away! When did you get an idea of how enthusiastic the reception to the movie was going to be?

ZS: Honestly not until the opening weekend!

TO: In 1999, the nominees were American Beauty, The Cider House Rules, The Insider, The Sixth Sense, and The Matrix.

ZS: I was surprised, honestly. It wasn't out of the realm of possibility, but I'm the kind of person who likes to downplay these things. I was very fortunate to have been given phenomenal material. I was given some extremely challenging material that when it played out it allowed people to appreciate my work than that of other material.

TO: I want to shift to a film that I really enjoyed very much. That's Lord of War.

ZS: It's one of my personal favorites. You're entering a world that people are not familiar with and in this case, it's a very real world.

TO: We talked a bit about the disappointments that sometimes occur when an editor reads a script but when the footage comes in, it's not supportive of what promise the script held. With Lord of War, I suspect the two were very close.

ZS: What you're saying is absolutely true. It's thrilling to see what was written. When you read the script, you can imagine the mis-en-scene, the casting, the locations, or what the sets are going to look like. And with filmmakers like The Wachowskis or Andrew Niccol, their work takes the script to another level. Writing a great script is one thing but when you actually roll the camera, and choose lenses, and stage it, that's when the movie is made. And then, of course, there's the editing stage. One of the really fun things in editing Lord of War was that the Nick Cage voiceover was always in the script, but I had the writer sitting in the editing room. We could, and did, constantly re-write and adjust it to the emerging drama and rhythms of the movie.

TO: That's really great that you had the opportunity to do that. You notice a difference in working with writer-directors?

ZS: Yes. The material has become more organic to them. If the DP or someone asks a question, the writer-directors can usually answer from a deeply organic place because they know the material so well.

TO: You made the transition from editing on film to digital pretty early on.

ZS: I made the switch on La Pastorela in 1991.

TO: That was a Great Performances episode on television.

ZS: Yes.

TO: How has it affected the business?

ZS: Well, I love digital because of the flexibility. When I did Bound in 1995, I edited it on film and the reason was because we wanted to see dailies projected and we wanted to save money because we were working on a smaller budget. We did not have the money to both print film and rent Avids. I edited Bound on a KEM-Moviola combination. I could still edit a film on film if needed. But, I believe that the work of all artists is a response to materials and tools that are available to them. So, I think that digital editing has changed filmmaking. Just as acrylics changed painting. Artists always adopt technologies that enable them to do new things.

TO: Are there scenes you've edited where you were particularly challenged?

ZS: One of the things that I'm very proud of is the freeway chase in Reloaded.

TO: It's great because it's a nice blend of action and humor, too.

ZS: That's a really long scene and it has a tremendous number of cuts in it. At the time, we were cutting negative and the negative cutters were commenting about that.

TO: Yeah, but here's the difference. There's clarity in that cutting. In other words, the audience isn't lost as a result of that cutting.

ZS: You always know where you are. There are plenty of 12 frame cuts in there. It's heavily edited. (Both Laugh) But there's always a logic to it. And I can't stand not knowing where I am. I'm very fond of opening scenes on tight shots where it's a little abstract and then opening up so you can see where the scene is taking place.

TO: Are there any examples where you felt a film you edited should have done better than it did?

ZS: I was disappointed that Lord of War did not do better domestically, although we did great overseas.

TO: What films did you watch growing up?

ZS: I loved David Lean movies. I can still remember seeing Lawrence of Arabia as a kid in Morristown, NJ, at the Community Theatre. And I saw it multiple times. I thought it was thrilling beyond belief.

TO: Same reaction to The Bridge on The River Kwai?

ZS: Oh yeah. I love movies that have an epic quality about them—a big encompassing point of view. And then later on I really liked John Ford movies. It seemed like he was making studio movies but they all seemed to have something personal about him in them. The Searchers. The Grapes of Wrath. The Quiet Man.

TO: Other editors whose work you admire?

ZS: I like Hal Ashby's work a lot. And I was really lucky to work with him as an assistant on Lookin' To Get Out. And Michael Kahn has done a huge amount for modern editing. You can't really mention editing without talking about what he's done. His body of work is really amazing.

TO: What are some of the things you've learned during the course of your editing career that may not have been so apparent when you started?

ZS: Editing is an extremely political situation. You're sort of the hub of a wheel and the principal spokes are the director, producers, and the studio. You have to learn to be politically adept and have a bedside manner. You can have all the skills and knowledge in the world, but if you can't communicate that and can't work with people, you won't be able to get the work done.

THOMAS STANFORD

Photo courtesy of Thomas Stanford

SANTA FE, NEW MEXICO

Partial Credits: West Side Story, The Yakuza, Jeremiah Johnson, The Reivers, Hell in The Pacific, The Slender Thread, Suddenly, Last Summer, The Fox.

West Side Story. The cadence of the cuts, the choice of angles, the invisible way that you'd be in a wide shot and then in a close-up and not know or care how you got there. Thomas had been retired for some 20 years but could I come to Santa Fe? As a spry 92-year-old, he'd email me to downplay his achievements!

✂

TO: Thomas, you are an Academy Award recipient for West Side Story. How did you enter the film industry?

TS: My aunt had an acquaintance that was able to place me into a gofer job in a documentary film library; carrying cans, finding stuff in the vaults, making labels, and so forth. Then ('43), off to war and, after 3 ½ years in the army, a return to the old job, followed by a swift transition to the editing room.

TO: You then emigrated to the States; how did you get to Hollywood and enter feature film production?

TS: It all began in Berkeley as the film editor of Crusader Rabbit, Rocky & Bullwinkle and then as the first director of film operations at KPIX in San Francisco. This was in the heady days of early television (1949). Everyone was young, nobody knew anything and we all had a wonderful time. While trying to join the Editors Guild, it was back to animation editing, Mr. Magoo, etc. But there was a snag. No union membership, no job. No job, no union membership. A lovely Catch 22.

To keep paying the rent there were numerous small non-union gigs—including a brief stint as an apprentice in the first season of "I Love Lucy" before I was unceremoniously fired. Welcome to Hollywood.

Finally, I became a member of Local 776 as Assistant Editor for The Moon Is Blue with David Niven, William Holden, and Maggie MacNamara. It became infamous in its day for having David utter the line to Maggie: "You're nothing but a professional Virgin".

TO: How did you move up to Editor?

TS: The next seven years were spent both in California and, for two years, in Europe, working a multitude of gigs in all sorts of capacities from editing assistant and music editor to full editor in a variety of projects: television series, documentaries, commercials even. While in Rome, I contacted Hollywood Editor Bill Hornbeck who was there editing The Barefoot Contessa for director Joe Mankiewicz. Bill was one of the outstanding American editors. He was awarded the Academy Award for editing A Place In The Sun. I wasasked by Bill to be his assistant on two films: I Want To Live directed by Robert Wise and Frank Capra's A Hole In The Head.

TO: What was your first major credit as a feature editor?

TS: It was Joe Mankiewicz's film Suddenly Last Summer, with Katherine Hepburn, Elizabeth Taylor and Montgomery Clift — in England, under Bill's supervision. Editor, at last—and what a fantastic opportunity. It was a dream come true; besides, in the following year it led to Bob Wise asking me to edit "West Side Story."

TO: How did that come about?

TS: When I first asked Bob whether he would consider me to edit West Side, he demurred, telling me in the nicest way that he would prefer someone with more experience. Just a week or two before he began shooting his film, I visited Bob on the music recording stage at the Goldwyn Studios— and it was really just to say hello. Bob asked me to step inside his dressing room for a word. My heartbeat went into overdrive. "I decided against an older, more experienced man in favor of a younger, more flexible person, not afraid to try new approaches. And I was wondering if you would like to be my editor on West Side?" It was one of those rare, possibly unique moments in one's career when the world stopped its rotation.

TO: What was it like working for the editor of "Citizen Kane"?

TS: He was a consummate Gentleman—charming, calm, always polite, always flexible and open to new notions. He was modestly confident in his authority, knowledge and goals because he was enormously experienced in the making of a film. Bottom line: because he had been one himself—he was truly an editor's director.

TO: Does anything else stand out?

TS: Here's an interesting example. In The Rumble, there was a moment where I felt I needed more time to make it work dramatically given what was happening visually.

TO: Sure.

TS: And I wanted to stretch something out. I found a way of extending the music—and I think it was two or four bars in order to make it play visually.

TO: That's not a trivial thing to be doing to a musical score especially that one!

TS: Absolutely right. And I went to Bob and I said, 'I've done this.' And he said, 'Oh, my God… Let me look at it.' He came into the cutting room and said, 'You're right. We need that and what you did was absolutely perfect.' But I said, 'In the contract with Bernstein, we are not to change one semi-quaver of the score. Nothing can be changed. It's inviolate.' So, they sent Saul Chaplin, who was the associate producer to New York. And he took Lenny out to dinner, bought him some fine wine and sprung this on him. 'We need four repeat bars in this moment because we don't have enough visual time to make it work.' And he gave his assent.

TO: I've never heard this story. That's great.

TS: Well, those things happen.

TO: Yeah, but that takes a lot of conviction to do that.

TS: Well, you have to do what you have to do.

TO: What do you think are some of the essential things that students should know about the editing profession?

TS: Story—what's it about and what, if any, is the sub-text? The individual sequences — what are they about, how do they serve the overall story development, are they still in the right place when everything is together, do they themselves "deliver" in the present length? Or, can less be more to greater effect? Finally, the individual edits. Editors determine what is seen, when it's seen and how long it's seen. Very simple really—but ever so complex. There are no guides or instructions other than a few words in the script. It is a demanding task of critical examination of an enormous amount of filmed raw material that must be whittled down to many hundreds, possibly even thousands, of individual pieces assembled in various lengths and in differing continuity for content, impact and truth to make up the whole, final enchilada.

TO: What has changed in the profession during your lifetime?

TS: There are far more job opportunities for editors today than was the case for me and procedures have been subject to enormous changes during the almost quarter century since I retired.

TO: Anything else for students?

TS: Know it is a career with constant challenges, alongside enormous potential for having a life of varied work experiences that will enrich and reward you with a never-ending sense of accomplishment. It is a life of ups and downs, demanding self-reliance, mental, physical and emotional stamina, and one in which you very much make your own opportunities. The work is rarely dull or repetitive, and, by God, you will never be bored. It can be richly satisfying and fun; it can also afford endless chances for original thinking and creativity. Yes, there can be heartbreak — being fired. Hey, it's show biz! But yes, there can also be the glory.

NEIL TRAVIS, ACE

Photograph courtesy of the American Cinema Editors and ACE Eddie Awards

LOS ANGELES, CALIFORNIA

Partial Credits: Terminator 3: Rise of the Machines, The Sum of All Fears, Outbreak, Clear and Present Danger, Patriot Games, Dances with Wolves, Roots.

When I spoke with Neil about the book, he had retired from film editing and he was very enthusiastic—remarking about the value he felt it could have for students. Supportive, generous with his time, and very funny. Sadly, not long thereafter he passed away. Here is a great editor whose words—and work—are for us to learn from and experience.

✂

TO: Neil, you are an Academy Award, Emmy and ACE Eddie recipient for best editing. How did you get your start?

NT: My father was a sound effects editor at Twentieth Century Fox. I got a call saying that there was a job opening at Paramount, so I took the job and stayed for nine years.

TO: What were you doing?

NT: I worked in film shipping, and stayed there for—Oh, My God, I don't know—a long time! I worked in the film library. And I ended up assisting people bit by bit. You worked as an apprentice for approximately two years and then you could get a job as an assistant and you had to be an apprentice and an assistant for a total of nine years before you were eligible to edit.

TO: In 1965, you worked as an assistant to Adrienne Fazan on Billie. She won her Academy Award for Gigi. She did something like 70 plus films.

NT: Adrienne was tough. She was very straightforward and very outspoken. I learned a lot by paying attention to her. The first actual editing job that I got was a second editor on a television movie of the week and from there I was lucky enough to get a job with Jack Smight editing a picture called The Travelling Executioner.

TO: You worked on Roots which had 36 Emmy nominations and you received your Emmy award for your editing.

NT: I worked on three episodes. I worked on the first two and then one in the middle. The first episode was the one that I won the Emmy for.

TO: Did you have any inkling about how well it was going to be received?

NT: We all had a pretty good feeling about how unique a situation it was. A man telling his story—especially a black man telling his story—in a favorable manner about his family and his upbringing and his ancestors. It felt like an epic from the very beginning.

TO: Do you put things aside or just edit whatever comes in?

NT: When a scene is shot, I talk to the director about what he likes and doesn't like about the scene. Then all I need to do is find the starting point.

TO: How so?

NT: The first cut. Some image that I'm going to begin the scene with and then it just seems to flow. The first image calls for the second image and so forth.

TO: You worked on the big Tom Clancy books, Patriot Games, Clear and Present Danger, and The Sum of All Fears.

NT: Tom Clancy is a very detailed-oriented writer. He'll describe the shape of a nut and the bolt and he'll take forever to describe a scene. Every now and then people will say, 'I liked the novel better' or 'I liked the picture better' but they're entirely different.

TO: Are there different challenges for you when an actor is directing?

NT: Not really. Generally, the actor has a very good handle on what he wants. In the case of Kevin Costner on Dances With Wolves, he knew exactly what he wanted. I was really rather amazed. And I was surprised at where his emphasis was.

TO: In what way?

NT: He had all of the dialogue scenes in that movie planned. He knew exactly what he wanted. He shot maybe two takes and printed them. He knew what he had when he shot it because he had rehearsed it. The only things that gave him fits were the action scenes.

TO: It's not like choreographing a fight scene between two people.

NT: And he was not used to directing action. And he did a very good job, but he was not secure in that. He didn't know that he had done a good job. So he was constantly changing it. He was constantly looking for something else in all of the action scenes.

TO: Can you give an example?

NT: Like in the Pawnee raid and things like that. I remember Kevin kept asking for 'beefier shots' and I had no idea what he meant! And what he wanted was long lens group shots where the background is brought in and everything looks kind of thick and out of focus.

TO: Really dense shots.

NT: Yes.

TO: You were the editor on Jaws 2 which obviously was the follow-up to the enormously successful original done in 1975. Was there a lot of pressure because of what preceded it?

NT: I felt no compulsion to make it feel like Jaws because we did not have the material. It was an entirely different kind of movie. I remember having an ongoing conversation with Jeannot Szwarc that the star was not the shark. Jeannot kept saying that we had to show the shark more and I said just the opposite. If you look at Jaws most of the time the shark is represented by some yellow barrels.

TO: It's just like any great Hitchcock movie — your imagination provides the suspense in a situation like that.

NT: Right, once you see the shark, you know that it's made out of rubber and sometimes you get laughs. The only thing I can do is get every ounce of goodness out of that film that I possibly can.

TO: Let's talk about No Way Out. Did you have a lot of challenges keeping the secret from audiences?

NT: As far as keeping Yuri a secret, I don't think it was difficult at all. Because there was never really any exposition that I had to work around very carefully to keep the audience from guessing that Kevin Costner was, in fact, Yuri. As a matter of fact, every now and then we tried to give some slight hints that something was not exactly right. But, no one in the world would have guessed that Kevin Costner was the villain in the movie. It's such an unusual concept that the romantic lead of the movie ends up being the villain also. It's amazing.

TO: Dances With Wolves had a budget of $19 million and did $424 million in business. How did the project come about?

NT: I had called Kevin Costner to give me a recommendation based on No Way Out for another movie with a director that he knew. And he said, 'But I have this picture and I'd like you to consider doing it.' And I had pretty much the same reaction that other people did in the studios—you're going to make a long movie and most of it is going to be spoken in Sioux with English subtitles. 'You're out of your mind!' Nobody will sit through a western and read subtitles for three hours. But I was wrong, the other studios were wrong.

TO: It just took over that year.

NT: It ended up being my favorite movie. Everybody on the picture felt like family. We felt like we had been together before and this was a very important movie with a great deal of purpose. We even gave each other Indian names. My name was "Over The Hill". Our script supervisor who loved to laugh was called "Sand In Her Teeth" because the wind blew the sand all around out there.

TO: How was it to work with Kevin Costner on his first directing job?

NT: Oh, my heavens, what can I tell you? A lot of people thought that Kevin Costner was not going to ever be able to direct this movie. The movie is all his. He plotted it all out. He shot it exactly the way he wanted to. He cast it the way he wanted to. And when the picture got close to running out of money, he put his own money up for it. Every ounce of success that that movie has is well deserved.

TO: You had a lot of footage for the buffalo hunt.

NT: The buffalo hunt was enormous. They shot seven cameras and then most of them were no good because the buffalo went in the wrong direction! So we went back and shot again with inserts and pickups and oh, my, it was an enormous amount of film for the movie. We did some sort of calculation that if you unrolled it, it would reach from LA to Alaska. I edited that on film and it was my last film edited on film.

TO: Did you experience a lot of challenges with the subtitled sequences?

NT: Most of them had not been translated by the time we shot the movie.

TO: So you had to edit them without knowing how much timing to leave...

NT: Right, by the time we got the subtitles, we found out that we had a great deal less time required for the subtitles than we thought. In other words, the Sioux dialogue is a great deal longer than English. They may save five words that will wind up as one word in English.

TO: You had to go back.

NT: Right, I had subtitles written out in English, but I didn't have all of them. I had everything written in Sioux, but, again, I didn't have all of them. So we ended up trimming the picture afterwards, which really was to the benefit of the picture because we thought we were really going to have to lay in these long subtitles. The only thing that really helped me in editing was Kevin's narration. Kevin narrated through the whole thing and I recorded that myself in order to help time the movie.

TO: Did you preview it?

NT: We previewed in Arizona and then Seattle. And both previews were astonishing. The audience loved it.

TO: March 25, 1991. Dances With Wolves, Ghost, The Godfather Part III, Goodfellas and The Hunt for Red October. How did you feel when they called your name?

NT: Oh, it's amazing. By that time, a lot of people had told me that I had it locked, and I told them not to say that because if I didn't win it would just make me feel worse. My daughter had a dream that I was the only one from Dances With Wolves who won an award and I was so excited that I ran up on stage, tripped and fell down and got a bloody nose! That was a pretty complex dream that she had!

TO: And all this is going through your mind as you're walking up there!

NT: Yes. So, I walked up there very carefully, and I told her once I got on stage that I would touch my nose, but I forgot to do that! I forgot all kinds of things. That very night was our 30thwedding anniversary and

I forgot to even mention her!

TO: Oh, no!

NT: Which has put me in the dog house ever since!

Moving from Film to Electronic Tape-Based Nonlinear Editing
Photograph courtesy the American Cinema Editors and ACE Eddie Awards

TO: Did you make the transition from film to electronic nonlinear on
Deceived?

NT: Yes, I was working on the Montage then. Originally, it was
difficult for me. When you are used to editing on film, you pick up the
film, you cut it, you splice it, and it's right there. I've embraced digital
entirely.

TO: You've been editing for 50 years. What have you learned?

NT: I've learned a lot about relationships with directors and
relationships with other people. When I first started I thought, 'Okay,

you cut the scene until the last word and then you go to the next word in the next scene.' And I learned there's a lot to be said for silence.

TO: Can you give an example?

NT: I sometimes artificially make a pause longer than the actors had it and I make the distance between words and the distance between thoughts greater. Most of the things that I've learned are about timing.

TO: What films and editors do you like?

NT: John Bloom is a favorite of mine. Artie Schmidt. Fritz Steinkamp. I liked his work in Three Days of The Condor and I thought that was brilliantly edited.

TO: This has been a major part of your life. What's your favorite part?

NT: Actually, it is putting together the first cut. Sitting all by myself with nothing but film like an empty canvas and creating the picture for the first time.

MICHAEL TRONICK, ACE

Photograph courtesy of the American Cinema Editors and ACE Eddie Awards

LOS ANGELES, CALIFORNIA

Partial Credits: Tomb Raider, Straight Outta Compton, The 33, Act of Valor, The Jonas Brothers: The 3D Concert Experience, Hannah Montana / Miley Cyrus: Best of Both Worlds Concert Tour, Hairspray, Mr. and Mrs. Smith, Remember the Titans, Eraser, Scent of a Woman.

Michael had no plans of becoming a picture editor and was content as a music editor. But watch his work in Scent of a Woman or Mr. and Mrs. Smith and he's working to rhythms that may not seem so apparent, but they are there and in the hands of a very kind and gifted editor.

✂

TO: Michael, how did you get your start in the editing business?

MT: I was working for Gene McCabe Productions, and their primary function was making industrial films for the Chrysler Corporation. I started out in production: grip, gopher, gaffer, assistant camera, camera operator. I always gravitated towards the cutting room because those guys made sense of all the chaos of what we did. So I kind of nudged my way into the cutting room and became an assistant.

TO: What happened next?

MT: I wasn't an assistant for long. Two of the editors were also feature film music editors. I had no idea what a music editor was. I called one of the editors, a gentleman named Dan Carlin Sr. and slowly but surely, he taught me how to prepare units for the dubbing stage where you cut music into certain footage. And how to prepare a film, the black and white dupes for scoring, the basic tenants of music editing, and I thought I had died and gone to Heaven. Post-production supervisor Jim Potter put us in touch with a feature they were doing called Movie Movie, directed by Stanley Donen. So early in my career I found myself doing a musical with Stanley Donen and composer Ralph Burns. Out of that, Bob Fosse was able to talk to Stanley because I was up for All That Jazz. And I got Stanley's blessing to work with Bob on All That Jazz. And it was an astounding, mind-boggling experience working for Fosse.

TO: What was your big break as a picture editor?

MT: I was working as a music editor on a feature at Disney. And down the hall from me was John Wright. And he was cutting an after school special about a rock star and he asked me if I wouldn't mind cutting a song. Tom Rolf was the editor I was working with and I asked Tom if it was okay and he said 'Sure'. They gave me the film and taught me how to do it and that led to being asked to cut picture and music on Streets of Fire. This is the second film I did for Walter Hill. So I stayed in L.A. and did Streets of Fire. Walter shot like 80,000 feet of film for the song. I made it through that and then Billy Weber and Chris Lebenzon asked me to be the third editor on Beverly Hills Cop 2, which had a phenomenally quick schedule. So from that point on except for Predator, which I did as a music editor following Beverly Hills Cop 2, I've been pretty much exclusively cutting picture.

TO: How do you approach a film and get introduced to a project?

MT: When I read a script I try to read it as if I was in the audience and seeing the film for the first time. Not critically as an editor, but as someone who goes and pays their twelve bucks to see a movie. And if I respond to the material, I'll take it to the next step, which is usually an interview. You want to keep working, of course, but more importantly is who you're working with and the caliber of the person.

TO: Are there films that stand out where you were particularly challenged?

MT: I worked on Scent of a Woman and I was fortunate enough to be able to cut the tango sequence where Colonel Slade—Pacino's character—dances with this beautiful young woman in a restaurant and it was a culmination of my musical training, and my ability to recognize dance through my work with Fosse. And the emotional content of the film that Marty Brest shot was so poignant. Marty shot something like 100,000 feet—some crazy amount of film—for that scene. So it was just hours and hours of film that we pored through.

TO: What do people who go to see films not know about your profession that you wish they had a little bit more understanding about?

MT: I wish that they were aware of the choices—the infinite amount of choices that can be made in editing a scene. Where to cut? What performance to use? What size? What line of dialogue do you want to start a scene with? Where do you get out? What bit of action is the most visceral, the most exciting? And realize that the choices… I mean it's what I do, but it can be really overwhelming.

TO: From editing film, you've also lived through the transition to editing electronic nonlinear.

MT: On a personal level, it's made me a better editor, because it's allowed me the freedom to try more. When I was cutting on film I would generate more trims than anyone else in the cutting room and I got very self-conscious about it. I looked at Billy Weber's trim bin and Chris Lebenzon's trim bin and they had two or three pieces of film and I just had hundreds because I was trying so many different things. And it shows. And when I saw the possibilities of nonlinear editing, I embraced it and I've never looked back.

TO: Are there any films that come to mind where you really admire how they were put together?

MT: Always. I remember seeing City of God and to me that's one of the best cut movies I have seen in the past fifteen years.

TO: Daniel Rezende.

MT: Yes, Daniel cut it. It was miraculous. And just to see what he did was phenomenal.

TO: Are there particular genres that you find yourself gravitating towards?

MT:You know, I love working on musicals. It seems like it's the natural extension of my background. And to me, cutting dance sequences is like dessert. I find it exhilarating.

TO: Is there anyone whose editing work you particularly admire?

MT: Well, I mean obviously Dede Allen was a tremendous innovator, and Billy Weber and Chris Lebenzon—these are guys I worked with and I see the work that they do. Jim Clark, Artie Schmidt, Joe Hutshing, Bill Steinkamp, Dennis Virkler, Peter Berger. I've seen first-hand how they work and am in awe of what they do.

TO: The dinner scene in Mr. and Mrs. Smith—there isn't a lot of dialogue. A raised eyebrow, a look...

MT: Yeah, yeah.

TO: But there's humor and danger at the same time.

MT: It was delicious. It was like a banquet—the material that I got on the film in terms of the performances. So sometimes the most crucial cuts are non-verbal—the reaction shots of someone listening. And what do you see on their face? And that sometimes is as important as what's being spoken itself.

TO: You're flipping through the television channels. What film is on that you just have to stop and watch?

MT: Oh, it's The Godfather. Because I savor every performance, every line of dialogue, everything about it. I was flipping through the channels recently and came across Cast Away. Just one character. And

I've seen it many times, but I am always entertained by it. When you're in the hands of a confident, imaginative filmmaker, I loved being in that world. But The Godfather is the one that immediately comes to mind.

ANGUS WALL, ACE

Photograph courtesy of the American Cinema Editors and ACE Eddie Awards

LOS ANGELES, CA

Partial Credits: The Girl with the Dragon Tattoo, The Social Network, The Curious Case of Benjamin Button, Zodiac, Panic Room, Fight Club (Editorial Consultant).

Back to Back Academy Awards for best editing—really an amazing feat—is not something that Angus Wall dwells upon. He has a total devotion to exploring every possible way that the elements of a scene can be orchestrated. That is the great responsibility he feels—that for one moment, if he looks away, he may miss the very best piece of a performance. This is the emotional engagement bond that Angus makes with his craft.

✄

TO: Angus, you are a two-time Academy Award recipient for your work on The Girl with the Dragon Tattoo and The Social Network. Has digital acquisition as opposed to film acquisition changed the way you approach editing a film?

AW: It's interesting because, no, it hasn't. I tend to do a lot in post in terms of resizing and what would in the days of film be very expensive scratch and dent type of work. And all of that is easier because of digital. You can do all of it in After Effects, essentially.

TO: If you don't have a character in the frame, you can add it. If you need a particular focal length that you don't have, you can manufacture it. I think that's exciting.

AW: Yeah and I've always done that regardless of whether we were on film, but with digital you're not just editing pieces together. You're actually working within the shot itself. You're editing the actual elements of the frame and you're editing the actual time within the shot.

TO: I call this intraframe editing, where you're editing at the pixel level. Not at the shot level.

AW: What we do as editors and filmmakers is an accumulation of details. And every detail that you can make better is going to add to the overall impact of the piece. All those minute decisions really do add up into something that is quantifiable. We've never had that flexibility to such a degree during the post stage. It underlines the fact that filmmaking is such a plastic process in terms of malleability. And that's very exciting. You're not just splicing shots together. You're helping to orchestrate things within the frame which is very fun.

TO: There have been books about editing. But there hasn't been a book about what's next for the craft and I think you're highlighting a lot of that now. And what you're talking about is really exciting—where every element is addressable. Are there cons?

AW: I don't see anything bad about having an all-digital workflow. What strikes me is that we've only begun to utilize computers to corral and understand what we have. A lot of software development—particularly of editing software—is kind of at a standstill.

TO: Right. It's sort of stuck.

AW: It's stuck in this old paradigm and I think we're in this period where there are certain legacy concepts that are really critical to maintain. But there are also a lot of things that we're not getting the computers to do for us yet. And it's going to be interesting to watch the next 10, 20, 30 years to see how much computers and technology can help so that we can work better.

TO: Right. One example that comes to mind is image recognition. Why can't you click on a piece of footage and have the system find everything that looks like that?

AW: Right. You do need to watch everything. You need to soak in what was captured during principal photography. You need to catalog in your brain what you have. And then you can start to attack with the full knowledge of what you have to work with. Then you can shape something. In my mind, I have to stick to the methodology of watching everything, thinking about it, and then planning my approach.

TO: Sure, and each time you see something you file it away, mentally.

AW: When you start learning how to edit, very often you're really thinking about cutting. But to me, editing is about shot selection. It's about finding the best pieces of footage, whether they're intentional or not. And it's being incredibly diligent that you find the best pieces and put them together in a way that is provocative. It's not about the cutting. It's all about selecting and sequencing.

TO: You were an Editorial Consultant on Fight Club. What did you learn and how did it prepare you for your work in features?

AW: I was lucky enough to meet (David) Fincher when I was 21. I had gotten a job at Propaganda Films in the vault. David brought me on Fight Club just to help out with the editing. He has been very generous to me, but that was one of the most incredibly generous things ever. He put me in a position where I could only succeed, because I didn't have the pressure of the whole film on my back. I was helping eliminate options, in a way.

TO: Between features you still work on the top commercials coming out of advertising agencies. How does that help your feature work?

AW: I think that whenever you make something you're sort of inventing the language of it. The great thing about commercials is you can reinvent that language and find a lot of different ways to tell the story. Sometimes people show up who have shot some stuff and you have to make something out of it. Which is really fun, terrifying, and exciting all at the same time. You have to figure out how to rub two sticks together and make fire. (Both Laugh) And that really helps you when you are working on the more disciplined aspect of a narrative film.

TO: Are there certain techniques that you could use in commercials that may apply to films and some conventions that may not?

AW: There are things that you learn in cutting commercials like how little you actually need in order to tell a story in a very small amount of time. The jump in time that you can get away with, that actually helps because it's more propulsive, is an example where commercials really help films.

TO: It's sort of hard to call you an editor these days—maybe there's a new term—it's not a cut-cut-juxtaposition thing anymore. I haven't figured out how to describe all the new things that some editors are doing. When you're working on these films that have these newly integrated characters and changing performances are there new challenges?

AW: A lot of the movies that David shoots are in layers. You're editing to get the best pieces but it's a more involved form of editing than you're used to. Because you're actually editing in layers in a way. Almost like you would in Photoshop—where in some shots you're choosing the foreground and background. You can really isolate different elements and makes sure that you have the very best pieces to combine to make something.

TO: You wrote an email to me about something you wanted to make sure we covered: "Skills needed at different stages of a film." What did you mean?

AW: Sometimes you have to be able to think about a film in its entirety and sometimes you have to make a choice about the readings of a syllable of a word. And there's a lot of joy in doing that—in going through the footage and responding to it and highlighting the things you like and disregarding the stuff that you think won't have a snowball's chance in hell of making the final version! (Both Laugh) With commercials, you don't get into the bigger structural skillset as much as you do with movies. And that makes movies more challenging and more rewarding. It's more difficult because there are a lot of moving parts. It's like you're putting together giant Lego structures. And then you have to say, 'These structures have to be presented in a different way.'

TO: What have you learned along the way?

AW: You suffer a great anxiety as an editor if you're really taking the job seriously. You're responsible for finding the best pieces of work that have required multiple man years of labor to be willed into existence. You have got to focus and clear your mind of everything because you're the last person in the chain. It's up to you to make sure you find the very best pieces and if you look away for a second, you could miss the best piece where the actor was giving his all and it may be the best piece you have in all of the dailies.

TO: You really have to be diligent.

AW: Yes. And in a way the methodology I use allows me to sleep at night. I have a system where I watch every single take. And then I methodically sift through the material and make sure I haven't missed anything.

TO: By and large, the editors I've talked with seem to have very high image recall skills.

AW: My brother has an absolute photographic memory and he's a high-powered attorney. I can't claim to have that. What I have is O.C.D. (Both Laugh) I know, within three seconds, that I can find anything because it is all organized. (Laughs) And I created that system for myself almost as a way to be able to say, 'I know I'm going to be able to sleep tonight because I have everything organized.' And if you have a good piece and it's a contender, then start to build the scene around that. Or start with the fattest bunch of selects possible and know that every piece of the scene is within this group of selects.

TO: Right.

AW: Somewhere I read someone say, 'performance versus structure', which I thought was a really interesting way to think about it. You're guiding people through this experience in terms of the structure of the scene. But you have this other element which is the performance of the actors which in any given moment may be best in a close-up. So you have to weigh the structural aspect of the storytelling against that performance.

TO: That's a really concise way of explaining those two things you have to balance.

AW: And particularly in cutting David's movies—he gives you so many options. You're going to have a performance for every moment of the scene within each setup. So you have the option to go where you want to go.

TO: The special edition of The Social Network does a great job of showing all the coverage on one of the deposition scenes. It's very educational.

AW: Yeah and there are these little magical moments where everything starts to click together. And those become your tent poles for how you're going to structure the scene.

TO: I don't think there's an appreciation for the mental exhaustion. But to have that 'always on' concentration to not miss the moment is tiring.

AW: Yeah, it's true. I also think that to do a really good job, you have to have a relationship with the characters. You're sort of a silent witness, a silent performer, and you're interacting emotionally with these characters. It's the only way that you can actually judge a good performance from a bad performance. You have to emotionally engage. So if you think about doing that—8, 10, 12, 14 hours a day—it does get emotionally exhausting.

TO: And some of the scenes can be rough—rough material.

AW: Yeah. I mean on Dragon Tattoo, as crazy difficult as it was, I always looked forward to cutting the chase scene on the bridge at the end of the movie.

TO: Why?

AW: Because it was just mechanical. It was just pure filmmaking. It wasn't exhausting because you didn't have to judge for performance. The parameters were "Is the bike in the right position in relation to the Land Rover? Are they far enough along on the bridge?" It was a relief because it was just action.

TO: What films that you worked on do you think should have done better?

AW: I have a soft spot in my heart for Zodiac.

TO: It's terrific. The period piece of it—the costume design.

AW: I just like the film. Part of me wishes it had done better and that more people had seen it.

TO: Are there genres you'd like to work in?

AW: A great story is a great story. I like comedies but I also know how incredibly difficult it is to edit comedies. There is a certain kind of diligence to get those right.

TO: Has it sunk in that you've accomplished so much in your career at such a young age?

AW: The interesting thing is that I feel that I'm just beginning. If there's anything good about being recognized for what you do it's that it opens up opportunities to do more. And because of that it always feels like you're starting over. And it's exciting and terrifying.

TO: Everyone thought that because you and Kirk (Baxter) didn't win the ACE Eddie for Dragon Tattoo that you were not going to win the Oscar. It was a big surprise for you and Kirk.

AW: Yeah, it was. Embarrassing. I think the greatest regret of my life was not thanking my wife and children before everyone else. There are proactive parts of filmmaking and there are reactive parts of filmmaking. Editing is reactive. You are reacting to footage and putting pieces together as a byproduct of that reaction. As editors we're so absolutely dependent on the ingredients that are provided to us. It's really hard to take credit for a film.

TO: What films and editors do you admire?

AW: There are so many. My favorite movie is Apocalypse Now. I watch it probably more than I should! (Both Laugh) I'm always fascinated to see what Scorsese and Thelma Schoonmaker do. They're always doing something adventurous even if it's the most mundane scene. I love to see what Hank Corwin does. When he's at his best he's creating meaning out of scraps which I think is fascinating. We've collaborated on a couple of projects which has been fun.

TO: He is a very humble person. I think Natural Born Killers is amazingly done.

AW: And in J.F.K. I believe he did the majority, if not all, of the work on the title sequence which I think is really a masterpiece of sleight of hand. I saw Senna and Restrepo and they were fascinating. Senna is a documentary that uses archival footage and no voiceover. Restrepo is a very sneaky, amazing, film. I've talked to veterans about it, and they say it feels as close an experience to being in real combat as there is. It has this sense of dread that's amazing. They're both cut masterfully in completely different ways. They're not fancy Hollywood movies at all.

TO: Your Emmys are for title sequences.

AW: I designed and directed the titles sequences for Carnivàle and Game of Thrones. And those are fun because you're creating a whole new world. I really love working with other people and one thing about editing is that it is a very solitary exercise. I actually find it—particularly on the feature side—very lonely. And that's why I enjoy collaborating. I like cutting commercials because you sit in a room with other people. And you have interesting conversations and at the end of those conversations you have a piece of work to show for it. I really cherish any process that allows for that.

TO: If you weren't editing, what do you think you'd be doing?

AW: I'll give you the answer and I guarantee no one else has given you this answer! (Laughs) I would probably be an outdoor instructor in mountaineering, river rafting, kayaking. I was a Maine Guide for two summers during college. And it's not easy to become a Maine Guide. I would probably be a mountaineer. (Laughs)

TO: I can confirm you are the first to give that answer! (Both Laugh)

MARTIN WALSH, ACE

Photo Courtesy of Martin Walsh

LONDON, ENGLAND

Partial Credits: Wonder Woman, Eddie the Eagle, Cinderella, Jack Ryan: Shadow Recruit, Prince of Persia: The Sands of Time, Clash of the Titans, V for Vendetta, Chicago, Iris, Strictly Sinatra, Bridget Jones's Diary, Roseanna's Grave, Feeling Minnesota, Funny Bones, Backbeat, The Krays

The expertly timed and edited book signing scene in Bridget Jones's Diary. And it was apparent mid-way through "Cell Block Tango" in Chicago that Martin is terrifically talented. Whether small films or huge summer films, he strives for diversity in his choices and excels.

✂

TO: Martin, you are an Academy Award and ACE Eddie award recipient. How did you get your start in the film business?

MW: After school I got a job at a company called Cinephoto in a six-man film unit making films for industry. Between us we would write, shoot on 16mm, edit and mix films for aircraft manufacturers, oil companies, bridge builders, you name it. It was through this company I discovered my love for editing pictures and sound.

TO: What was your big break as a picture editor?

MW: I guess my first break came when the BBC offered me a short-term contract as an assistant and I jumped at the opportunity. From there I went freelance and worked my way round various TV stations in both the BBC and ITV. I cut my teeth in news and current affairs, graduated to documentaries and finally small drama shows. In 1995 I cut my first full length movie, Sacred Hearts. I remember a producer doubting my ability to make the jump from cutting lowly 16mm for television to the dizzy heights of 35mm for movies.

TO: You've edited many films where music and musicians are the centerpieces. Is this by design?

MW: Absolutely! I love music and as a frustrated – failed really—musician any script I get that involves music is one I'll pay special attention to. One of the criticisms aimed at me after Chicago was that it was cut too fast, or that it was – an over-used phrase—"MTV cutting". Well I'm too old to have ever been influenced by MTV and the film was shot to be cut in a particular style. Some critics couldn't understand why we didn't spend longer on the lovely wide shots, the suggestion being they wanted to see the whole company doing the steps and cutting was somehow cheating. Was that actually Richard Gere tap-dancing brilliantly in the courtroom sequence or did we use close ups of a double's feet? Did Catherine Zeta Jones do all her own singing or was she dubbed? The answers are yes and yes. All the actors sang their own songs and danced themselves silly day in, day out, for 4 months. If we did stay for a few more frames on a cut something in the frame – a hand, a foot or a dancer—would be off sync and spoil the frame and the cut would fall out of time with the rhythm of the music. That's no good in a musical and that's why we cut to another shot.

TO: Bridget Jones's Diary was a huge hit. It was made for $26 million and grossed almost $282 million.

MW: It was a great film to work on with a brilliant script and a fantastic cast. Comedies are arguably the hardest genre to get right. You need plenty of coverage in order to help make gags work. The reaction shots in the scene at the book launch are calculated to make the scene as excruciatingly embarrassing as possible for Bridget. She starts off her speech on the wrong foot and gradually digs herself into a massive hole. Again!

The thing with comedies is to maintain objectivity. The danger comes when, after numerous screenings of the cut it begins to feel stale and you start to lose faith in the material. If something made you laugh in dailies and you put a big red asterisk next to it in your screening notes chances are it will be just as funny six months later for a new audience. Put the cut it in front of a crowd as often as possible. You very quickly discover what's working and what is not.

TO: Iris has wonderful performances. Can you recall getting the dailies and your impressions of the performances?

MW: Iris was the easiest job I've ever had. With Jim and Judi as the older couple and Kate and Hugh playing their younger selves I didn't have to do much. Richard Eyre's direction was spot on. Nothing had to be forced. The thing I remember from dailies after seeing a few close ups of Judi Dench was thinking, "Why would you cut away from that performance?" So, I didn't unless Jim had a line or a crucial reaction to make. Bliss!

TO: How did you come to edit Chicago? Your work on the film is truly amazing. When I saw the film in the theatre, as I was watching "Cell Block Tango" I just sat there thinking that this is the film that will win best editing.

MW: Thank you. Pretty much everyone who saw my first cut of the picture said the same. The expectation was huge. The most challenging aspect of Chicago was the amount of footage to get through, about a million and a half feet I think. Each musical number was shot over a period of three or four days using up to five cameras so the number of choices I had were immeasurable and it took a long time to get right – if anything's ever right. My favourite number is probably "We Both Reached For The Gun". I love the staging, lighting and choreography of that scene. The use of the puppet and reporters was inspired.

TO: March 23, 2003. Chicago, Gangs of New York, The Hours, The Lord of the Rings: The Two Towers, and The Pianist. Were you surprised when your name was announced?

MW: No. Nervous? Absolutely! Sweaty palms, dry throat. The ceremony goes on for so long you begin to wonder if they'll ever put you out of your misery. I don't remember much after my name was called out except getting a hug from Thelma Schoonmaker and a handshake from Marty Scorsese. Almost better than winning an Oscar! The rest is just a fog.

TO: You have quite a lot of experience editing films that have a large amount of visual effects, such as Prince of Persia: The Sands of Time, Clash of the Titans, Inkheart and V: For Vendetta. Does having a large amount of visual effects present different challenges for the editor?

MW: I'm not sure what difference it makes to the editing process, if any. There are still actors and performances to consider and the story and plot to keep track of. Schedules on big VFX movies are such that we have to "turn over" scenes involving VFX work as early as possible so that the work can be of the highest quality possible. The downside is that, unlike a Bridget Jones or a Chicago, where you can tweak and fiddle and experiment to your hearts content, the VFX movie is getting finished almost before it's got going resulting in films with spectacular(ly) overlong VFX sequences and lousy stories. No names mentioned!

TO: You've worked with a variety of directors. What are some of the things you've taken away from those experiences?

MW: Editing is collaboration. Spending all day every day in a small room with the same people – the director and an assistant – can, at various times, be stressful, tense, intense, tedious and certainly long, but will also be exhilarating, satisfying, and above all enjoyable. The directors you mention are just a few of the people I've worked with. All of them are very different personalities and therefore bring quite different ways of working.

TO: Are there films that you have worked on that didn't do as well as you thought?

MW: One film I would like to revisit is Funny Bones, a misunderstood work of genius, badly overlooked by a studio that just didn't get it. We were so close. There was a cut of about twenty minutes longer than the eventual release that had all the missing detail, all the character development and all of the various storylines resolved beautifully. I loved that film but the studio couldn't come to terms with the length and we were forced to cut it.

TO: What are some of the things you've learned during the course of your editing career that may not have been so apparent when you started?

MW: Nothing's ever finished.

TO: What are some of the films that you really admire?

MW: Too many to list really... Martin Scorsese & Thelma Schoonmaker have worked together since the 70's and it shows, Raging Bull is brilliant, as is Goodfellas. Their use of music is simply the best. Billy Wilder's The Apartment, Ace In The Hole, Some Like It Hot.

All That Jazz edited by Alan Heim was one of the movies that nudged me towards editing. Some of the best editing is done with the worst dailies and goes unnoticed by all but those involved. It is possible to make a silk purse out of a sow's ear. I can watch a movie as a regular cinemagoer but if I find myself checking out the cutting or being thrown by it I know the movie's not working for me. If it's working, I would be immersed in the story.

HUGHES WINBORNE, ACE

Photograph courtesy of the American Cinema Editors and ACE Eddie Awards

GREENWOOD, MISSISSIPPI

Partial Credits: Fences, All I See Is You, Pixels, Guardians of the Galaxy, Charlie Countryman, The Help, Seven Pounds, The Great Debaters, The Pursuit of Happyness, Crash, Employee of the Month, Sling Blade, Comfortably Numb

Perseverance. Here is Hughes Winborne, a house painter who loved movies, making $35 for 18 hours of work, not knowing how the rent would be paid, and almost walked away from the profession. And, as usually happens, opportunity was just around the corner. He says he was lucky, but, looking at the films he's edited, I'd say talent was much more the case.

TO: Hughes, you are an Academy Award and an ACE Eddie recipient for your editing of Crash. How did you get your start?

HW: I grew up in North Carolina. I came from a family of attorneys and I became a paralegal and I pretty quickly came to the conclusion that I didn't want to be a lawyer so I became a house painter. I always loved film all through my high school years. And that period—the late '60s and '70s—was a great period for film.

TO: I loved that period—Serpico, Dog Day Afternoon, The French Connection—there are so many of them.

HW: I remember the day I saw Barry Lyndon in the Crabtree Valley Mall and I walked out and thought 'You know, it would be fun to be involved in making something like that.' And I found out from the New York Times that there was a summer film school, called Sight and Sound. So I sold my great 2002 BMW, paid for my tuition, and went to

New York.

TO: You took this great jump.

HW: It was for six weeks and it was an intensive 16mm film class with four people in each group and we made three or four films.

TO: Okay, so what happened after the six weeks?

HW: I went back to North Carolina, packed my bags, and moved to New York. I finally got a job as a P.A. working on commercials. And after the first day, and working 18 hours for $35, I was crying to the cab driver about why in the world I moved to New York! (Both Laugh) I had been in New York for about three months doing a few commercials and making almost no money. I was reading books about films and I read Ralph Rosenblum's book, "When the Shooting Stops, The Editing Begins".

TO: Sure, a great book.

HW: One Sunday morning, my phone rang and I had too much to drink the night before. I answered it and the voice said, 'I'd like to speak with Hughes Winborne. This is Ralph Rosenblum.' And I said, 'Who?' And he said, 'This is Ralph Rosenblum. You wrote me a letter about my book.' And I said, 'Oh yeah, wow, how did you work in this business? These people are all insane!' (Both Laugh)

TO: That's great.

HW: He was so nice to call me—I couldn't believe it. And he didn't say very much but he listened. And he said, 'I don't know. I just hung around and it can be swell.' Then I got a job at a company run by George George who was Rube Goldberg's son and I was syncing dailies on 16mm. And to me it was fantastic. Ironically, I got a call from my father, telling me that in Atlantic, North Carolina, there was an attorney who was going to make a horror film on the beach. His name was Buddy Cooper. So I talked to Buddy and said that I would try to find him an editor if he'd hire me as an assistant because I didn't really know my way around an editing room yet.

TO: Okay, this would have been 1985 and the film was The Mutilator.

HW: Right. So I called up a couple of editors and one of them was Steve Mack. He cut Robert Duvall's first film, Angelo My Love, which is a pretty good film. So I got Steve the job and we both came on. We got about eight weeks into the director's cut and Buddy was on a barstool and was with Steve. And Buddy looked at me and asked me to go and have a cup of coffee and to come back in 20 minutes.

TO: And you knew something was up.

HW: Sure and 20 minutes later, Steve's not there and Buddy says, 'Would you like to finish editing the film?' And I said, 'Okay.' I think, frankly, if he had called me on the phone I would have chickened out because I didn't think I had the experience or was ready for it. And this was all on film. The pressure was incredible. I was working 14 hours a day but when I went home I was shaking for the first month. And Buddy said—and I'll forever be grateful for it— 'Look, if you're feeling pressure, it's not coming from me.'

TO: That's great.

HW: And from that point on, everything was fine. The big lesson for me on that movie was that Buddy was a first-time director and I think he felt that Steve wasn't taking his suggestions seriously. It was very low budget and a lot of things had to happen in the editing to give the illusion to make things work. And that was a huge lesson for me. You have a responsibility to try and you never know what will work. When I got back to New York, I couldn't get any feature work. I got a call and did a film job and it was on an upright Moviola. And I was so bad, I lasted two days.

TO: Really?

HW: Yeah, I have to say, it was one of the darkest moments in my career. I was ashamed of myself—just walking away and quitting. But I got a call a couple of weeks later. I was working out of this company called Fantasmagoria. I was cutting music videos for B.B. King and others and I was having a great time. By then, I was cutting tape-to-tape and I got a job cutting industrials. I was in heaven—I was cutting and getting paid! I was making $175 a day! And you have to remember, Tom, I had no money. I was in New York, living on five thousand dollars a year and that barely paid my rent.

TO: You had nothing.

HW: I did a job for PBS called Faces of Japan and on these documentaries I learned so much about cutting and using sound and every bit of material that I had. And that carried over to CBS with 48 Hours, which was even more intense. On Faces of Japan, I was doing a piece on Little League Baseball in Japan. I had two weeks to do it and had 100 hours of footage.

TO: And if it was an hour doc, that's still a 100:1 shooting ratio.

HW: And it was a really good show because they had such great characters—and that is really the key to everything.

TO: How did you move from television to feature films?

HW: My dream had always been to cut dramatic material. And, during this time, I did a pilot for David Seltzer.

TO: Sure. He wrote The Omen.

HW: Right. I had been doing documentaries, commercials, and industrials for six years or so and this was a return to dramatic material. It was called Urban Anxiety and it was really ahead of its time. It had Mandy Patinkin, Mercedes Ruhl, Bob Balaban, Robert Wuhl, Kevin O'Connor—it was a great cast. And it was hard to put together because it really was like a documentary. David Seltzer moved on and he wanted me to cut this feature called Shining Through with Melanie Griffith.

TO: Sure.

HW: David said that he wanted me to cut it but that the studio wouldn't let him hire me. So, Craig McKay cut it and I met him and he told me that Jonathan Demme's nephew, Ted, was going to be doing a short.

TO: Makes sense. Craig cut The Silence of the Lambs for Jonathan.

HW: And Craig recommended me as the editor and this is where my career starts to move in a different direction from 48 Hours. I worked with Ted on this short called The Bet. From there I cut a film called The Drunks for Peter Cohn, who directed it. While I was working on that, The Shooting Gallery was about to do a movie called Sling Blade. I called the folks at Shooting Gallery, talked to Billy, and got the job.

TO: Just like that.

HW: Just like that.

TO: That's amazing. That's persistence.

HW: And Sling Blade was so successful—I knew it was good. I came out to L.A. to cut it on D-Vision. And it was horrible—it kept crashing. It was so hot that Billy and I kept falling asleep. Billy had to go to New York for a meeting with Miramax and while he was gone, I was trying to get the film down because it was really long. So I started cutting out material and when he came back, he almost fired me! (Both Laugh) Sling Blade was a huge lesson for me.

TO: What did you learn?

HW: You get coverage and if you haven't had a lot of time talking with the director, you have to figure it out. And what I learned was that just because you have the coverage, it doesn't mean you have to use it.

And Billy didn't want or shoot a lot of coverage. He wanted everything to play, as much as possible, in a master. But you know, there's something that I learn on every film—it's the same lesson.

TO: What's that?

HW: I learn to get out of the way.

TO: Can you explain?

HW: I mean if the performances are great and the story is great, you don't want people to know you're there. Every time you make a cut, you're drawing attention to the process. I learned it again on The Pursuit of Happyness with Gabriele Muccino. When I started showing him what I had done, he said, (uses Italian accent) 'You are making my film like a Hollywood film. Stop cutting so much!'

TO: Crash is a drama that has multiple, intertwined storylines. Your work in balancing these storylines and creating tension is brilliantly done.

HW: On Crash, it's the multiple characters and storylines and juggling those storylines. All of those balls that had to be in the air at the same time and couldn't be allowed to hit the ground. That really is a television series structure. Paul (Haggis) came out of television and he wrote for L.A. Law and the whole parallel storylines was not new to him. What we did was to take out the commercial breaks!

TO: That's funny.

HW: Now, that's not a small thing because the commercial breaks in television have conditioned the audience that there is a pause in the drama. And with a film, things have to keep going. There is no break. The audience is not going to pause. Was it hard? They're all hard, Tom. What I think is great is the writing and Paul is an incredible writer. What he and I did, more than anything once he was in the editing room, is that rather than trimming the ins and outs of scenes, we really condensed internally the scenes.

TO: What was the reason?

HW: We needed to make sure that we didn't stay with a character too long so that the audience wouldn't forget the other characters and to keep the flow going. We did a little restructuring—but really not a lot. Paul cares tremendously, and he is there all the time.

TO: Lara and the gun is really hard to watch.

HW: Yeah, to me, that scene shows the genius of Paul. First of all, children and guns gets you right away. And all of the characters are sympathetic—there's not really a bad guy out there.

TO: Right.

HW: That was one of the earlier scenes that I put together. That scene changed very little. There were definitely some problems with the film that we had to work out.

TO: Can you say more?

HW: Well, later in the movie when Don Cheadle has to make the decision on what he's going to do about his brother, he has the conversation with Brendan Fraser. When they shot that scene, half the crew was sick with food poisoning.

TO: What did you do?

HW: So, we had to get stand-ins to get the over-the-shoulder shots. The problem was that we had this major scene at the end of the movie where Brendan Fraser just disappears. Paul brought in Bill Fichtner to be the D.A. because Fraser wasn't available for these re-shoots. And the scene was fantastic with Cheadle but the problem was that Fraser disappears. And this was my big save—it doesn't seem like it now—but then it was.

TO: What did you do?

HW: I went back and I pieced together some of the stuff from those sick days when Brendan was there and I think it was only 15 seconds of material of him talking to Cheadle. And we popped it in there and it was just what we needed.

TO: That's great. Where were you when you heard you were nominated?

HW: (Laughs) I was in bed. What was it like? Well, I can tell you, without a bit of irony or being disingenuous—I never in my mind or in my life thought about getting an Oscar. I mean that honestly. I never thought about it. I never fantasized about it.

TO: You mentioned earlier that you were just happy to be working.

HW: Exactly. I wasn't thinking about statues and recognition from my peers. I just wanted to keep working.

TO: That year the best editing nominees were Crash, Cinderella Man, The Constant Gardener, Munich, and Walk the Line. Do you remember the moment?

HW: I was sitting in the aisle, close to the podium and Michael Kahn was on the other end. I don't like getting in front of an audience and honestly, I don't really remember it.

TO: What films do you like watching and are you conscious about the editing?

HW: I don't think there is an appreciation for how difficult it is to put together a dramatic dialogue scene. People just don't know and they can't see what went into making that dialogue scene work. What the choices were as far as performances and the structure. The number of decisions and choices you have—even if you only have two shots—are incredible. The different way you can go and the impact you can have is mind-boggling. You can be subtle or not so subtle.

TO: What other editors or films do you like?

HW: It's very hard to judge other editors because you just don't know what they had to work with. But I will tell you this—what's the film that Dede Allen cut with Michael Douglas?

TO: Wonder Boys?

HW: Yes. The cutting in that film is very, very interesting. It's jaggy and very dirty in a lot of ways and I admire it because it flows. There's not a lot of attention to crossing the line, screen direction or continuity. She did an incredible job.

TO: What's your advice for people starting out who want to get into editing?

HW: After I won the Academy Award I got a lot of requests to give talks at schools. And one of the things that I was asked a lot was how I had gotten to that point and how had I laid out my career. And I said that there was no laying out and that it was a lot of luck and that, more than anything, I hung around. I didn't leave.

TO: You didn't give up.

HW: Right. I hung around enough that I got lucky.

CPSIA information can be obtained
at www.ICGtesting.com
Printed in the USA
FFHW02n1853151018
48819663-52986FF

9 781925 819564